# Perpetual Contact

The spread of mobile communication, most obtrusively as cell phones but increasingly in other wireless devices, is affecting people's lives and relationships to a previously unthought-of extent. Mobile phones, which are fast becoming ubiquitous, affect every aspect of our personal and professional lives either directly or indirectly. They have transformed social practices and changed the way we do business, yet surprisingly little serious academic work has been done on them. This book, with contributions from the foremost researchers in the field, will be the first study of the impact of the mobile phone on contemporary society from a social-scientific perspective. Providing a comprehensive overview of mobile phones and social interaction, it comprises an introduction covering the key issues, a series of unique national studies and surveys, and a final section examining theoretical and practical implications.

James E. Katz is Professor of Communication at Rutgers University. His publications include *Congress and National Energy Policy* (1984) and *Connections: Social and Cultural Studies of the Telephone in American Life* (1999). Katz has authored more than thirty peer-reviewed journal articles; his works have been translated into five languages and republished in numerous edited collections.

Mark A. Aakhus is Assistant Professor of Communication at Rutgers. He has published in technology and communication journals, and his work appears regularly in international publications on argumentation and disputing processes.

# Perpetual Contact

*Mobile Communication, Private Talk,*
*Public Performance*

*Edited by*

James E. Katz and Mark A. Aakhus

CAMBRIDGE
UNIVERSITY PRESS

PUBLISHED BY THE PRESS SYNDICATE OF THE UNIVERSITY OF CAMBRIDGE
The Pitt Building, Trumpington Street, Cambridge, United Kingdom

CAMBRIDGE UNIVERSITY PRESS
The Edinburgh Building, Cambridge CB2 2RU, UK
40 West 20th Street, New York, NY 10011-4211, USA
477 Williamstown Road, Port Melbourne, VIC 3207, Australia
Ruiz de Alarcón 13, 28014 Madrid, Spain
Dock House, The Waterfront, Cape Town 8001, South Africa

http://www.cambridge.org

First published 2002
Third printing 2003

Printed in the United Kingdom at the University Press, Cambridge

*Typeface* Plantin 10/12 pt.     *System* LATEX 2$_\varepsilon$   [TB]

*A catalogue record for this book is available from the British Library*

*Library of Congress Cataloguing in Publication data*

Perpetual contact: mobile communication, private talk, public performance /
edited by James E. Katz and Mark Aakhus.
      p.   cm.
ISBN 0 521 80771 9 (hbk) – ISBN 0 521 00266 4 (pbk)
1. Cellular telephones – Social aspects.   2. Wireless communication systems –
Social aspects.   I. Katz, James E.   II. Aakhus, Mark, 1964–
HE9713 .P47   2001
302.23′5 – dc21       2001043082

ISBN 0 521 80771 9 hardback
ISBN 0 521 00266 4 paperback

Ronald E. Rice
*Primus inter primos*

# Contents

# Figures

# Tables

# Notes on the contributors

*Editors*

JAMES E. KATZ
*Rutgers University, USA*
Dr. James Katz is the author of several books in the field of technology and society. His latest book, co-authored with Ronald E. Rice, is *Social Consequences of Internet Use*, published by MIT Press (Cambridge, MA) in 2002. His 1999 book, *Connections: Social and Cultural Studies of the Telephone in American Life* (New Brunswick, NJ: Transaction Publishers), was included in the 37th "Outstanding Academic Titles" award, given by the American Library Association's journal *Choice*. His book *Congress and National Energy Policy* (New Brunswick, NJ: Transaction Publishers, 1984) was nominated for the American Political Science Association Gladys Kammerer prize for best political science publication in 1984. Another of his recent books, co-edited with Ronald E. Rice, is entitled *Internet and Healthcare Communication* (Thousand Oaks, CA: Sage, 2000). In 2000, he won the Rutgers Department of Communication Researcher of the Year award. Katz has authored more than thirty peer-reviewed journal articles; his works have been translated into five languages and republished in numerous edited collections.

He earned his PhD in 1974 from Rutgers; in 1997, he joined its Department of Communication as professor. In between those years he won postdoctoral fellowships at Harvard University and MIT, served on the faculties of the University of Texas, Austin, and Clarkson University, and headed the social science research unit at Bell Communications Research (Bellcore). He was also granted national and foreign patents on his inventions in telecommunication technology.

The national electronic media frequently interview Katz; and he has appeared on numerous network news programs. He has been quoted on the front pages of leading newspapers including the *New York Times, Wall Street Journal, Boston Globe*, and *USA Today*. He serves on the boards of several leading social science journals and charitable and educational foundations. His teaching and research interests include research methods, the social aspects of communication technology, the contest between privacy and publicity on the Internet, and of course mobile communication and computing.

MARK A. AAKHUS
*Rutgers University, USA*
Dr. Aakhus is assistant professor of communication at Rutgers. He investigates how new media and communication formats are designed and implemented to solve problems of human communication. Within this domain, Aakhus is especially interested in investigating how such innovations affect the quality of human activities in the areas of learning, organizing, decision-making and conflict management. He has published in technology and communication journals. His work appears regularly in international proceedings on argumentation and disputing processes. He earned his PhD at the University of Arizona in Communication, with a specialization in Management Information Systems. He is past co-chair of the National Communication Association's Human Communication and Technology Commission. He is dispute-mediator and has invented a distributed learning application for educating professionals.

## Contributors

AKIBA COHEN
*Tel Aviv University, Israel*
Dr. Cohen is chair of the Department of Communication at Tel Aviv University. Previously he was chair of the Department of Communication and director of the Communication Research Institute at the Hebrew University. He has had visiting appointments at Michigan State University, the University of Minnesota, the University of Maryland and Mannheim's ZUMA Institute. He serves on the editorial boards of the *Journal of Communication, Human Communication Research,* the *Journal of Broadcasting and Electronic Media,* and *Communications.* He is a member of several scholarly associations and is a past president and fellow of the International Communication Association.

LEOPOLDINA FORTUNATI
*University of Trieste, Italy*
Dr. Fortunati teaches sociology of mass communications and sociology of education at the Faculty of Sciences of Education of the University of Trieste and is vice-chair of the European Union's COST 269. She has conducted many research projects in the field of gender studies, cultural

processes and communication technologies. She is the author of *The Arcane of Reproduction* (Autonomedia, 1995) and the editor of *Gli Italiani al telefono* (Angeli, 1995) and *Telecomunicando in Europa* (Angeli, 1998).

KENNETH J. GERGEN
*Swarthmore College, USA*
Dr. Gergen is an authority on cultural change, personal identity, and language and communication. Gergen's best-known book, *The Saturated Self: Dilemmas of Identity in Contemporary Life* (Basic Books, 1991), examines the effects of the increasing immersion in images, information and relationships on the collective psyche of contemporary society. He is an endowed professor at Swarthmore College.

In one recent research project, Gergen monitored an online suicide hotline to explore the human interactions that take place in the world of "virtual" community. He is also the author of two books dealing with the conception of knowledge in the human sciences and society more generally. In over twenty-five years of teaching, Gergen has been awarded three Fulbright grants as well as a Guggenheim Fellowship, the Alexander von Humbolt prize in the Humanities, and honorary degrees from Tilburg University and the Saybrook Institute. Gergen maintains professional relationships with several psychological associations; most notably, he has served as president of the American Psychological Association divisions of Psychology & the Arts and Theoretical & Philosophical Psychology. Gergen earned a BA from Yale University in 1957 and a PhD in psychology from Duke University in 1962.

CHANTAL DE GOURNAY
*France Telecom Research*
Mrs. de Gournay studied political science at the Université Laval, Québec (Canada), and sociology and urban planning at the Université Paris XII, Institut d'Urbanisme de Paris. Since 1983, she has been a researcher on the social uses of information and communication technologies (ICTs) in France Telecom Labs (CNET). Her books include *Information Technology: Impact on the Way of Life* (Commission of the European Communities, Tycooly International Publishing, Dublin, 1982), *Télévisions déchaînées* (with P. Musso and G. Pineau; La Documentation Française, 1985), *"1984" et les présents de l'univers informationnel* (with J.L. Weissberg, as editors; CCI-Centre Georges Pompidou, collection Alors, 1985) and "Telephone Networks in France and Great Britain" (with G. Dupuy and J.A. Tarr, eds.) in *Technology and the Rise of the Networked City in Europe and America* (Temple University Press, 1988). She has also widely published articles on social aspects of telecommunications.

JEAN-PHILIPPE HEURTIN
*France Telecom Research*
Dr. Jean-Philippe Heurtin earned his PhD in political science. Currently he is a researcher in the social and cognitive sciences laboratory at CNET, a major R&D center associated with France Telecom. Among his projects are an investigation of the uses of mobile telephony and the sociology of sociability.

EIJA-LIISA KASESNIEMI
*VTT Information Technology*
Ms. Eija-Liisa Kasesniemi headed the project "Mobile Phone Culture of Children and Teenagers" from 1997 to 1999. She currently is a researcher at VTT Information Technology, Human Interaction Technologies, where she is involved in a research project on Wireless Application Protocol to examine adapting Internet services to mobile terminal devices. Ms. Kasesniemi is also working in the publication projects of the Information Society Research Center of the University of Tampere. She received her MA degree at the University of Jyväskylä and is currently pursuing her dissertation on the text messaging culture of Finnish teenagers.

SHIN DONG KIM
*Hallym University, Korea*
Dr. Shin Dong Kim received the BA and MA in mass communications from Korea University in 1986 and 1988 and a PhD from Indiana University in mass communications in 1997. His experiences include having worked for the *Joongang Daily* to produce the Korean version of *Newsweek International*, and for the Korea Press Foundation as a research fellow. Most recently, he was appointed a visiting assistant professor at Dartmouth College for the winter term of 2000. Among his research interests are media policy in globalization, modernity and media, and social/cultural issues of information society.

CHRISTIAN LICOPPE
*France Telecom Research*
Dr. Licoppe has a doctorate in the history of science and technology. Currently he is head of the social and cognitive sciences laboratory at CNET, France Telecom's R&D center.

RICHARD LING
*Telenor Research, Norway*
Dr. Richard Ling is a sociologist at Telenor's research institute located in Kjeller, Norway. He received his PhD in sociology from the University of Colorado, Boulder. He taught at the University of Wyoming in Laramie before going to Norway on a Marshall Foundation grant. Since

that time he has worked at the Gruppen for Ressursstudier (the resource study group) founded by Jergan Randers and has been a partner in a small consulting firm, Ressurskonsult, which focused on studies of energy, technology and society. Since 1994, he has worked at Telenor, focusing on researching issues associated with new information technology and society.

ENID MANTE
*KPN Telecom, the Netherlands*
Dr. Enid Mante is an organizational sociologist. After a scientific career at Leyden University, she moved to the research department of KPN Telecom. There she did research on changing organization processes within KPN and on the acceptance of information/communication technologies by consumers and organizations. Currently she is project leader of a EURESCOM project on information and communication technologies in everyday life that studies cultural differences in the acceptance of them in Europe. Since 1996, she has been associate professor at the University of Utrecht, Center of Management and Management Policy in the field of Management of Changing Organizations.

DAWN NAFUS
*Cambridge University, UK*
Ms. Dawn Nafus is a social anthropology PhD candidate at the University of Cambridge, Sidney Sussex College. Her research interests include the social construction of time and space, consumption, and the political economies of post-socialism. Her dissertation, based on fieldwork in provincial Russia, examines the ways in which transformations of communications and transport infrastructures and the social processes engender new survival strategies and spacio-temporal ideologies. Before beginning her PhD she was a management consultant with the Corporate Executive Board working in the corporate banking sector.

JUKKA-PEKKA PURO
*Turku School of Economics and Business Administration*
Mr. Jukka-Pekka Puro is a PhD Docent and Programme Manager at the Business Research and Development Centre, Institute for Executive Education, Turku School of Economics and Business Administration, Turku, Finland.

PIRJO RAUTIAINEN
*University of Tampere, Finland*
Mrs. Pirjo Rautiainen has been working on the research project "Mobile Phone Culture of Children and Teenagers in Finland" since January 1998 at the Information Society Research Center at the University of Tampere.

She earned her MA degree in the Department of Ethnology of the University of Jyväskylä, where she majored in cultural anthropology. Her MA thesis is based on the fieldwork she did in Menominee Indian Reservation in Wisconsin, USA. Currently she is researcher-in-charge of the "Mobile Phone Culture of Children and Teenagers in Finland," which is partly supported by Nokia and Sonera.

KATHLEEN ROBBINS
*Cellular One, USA*
Ms. Kathleen Robbins has a BSc in engineering from the US Air Force Academy and an MBA from California State University, Sacramento, and is a Doctor of Ministry candidate. Her work experience includes a management role at Procter & Gamble and nine years in the telecommunications industry. Currently she is General Manager of Cellular One of East Central Illinois. Before joining Cellular One, she worked as a telecommunications consultant and her clients included GTE and Nextel.

JAMES B. RULE
*State University of New York (SUNY), Stony Brook, USA*
Dr. James Rule was born and reared in California. He earned his doctorate in sociology at Harvard University. He taught and carried out research at Oxford, Cambridge and the University of Bordeaux before joining the sociology department at SUNY, Stony Brook. Dr. Rule is the author and co-author of many books and monographs as well as a variety of articles. He has been highly active on the editorial board of *Dissent* magazine. His core interests include information issues, especially their privacy and surveillance aspects. He has been awarded fellowships at the Russell Sage Foundation, the Institute for Advanced Study and the Center for Advanced Study in the Behavioral Sciences.

EMANUEL A. SCHEGLOFF
*University of California, Los Angeles (UCLA), USA*
Dr. Emanuel Schegloff holds degrees from Harvard University and the University of California, Berkeley. He earlier taught at Columbia University and since 1972 at UCLA. He has also been a fellow at the Netherlands Institute for Advanced Study in the Social Sciences and Humanities (1978–79) and at the Center for Advanced Studies in the Social Sciences at Stanford (1998–99), the latter while he held a Guggenheim Fellowship. He has lectured widely in the United States and Europe, and has published over seventy papers and chapters on a variety of topics concerning conversation and other forms of talk-in-interaction as the primordial site of human sociality.

AMIT SCHEJTER
*Tel Aviv University, Israel*
Dr. Amit Schejter joined the communication department at Tel Aviv University in 1997 after serving four years as director of legal affairs and international relations of the Israel Broadcasting Authority in Jerusalem. He also served as policy adviser to two education ministers charged with overseeing public and educational broadcasting. He has sat on the Administrative Council and Legal Committee of the European Broadcasting Union and chaired the Israel Audience Research Board. He is a graduate of the Hebrew University of Jerusalem Law Faculty and earned a Master's degree in mass communication at Boston University and his PhD at Rutgers University.

BERIT SKOG
*Norwegian University of Science and Technology, Trondheim*
Dr. Berit Skog is an associate professor in sociology in the Department of Sociology and Political Science at the Norwegian University of Science and Technology (NTNU), Trondheim. Her work focuses on issues concerning gender and social class in education, youth and technology, and gender as an aspect of academic culture. Recently she has been leading research projects entitled "An Evaluation of the Mentor Project, NTNU" and "Analogue and Digital Learning Material: Pupils and Teachers in the Information Society."

GEORG STRØM
*Ericsson, Denmark*
Dr. Georg Strøm, a Danish citizen, earned his BA in anthropology 1981 and an MSc.Eng. in 1982. He received his PhD in computer science in 1996. Earlier in his career, Dr. Strøm worked on GSM specifications for the Danish Ministry of Post and Telegraph (PTT) then as a product manager in communication for Motorola. Presently he is usability coordinator in L. M. Ericsson A/S. He has published many popular articles in Danish on the use of electronic equipment and is the author of three books. His personal web page is www.georg.dk. He last visited the Philippines in 2000.

KARINA TRACEY
*British Telecom, UK*
Mrs. Karina Tracey graduated from Queens University, Belfast, in 1995 with a BSc Hons. in Psychology. She joined BT in 1997 after completing an MSc (Eng.) in work design and ergonomics at Birmingham University. She works in the Advanced Communications Research Group at Adastral Park, BT, and is currently working on a longitudinal project looking at consumer lifestyles, behavior and attitudes in households in Britain.

MARTHA TURNER
*Rutgers University*
Ms. Martha Turner is a PhD student at Rutgers University in the School of Communication, Information and Library Studies. She studies electronic and other forms of mediated communication. Before coming to Rutgers she worked at the US National Science Foundation, located in Washington, DC.

VALENTIN VARBANOV
*B&G Ingenering*
Mr. Valentin Varbanov is a professional electrical engineer who is the head of his own consulting company in Ruse, Bulgaria. He graduated from the University of Ruse in electrical engineering and has served there as an assistant professor. Among the positions he has held was managing director of Agroelmontagstroi, a state enterprise for agricultural electrical engineering and construction. He has received several awards for his inventions related to equipment assembly.

BIRGITTE YTTRI
*Telenor Research, Norway*
Dr. Birgitte Yttri is a sociologist at Telenor Research Institute located outside Oslo, Norway. She finished her studies in sociology at the University of Oslo in 1998, and did her main thesis on the relationship between the private and public sphere among home-based teleworkers. Since that time she has worked in the group called Future Users researching new information technologies in their social context.

# Preface and acknowledgments

Stopping at a Princeton, New Jersey, construction site, we half-consciously summarized the communicational situation. Before quite realizing it, we found in that buzzing, blooming confusion we could readily spot the person in charge. He was a man in his late 40s nestling a mobile phone in his meaty fist. The mobile phone was not what tipped us off – most workers at the site had cell telephones or pagers dangling from their belts. The boss carried his in his hand, its stubby antenna poking forward like an extra digit.

What you wear, and how you wear it, is a powerful form of communication. In this case, the boss's unconscious positioning of his communication device relative to his body was wonderfully indicative of his status and power. By otherwise occupying his hand with a mobile phone, he showed he had no intention of picking up a tool or performing manual labor. He used the phone's abbreviated antenna to point and gesture, in the manner of a nineteenth-century English army officer using his riding crop to dictate who needed to go where and do what.

The boss was also presumably more likely than his workers to be receiving a phone call, and thus needed to have his phone at the ready; the others, requiring it less often, could make do with a fumbling recovery from their belts. By having his telephone so primed for action, the boss could summon whatever manpower, materiel or expertise the project might require. Thus his cell phone also served as the symbolic equivalent of an ancient Egyptian overseer's whisk: others would be doing his bidding.

A few days later, strolling through the village green in Morristown, New Jersey, we caught a sidelong glance of a man sitting on a park bench. Like the foreman, he also looked to be in his late 40s. Unkempt, his gaze was fixed firmly on the horizon. Although by himself, he was nonetheless talking animatedly in a too-loud voice. Other passers-by, we noticed, inflected their path so as to provide him a wide berth. We did likewise. After transiting to his other side, we glimpsed backward nervously to see whether we could discern the telltale cord running from his ear to disappear beneath his clothes. Under the bulky sweatshirt, one hoped, the cord would connect to a cell telephone. Such a tether would allay our anxiety, allowing us to slacken our pace. Without it, we'd want to maintain our speed.

These two New Jersey vignettes encompass many of our themes. They include symbolism, power, order and command, issues reflected in the first vignette. Other themes, encapsulated in the second vignette, are the choreography of interpersonal communication, negotiation and maintenance of the social order, as well as the regulation of conversational interaction and self-presentation.

The disheveled man in the park was emblematic of the problem societies had been facing for millennia. Was this person in contact with a distant sentience or simply out of touch with quotidian reality? If the former, in historical times the individual would be a powerful and important religious figure. If the latter, an object of disdain. Nowadays we generally assume that such pre-Industrial Age "long-distance callers" never did have anyone at the other end of the telepathic line, whereas we give benefit of doubt that today's "plugged in" mobile phone users do.

Indeed the power to converse instantaneously and comfortably across vast distances was once a power reserved in human imagination only for the greatest gods. By contrast, today people with a few dollars can, from any geographically favored place, avail themselves of this ability. Hoi polloi of the twenty-first century enjoy ease of communication (not to mention physical comfort) far beyond the ken of the nineteenth century's richest potentate.

Our book is about how this godlike power is used by those who are far less than angels. We look at how people's lives are different now that copper tether and monopolistic tariff no longer constrain communication-at-a-distance. We also assay how organizations and societies, or, more precisely, social arrangements in physical space, have become transformed as a result of people exercising these powers. It is about how the internal psychological feeling of being accessible or having access changes social relationships. We want to understand how the "life feel" of the lived experience may be altered owing to the availability of this technology.

Yet we also want to know what has not changed. Like the construction site boss, people still need to arrange their lives so important tasks can be coordinated and executed. They still must struggle for a place in the social hierarchy, for money and economic resources and for control of their social environment. They want to express their will and sustain and nurture their social connections. To explore these issues we use several analytical perspectives that focus on the levels of national social structures, comparisons across cultures, social interaction rituals and the choreography of communication. We also seek to understand how these tools in turn can be used to gain insight into the human communication process.

To avoid confusion and disappointment, it is important to note what this book is *not* about. It not an analysis of the technology underlying the mobile phone industry or of its economic and marketing aspects. Nor is it about the safety aspects of mobile phones (such as are entailed in questions of their contribution to highway accidents or brain cancer).

A few comments about the book's genesis: most papers herein were first presented at a workshop convened at Rutgers University, New Brunswick, December 9–10, 1999. We think that this was the first international workshop aimed at codifying what is known about the social aspects of mobile communication on national cultural or comparative bases. Participants saw the endeavor as first steps towards building a multidimensional conceptual framework and outlining what is known and what needs to be learned about the social aspects of mobile communication. This volume is the first fruit of that gathering.

One cannot create an edited book without also creating a substantial intellectual debt. In our case, though, our profligacy and shameless imposition on colleagues could rightfully land us in intellectual debtor's prison. By no stretch can we discharge that debt here, though we can at least acknowledge it.

A crisp salute is due the excellent colleagues of our Department of Communication at Rutgers since they have helped create a positive intellectual atmosphere that encourages endeavors such as the "Perpetual Contact" exercise. Brent Ruben, Linda Lederman and Lea Stewart continuously work to foster a cooperative intellectual environment. They, like we, want the Department to be always a unit that conducts original research and produces heuristic insights. We also appreciate the judicious leadership of our colleague, Gustav Friedrich, who in his role as Dean cultivates these goals throughout the entire School of Communication, Information and Library Studies. Our gratitude goes as well to Vice President for Academic Affairs Joseph J. Seneca, whose fair-minded and astute leadership helps maintain Rutgers' position as an internationally recognized institution of higher learning.

As to the workshop itself, several departmental colleagues were instrumental in its success. Hartmut Mokros, then chair, encouraged us to hold a conference. He exerted himself tirelessly to encourage creative thinking throughout the Department. Jenny Mandelbaum gave generously of her time and sapience as unofficial senior counselor to the workshop, and lent important assistance at every turn with wry humor and efficiency. Ron Rice served as a conduit to what can verily be said was a worldwide talent pool. Additionally he helped provide an intellectual context for our activities and contributed mightily thereto both during and after the conference.

Among our workshop contributors, Richard Ling was our first recruit; he heartened us with his enthusiasm and assiduousness. Another early supporter was Enid Mante, whose dedication and thoughtfulness were important elements in the conference's overall success. Emanuel Schegloff provided us with our keynote address, and bestowed upon us manifold insights and constructive advice. His comments helped delineate and clarify our discussions; he also politely but firmly encouraged us to move in a heuristic direction. He is an important figure in the social study of the telephone, having contributed to the classic volume on the subject, *The Social Impact of the Telephone*, edited by Ithiel de Sola Poole. Since he provided the first words to our conference gathering via the keynote, it is also appropriate that, as the reader shall see, to him goes the volume's the last word.

We greatly appreciate the acuity and energy of colleagues who by their presence and papers allowed us to consummate the workshop. They are: Stephen Duck, Akiba Cohen, Chantal de Gournay, Leopoldina Fortunati, Shin Dong Kim, Christian Licoppe, Dawn Nafus, Jorge Quitegui, Sheizaf Rafaeli, Pirjo Rautianinen, Kathleen Robbins, James Rule and Amit Schejter.

We also thank those who, though unable to attend the workshop, were still kind enough to formulate their thoughts in writing. Their efforts greatly expanded our understanding and have also yielded thoughtful papers. These scholars include Kenneth Gergen, Jean-Philippe Heurtin, Eija-Liisa Kasesniemi, Jukka-Pekka Puro, Daphne Raban, Berit Skog, Georg Strøm, Karina Tracey, Martha Turner, Valentin Varbanov and Birgitte Yttri.

We were ably assisted during the workshop by a cadre of top-flight students. They included June Anibogu, Susan Bagley-Coyle, Jo-Tzu Chi, Victoria Kozol, Liliana Pinilla, Jeannie Rodriguez-Diaz, Peter Alexander Stepman and Angelica Weber.

Irving L. Horowitz, Barry Wellman and William H. Dutton provided acute comments on the manuscript. Mauricio Arango, Richard Buttny, John T. Carey, Claude Fischer and Oscar Gandy, Jr., shared their valuable ideas generously and graciously. At the project's early stage, Bill Caldwell lent valuable guidance and expertise; he remains a unique inspiration in his selflessness and thoughtful efforts to build a better world. Sarah Caro and Gillian Dadd of Cambridge University Press were wonderfully supportive throughout the publication preparation process. To all these colleagues and friends we offer our heartfelt gratitude.

*New Brunswick, New Jersey*                                          J.E.K.

M.A.A.

# 1  Introduction: framing the issues

*James E. Katz and Mark A. Aakhus*

## Greater than gods

With the invention of the telephone in 1876, it was possible for the first time in history to have real-time conversational interaction at a distance.[1] Back then, the technology was astounding. Early demonstrations of its capability attracted large crowds, most of whom were awe-struck, though some thought it mere legerdemain. By contrast, in the twenty-first century the telephone has for a billion people become, literally, a fixture of everyday life. Only by its absence do we deem it worthy of comment (such as in school classrooms and prisons or in poor countries). The miracle of telephone conversation is too readily forgotten by laypeople and scholars alike. However, the telephone's becoming mobile has re-familiarized many people with the amazement felt by its early witnesses. The exquisite value of the telephone can best be appreciated if one considers the plight of a villager who wants to know if there might be work available in a nearby town, or who needs to summon aid for a sick family member.

Over the years, the telephone has dramatically changed how people live their lives and see their world. Another change of perhaps similar magnitude is in the offing with the mobilization not only of speech but also of a novel array of computer-supported communication and social interaction. Bursty chip-to-chip chats will arrange everything from grocery deliveries to a blind date between two co-located individuals of matching interest profiles. But even today's powers of the mobile phone are extraordinary. In the words of one of our students: "Although my family and I now live in America, I am originally from China. If I want to talk to one of my aunts or uncles, anytime day or night, I just press a button or two on my mobile phone and begin visiting with them."

---

[1] To be technically precise, there had been something that existed somewhat earlier, sometimes called "the lovers' telephone," which was the equivalent of two tin cans connected by a taut string. Since the mechanical energy of this system dissipated after a few score meters, it cannot be considered a distance-spanning real-time conversational communication technology.

The telephone and its latest mobile incarnation have a unique place in the history of humanity's development. Cars and airplanes were adumbrated respectively by horse-drawn vehicles and birds; as such, humans were at least familiar with what might await once the right technology had been puzzled out. By contrast, nothing in the animal world could allow humans to anticipate the power bestowed by the telephone. In the history of human imagination the power of real-time interactive oral communication over great distances had been a power so great that even most divine beings were considered incapable of it: Zeus, king of the Greek gods, and the rest of the pantheon, had to rely on messenger-boy Mercury. Today a good many messenger boys have their own mobile phones.

## A mind- and society-altering technology

The spread of mobile communication, most obtrusively as cell phones but increasingly in other wireless devices, is affecting people's lives and relationships. Cell phones speed the pace and efficiency of life, but also allow more flexibility at business and professional levels as well as in family and personal life. They are a boon for those who feel they are not accomplishing enough. People can harness spare time, or time previously spent in tasks that seem not to require full attention (for instance, waiting on a shopping queue, or, far more disturbingly, driving). They can use this time to plan and coordinate with others, get information or messages. They can even shop remotely by phone while at the same time themselves shopping in person.

Mobile technology also affects the way people interact when face-to-face or, rather and increasingly, face-to-face-to-mobile-phone-face, since people are ever more likely to include the mobile phone as a participant in what would otherwise be a face-to-face dyad or small group, and even parties.

On the other hand, those who treasure respite may find themselves pressured to replace otherwise excusable isolation with productive tasks. Once upon a time, being aboard an airplane excused an executive from having to interact with colleagues. No more, for the fax and phone now follow even at six miles high; nor are the seashore and mountaintop immune to their reach. An age of perpetual contact, at least in terms of potential, is dawning.

Neither should we underestimate the mobile phone's ability to help effect large-scale political change. Having recently become wildly popular in Manila, mobile phones were instrumental in organizing public pressure in response to personal corruption charges that forced Philippine president Joseph Estrada from office in January 2001. Throughout 2000, anti-Estrada text messages, such as hostile slogans and satirical jokes, were aggressively propagated over the system. One government response was to encourage citizens to "just turn their cell phones off" (Brown, 2001). As the crisis intensified, anti-Estrada leaders began using "phone trees" to quickly organize massive demonstrations against Mr. Estrada. When riot police would maneuver to contain demonstrators, protest leaders would use mobile phone messaging to redirect the crowds. These efforts culminated with the ouster of Mr. Estrada. When he was arrested for "plundering the public treasury" a few months later, Mr. Estrada spent his first few hours in jail giving lengthy interviews to television stations – via *his* mobile phone (Chandrasekaran, 2001, p. A3). The mobile phone, a quintessential instrument of two-way interpersonal communication, can also work as a tool to spur and coordinate the actions of masses for political change.

### Scholarly lacuna

Given the ever-expanding changes enabled by the ever-shrinking mobile phone, it is high time to give the subject concentrated scholarly attention. Yet, despite billions of dollars and hours spent on mobile communication, there is but slight academic interest in the social aspects of these processes. To fill this disquieting void we have assembled leading and rising scholars to analyze and report on the changes mobile communication has wrought in the way people conduct their lives and relationships. This volume presents their research findings.

Our investigation proceeds along three avenues. First, we want to see how the mobile telephone as a technology has been affecting people's lives. We wish to specify at several levels across ten cultures what these changes are and what they portend. Second, we see that the mobile telephone as a technology can sharply illuminate human behavior. The novelty of mobile phone technology, and its intrusive power into people's lives, allow us to observe aspects of the human communication process that would otherwise escape our attention, or at least be extremely difficult to discern. Finally, we introduce a new communication term to describe the mobile communication phenomenon.

Mobile communication technologies are already modifying well-established communication patterns, amplifying and substituting for them. Indeed, even creative and unanticipated uses are proliferating, with consequences for the pace and content of all walks of life. There has been a rapid and continuing merging of formerly separate modalities of mediated communication. These include the Internet, the telephone, portable computers, personal digital assistants, radio broadcasting, wireless and infrared technologies, digital audio and video, and, traditionally, paper. The last time a communication technology had such a large effect on so many people was nearly a half-century ago when commercial television was introduced; as we will note next, a legitimate question is whether the mobile phone will surpass TV. What is not a question, though, is that for many, especially those outside the United States, the consequences of mobile communication dwarf that of the Internet.

## More popular than TV

Comparative international statistics convey the magnitude and speed of these changes and the growth of the mobile phone. As the estimates in figure 1.1, suggest, people worldwide are more likely to own a telephone

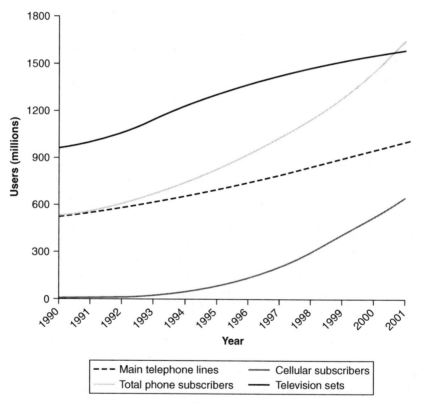

Figure 1.1 Worldwide ownership of telephones and mobile phones vs. TV. *Source:* World Telecommunication Development Report, cited in *Communication International* (November 1, 1999).

Table 1.1 *Estimates of mobile phone ownership, 2001*

| Region | Penetration rate (%) |
| --- | --- |
| "Four tigers" (Hong Kong, Singapore, South Korea and Taiwan) | 72.4 |
| Western Europe | 72.1 |
| Japan | 53.4 |
| Australasia | 49.6 |
| North America | 42.7 |
| Latin America | 15.6 |
| Middle East | 12.1 |
| Central Europe | 8.6 |
| Rest of Asia | 4.2 |
| Africa | 3.2 |

*Source: Financial Times,* June 14, 2001, p. 26.

than the more celebrated "miracle" of communication technology, the
TV. These figures bolster our position that the mobile phone is indeed a
revolutionary technology in terms of its ramifications for individual lives
and social organization, both formal and informal.

In terms of penetration rates, table 1.1 clearly shows that the Northern
European nations have some of the world's highest rates. These were
among the earliest countries to have mobile phones available. As will be
seen in subsequent chapters, the mobile phone has indeed transformed
life in these societies. However, the question of early availability might
not alone be enough to explain the uptake of mobile phone technology.

The economic profile of the mobile phone, or, more specifically, the
cost per minute of usage, appears to be an important predictor of its
mass penetration rate. Figure 1.2 shows the correlation between the cost
per minute for mobile phone use and its penetration. Correlation does
not mean causation, and there are obviously other variables that help
account for both penetration rate and cost. These include the cost of
handsets, population dispersion, the gross national product of the society and the extensiveness of service availability. However, it is known that
consumer behavior of other "utilities" such as natural gas for home heat-
ing is strongly influenced by metering and awareness of unit consumption
and pricing. So it is not much of a stretch to argue that the consumer cost
awareness of the per minute pricing plans of the service provider, along
with a consumption meter (such as is displayed on most mobile phones),
would lead to users being exquisitely sensitive to price. This is all the
more the case since, in our surveys, of those who have dropped their service for mobile phones excessive bills caused by inattentive consumption

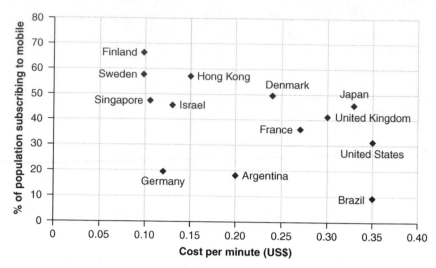

Figure 1.2 Penetration rates and cost per minute of mobile phone use, by country. *Sources:* D. Wilson, "The Future Is Here. Or Is It?" *Scientific American* 283 (October 2000): 50–51. Based on International Telecommunication Union, European Commission, eMarketer, and national telecom agencies and carriers.

of minutes is frequently mentioned as a reason for terminating service. Thus price would seem an attractive explanatory approach. One consequence of this argument is that, if costs per minute continue to decline at their historical rates, the worldwide proliferation of the mobile phone will accelerate over the near-term.

## Framing the mobile phone

As a result of the mobile phone's extensive impact, rich stores of everyday discourses have accreted about the meaning of the mobile telephone for individuals and society. These discourses are visible in the wide range of accounts exchanged about the mobile telephone, especially regarding social etiquette. Whether these accounts concerning mobile phones are made in personal complaints, news stories, or advertisements, they serve an epideictic function. An epideictic function, as Aristotle wrote, is the use of speech to prove a person and their possessions or actions as worthy of honor or censure (Aristotle, 1954, pp. 31–33). Epideictic discourse stands in contrast to forensic discourse, which is the use of speech to determine what happened (Fahnestock, 1993, p. 19).

One might be tempted simply to ignore epideictic discourse that occurs in everyday cultural expressions made by ordinary people (referred to as "folk") about the mobile telephone and seek instead the directly revealed insights of topical forensic discourse experts. But, in terms of contemporary discourse about mobile communication, we discern a puzzle: folk views are abundant in observations and explanations, whereas expert discourse is relatively impoverished.[2] This puzzle is not a barrier to understanding the mobile telephone but an opportunity to formulate new grounds from which to explain the mobile communication phenomenon, in particular, and the tools humans invent to communicate, in general. The points of controversy potentially reveal more general, yet inchoate, philosophy about technology and communication common to the participants in the epideictic discourse about mobile telephones. Based on our focus group research and interviews, we can suggest some lines along which an inquiry might proceed.

The everyday epideictic discourse about the mobile telephone suggests a struggle to make sense of mobile communication and the technology that makes it possible. The contest over the meaning of the mobile telephone invokes well-formulated and nascent folk theories about the purpose and consequence of mobile communication and points to broader contest over the material and ideological condition of communication in contemporary societies. If the contest about the meaning of the mobile phone in everyday life contains dramaturgical elements, our goal is to articulate the staging, the framing, that makes the drama possible. We turn to the folk and expert framing of the mobile telephone.

### Folk framing

Mobile telephones are praised, on the one hand, as devices that will liberate individuals from the constraints of their settings. Individuals who master these devices are shown as people who control their destiny. Stories circulate that focus on how people manage the contemporary demand to

---

[2] The situation in terms of expert discourse is, happily, improving. Two recent studies addressed the status symbol function of the mobile phone. The first (Lycett and Dunbar, 2000) looked at it in terms of displays and other manifestations of mobile phone ownership and use in a pub. The authors called this "lekking" behavior (a lek is an area where male members of a species congregate for elaborate courtship displays, while females observe performances to choose a mate). A second study (Charlton and Bates, 2000) claimed, on slender evidence, that mobile phone usage was a substitute for achieving the social recognition earlier conferred by cigarette smoking. Thus, the authors argued, as mobile phone usage among teens rose, cigarette smoking declined. Neither study was particularly persuasive, but the international press attention they received should spur further intellectual inquiry.

be in multiple places at one time or to simultaneously serve multiple roles and present multiple faces. These stories heap praise and honor on those who pull off such an elegant performance through the use of technology.

One theme in accounts about the mobile phone concerns its role as an instrument for managing practical affairs. The mobile phone is praised as a means to handle or avoid the emergencies and crises that otherwise disrupt the smooth flow of everyday life. Within this view, the mobile telephone is a tool that forestalls tragedy or tragi-comedy. For instance, one family, who lives on a farm on the northern plains of the USA, used a cell phone to dispatch emergency services when the father suffered a heart attack while working by himself miles from the nearest person or wire-telephone. The cellular industry gave members of the family a free trip to Washington D.C. where they recited their story to industry stakeholders and the press (*The Fertile Journal,* 1999). Less dramatically, the mobile phone is praised as a means to facilitate the planning and coordination of everyday matters. It is also a means to "be in touch" to offer socio-emotional support. One of the common uses mobile telephone users report with praise involves one family member simply checking in on another to find out "how it is going" or to report that "I'll be home in a few minutes." The praise thus draws attention to the mobile telephone as a means for friends, family, and other social networks to retain accessibility when they would otherwise be isolated from each other. Sometimes individuals, particularly men, even cite the belief they earn "points" in the relationship for having done so.

Mobile telephones are blamed, on the other hand, as the cause or catalyst of the loss of control over life. The mobile telephone, in these accounts, is often dramatized as a means to victimize people, thus robbing them of their humanity. The ability of people to manage the access others may have to them is a central premise upon which blame is formulated.

One theme in accounts about the mobile telephone concerns how the mobile is implicated in the loss of control over one's accessibility and the subsequent acceleration of the erosion of the public–private distinction. The mobile phone is blamed in the loss of leisure. A recent news story reported on a man who, while vacationing at Yellowstone Park, hooked up a pay phone to his personal computer. He did this "just to be in touch" with his office. An implication of the news story is that a mobile phone with wireless Internet access could have circumvented this situation. Yet, the story itself was told to portray the man as a depraved, communication junkie seeking his next fix. Rather than creating more time or better use of available time, the phone is seen to usher in an ever more quickened and hectic pace to life. In other cases, the blame highlights how people are victims of others' excesses. People report frustration when one person's chat and talk with an absent other via the phone spills over into the public arena. News accounts report rules established against mobile telephones in public arenas such as restaurants and theaters. These accounts dramatize how public space is destroyed, and even colonized, by private talk that interferes with ongoing interactions or that prevents spontaneous public interaction. Finally, the images of the mobile phone and related services portrayed by industry and marketers are seen to be false images of technology use that only spur consumption. The blame then emphasizes how the mobile telephone is an opportunity for the loss of control over contact and accessibility with others.

The struggle in folk discourse about mobile telephones and mobile communication signals a contest over deeper issues about sociality such as openness, availability and access. Indeed, the struggle to gain access and prevent access to one's self appears to animate social and technical innovations (Hopper, 1992).

The accounts about the mobile telephone tend to fix either praise or blame on the purpose and consequence of mobile communication, yet these accounts also depend on similar presumptions about communication and technology. The virtue and vice people find in the availability of the mobile telephone and its uses represent concerns about control over the new degree of contact and availability the mobile telephone makes possible. The praise and blame offered about mobile communication are generated concerning the mobile phones' facilitation or obstruction of a presumed natural progression of humans toward the ideal of open, transparent communication. The praise heaped on the mobile phone and its elegant use suggests that the good person communicating well maintains both contact and availability. Yet, the mobile telephone is also a foil in this teleology. The blame heaped on the mobile telephone or its dishonorable use suggests that a person is bad and communication is poor when a person is prevented from being an open, authentic communicator. The judgments are generated from a philosophy about humans and communication that embraces the Romantic image of Rousseau's natural man. The judgments about the technology stem from its transparency and presumed non-interference with human communication.

### Expert framing

What the folk have noticed the experts are missing. The mobile telephone, and mobile communication, are now sufficiently prominent for the intellectual community to see them as consequential in understanding communication behavior. Moreover, new forms of communication behavior do not eliminate the problem of each form; yet saying there is no change to daily life is contrary to commonsense and fact. It is worth understanding how lives are changed because of the mobile phone and, therefore, it is important to have technology in a theoretical picture.

Theories about communication ignore technology, except as a mass medium. Even in mass media studies, there is traditionally a preoccupation with media effects. Upon reading literature on communication technology, one might think that communication technology is a television or a personal computer linked to a network. Further investigation would lead one to think that the purpose of technology is to deliver entertainment packaging or to make organizations more efficient and effective. In this connection, we would also point out that mobile phones are in a transitional state, their status in public and the norms governing its use still transmogrifying – as is evident in the folk framing.

The mobile telephone is a technology that can sharply illuminate human behavior. Yet with notable exceptions – such as Hopper (1992), Fischer (1994), and, of course, Schegloff (see the Appendix to this volume) – experts have largely ignored the telephone and in particular the mobile phone. There are at least two important reasons for this theoretical situation. First, the media of everyday life, in particular the phone and mobile phone, are neglected as material to the conduct of everyday action. Although the telephone has assumed a central role in contemporary life, even Goffman, arguably the most astute observer of the routine and the mundane, seldom talked about the phone. Thus, the problematic ordering of behaviors is taken for granted. Second, the sociology of knowledge regarding communication makes it difficult to engage the scholarly community of people interested in communication. It appears that the experts have difficulty discovering and interpreting even the communication taking place right in their own ears. Save for computer-mediated communication, little interest is devoted to personal communication devices. This emphasis raises questions too. Why, for instance, have fewer than five articles been published over thirty years in the scholarly literature on the communicative aspects of Citizens' Band radio when millions use it each day? In stark contrast, more than an average of five articles are published daily on computer-mediated communication.

*A new perspective and a new term: the convergence of the folks and experts*

On the one hand, the folk framing and empirical evidence show the importance in daily life and human meaning of the mobile and other personal communication technologies (PCTs). On the other hand, the theorists whose job it is to give us social analytic tools to explain and predict human behavior have been as reticent on the subject as the public has been voluble. Given the omnipresence, the expansive multitasked functions, and the far-reaching social implications of the mobile and personal communications technology, it would seem worthwhile to make it a focus of theoretical investigation.

We propose a term that brings the focus squarely upon the human use and consequences of PCTs. Therefore, we coin a new term that encompasses the intersections of these two domains, namely the social person and the mobile machine. It seeks to encompass both the folk and the expert frameworks; tangible and intangible aspects; material and social issues; and, quintessentially, the machine and "spirit" elements of flexible interaction with assistive technology. For this we propose the term *Apparatgeist*, which originates from Latin and here is derived from the German and Slavic word, *apparat*, meaning machine. The Germanic suffix, *Geist*, denotes spirit or mind. The potential use for such a bridging term and model will become evident throughout this volume as the social, cultural, and material aspects of the mobile are explored (see chapter 19 for an extensive argument for *Apparatgeist*). We anticipate that the new perspective will allow us to discern with greater clarity the ways PCT use is socially transformative as well as a lens through which human communication behavior can be examined. We of course welcome the thoughts of other communication scholars on these questions.

### Looking forward

In presenting this volume, we have three goals and use the empirical data and theoretical arguments of the chapters in their pursuit. These goals are to identify and analyze mobile communication technologies in terms of:

1. ways they change (as well as leave unchanged) our social lives and organizations;
2. how they create, destroy, and reinforce various communicational forms;
3. potential conceptual framings that offer new ways to understand both the mobile communication phenomenon and the role of communication technology in everyday life.

Throughout the book, though, our emphasis is less fatidic than analytic.

The chapters are wide-ranging in terms not only of research method and theoretical perspective, but of cultural context and focus of analysis as well. Like our subject – the mobile telephone – the chapters engage social interaction at all levels from micro to macro and from monads and dyads to organizations and societies.

The volume has three parts addressing, respectively, (1) mobile communication, (2) private talk, and (3) public performance. Part I presents national studies exploring the culturally specific reception and adoption of the mobile phone, as well as the relationship between national values and communication behaviors involving the mobile phone. These studies are presented in approximate order of magnitude of mobile phone penetration rates, with pride of place going to Finland. (There is much variation in precise ranking owing to the rapid adoption of the mobile phones.) Another theme of the section is the value of the mobile phone in relationships at all levels, including the family and cliques. Yet it can also suggest meanings for when the mobile is not available, as well as the cultural significance of its arrival in a former dictatorship.

Part II explores the micro-level of communication and the interpersonal and nuance management it requires. It highlights how communication technology is folded into the warp and woof of life through private talk. We see how the technology is embraced and mastered by some social groups while being tolerated or resisted by others. Each chapter highlights the negotiation of the social-communicative order involved in the way people bring together the technical and the social.

Part III examines the role of the mobile telephone in public performance, with special attention given to the unique characteristics of the mobile phone relative to other personal technologies and the prospects of what we, with only slight exaggeration, call perpetual contact. The part also looks at what life means without the mobile phone and thus how the mobile phone indexes aspects of social life that may otherwise go unnoticed. It also examines how the telephone can be used to gain insight into vital but ephemeral constituent elements of social interaction.

This latter purpose extends to the Appendix, which allows us the special privilege of presenting for the first time in published form the early and still highly fruitful theories of Emanuel Schegloff, a seminal figure who has helped illuminate our field. His discussion of "Opening sequencing" is as fresh and acute today as it was when it was written. It is particularly germane to the problems outlined in the folk framing of mobile communication because Schegloff examines how people manage – through conversational practices – access to each other and appropriate identities to be taken up in an interaction. His discussion puts into perspective the class of social problems characterized by stories of speaking loudly, and often ambiguously, in public to an indeterminate "other."

In this sense, the Schegloff appendix is even more useful when considered in the context of mobile phone technology's use in public places. In the contemporary world, a man walking down the street can, while looking at passersby, shout emphatically, "You're a jerk!" If the individual doing the shouting has a mobile phone pressed against his head, he will, after being scrutinized suspiciously, be ignored and forgotten; without such an exculpatory device, a nasty engagement would probably ensue. Desperate searches for gaining one's conversational and raptorial bearings, often impelled by telephone technology, are the enduring relevant themes included in Schegloff's analysis.

Beneath the material descriptions and phenomenological insights presented in this volume we can discern, in certain consistent patterns of relations between people and their communication technology, a sleeping giant. In our concluding chapter, we will return to this theme and probe for potential insights.

## References

Aristotle (1954). *The Rhetoric and the Poetics of Aristotle* (W. R. Roberts and I. Bywater, trans.). New York: Modern Library College Editions.

Brown, Rick (2001). "Cell Phone Revolt: Filipinos Wage Wireless War." Office.com Telecommunications News Page, January 19. Accessed on July 27, 2001, from http://www.office.com/global/0,2724,9-21932,FF.html.

Chandrasekaran, Rajiv (2001). "Police Arrest Former President." *Washington Post*, April 26.

Charlton, A., and Bates, C. (2000). "Decline in Teenage Smoking with Rise in Mobile Phone Ownership: Hypothesis." *British Medical Journal* 321 (November 4): 1155.

Fahnestock, J. (1993). "Accommodating Science: The Rhetorical Life of Scientific Facts." In M. W. McRae (ed.), *The Literature of Science: Perspectives on Popular Scientific Writing.* Athens, GA: University of Georgia Press, 17–36.

*The Fertile Journal* (1999). "Local Family Wins Trip to Washington, D.C." May 26, pp. A1, A9.

Fischer, Claude S. (1994). *America Calling.* Berkeley: University of California Press.

Hopper, Robert. (1992). *Telephone Conversation.* Bloomington, IN: University of Indiana Press.

Lycett, John E., and Dunbar, Robin I. M. (2000). "Mobile Phones as Lekking Devices among Human Males." *Human Nature* 11(1): 93–104.

*Part I*

# Mobile communication: national and comparative perspectives

Hundreds of millions of people worldwide are enthusiastically embracing mobile digital communication. In this part, we explore through the lens of national cultures the social scientific and communication issues that arise from this process. Authors representing eight countries provide information and interpretation of this process; they tell us what is happening in their countries and some possible reasons why. We present the chapters in roughly the order of penetration of mobile phones at the beginning of the millennium. Pride of place goes to Finland.

The nations examined range from those that have more mobile phone than wireline subscribers (Israel) to those in which mobile phone subscription is a rarity, costing several times the average monthly wage (Bulgaria). The respective national situations represented among the chapters are variegated in terms of cultural practices, economic development and geography. Mobile phone practices also vary somewhat among these nations. But what is perhaps even more striking is the way denizens of these national cultures, despite their respective uniqueness, nonetheless often converge on a common set of mobile phone practices, give voice to a common set of social conduct concerns and find themselves grappling with comparable negotiations of time, space and identity. These nation studies yield a snapshot of the emerging contested domains of local culture, family control and the new low-level uses and abuse of public and private places. They also address the inevitable conflict between, on the one hand, the external world of work, strangers and sales people, all with their inexhaustible demands, and, on the other, the warm circle of family and friends. Yet even within each of these two clusters of obligations and dependencies there are highly charged divisions and cross-pressures. The tighter knit situation that the mobile phone allows brings the future user face-to-face with a blessing and a curse. That is of course the promise and peril of perpetual contact.

With a focus on Finland, *Jukka-Pekka Puro* probes the meaning and demographics of mobile phone usage in Finland. He explores how Finns,

15

who are traditionally thought of as "silent," suddenly appear extremely voluble when their communication is piped through a mobile phone. Finland also lives in the shadow of its own creation, the technological giant, Nokia. The penetration of the mobile phone draws traditional Finnish culture into a clash with an emerging mobile information society. Puro shows unexpected patterns of ownership by Finnish families and usage by women and men. As Finns fold the tool into their lives, they develop communication practices and expectations that challenge fundamental aspects of self-identity, including the use (and possible abuses) of speech culture. This chapter provides insight into many issues that other nations and cultures may face.

In their chapter on Israel, *Amit Schejter and Akiba Cohen* seek to explain the unprecedented growth of the mobile phone market in Israel. They examine various data and exemplars to argue that the characteristics of the medium and the Israeli culture are mutually reinforcing and extending. They explore three areas in this regard. The first is functions and uses (including uses and gratifications, status symbols and identity creation, selection and use of mobile phone features, and parental control over children). The second is ethics, etiquette and values (including the blurring of public and private space, pedestrian and driver behavior, advertising for mobile phones, and tone, volume and manners). The third is policy questions (including social aspects of market policy, competition, universal service obligations, privacy, and regulation of behavior in public).

*Leopoldina Fortunati* analyzes the social identity of the mobile phone in Italy in comparison with the rest of Europe. Her data come from three research projects: one a telephone survey sample ($n = 6,609$) in Italy, France, Germany, Spain and the UK. Her second sample was of Italians only ($n = 1,400$) as well as a free association test of a subsample. Her third dataset also comes from a telephone survey ($n = 1,400$). She uses these data to put into critical perspective some common assumptions about the use of the mobile phone, specifically that it presents itself, as it were, as a communicative, mobile, metropolitan, portable, intimate technology. She shows with her data where stereotypes are supported and where they are refuted. She also seeks to account for the mobile phone's success in an Italian setting as well as some of the problematics of the technology in relation to the body. She also argues that the symbolic and social dimensions of the telephone are important. It is especially intriguing that Italians are very light users of the landline telephone (less than a quarter of US usage), and have not increased their landline use over the past few decades to any substantial degree. They have, however, embraced the mobile phone enthusiastically and are among Europe's heaviest users. To explain this, she relies on explanations that extend beyond the functional.

Drawing upon detailed analysis, *Shin Dong Kim* argues that, aside from economic and pragmatic rationales, which go a long way towards explaining the meteoric growth of the mobile phone in South Korea, there are also some important socio-cultural ones. He presents explanations as to why this technology has been so heartily embraced in Korea, a society known for its regularized and formal interactions. This is all the more intriguing given that the seemingly casual and social-barrier-penetrating qualities of mobile communication are taken up with such enthusiasm in a highly collectivist and hierarchical culture. Kim's analysis draws attention to the subtle changes in communication practices and expectations that accommodate the mobile phone into everyday life, which, in turn, lead to more dramatic shifts in expectations about appropriate and competent communication. These issues parallel the issue raised by Puro's analysis in chapter 2 of mobile communication culture encroaching on traditional Finnish culture.

Turning to the United States, *Kathleen Robbins and Martha Turner* point out that, when AT&T initially developed the cell phone in the early 1980s, the company estimated that the US cellular phone market would reach 1 million users by 2000. The actual number of US subscribers in the year 2000 was nearly 100 million, or about 35% of the population. Yet, as impressive as the penetration rate appears, the USA lags its industrialized counterparts in other parts of the world. So their purpose is to explore why the USA lags so far behind Europe and the Pacific Rim countries in terms of penetration in the usage. Some of the reasons arise out of the US regulatory background. However, we also believe that there are aspects of the American character and national policy that yield the unique configuration found in the USA. These aspects also fit into the questions of a digital divide as well as the role of the federal government in enhancing cell phone security. Robbins and Turner also are able to give an update to the profile of users (and non-users) as the mobile phone becomes an ever-more pervasive aspect of daily life in the USA. They show, for instance, that more women are now mobile phone subscribers than men. They also raise issues about how perpetual contact presents a reciprocal danger in monitoring and privacy deprivation. This important issue cannot be explored in any detail in this volume, but we do note its social and policy importance. Also, James Rule picks up this theme in Part III.

*Christian Licoppe and Jean-Philippe Heurtin* report on a 1997 French study of 1,000 mobile phone users in Paris and Toulouse. They gathered both quantitative traffic data and qualitative interviews. They found that the telephone is dramatically affecting norms and manners in France.

Traditionally, the telephone has been seen as a highly formal instrument. However, the proliferation of the cellular mobile telephone is leading to its being seen as an informal and casual way of communicating. This, according to the researchers, has significant but undesirable implications for those of the middle and petit-bourgeois classes in French society. However, they note that teenagers have embraced the new technology with fervor.

*Enid Mante* compares the Netherlands with the USA and is surprised by the similarities, despite the fact that the study was aimed at highlighting differences. She holds that, with the general globalization tendencies and widespread use of information and communication technologies (ICTs), a world is developing with blurring boundaries between countries and regions, between home and work, between work time and leisure time, and between time zones. One of the aspects of this blurring phenomenon is that a sense of location, and a sense of the home base, is becoming lost. To better understand this phenomenon, she reports on two studies that she supervised. The first was conducted cross-nationally in the USA and in the Netherlands to see if the USA could serve as a benchmark for the Netherlands of the adoption of an array of mobile telecommunications services. Also of interest was to assess the public's view of the convergence of mobile telephony and the Internet. The second study was an international comparison between six European countries. Perhaps one of the most intriguing findings was the remarkable similarity between the USA and Netherlands in terms of attitudes towards ICTs. That is to say, that Dutch and Americans have convergent meaning structures for understanding and using (or criticizing) the mobile phone technology. Indeed, when people of similar perspectives were brought together in focus groups, they had a wonderful time reinforcing each other's views and trading stories about the blessings (or horrors) of the mobile phone.

Bulgaria is an interesting case because it is both a post-communist nation and relatively impoverished. *Valentin Varbanov* discusses how, by contrast to the richer countries, symbolically important a mobile phone can be. He highlights its practical value, but also shows how it has entered the symbolic constellation of values and desires of the population of a country that suffered the rigors of a totalitarian state.

# 2    Finland: a mobile culture

*Jukka-Pekka Puro*

## Introduction

Compared with any other nation, the number of mobile phones per head of population in Finland is the highest in the world. The population of Finland numbers nearly 5 million and, at the close of 1999, there were 3.2 million mobile phones in use in the country. At the end of 1999, there were 2.35 million households in Finland and 78% of them owned a mobile phone. Furthermore, the number of mobile phones in use is still increasing rapidly. The number of mobiles per household has nearly doubled since 1996. Between 1998 and 1999, the number of mobile phone owners rose by 60,000 every month, and the trend seems to be the same in 2000. It is hardly surprising that Finnish communication scholars, sociologists and psychologists have taken special interest in how the mobile phone affects everyday Finnish life.

The rate of mobile phone penetration in Finland points to a puzzle first articulated by Roos (1994): why do Finns, "silent in two languages," have the highest density of mobiles in the world? This mystery has led academics in two directions. First, studies such as those by Nurmela (1997, 1998; Nurmela et al., 2000) examine the quantitative dimensions of the mobile phone culture. These studies demonstrate, for instance, the extent to which mobiles are used in Finnish households. Second, studies by Roos (1993, 1994), Kopomaa (2000) and Mäenpää (2000) examine the qualitative aspects of mobile phone culture. These studies suggest how deeply the mobile phone affects Finnish cultural and social patterns.

The dramatic changes represented by the penetration rates of the mobile phone suggest that the manner in which Finns interpret and understand their everyday interactions and interpersonal relations is also changing. In the following sections, I shall consider how Finnish culture is changing in this era of mobile telephony. In particular, I will explore and challenge assumptions about mobile communication culture as it is emerging in Finland.

## Ownership

*Age and household.* It is widely believed that the success of mobile phones reflects the lifestyles of young, single and independent people
who live in Finnish cities. The urbanization process is one of the topics in
discussion concerning mobile phones in Finnish life. The mobile phone
is seen as an extension of the urbanization of Finnish youth, which reflects deeper attitude and value changes in Finnish youth. The evidence,
however, does not support this belief (see table 2.1). The difference in
ownership between young and old is much smaller than might be expected. Older people and households with two or more members have
ownership rates equal to and sometimes greater than single, young individuals. People over 60 who live alone are the only group that so far
manage without mobile phones.

The most significant change during the past three or four years has
been that the youngest households have begun to prefer mobile phones
over landline phones and the change has been both rapid and effective.
Younger people are considered to be a significant factor in the mobile
phone business, because they have quickly learned how to use mobiles as
fully as possible. As a matter of fact, the position of younger people could
be even stronger if Internet connections did not require conventional

Table 2.1 *Ownership of mobile phones, wired phones, PCs and CD-ROM
drives in Finnish households (%)*

| Type of household | Owns a mobile phone | Owns a wired phone | Owns a PC | Owns a CD-ROM drive |
|---|---|---|---|---|
| 1-person under 30 | 93 | 28 | 34 | 28 |
| 1-person 30–39 | 83 | 38 | 33 | 23 |
| 1-person 40–59 | 64 | 74 | 22 | 18 |
| 1-person over 60 | 33 | 60 | 3 | 3 |
| 2-person under 30 | 91 | 49 | 49 | 45 |
| 2-person 30–49 | 97 | 68 | 49 | 39 |
| 2-person 50–64 | 86 | 97 | 35 | 27 |
| 2-person over 65 | 63 | 100 | 22 | 1 |
| 3-person households | 90 | 93 | 54 | 49 |
| 4-person households | 98 | 91 | 69 | 64 |
| 5 + -person households | 95 | 90 | 83 | 71 |
| All households | 78 | 77 | 39 | 30 |

*Source:* Nurmela et al. (2000).

phone techniques. If people could use their PCs without wired lines, they would not need traditional phones at all.

*Gender.* It is widely believed that the mobile phone is primarily used by males. This view has been approached from two perspectives. First, it has been argued that men adopt new technology first because men are more interested in new communication devices than women (Grint and Gill, 1995). Second, it is claimed that mobile phone ownership is in fact an aspect of employment and that employers offer mobile phones to male more than to female workers. Men, then, are given a preferential position in the mobile phone business.

Both arguments fail to find support in the evidence. The first argument is especially weak, while the latter receives some support, as table 2.2 shows. Males and females have similarly high ownership rates, especially in the age groups between 15 and 49. There appears to be some higher ownership via work by males, which is most evident in the age groups 30–39 and 50–59.

The mobile phone has penetrated most walks of life in Finland. It is not a communication device used primarily by urbanized, young people or a device used primarily by men. Indeed, the mobile phone is owned by multiple-member households and relatively equally across gender and age. Widespread ownership, of course, raises questions about how the mobile is used in everyday life and the consequences its use has for the texture of everyday life.

Table 2.2 *Ownership of mobile phones by gender, age, and work (%)*

|  | Age group | | | | | | |
|---|---|---|---|---|---|---|---|
|  | 15–19 | 20–29 | 30–39 | 40–49 | 50–59 | over 60 | All |
| *Men* | | | | | | | |
| Owns a mobile phone | 77 | 87 | 81 | 72 | 68 | 39 | 73 |
| Mobile phone from work | 0 | 6 | 26 | 19 | 26 | 6 | 16 |
| *Women* | | | | | | | |
| Owns a mobile phone | 77 | 85 | 72 | 62 | 50 | 19 | 61 |
| Mobile phone from work | 0 | 2 | 17 | 15 | 7 | 0 | 7 |

*Source:* Nurmela et al. (2000).

## The communicative and social aspects
## of the mobile phone

*Work and leisure*

Finns carry their mobile phones everywhere, all the time, because they do not want to lose their instant contact. For example, 93% of both men and women stressed that one of the main reasons for obtaining a mobile phone is availability (Nurmela et al., 2000). Whereas a traditional phone call is connected to one place, the mobile phone is on hand all the time. The mobile phone then makes it possible to be reached wherever you are; thus one is less likely to miss opportunities. Perpetual availability, however, could be seen as a tie as well. One runs the risk that others assume the mobile phone owner will accept messages regardless of place or time. Indeed, a mobile phone does not necessarily offer "more free time" or "more personal possibilities," as people thought at the beginning of the 1990s. A mobile phone does not imply that one has more freedom than before. On the contrary, a mobile phone may be a means of control.

Availability via the mobile phone is a real problem in Finnish business life. The complexity is heightened owing to the fact that most Finns own their own phones and do not receive one through their workplace. Personal free time or a holiday, for example, does not imply that you are not available. In that sense, the mobile phone means that you are at work, wherever you are. As Kopomaa (2000, p. 47) puts it: "Personal and professional messages become intertwined, Sundays are no different from Mondays, nor February from July." Some superiors may call their subordinates' mobile at any time, as the interviews by Kopomaa and Mäenpää make clear.

A mobile phone changes people's attitudes towards the workplace and office hours. Those interviewed do not make a clear distinction between personal issues and work-oriented calls. With mobile phones, work and leisure are mixed: for example, you may call your business partner in the evening, after official working hours, in order to chat about daily projects. It seems only natural not to abide by office hours with a mobile phone. In short, it is not thought to be disruptive to use a mobile phone after official working hours. Finns currently struggle to draw a line between work and leisure. The consequence, at its worst, may be the formation of a digital version of Foucault's panopticon where there is no room for choice between work and personal needs (Mäenpää, 2000, p. 143).

The different patterns of mobile phone usage between men and women shed some light on how Finns draw the line between work and leisure. According to *Statistics Finland*, 91% of men and 83% of women state that their reason for owning a mobile phone is to deal with everyday business. Yet, everyday business appears to mean something different to men and women. For example, 70% of women keep their mobiles on all the time, whereas half the men turn their phones off at night. Although both men and women want to be available all the time, the different mobile phone habits of men and women treat everyday business and accessibility differently. Indeed, women see their mobile phone as serving a wider range of purposes than men do. Women use their mobiles for all types of social purposes, such as keeping in contact with children, relatives or friends, in addition to non-household work-related uses (Kopomaa, 2000, p. 28; Nurmela et al., 2000). Furthermore, women emphasize such issues as care and security more than men and see the mobile phone as a means to care for people (Roos, 1993, p. 454).

### Public and private

One of the most distinctive characteristics of a mobile phone is that it privatizes public places. That is, as someone talks on the phone, one is in her or his own private space. Talking on the mobile phone in the presence of others lends itself to a certain social absence where there is little room for other social contacts. The speaker may be physically present, but his or her mental orientation is towards someone who is unseen.

Privatization of public spaces is evident in people's behavior on the street. When someone talks on the phone, he or she leaves the most crowded places, tries to find a quiet corner, and usually talks as quietly as possible. The non-verbal performance of mobile phone usage is commonplace: the mobile phone user turns his or her back toward other people and then talks and either stares at the floor or walks slowly around. The purpose of these actions is to indicate that the mobile phone user has moved into his or her own private place and that he or she is concentrating on the phone call. Non-verbally, the mobile phone leads to "closed" and "passive" public behavior. Such mobile phone use, as both Kopomaa and Mäenpää have noted, appears as an autistic form of public behavior. In contrast to the non-verbal performance involved in making and receiving calls, it is almost ironic the extent to which people are willing to talk about their private matters in public. The consequence is that public space is doubly privatized because mobile phone users sequester themselves non-verbally and then fill the air with private matters.

The privatization of public space represents a dilemma for a common understanding of "closedness" and "openness" in a mobile information society. People must reconsider the norms and rules of interaction. Social efficiency, for example, which is one of the main characteristics of a mobile information society, is double-sided. The mobile phone may be understood "in terms of increased contacts and immersed, synchronized living" (Kopomaa, 2000, p. 123). At the same time, social efficiency implies controlled social relations. Mobile phone users may "choose the person who most closely satisfies their preferences at any given moment" (Kopomaa, 2000, p. 124). It is possible that so-called social relations change when mobile (Mäenpää, 2000, p. 134). That is, one may have a wide social network, but meet most of those people relatively rarely. They are "friends," but, in particular, "mobile phone friends."

The mobile phone presents communicators with situations where their private communication is potentially open and shared. In a bus or in a train, for example, neither speaker nor bystander can avoid the phone call being more or less shared with other people. It does not matter how quietly you talk if there is someone sitting or standing right next to you. In fact, one of the main reasons Finns resist the mobile phone is the feeling of intrusion. Communicating via mobile phone exposes their intimate interaction to a verbal openness they do not like, whether they are the communicator or the bystander. As one interviewee in Kopomaa's study put it: "I wouldn't like to hear about people's private things. It's like opening someone's envelopes." Finns often feel that they are forced to listen to a stranger's problems or plans and that is annoying.

The mobile phone leads to a certain extempore lifestyle that exposes Finns to another intellectually interesting dilemma. "Both shared and private decisions are expected to be taken rapidly, and schedules are not determined precisely, because they can be adjusted along the way" (Kopomaa, 2000, p. 125). At the same time, there exists the possibility of changing decisions all the time, thus being "liberated from fixed schedules." This does not necessarily lead to a feeling of freedom. One may be dependent on connections and feel constant worry over accessibility, as though one were addicted to the connections the mobile phone makes possible. Thus, the dilemma ushered in by the mobile phone is that "contemporary individuals have both the freedom and the obligation to plan their life and make choices" (Kopomaa, 2000, p. 127).

### The mobile phone and Finnish speech culture

There is a belief that Finns have embraced the mobile phone because it is a technical means to overcome their inherent shyness and reticence, in much the same way that Finns have apparently embraced ballroom dancing and the tango. This account, which is perpetuated in news stories by the American television show *60 Minutes*, perpetuates the stereotype of the "silent Finn." While recognizing that communication technology can be a catalyst for cultural change, this view shows a lack of understanding of Finnish speech culture and the influence of technology on everyday communication. The ascendancy of the mobile phone in Finland is probably not caused by deep fears of social interaction. However, the pervasive presence and extensive use of the mobile telephone introduce some communication situations that may challenge the patterns of talk in Finnish speech culture. If the mobile phone influences Finnish speech culture, it is likely to be evident in the role of silence and small talk in Finnish social interaction.

Even though Finnish culture has changed rapidly during recent decades, Finns still appreciate silence (Lehtonen and Sajavaara, 1985). Finns traditionally have a lot of patience regarding uncertainty and do not worry about silence. They enjoy it and do not have the same need for contentious and intensive social encounters that people may have, for example, in the United States (Carbaugh, 1995). It is often culturally and socially inappropriate to break the silence, which is also evident in a general presumption against small talk. The respect for silence in Finnish speech culture points to an expectation to be direct in one's talk. Thus, when someone does speak they have something substantive to say and are justified in breaking the silence. Finns follow principles of matter-of-fact talk, or "*asia*," which is a Finnish term that indexes a broader cultural code that defines social interaction as the "mutual attention to some matter" (Wilkins, 2000). This is an "infocentric" view of social interaction that, as Wilkins explains, stands in contrast to the egocentric code for social interaction in Anglo-American culture and the sociocentric code in Ilongot and Colombian cultures.

Finland represents a confluence of a "mobile information society" that idealizes communication at "anytime and anyplace" with an existing speech culture that respects silence and prefers that speakers err on the side of reticence rather than expressiveness. What will happen as these two communicative ideals come into contact is not knowable at this time but some important aspects of the conflict can be articulated. The mobile phone and the mobile culture may draw people into new and unfamiliar communication patterns. Mobile phone discussions in Finland are typically short and informative. These discussions tend to last no longer than two minutes. People tend to concentrate on the near future, such as where and when they could meet and continue the discussion. In most cases, discussions are organized around a few questions such as "Where are you?" or "What are you doing?" and answers such as "I'm here in the square" and short-term decisions such as "Let's meet right there in a few minutes." When using the phone, there is an expectation to concentrate on crucial matters. In Finnish speech culture, there is little expectation of social pleasantries, idle chitchat or insincere flattery when one is on the phone. Compared with other closely related nationalities, such as Germans, Finns have always used phones briefly, without small talk. Short and informative discussions are understandable and follow the everyday norms of phone conversation (Tiittula, 1993).

Yet, the mobile phone, in terms of everyday interaction, raises the possibility of being open and outgoing. In particular, the mobile phone encourages new contacts and enlarges one's social network. Mobile phone calls may typically be short but – in particular among younger people – the number of daily contacts via the mobile may be high. Each encounter increases the potential that the feelings and emotions of others must be dealt with at any time and anywhere. This situation is made more complex by the fact that an ever-available network of mobile contacts increases the opportunity for openness with non-intimates. The availability made possible by mobile phones seems to undermine the value of silence and directness and to require a revision in speech behavior and interactional expectations for communicators.

The perplexing interactional question that emerges with the mobile phone, especially from the perspective of Finnish speech culture, is whether or not interest in another's private issues must be shown or feigned. Even if one is not interested in asking for information and it is not needed in terms of coping in one's social life, people may look for information because it may be necessary to keep one's network of contacts in good social standing. These situations call for a form of transparency (Jourard, 1971) that gives the appearance of openness but is actually closed because people do not in fact disclose matters of emotional importance to each other during their interaction. The mobile phone introduces new communicative demands for which silence and *asia* may hold no immediate solutions. Indeed, the mobile phone seems to increase the demand to have conventional forms of speech, such as small talk, to manage the boundary between public and private and appropriately explore the type of talk to which the other is open. Yet, it remains to be seen whether and how small talk will evolve in Finnish speech culture and whether the principles of Finnish speech culture will change as a result of the introduction of communication technology. If there is a change it may be in how silence is understood within Finnish culture itself. For instance, there is some evidence that Finns perceive their own communication abilities as poor (Sallinen-Kuparinen, 1986) and there is increased concern with questions about speech anxiety, reticence and shyness. The standard code against which communication competence is judged may be shifting toward a different communicative ideal, such as is expressed in the image of the mobile information society.

### Mobile phones, emotions and lifestyle

Participating in the mobile information society is not only a matter of getting a phone or calls, but how a phone is used in everyday life. It is obvious that two characteristics of the mobile information society – the speed of interaction and the extempore lifestyle – are not in harmony with the traditional Finnish lifestyle. Stereotypically, to be a Finn implies that you are allowed to be a little bit slow in your social life and that you do not have to talk if you are not interested. When you open your mouth, there is a reason for it. There used to be plenty of time to plan social occasions and well-understood communication scripts. In that sense, the mobile information society is a revolution in Finnish lifestyle. It changes familiar communication codes and leads to new uncertainty that can render the social environment strange, if not hostile.

The mobile phone, following Goffman (1967), is a new kind of stage where the mobile information society is acted out. However, the observation that mobile interactions are not necessarily deep raises questions about the freedoms and burdens that come with this new interactional stage. A mobile phone is, in many respects, a place where one can go to chat about anything. With a mobile phone, one can feel that one is in a place where emotional arguments and friendly laughter, for example, are appropriate. It is a stage that resembles a virtual cafeteria or marketplace where people meet each other. A marketplace is not simply a place to buy something but also a place just to be with others and to meet people (Oldenburg, 1989).

The mobile phone, relative to the respect for silence and matter-of-fact talk in Finnish speech culture, may be creating an obligation for talk without a reason for the talk. Although it may open up Finnish speech culture to expectations other than *asia* talk, in the long run this may result in forms of interaction that are emotionally empty and, in retrospect, rather depressing. The social distance between people, on the mobile stage, is small but the emotional bond may be weak. So, mobile phone contact may increase contact but also increase loneliness. The fact that people are around you does not imply that you have a social relationship with someone and, by extension, the perpetual availability of others does not imply that you actually find anyone with whom to make contact. It is plausible then that the mobile phone may also arouse feelings of being an outsider rather than one who is in touch. It could be similar to the feeling of being alone in a crowded place. The mobile phone increases people's awareness of their social environment, particularly if that environment is empty. A mobile phone may not be the key to social satisfaction and happiness that it is often said to be. As regards one's loneliness or unhappiness, for example, the social world is the same with a mobile or without it. It is possible that a mobile phone, in fact, leads to even greater loneliness: if you are not socially active and if you are not willing to follow the communication style of a mobile information society, you are outside your community. As Kopomaa (2000, p. 78) put it: "In the center of Helsinki, for example, it is almost exceptional *not* to see people using mobile phones." Seeing how everyone talks on the phone, one realizes that there is a mobile community and that one is not part of it. In the mobile information society, people may feel that they are obligated to forms of interaction without meaningful and emotionally loaded relations. That is, it may be difficult to change the nature of constant mobile chat to interpersonally fulfilling relationships.

## Summing up

A mobile phone is, undoubtedly, more than just a communications device. Its rapid adoption in Finland raises many questions about the relationship between mobile communication and Finnish speech culture, self-image and the social environment. The mobile has, for example, been a fairytale for Finnish industry and economic growth (Ali-Yrkkö et al., 2000). Socially and culturally, however, the story is more complicated. Finns have been eager to buy, test and use the new telecommunications equipment. The step from testing to everyday use has been taken quickly and yet, surprisingly, the way in which people manage within two cultures – a mobile information society and traditional Finnish social life – remains largely unexamined.

Younger people in particular are right now adopting and so shaping the rules of the new culture. It is thus easy to understand why some ongoing research projects are very interested in youth culture. In Finland today, it seems as if people are almost born with their mobiles; children learn at a young age that the mobile culture follows people everywhere. Every child in Finland learns that there is one name, Nokia, that is somehow very special in Finnish life. It is something monumental and important and affects everyone's life in Finland. So children face no problem in a society where the phone may ring at any time and social life is based on constant connections. It is, after all, a logical aspect of "*nokialization*." Elderly people, of course, may think little is left of traditional Finnish life; but then again, it remains to be seen whether and how the mobile information society will evolve and which aspects of Finnish culture will remain and which will change.

# References

Ali-Yrkkö, J., Paija, L., Reilly, C., and Ylä-Anttila, P. (2000). *Nokia – A Big Company in a Small Country.* Helsinki: Research Institute of the Finnish Economy.

Carbaugh, D. (1995). "Are Americans Really Superficial? Notes of Finnish and American Cultures in Linguistic Action." In L. Salo-Lee (ed.), *Kieli & Kulttuuri* [Language and Culture]. Jyväskylä: University Press.

Goffman, E. (1967). *Interaction Ritual.* New York: Doubleday.

Grint, K., and Gill, R. (1995). *The Gender–Technology Relation. Contemporary Theory and Research.* New York: Taylor & Francis.

Jourard, S. (1971). *The Transparent Self.* New York: Van Nostrand Reinhold.

Kopomaa, T. (2000). *The City in Your Pocket. Birth of the Mobile Information Society.* Helsinki: University Press Finland.

Lehtonen, J., and Sajavaara, K. (1985). "The Silent Finn." In D. Tannen and M. Saville-Troike (eds.), *Perspectives on Silence.* Norwood: Ablex.

Mäenpää, T. (2000). "Digitaalisen arjen ituja. Kännykkä ja urbaani elämäntapa" [The shoots of day-to-day digital life. The cell phone and urban lifestyles.]. In T. Hoikkala and J. P. Roos (eds.), *2000-luvun elämä* [Life in the 21st Century]. Helsinki: Gaudeamus.

Nurmela, J. (1997). *The Finns and Modern Information Technology.* Reviews 1997/12. Helsinki: Statistics Finland.

  (1998). *Does Modern Information Technology Select Its Users?* Reviews 1998/5. Helsinki: Statistics Finland.

Nurmela, J., Heinonen, R., Ollila, P., and Virtanen, V. (2000). *Matkapuhelin ja tietokone suomalaisen arjessa* [The cell phone and laptop in day-to-day Finnish life]. Reviews 2000/2. Helsinki: Statistics Finland.

Oldenburg, R. (1989). *The Great Good Place.* Paragon: New York.

Roos, J. P. (1993). "300000 Yuppies? Mobile Telephones in Finland." *Telecommunications Policy,* 446–458.

  (1994). "A Post-Modern Mystery: Why Finns, 'Silent in Two Languages', Have the Highest Density of Mobiles in the World?" *Intermedia* 22: 24–28.

Sallinen-Kuparinen, A. (1986). *Finnish Communication Reticence.* Studia Philologica Jyväskyläensia 19, University of Jyväskylä.

Tiittula, L. (1993). *Kulttuurit kohtaavat. Suomalais–saksalaiset kulttuurierot talouselämän näkökulmasta* [Cultures meeting. Finnish–German cultural differences from the economic perspective]. Helsingin kauppakorkeakoulun julkaisuja D-190. [Helsinki School of Economics and Business Administration Publications D-190].

Wilkins, R. (2000). "Infocentrism: An Interactional Code in Some Finnish Educational Scenes." Paper presented at the National Communication Association's conference on "Rhetoric and Communication in the 21st Century," Jyväskylä, Finland, June 14–16.

# 3 Israel: chutzpah and chatter in the Holy Land

*Amit Schejter and Akiba Cohen*

> *On a summer evening in 1999, a fully loaded bus traveling from Tel Aviv to Jerusalem had just climbed to one of the highest points overlooking the city, ten minutes from its final destination. A young lady sitting a few seats behind the driver slipped her mobile phone from her purse, dialed a number, and put the phone to her ear. To the person on the other end of the line she said: "Okay, we've just passed Mevasseret [a suburb of Jerusalem], so we'll arrive in about ten minutes. Start moving and pick me up across from the Convention Center." The bus driver, who had been busy maneuvering the complicated turns, suddenly looked up in his rear-view mirror and shouted: "No, lady, there's no stop there anymore!"*

It seems every tourist visiting Israel in recent years comments on the omnipresence of mobile phones. The above anecdote is a wonderful example typifying not only the sheer numbers but also the particular nature of mobile telephone usage in Israel. In this chapter, we describe as well as seek to understand the unprecedented growth of mobile phone ownership and use in Israel. We also point out some unique characteristics of this medium, which seem to suit the Israeli culture and mentality so well, and hence make it ubiquitous.

Israelis spend impressive amounts of time talking on mobile phones. Studies quoted in the media claim Israelis spend an average of 450 minutes per month talking on their cellular phones, close to double the average in Europe and almost four times the US average (Maltz, 1999). By 2002, there were more than 4.8 million subscribers, a 76% penetration rate. Yet we know little about human communication behavior on the mobile phone; as with the old-fashioned telephone, there is virtually no research on its use.

If one were to ask Israelis why mobile phones are so popular – they are among the world's usage leaders – answers would vary. Policymakers would say it is an example of success in navigating the adoption of the new technology. Social psychologists would probably choose explanations stemming from the unique history or cultural norms of Israeli society. Whatever the reason, mobile phones are everywhere.

## Cellular telephony in Israel: a pattern of growth

No one predicted accurately the growth rate and popularity of the cellular phone when it made its debut in the Holy Land. In 1984 the government handed over basic telecommunication services, which it had previously controlled, to a newly created government-owned corporation – Bezeq – which came to be a new word in the Hebrew language, literally meaning "telecommunication." Three years later, cellular phones made a modest appearance of their own, again by introducing a new term to the Hebrew language: the Pele-Phone, combining the sound of the word "telephone" with the Hebrew word for "wonder" (*Pele*), thus referring to the perceived wonder of having a telephone wherever one goes.

Pele-Phone was a joint venture by Bezeq and the Motorola Corporation. During the first seven years of operation there were only 125,000 subscribers out of a population of 5.3 million at the time (a penetration rate of 2.4%). In 1990, the government appointed a committee of experts (the Boaz Committee) to recommend a restructuring of the telecommunication market. The then-CEO of Bezeq was sufficiently influential to force the committee members to compromise on liberalization, recommending a limited divestiture of the powerful government-owned corporation along with its gradual privatization. Bezeq was to limit its activities to basic domestic telephony, while the rest of its services, including cellular telephony, international service, broadcasting facilities, end-equipment sales and value added services were to open to varying levels of competition. The first stage of implementing the new policy, following the sale to the public of 25% of the corporation's shares, was the introduction of choice in cellular telephony. This policy was concomitant with the formation of the Rabin government in 1992, which promised a platform of "changing the national priorities." This change included massive investment in infrastructure and education, and the opening of the markets to competition and privatization. The telecommunication market was first to respond to these changes, and did so with a vengeance.

The revolution in the provision of telecommunication services by corporations other than Bezeq was preceded by another major policy step. In 1993, the Ministry of Communications ordered Pele-Phone to change its pricing structure by introducing a concept uncommon in the world at the time, that of "Calling Party Pays" (CPP). Until then, both caller and receiver of cellular calls paid for the "air time," the transient use of bandwidth. The policy was based on recognizing cellular telephones as wireless communication devices rather than as a landline telephone. The regulators viewed as unjust that those who received telephone calls had no way of controlling who called them, and thus their charges. This in turn was seen as obstructing the growth of mobile telephone usage because mobile phone subscribers apparently were reluctant to have their number known owing to that lack of control.

The price for owning and using a mobile phone at the time was exorbitant: the basic mobile unit cost the equivalent of US$1,500, to which a US$150 connection charge was added. Monthly usage fees were set at US$25.00 and each minute of airtime at US$0.23 (Teitelman, 1994).

According to the Boaz Committee recommendations, cellular telephony was to open gradually to limited competition. The first step, the introduction of a second mobile phone operator, was taken in 1994 by publishing a public tender. The tender designers sought to achieve an outcome that would make mobile phones a popular commodity. Many Israelis still remembered the 1960s phrase "a car for every worker" coined by Minister Shimon Peres; now it seemed to be replaced by the goal of "a mobile phone for every worker." If in the 1960s the automobile symbolized social status, wealth and success, in the 1990s the mobile phone, portable and visible to all, seemed to fill the need.

The government decided that the new service would be a digital service from the outset, and bandwidth was allotted for the introduction of the American-based technology known as Time Division Multiple Access (TDMA). The scoring table for the bidders was designed so that the price offered to consumers counted for 50% of the final score, with the timetable for digitalization and territorial coverage, as well as an overall impression of the bids, being the other, less important, components. The results announced in mid-1994 reflected this policy and created a new environment for cellular telephone ownership.

During its first year of operation, the winning corporation, Cellcom, committed to provide service at the rate of US$0.025 per minute during peak hours. During the first five years no connection fee was to be charged. The same applied to the first two years of monthly usage fees, which would then rise to US$5 from the third through the fifth year. By the fifth year the per-minute charge too was to remain low, at US$0.09. The market responded with previously unheard of enthusiasm. On the day Cellcom began to accept subscribers, the media reported that customers literally stormed the doors of the branch offices of the new operator. Numbers were given to people waiting on line and the police were called to maintain order. It has often been said that in economic and consumer behavior Israelis tend to demonstrate a herd mentality; in this particular case the magnitude of the phenomenon was unique. Even a major breakdown in the Cellcom system during the first months of its

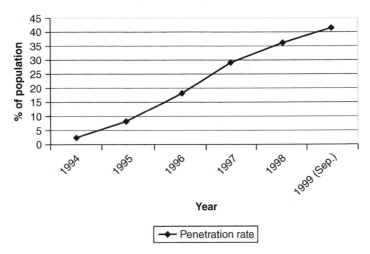

Figure 3.1 Penetration rate of cellular phones in Israel. *Source:* Ministry of Communications (1999).

operation, which made using the phones almost impossible, and the fact that the TDMA system caused the speaker on the receiving end to sound unclear, could not stop the popularity of the new device and the huge demand for its service.

By the end of 1995 the number of mobile phone subscribers in Israel more than tripled to reach 445,000. The penetration rate, which, as mentioned, had reached 2.4% on the eve of the introduction of the Cellcom service, rose to 36.5% by the end of 1998 (see figure 3.1). The growth in the cellular telephony market led the government to publish a second tender, for a third operator in 1998.

This time, however, the tender was based on a different principle altogether. Instead of seeking a low fee for the consumer (a goal provided by Cellcom), the government sought to receive a good price for bandwidth allocation. The criterion set for the tender for the third operator, was to operate within the 900MHz spectrum using the European GSM (Global System for Mobile Communications) technology, and was to be decided by an initial payment by the highest bidder. Thus, the Partner Communication Company, which offered US$400 million, received the license. Entering what seemed at first a saturated market, Partner (which later teamed up with Orange, its rival for the bid) is currently being marketed under the international Orange trademark. In November 1999, Orange announced that it had reached 300,000 subscribers during its first year of operation. By then, the total number of mobile

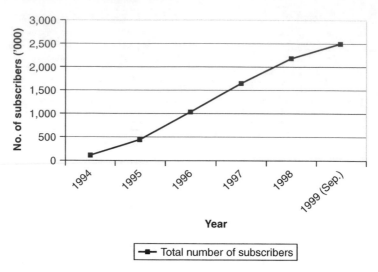

Figure 3.2 Total number of cellular phone subscribers in Israel. *Source:* Ministry of Communications (1999).

telephone subscribers in Israel had passed the 2.5 million mark (see figure 3.2).

The success of the Partner–Orange group came on the heels of another development, this time a shrewd business decision rather than one made by policymakers. As late as June 1999, analysts viewed the cellular market in Israel as reaching its peak with the new tripartite structure. A local analyst estimated the value of Pele-Phone and Cellcom (both private corporations not traded on any stock market) at US$1.4 billion each (Friedman, 1999). But, in October 1999, Partner, which is significantly smaller than either Pele-Phone or Cellcom, made an initial public offering on the New York and London stock exchanges and was able to establish its worth at US$2.4 billion (Allalouf, 1999). Although these figures did not reflect any profit that the smallest of Israel's mobile phone companies was making (in fact it is still losing money), they reflected the faith of the international business community in the future growth of the market.

The growth in cellular telephony ownership is even more striking when one compares it with the high level of fixed telephone service provided in Israel, and especially its growth curve over the years. The penetration of fixed lines too has grown rapidly. In 1980, on the eve of the creation of Bezeq, 208,000 Israelis were waiting for a telephone line, some of whom had been waiting for years. This was due to the lack of infrastructure. By 1997, only 9,000 were waiting for a phone (Central Bureau of

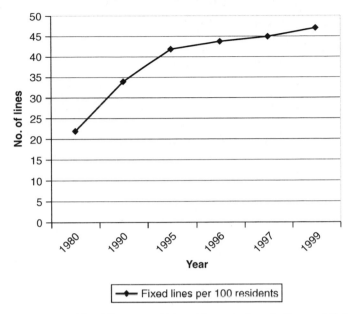

Figure 3.3 Fixed lines per 100 residents in Israel. *Source:* Ministry of Communications (1999).

Statistics, 1998).[1] As of December 1999, the fully digital system consisted of 2.8 million fixed phone lines, or 47 per 100 residents (see figure 3.3), which is on a par with most developed nations; for mobile phones, the corresponding figure was 2.9 million subscribers (Ministry of Communications, 1999; Zrahiya, 1999). Mobile subscribers outnumbered landlines!

As mentioned above, the policymakers' analysis of this situation leads to the conclusion that policy alone caused this remarkable and extraordinary growth of the market. Policymakers cite price, Calling Party Pays, nationwide high-quality coverage (dictated by the tenders), and competition. But, considering the initial problems Cellcom had upon launching its service, and the fact that at the end of 1998 Cellcom and Pele-Phone had similar numbers of subscribers even though Pele-Phone prices were much higher, a more sophisticated explanation is needed.

## Israelis and technology: a love story

One probable explanation for this phenomenon is the infatuation that Israelis have with new technologies in general and communication

[1] The Central Bureau of Statistics refrained from following up on this particular element of data after 1997.

technologies in particular. A good example is the history of the introduction of television in Israel, although the growth in ownership of cellular telephony, as well as the level of and expenditure on its use, dwarf these figures. Back in 1961, a team acting on behalf of the United Nations Educational, Scientific, and Cultural Organization provided the Israeli government with a plan to introduce television (Cassirer and Duckmanton, 1961). The international experts envisioned that within twelve to eighteen months of the commencement of broadcasting, the purchase of 20,000 sets in Israel would be a "reasonable estimate." But, by 1965, three years *before* the introduction of television broadcasts in Israel, 30,000 Israelis already owned television sets. This seeming peculiarity may have been due at least in part to the fact that in some regions of the country it was possible to pick up broadcasts from neighboring countries. In 1965, a governmental committee was established to implement the decision to launch a television service. It estimated that by 1972, which was to be the fifth year of broadcasting, the number would rise to 300,000 (Bendor, 1965). In fact, by 1971, which was only the third year of broadcasting, the number of sets rose to more than 400,000 (Central Bureau of Statistics, 1971), which corresponded to 53% of households at the time.

A similar pattern appears with the introduction of video-cassette recorders (VCRs). The high penetration rate (43.5%) in 1991 (Central Bureau of Statistics, 1994) could have been attributed to the fact that there was no choice in television fare, as only one channel was available at the time. But in 1999, only eight years later, 70.9% of Israeli households owned a VCR (up from 61.9% two years before). This was the case even though cable television has also become a big hit, despite its relatively high cost (around US$40 per month), and 75.5% of all Israeli households are currently subscribers (Israel Audience Research Board, 1999). It is interesting to note that, as part of the Israelis' passion for technology, they would purchase VCRs with the most advanced features although many did not know how to use them and hence could not benefit from them (Cohen and Cohen, 1989). Finally, in a pattern reminiscent of the 1960s, 7.2% of households owned satellite dishes in 1999, although a direct broadcasting satellite (DBS) service commenced only in the summer of 2000.

### Patterns of use

Additional explanation may be sought in Israelis' patterns of usage of their mobile phones, both in the amount of usage and in the types of uses. In an environment in which the number of mobile units was about equal to fixed lines, it would be logical to assume that Israelis made choices concerning which of their telephones to use on the basis of the cost factor. Yet, as official figures demonstrate, this was not the case. The rate of expenditure on both systems was almost equal at about 40% in 1999.

The marketing strategies of cellular phone operators too can be indicative of what it is that makes Israelis talk so much on the mobile phone. One of the characteristics of the mobile phone market in Israel has been the growing sophistication of the marketing strategies of the different operators.

As expected, Cellcom launched its service based on its low price. Pele-Phone responded by emphasizing the clarity of the sound on its phones and the quality of service. The next stage of growth occurred when Pele-Phone introduced the "Mango" service, which was a unique cellular phone developed by Motorola for the Israeli market that can receive calls but make outward calls to only one pre-selected number. This was a remarkable device aimed at providing children, elderly people and those with similar "tracking" needs with the ability to be located and to call the singular number (usually home). In addition, it was very beneficial for employers who provide their employees with a cellular phone in order to keep track of their whereabouts without paying for their personal calls (of course this service was named "Mango-Pro"). Cellcom kept pace when it introduced the "TalkMan," a cellular phone for which calls are pre-paid, using a credit-card-like device, which also can provide parents and employers with both surveillance and cost control.

Upon the arrival on the scene of Partner–Orange, more sophisticated schemes were developed. In general, all mobile phone companies must have learned from their marketing research that most people use the mobile phone to call a limited number of people. This tendency was thus targeted with pricing schemes that allowed for cheaper calls to selected numbers. The "packages" of numbers were designed around three main reference groups: family, business and friends. The "friends" were again divided into certain social groups. Thus a special package was devised for soldiers serving in outlying areas, another for students (providing cheaper calls when dialed from campus) and a third for calls within a designated area close to the subscriber's home. A unique marketing scheme of this sort is a special "club" for religious Jewish owners of cellular telephones, which Cellcom introduced in early 2000. Among other features, members' needs such as finding the times for conducting prayers or kindling Sabbath candles can be reached by dialing *613 – 613 is the number of *Mitzvot* (prescriptions) that an observant Jew is required to perform. Needless to say, by the time these packages were being marketed, the telephones themselves were being offered virtually free of charge, as long as the subscriber agreed to a long-term contract with the operator and a minimum monthly fee.

## The social setting for interpreting mobile phone usage in Israel

As noted, the rate of adoption of mobile phones in Israel has been rapid and profound. In addition to the fact that Israelis are very fond of communications technology, there seem to be some particular characteristics that augment their obsession with and use of mobile phones: their need to be connected, their need to chatter and their basic audacious (*chutzpadic*) temperament.

Given its historical and geopolitical situation, Israel is highly security conscious. In addition to several wars with its Arab neighbors since it became a state in 1948, the past few decades have seen devastating acts of terror committed against its citizens. When they turn 18, most young men and many young women serve in the Israeli army for a period of three and two years, respectively. Many continue to serve as reservists and are called to active duty for several days to several weeks per year until their mid-40s.

The position of the army regarding the cellular phone is somewhat ambivalent. On the one hand, the Supreme Command several years ago issued a clear ban on the use of privately owned mobile phones while soldiers are engaged in military activities, including training and combat. This ban is owing to the fear of distraction by the device and the threat of revealing classified information, including the whereabouts of the soldiers, which the enemy might detect from signals emitted by the phone. During off-duty hours, however, the enforcement of the ban had been virtually impossible; hence the army's ombudsman, who was approached on the matter, has responded with a more liberal policy. Thus, soldiers can get in touch with their families and girl/boyfriends from wherever they happen to be, including outlying areas. As noted, special rates have made it extremely cheap for soldiers to keep in touch, and indeed they do. When the Israeli army pulled out of southern Lebanon in May of 2000, some of the cellular operators reduced prices for calls originating from Israel's boundary with Lebanon, making it cheaper for soldiers arriving safely at the border to call home.

Two recent events during the renewed Intifada in the West Bank and Gaza provide additional dimensions in the realm of security-related mobile phone use. When initial radio reports told of two Israeli soldiers who had been apprehended by Palestinian policemen and taken to the Ramallah police station, the wife of one of the soldiers, worried by the report, called her husband's cell phone. Somebody answered and said: "I just killed him," and hung up. Within minutes it was learned that the soldiers had been beaten to death by a mob. In another incident, when a group of Israeli settlers on a controversial excursion near a Palestinian refugee camp exchanged fire, several wounded Israelis were interviewed over their mobile phones by television and radio reporters, in real time, from the scene of the event while they waited to be evacuated.

As for terror, when such incidents occur, people are able to check with their loved ones to be sure that they are all right. In fact, on several occasions when major terrorist acts have taken place, the cellular system crashed because of the overload of people trying to contact others.

One aspect of contact is being and keeping in touch. In many ways, the myth of the Jewish Mother is not a myth at all. The obligation to report on what is going on is part of the way of life. Many Israelis travel abroad, but calling home is almost mandatory. In fact, in the mobile phone age, as the airplane touches down at a foreign airport, even while still in the plane, many Israelis pull out their mobile phone and report that they have arrived safely. They often do the same upon returning home.

As in our opening case, Israelis do not mind sharing their travel plans with others, including the anxiety of making certain they will be picked up at the particular spot as planned. Social ties established during adolescence often remain throughout life. Strong relationships formed during years spent together in the same class, in the youth movement and in the military unit are enhanced by frequent social gatherings as well as by talking on the phone. Israelis are often amazed by what they see as thriftiness, particularly by Americans, when it comes to minimizing long-distance phone calls. Israelis have no qualms about speaking at length, especially if somebody else (parents or employer) is paying the bill. Cellular phones are often given to employees by their employers, and are an almost fully tax deductible expense, thus adding to the popularity of their usage, albeit the level of expenditure for personal use is determined by the employee's status and position. Israelis love to gossip and talk about rumors. There is even a metaphor that certain rumors have rankings, comparable to those of major, lieutenant colonel and even colonel. And what is the quickest way of spreading a rumor if not by talking on the phone (or the mobile phone)? In short, Israelis love to talk.

Israelis have never been known for their exemplary behavior, courtesy and elegant manners. The *sabra*, the native-born Israeli (nicknamed after the prickly pear), has been characterized as the straightforward *dugri* type (Katriel, 1986) who says what he or she thinks, both in private and in public. Israelis are not prone to be *freiers* – or suckers – either (Bloch, 1998). Finally, audacity, or *chutzpah*, has always been part of the culture, and contemporary notions of political correctness are not the typical Israeli's cup of tea.

So it is with the mobile phone. There is virtually no place where Israelis do not use their mobile phone: on public buses and trains, in restaurants, banks, offices, clinics, theaters and classrooms, and of course in the street. Judging by its omnipresence, it seems that there are few limits and restrictions that people abide by. In fact, it is not uncommon for people to use their mobile phone in places where it is prohibited by law, such as in certain parts of hospitals and gas stations. There has even been an anecdote reported of an undertaker's phone ringing inside a grave as the deceased was being put to rest. This event grabbed national media attention alongside ten (!) interruptions during a production of *One Flew Over the Cuckoo's Nest* at the National Theater and several interruptions during *Don Pasquale* at the New Israel Opera, as well as in other cultural events (Lori, 1999). Bezeq has been running a public service announcement on television requesting people to switch off their cellular phones in public places. Some restaurants now carry a "no cellular telephone" sign next to the obligatory "no smoking."

Given this background and setting, it is no wonder that the mobile phone has been well received (or at least much used) in Israel. We are not suggesting that these factors are unique to Israel; we do believe, however, that they are particularly conspicuous in Israel.

## References

Allalouf, E. (1999). "Partner raised $525 million according to market value of $2.4 billion; Pricing closed at $13.5." *Globes*, October 28 (in Hebrew).

Bendor, S. (1965). "Report of the Inter-ministerial Committee on General Television." Unpublished report on file with authors (in Hebrew).

Bloch, L.-R. (1998). "Communicating as an American Immigrant in Israel: The 'Freier' Phenomenon and the Pursuit of an Alternative Value System." *Research on Language and Social Interaction* 31(2): 177–208.

Cassirer, H., and Duckmanton, T. (1961). "Educational Television in Israel: Report of a UNESCO Mission." Unpublished UNESCO report on file with authors.

Central Bureau of Statistics (1971). A Poll on Listening to the Radio and Watching Television." Unpublished report (in Hebrew).

—— (1994). *Statistical Abstract of Israel 1993*. Jerusalem: Hemed Publishers (in Hebrew).

—— (1998). *Statistical Abstract of Israel 1997*. Jerusalem: Hemed Publishers (in Hebrew).

Cohen, A.A., and Cohen, L. (1989). "Big Eyes but Clumsy Fingers: Knowing about and Using Technological Features of Home VCRs." In M. Levy (ed.), *The VCR Age*. Beverly Hills, CA: Sage Publications, 135–147.

Friedman, S. (1999). "Gmul-Sahar: Pele-Phone and Cellcom worth only $1.4 billion each." *Globes*, June 21 (in Hebrew).

Israel Audience Research Board (1999). *The 1998/99 Establishment Survey of the People-Meter System for Measuring Television Viewing.* Jerusalem: Israel Audience Research Board.

Katriel, T. (1986). *Talking Straight.* Cambridge: Cambridge University Press.

Lori, A. (1999). "Cellphones Can Drive You Cuckoo." *Haaretz Magazine*, November 19, p. 4.

Maltz, J. (1999). "The Hard Cell." *Jerusalem Report*, November 8, p. 40.

Ministry of Communications (1999). *Telecommunications in Israel.* Jerusalem: Ministry of Communications.

Teitelman (1994). "Love Me Tender." *Communications International*, October, pp. 83–86.

Zrahiya, Zvi. (1999). "It's Official: Cellphones Outnumber Landlines." *Ha'aretz* (Tel Aviv), December 10 (on-line edition).

# 4    Italy: stereotypes, true and false

*Leopoldina Fortunati*

## Introduction

The data for this chapter come from three research projects sponsored by Telecom Italia over the years 1996 to 1998.[1] The first, 'Verso uno scenario europeo delle telecomunicazioni' (Towards a European Scenario of Telecommunications, 1996a) consisted of a telephone survey in 1996 in five European countries (Italy, France, Germany, Spain, and the UK) with a sample of 6,609 subjects. The second, 'La rappresentazione sociale delle telecomunicazioni' (The Social Representation of Telecommunications), was conducted in 1996 in Italy on two different samples. The first sample consisted of 1,400 randomly selected individuals who were interviewed over the phone and who also responded to a free association exercise, also given via telephone. The second group consisted of a convenience sample of 303 selected subjects, of 15 years of age and over, who filled out a questionnaire containing a semantic differential with twenty-five concepts and twenty-three scales (1996b).[2] The third research project, entitled 'La competenza d'uso delle tecnologie comunicative' (Competence in Using Telecommunication Technologies), was a 1998 telephone survey in Italy with a sample of 1,400 subjects.

---

[1] The preliminary results of the first project were published in Fortunati (1998). The results of the second project are described in Fortunati and Manganelli Rattazzi (in press). Some results from the third project have been published in Chiaro and Fortunati (1999).

[2] The semantic differential was applied following the indirect method, elaborated by Hofstätter (1963), with which the representational field and its dimensions are defined. The twenty-five concepts proposed consisted of seven inductor terms – fax, telephone, mobile phone, TV, telecommunications, computer and radio – and another eighteen concepts to arrive at the metaphorical meaning of telecommunications: tyrant, democracy, feminine, friend, culture, love, masculine, isolation, work, noise, information, communication, hate, innovation, amusement, home, participation and company. The twenty-three scales consisted of the following pairs of opposing adjectives: delightful/disgusting; merry/sad; dangerous/safe; superfluous/indispensable; easy/difficult; intimate/extraneous; bad/good; dynamic/static; far/near; stressful/relaxing; strong/weak; open/closed; satisfactory/frustrating; powerful/impotent; fast/slow; superficial/deep; cold/warm; harmful/beneficial; pleasant/unpleasant; passive/active; heavy/light; desirable/undesirable; liberating/constricting.

Apart from the semantic differential group, the samples were representative of the broader Italian population in terms of gender, age and geographical area of residence. Incidentally, the research program explored all major means of communication. The mobile phone was not a particular focus, so we do not have as much data on this particular technology as one might wish. Still, our research projects did enable us to investigate three aspects of the mobile phone that are crucial to understanding the cultural location and identity of the mobile phone. These are: (1) the basic physiognomy of the mobile phone; (2) the reasons for its success in Italy; and (3) the mobile phone in relation to the human body, especially the seeming compromises the ever closer connection creates.

## The basic characteristics of the mobile phone

### *Is the mobile phone seen as a communicative instrument?*

Our first, somewhat counterintuitive, finding is that the mobile phone does not seem a very communicative instrument.[3] Despite its appearance as a modern form of the telephone and despite the fact that many people think it will replace the fixed phone, our research highlights the way it frustrates users' attempts to communicate. Doubtless the mobile helps us to overcome limits inherent in both traditional and telephone communication modalities. However, movement itself brings with it a certain difficulty that ends up by affecting use of the mobile. Just think of the position of the body when one walks along in public space using a mobile, or the difficulty one faces in defending the space within which one would like to isolate one's voice.

The substantially higher cost of using a mobile, compared with a fixed phone, argues for its sparing use, and a careful decision whether to use it even for brief calls. The questionnaire part of our 1996b research project highlights that Italians are more likely to engage in other activities while using the mobile phone compared with fixed line phones, and even these actions tend to be of a different scope. Specifically, actions carried out while speaking on the mobile phone involve the speaker's attention much more. Thus, only 31% of those who use a mobile do nothing else while they are phoning, compared with 38% of those using a fixed phone. But if we add to this percentage those who have activities ancillary to talking on the phone itself (for examples, making themselves comfortable, observing, scribbling), the figures for the mobile phone total are 53% who do nothing else compared with 89% for the fixed phone.

[3] De Gournay (1997) and Heurtin (1998) proposed that it should be seen as an individual and personal technology rather than a mobile one.

The severe restriction of one's personhood – what we call "communicative asphyxia" – that accompanies the use of the mobile is confirmed by other evidence. In our 1996b free association study, the word "communication" is rarely associated with the mobile (3% of cases); more people associate the telephone with the word "communication" (11%). Evidently the mobile is considered an instrument that is not very suitable for communication, but is perhaps more suitable for a rapid exchange of information. The impossibility of sustained communication over long periods, therefore, has led to a new cultural interest in brevitas (the Latin virtue of brevity), and, paradoxically, has reconciled many people to writing who would not otherwise have done so. (Observe the explosion from 1999 onwards of short written messages, or SMS, sent via a mobile.)

## Is the mobile phone really a mobile technology?

If by mobile instrument we mean an instrument that accompanies human movement (as opposed to "moving" – see Virilio, 1993), then the mobile phone is not very mobile. In Western Europe, only about a fifth of users say they use it in the street (these users are disproportionately Italian) (Telecom Italia, 1996a), while another fifth use it in enclosed spaces, such as at home, in other people's houses, in the workplace, restaurant, bar, or pub. This is shown in table 4.1.

If by mobile we mean, on the other hand, an instrument that can be used when the body itself is still, though being conveyed through space, such as occurs when one is in a railway carriage, then the proportion of our respondents who use it in a means of transportation involves 42% of cases (table 4.1). This means that the mobile phone, even if we use the concept of mobile instrument in the most liberal way, is used in mobile situations in only 62% of cases.

An interesting macro-measure of mobility, moving home, surprisingly has no correlation with possession and use of a mobile. Italy for instance, which is the European country with the largest number (though not the highest penetration rates) of mobiles, is the least mobile in terms of residence (the Italian interviewees reported staying in the same house on average 17.0 years versus 13.7 years in France and 13.1 years in the UK; ISTAT, 1998, 1999). The Italians are also lower on a range of factors traditionally considered as indicators of mobility.

It may be more valuable to look at shorter-range indicators of mobility. Among these, we have examined forms of communicative sociality such as: meeting friends or relatives; going to public events such as cinema, theater, exhibitions or library; going to a restaurant, bar or club; going out with friends, including walking, shopping and sporting events; playing

Table 4.1 *Where people most often use the mobile phone in Europe*

| | | Country | | | | | | | | | | | | | | | | |
|---|---|---|---|---|---|---|---|---|---|---|---|---|---|---|---|---|---|
| | France | | | Germany | | | Italy | | | Spain | | | UK | | | Europe | |
| Location | No. | % of Europe | % of country | No. | % of Europe | % of country | No. | % of Europe | % of country | No. | % of Europe | % of country | No. | % of Europe | % of country | No. | % of country |
| In a vehicle | 25 | 8.2 | 27.8 | 70 | 22.9 | 58.3 | 68 | 22.2 | 27.9 | 18 | 5.9 | 25.0 | 125 | 40.8 | 64.1 | 306 | 42.4 |
| In the street | 18 | 12.7 | 20.0 | 6 | 4.2 | 5.0 | 87 | 61.3 | 35.7 | 16 | 11.3 | 22.2 | 15 | 10.6 | 7.7 | 142 | 19.7 |
| In a restaurant | 0 | 0.0 | 0.0 | 2 | 25.0 | 1.7 | 2 | 25.0 | 0.8 | 1 | 12.5 | 1.4 | 3 | 37.5 | 1.5 | 8 | 1.1 |
| In a second home | 1 | 7.7 | 1.1 | 3 | 23.1 | 2.5 | 4 | 30.8 | 1.6 | 4 | 30.8 | 5.6 | 1 | 7.7 | 0.5 | 13 | 1.8 |
| At your home | 30 | 41.1 | 33.3 | 12 | 16.4 | 10.0 | 16 | 21.9 | 6.6 | 4 | 5.5 | 5.6 | 11 | 15.1 | 5.6 | 73 | 10.1 |
| At other people's home | 2 | 50.0 | 2.2 | 0 | 0.0 | 0.0 | 1 | 25.0 | 0.4 | 0 | 0.0 | 0.0 | 1 | 25.0 | 0.5 | 4 | 0.6 |
| At your place of work | 3 | 4.8 | 3.3 | 9 | 14.3 | 7.5 | 26 | 41.3 | 10.7 | 6 | 9.5 | 8.3 | 19 | 30.2 | 9.7 | 63 | 8.7 |
| Elsewhere | 7 | 14.0 | 7.8 | 8 | 16.0 | 6.7 | 18 | 36.0 | 7.4 | 10 | 20.0 | 13.9 | 7 | 14.0 | 3.6 | 50 | 6.9 |
| No Response | 4 | 6.5 | 4.4 | 10 | 16.1 | 8.3 | 22 | 35.5 | 9.0 | 13 | 21.0 | 18.1 | 13 | 21.0 | 6.7 | 62 | 8.6 |
| Total | 90 | | | 120 | | | 244 | | | 72 | | | 195 | | | 721 | |

sports; taking part in associative activities (religious, political, trade union or social gatherings). Our aim with this part of the research was to see if those with a locally mobile lifestyle were likely to adopt mobile phones. We did indeed observe that in the Latin countries – Italy, France and Spain – those who were more likely, for example, to meet friends, and especially in Italy to meet relatives, were also much more likely to be mobile phone adopters. The rate of use of the mobile also varied according to the frequency of restaurant going. Those who go to restaurants several times a week made more calls, on average, than those who went rarely ($M = 25.61$ calls per week compared with $M = 14.55$).[4] This great use of the mobile by restaurant goers probably explains why, even though relatively few of the overall users activate their mobile phones in restaurants (1%), mobiles are still so readily apparent in terms of their perceived intrusiveness and cultural violations. Those who go to see relatives, and especially those who go to a cinema several times a week, receive significantly more mobile calls per week on average ($M = 34.32$ and $M = 41.79$) than those who do not engage in these activities ($M = 28.36$ and $M = 23.85$, respectively).

Although many variables influence people's use of mobile telephones, we can summarize what seems to be the major determining factor. This factor is a lifestyle that is urban and highly mobile, although that mobility is generally constrained to a short range.

### Is the mobile phone a metropolitan technology?

Without detailed empirical investigation, it is temping to say that mobile technology is emblematic of complex metropolitan life. The urban and suburban sprawl requires people to travel enormous distances. But this very necessity makes mobility itself difficult because of the large number of other people who likewise on the move. It also seems that complex urban lifestyles require a great deal of face-to-face interaction to achieve the coordination necessary for efficiently conducting social and commercial lives.

### Is the mobile phone a really portable technology?

To what extent is the mobile telephone a truly portable technology? If we look at the phenomenology of its use, its position on the surface of the body is both precarious and uncomfortable.

On the male body, for example, it sometimes goes in an inside pocket of clothes, sometimes in the back trouser pocket, or slung on the belt

---

[4] All differences between means ($M$) reported in this chapter were significant at the .05 level in a one-way analysis of variance with Bonferroni corrections applied.

or in a briefcase. Nowhere in male clothing does it have a stable place, so the mobile is destined to be accommodated as other objects that have historically had analogous functions, such as a gun slung on the belt. This of course makes sense both from a human factors perspective and from a symbolic perspective of masculine identity reinforcement. (Interestingly, one manufacturer has a clothing accessory for men called the e-holster, which is designed to be worn under a jacket in a manner similar to an undercover police officer's hidden pistol.)

In women's clothing, the mobile is more stable, in that it is generally placed in a handbag and is also kept further away from the body. Any solutions that users come up with seem crude, because they do not fit with the formal aesthetic of the original fashion designer. (At the same time, this problematic of clothing is being recognized by mobile phone manufacturers. Nokia, for example, has teamed up with a European fashion house to create clothes specifically designed to incorporate mobile communication technologies.)

This difficulty of finding a place for the mobile phone on the body limits its wearability because, even when the problem has been resolved temporarily, the tendency is to free it from its new place at the earliest opportunity and put it somewhere else. At meetings, for instance, where everyone arrives with their own mobile, one of the first things they do is to place it on the table where they are going to sit. This also happens in restaurants, bars, cars, trains, in fact in all possible situations and on any means of transport where there is a flat surface. It matters little where we are; as soon as possible we make ourselves comfortable, which means we take out our mobile and set it aside. Nevertheless, the fact that we frequently take out this prosthesis means that it is easily forgotten. It is not a coincidence that, in the London lost property offices, mobiles have reportedly replaced umbrellas as the most frequently turned-in item.

The European research (Telecom Italia, 1996a) found that one owner out of five never used their mobile phone outside the four walls of the house. Therefore, the function of the mobile, in this case, was as a substitute for a cordless phone. Another fifth of owners maintained that they took it with them only occasionally, thereby using it in a fragmentary and episodic fashion. A barrier to use is that mobile phones, unlike the fixed phones, require a certain level of management and maintenance (for example, charging the batteries, buying pre-paid mobile phone cards). Above all, to be useful outside the home, users must remember to take the mobile phone with them when leaving the house or place of business. In practical terms, just the simple action of having to remember to take the mobile phone serves almost to halve use. Although people increasingly

*[handwritten margin note: Makes sense if mobile replaces landline]*

take the mobile phone with them, this routine is not yet automatic (except for the youngest generations), unlike taking one's wallet or keys, although there are of course painful exceptions even to this well-established routine in one's life.

The problem of the wearability of the mobile phone may be satisfactorily resolved only when this instrument is totally incorporated into fashion. This suggests that the firms producing the technology would want to be involved in addressing wearability issues. Indeed, as noted above, there is already progress in this direction.

Another element in equation is personal health and safety. Even if there were definitive research showing that mobile phone radiation is not harmful, questions and doubts would remain. Since there are no such data, concerns are quite pronounced. There is also great concern about mobile phones causing motoring accidents. This has led to legislation being advanced governing the use of the mobile phone while driving. Therefore, the problem of mobile phone wearability is not only aesthetic and technical in nature, but ecological as well.

### Is the mobile phone a technology of intimacy?

I would argue that, of all mobile technologies, the mobile phone is the one most intimately close to the body. If the Walkman "dresses" the ear, and microchips remain inserted in the body for long periods, the mobile involves not only the ear but also the mouth and voice. To involve the voice involves a most intimate part of our body, because the voice emerges from within the body's intimate core, and is connected directly with one's sexuality. Users are also increasingly connected to this technology throughout the day, thus the mobile phone tends to stay on the body for longer periods during the day, maintaining this intimate dimension even longer. Perhaps this is the reason why it is the communicative instrument that, potentially more than any other, can influence the traditional management of intimacy and distance (Morris, 1971).

In fact, the mobile seems to be contributing to dissolving the traditional separation of intimacy and extraneousness and of public and private. The process of attacking this historically delimited separation was accelerated in the 1960s and 1970s with the re-mobilization of women (under the slogan of "the private is political"). Since that time, this political theme has expanded across the social spectrum. The use of the mobile phone amplifies the process already under way of ever more frequent exposure of private matters and intimacy in the public sphere. In an interesting counterpoint, though, it also represents the encroachment of intimacy on the territory of extraneousness and of the private on the public.

We now see two sets of opposing concepts (intimate/extraneous and public/private) and their relative dimensions, bordering on each other but different, merging together, often indistinguishably. The concept of intimate is linked to touching; – coming into contact with the other's body, eliminating the distance that lets us control the observer's gaze. Intimacy belongs to the pleasures of the body, affections, sexuality, the concept of the body as a way of exchanging energies. Therefore, intimacy is connected with affective innerness and/or sexuality. This exquisitely important sphere is managed by (and often left to) the inner sphere, the private. Communicative intimacy obviously illumines this sphere.

Intimacy is usually considered a positive value, as opposed to extraneousness, which is seen as the negative pole. The situation is more properly described as one in which the intimate relationship is viscous and selective, excluding large numbers and creating dependence because it allows reciprocal control. It is no accident that romantic love cements complicity and solidarity against others, the outside. On the other hand, extraneousness also has a positive side, because it is the dimension that has aided the development of modernity, science and the freedom that derives from anonymity and distance from others.

Intimacy has been used as a synonym for privacy. However, the concept of privacy is more connected with the individual sphere, with the family, with life lived sheltered from the absolute expansion of the public dimension. Privacy has developed as it were from the inside, in the domestic space, the everyday, the space of family life, and that intimacy has found a collocation in the private dimension. By contrast, the public is a dimension in which negotiation and collective contracting take place, it is the dimension of the sharing of norms and procedures that regulate social coexistence, it is the dimension that tends towards transparency in languages (whereas the private also exists in the shady part, in the unconscious). Value-attribution in the case of the public/private pair is, however, more equally distributed.

The mobile phone is the communicative instrument that helps these opposing concepts come closer together by unifying them, and it favors the progressive encroachment of intimacy in the public sphere and of extraneousness in the private sphere. Since the appearance of the mobile, the connotations of these concepts and dimensions have changed radically. This instrument enables us to capture the intimacy of interpersonal relations while moving from one place to another, that is, in a public dimension, traditionally the place of extraneousness in social relations. At the same time, it enables members of the family to retain a personal dimension of intimacy even in the house.

If domestic intimacy has been a dimension experienced by the members of family together as internal cohesion in the face of an extraneous (and public) external dimension, today the mobile is opening up the possibility of conquering new intimate communicative spaces at a personal level in the home. One might say that this instrument allows us to strengthen personal intimacy inside family intimacy, apart from strengthening the personal identity of the public dimension. Hence, the development of personal intimacy opens up areas of extraneousness with other members of the family, whose possibility of control it limits. (Consider adolescents who shut themselves off from family members to check on their mobile for messages from friends).

In the same way, the exposing of intimacy in public highlights the values that can be placed on the positive characteristics of extraneousness (distance, anonymity and lack of control). In fact, these values can be seen in play when the mobile sometimes erupts into the public communicative space, which, as shown by the variety of normative pressures discussed in other chapters, jealously guards the anonymity of the crowd. It is not rare for one to overhear, in public spaces, along the street, on the train, in a restaurant, the most intimate things said by people who are totally anonymous to us. And, as Georg Simmel (1901) observed in the context of the stranger as a co-traveler, it is just their anonymity that allows them to speak so that all may hear their problems and personal affairs. Intimacy can be made public, mobile interpersonal communication can be listened to by the public, as long as that public cannot use the personal and intimate things that they have heard in any way to control or condition the person who speaks loudly in public. What remains to be said is that intimacy, which on the plane of the social negotiation of communication is a sphere profoundly linked to individual freedom and decision-making, is in these cases made public and imposed on those around without their prior assent and involvement. So, the extra freedom on the part of the speaker is taken away from those who are obliged to listen because of their proximity, often against their will. That is, they are forced into a listening situation that has not been mutually negotiated previously.

The possible advantages for bystanders are that they have the possibility of access to numerous intimate communicative spheres, recounted by those directly involved. Until recently, literature or the mass media handled access to others' intimacy. Nevertheless, in the first case the deforming filter of the author's presence overlies it, and in the second there is an awareness of the intimacy being put on display. The mobile instead leads to the spread of shared senses of the dimension of intimacy itself, even if it is an intimacy often mortified precisely because of its public exposure and limited by its being incomplete. What bystanders are able to hear directly is in fact one half of a dialogue; the other half is merely imputed. These half-dialogues can lead to guesses about the other half of the conversation, on the basis of the half that can be heard. However, few Europeans admit to listening in on the public mobile telephone conversations of others (less than 1%; see table 4.2).

The widespread use of the mobile for the conduct of intimate conversations has developed only recently. It was initially a tool of business. This can be seen in our European research of 1996 (Telecom Italia, 1996a), when only 13.5% of the interviewees reported using their mobile for private and intimate conversations that they did not want to have over a fixed phone. It is mainly the 14–24 age group who say they use the mobile in this way: 28% of adolescents and 26% of young people aged 18–24 make and receive intimate calls on their mobile. This use of the mobile helps defend and develop young people's sense of autonomy and identity, and allows them to escape the social control of others (members of the family, for instance) (Katz, 1999; Wynn and Katz, 2000). This conclusion notwithstanding, we argue, as will be seen below, that the mobile appears to strengthen rather than weaken social control over individuals.

The opening up of telephone conversation seems to vary according to whether the modality is mobile or fixed. We calculate that about 18% of users use the mobile to quickly convey a piece of information, with all the classic topoi of mobile communication: 'At the moment I'm at . . . ,' 'I'm doing . . .' This typical opening of the mobile call is less interlocutory compared with that of the fixed telephone. It tends to take and give information of control more than the traditional "Hello, I'm fine, how are you?"

If we analyze the data according to gender, women are more likely than men to phone to give their location. This could stem from many factors, such as the need of men and children to know where the woman is at any moment, and women's compliance in making themselves easily reachable by men, and especially by children. This aspect had already surfaced in research on the early users of mobiles in Italy. Based on a series of in-depth interviews, we learned that men found it difficult to accept that women, who were potentially reachable at work through their mobiles, should actually turn them off (Fortunati, 1995).

We find that the mobile tends immediately to become a strong booster of intimacy among those within the social network of the user. The purpose of the mobile is to be reachable not by everyone, but only by those with whom we want to communicate – intimate friends or selected others whom we want to contact us. The mobile is a good means of creating a niche of intimacy because it serves as a "hot line" or open line channel for those to whom one gives an acknowledged claim of access. At the same

Table 4.2 *Reactions to seeing someone using their mobile phone*

| | Country | | | | | | | | | | | | | | | | |
|---|---|---|---|---|---|---|---|---|---|---|---|---|---|---|---|---|---|
| | France | | | Germany | | | Italy | | | Spain | | | UK | | | Europe | |
| Reaction | No. | % of Europe | % of country | No. | % of Europe | % of country | No. | % of Europe | % of country | No. | % of Europe | % of country | No. | % of Europe | % of country | No. | % of country |
| Nothing in particular | 596 | 28.1 | 44.7 | 447 | 21.1 | 25.3 | 398 | 18.8 | 28.9 | 297 | 14.0 | 31.3 | 384 | 18.1 | 32.4 | 2,122 | 32.1 |
| Think how useful | 215 | 25.4 | 16.1 | 175 | 20.7 | 9.9 | 152 | 18.0 | 11.0 | 220 | 26.0 | 23.2 | 83 | 9.8 | 7.0 | 845 | 12.8 |
| It annoys you | 74 | 9.4 | 5.6 | 119 | 15.2 | 6.7 | 285 | 36.3 | 20.7 | 57 | 7.3 | 6.0 | 250 | 31.8 | 21.1 | 785 | 11.9 |
| Try to listen to | 13 | 26.0 | 1.0 | 8 | 16.0 | 0.5 | 13 | 26.0 | 0.9 | 3 | 6.0 | 0.3 | 13 | 26.0 | 1.1 | 50 | 0.8 |
| Think what a show | 341 | 15.0 | 25.6 | 886 | 38.9 | 50.1 | 429 | 18.8 | 31.1 | 273 | 12.0 | 28.7 | 349 | 15.3 | 29.5 | 2,278 | 34.4 |
| Think I would like one | 0 | 0.0 | 0.0 | 30 | 27.3 | 1.7 | 17 | 15.5 | 1.2 | 43 | 39.1 | 4.5 | 20 | 18.2 | 1.7 | 110 | 1.7 |
| Other | 62 | 23.0 | 4.7 | 77 | 28.5 | 4.4 | 47 | 17.4 | 3.4 | 30 | 11.1 | 3.2 | 54 | 20.0 | 4.6 | 270 | 4.1 |
| No response | 32 | 20.9 | 2.4 | 25 | 16.3 | 1.4 | 37 | 24.2 | 2.7 | 27 | 17.6 | 2.8 | 32 | 20.9 | 2.7 | 153 | 2.3 |
| Total | 1,333 | | | 1,767 | | | 1,378 | | | 950 | | | 1,185 | | | 6,613 | |

time, there are people who choose to call others only on their mobile, even though they know the other's home or office number. Generally, this is because they wish to show themselves, and the person being called, that they can overcome any barrier, thus shifting the center of communications gravity in their favor. Such a gesture also has collateral power significance that we cannot explore here.

### The reasons for the success of the mobile phone

An essentially stereotypical explanation given for the success of the mobile phone in Italy is that Italians are more communicative than are other Europeans. From the data of the European research (Telecom Italia, 1996a), though, this does not seem to be the case. Among Europeans, Italians most frequently say they have problems in talking freely in front of a large group of people.[5] They are also more irritated, together with the British, by other people's conversations on mobiles (see table 4.2). What is more, they do not generally show any great communicative competence: more than the others, Italians confessed to having difficulty in starting a conversation ($M = 3.38$ vs. $M = 4.06$ for the Germans). Also surprising was that Italians were less likely to agree than those in other countries that their friends speak to them about their problems ($M = 3.89$ vs. $4.08$ for Germans).[6]

Hence, the stereotypical explanation the success of the mobile in Italy does not appear valid. Neither can the success of the mobile in Italy be readily attributable to the Italians' enchantment with technology, because, on the contrary, the Italians often appear as technophobic. Our poll data (Telecom Italia, 1996a) confirm this negative attitude: Italians are among the least enthusiastic about technological progress. (Paradoxically, though, Italy is one of the European nations that have most widely adopted the mobile). Another admission from Italians fills out this picture: they have difficulties using new technologies. The Italians are the only Europeans who admit to having this difficulty.[7] So this would suggest, if anything, the opposite hypothesis: the mobile has been a great success in Italy because it was introduced not as a sophisticated technological instrument, but more as a friendly, easy-to-use gadget, a unique totem. So the early promotion surrounding the technology showed it

[5] $M = 3.26$ for Italy, 2.82 for France, 3.21 for Germany, 3.04 for Spain, 2.95 for UK; $p < .01$. The answers were rated on a 5-point scale where 1 = does not apply at all, and 5 = applies completely.
[6] $M = 3.93$ for France, s.d.1.30; $M = 4.02$ for Spain, s.d.1.32; $M = 4.03$ for UK, s.d.1.14.
[7] $M = 3.17$ for Italy, compared with 2.59 for Germany, 2.65 for UK, 2.73 for France, 2.83 for Spain.

not as a serious communication instrument, but rather as an easy-to-use toy – as simple to use as a wired telephone.

Another important reason for the mobile's success in Italy is that it has become "fashionable" by being incorporated into the aesthetic management of the body's perceived visual field (Alberoni, 1998). On this terrain, where socially shared values and feelings meet, like the famous Italian "beautiful tradition" and passion for aesthetic taste, the mobile has become more of a necessary accessory. Italians, who give special importance to dressing well, spend more on clothes than on leisure (6.7% vs. 6.0% of total expenditure by families in 1998; ISTAT, 1999, p. 187). Thus they could not forgo possession of such a powerful accessory; an accessory, we might add, that as late as 1996 still indicated to consumers that its owner belonged to the higher classes of Italian society. To the Italians, therefore, the mobile is an accessory that enriches those who wear it, because it shows just how much they are the object of communicative interest, and are thereby desired, on the part of others.

More consequential than the mobile's outward appearance, which at a minimum must be acceptable aesthetically, is its place within the aesthetics of communication (de Kerckhove, 1999; Costa, 1999). We find this underlying aesthetic expresses itself when users manage, from a stylistic perspective, their multitude of communication relationships.

Before the advent of the mobile, telephone users were, relatively speaking, alone in their communicative space. Today, mobile users may more commonly be traveling with an entourage. However, inasmuch as the exhibition of the vastness of our network of relations has become a form of mass behavior, what has begun to give users prestige is knowing how to use the mobile with ease. This leaves those who use it in too exaggerated a fashion to be accused of vulgarity. People who use it discreetly, who show that in its use they are not affected by the anxiety of continual contact, are in a better position to win tacit social approval. Indicative of this fashion sense was our result that showed that Italy was, in fact, the country with the highest percentage of people who refrained from readily giving their mobile number to family and friends. Italians showed greater caution in regulating the possibility of being contacted daily on their mobile. Italy notably is also the country where the mobile is most often left on in all settings: at home, in shops, in theaters, on public transport, at the home of friends, and in the car. This indicates a greater flexibility in use of the mobile, as if the Italians, for example more than the British, have learnt to modify its use according to changing circumstances.

The second hypothesis that we put forward is that the great success of the mobile in Italy is due, in great part, to its being a technology

Table 4.3 *Evaluation of the mobile phone as facilitating social relationships: mean scores and results of the Manova analysis*

|                          | Italy | Germany | France | UK    | Spain | Total Europe |
|--------------------------|-------|---------|--------|-------|-------|--------------|
| Mean agreement score     | 3.13  | 2.15    | 3.11   | 2.88  | 2.74  | 2.76         |
| Standard deviation       | 1.52  | 1.17    | 1.33   | 1.28  | 1.38  | 1.39         |
| N                        | 1,376 | 1,768   | 1,334  | 1,183 | 948   | 6,609        |

*Notes:* The answers were rated on a 5-point scale, from 1 (very little) to 5 (a lot). A Manova analysis, using "countries" as the dependent variable, gave highly significant results ($p < .001$).

of re-productive work.[8] It responds exactly to the sort of social living that the Italians love, neither intimate nor tied to the home, but rather lived outside, in the street. It is a particular feature of Italian sociality that one must neither be nor appear programmed. Regimented living and precise organizationally planned activities are abhorrent. Rather one must be and appear to be engaged in spontaneous activities with a posture of openness to being deflected onto another trajectory. This inherent sense of spontaneity and flexibility, which can also appear to outsiders as disorganization and incoherence, leads the mobile to be seen as the ideal instrument for rapidly adjusting the organizational fabric of daily living.

We find it illuminating in this context that, when we conducted research via free association techniques (Telecom Italia, 1996b), Italians tended to associate "emergency" with the mobile (78%), but were much less likely to do so with the fixed phone (22%). This implies the perception that emergencies are now much more likely to be encountered in external situations, that is, outside the home. This shift of focus for emergencies from fixed phone to mobile might be explained by reference to the crises connected with sudden changes in daily patterns of organization precipitated by unprogrammed events. In fact our Italian respondents, more than those of other countries, said they use the mobile to manage time and to get information, and that they regarded the mobile as a facilitator of social relations (see table 4.3).

---

[8] Re-productive work is all the unpaid work carried out outside the waged production of commodities or services. Such work, which takes place in the sphere of social reproduction (family, friendships, free time, and so on), serves to rebuild and recreate every day the energies consumed by people in the workplace. The main worker in this process of work continues to be the woman, but all individuals, even if at different levels, contribute to carrying it out.

Another interesting observation in this regard is that the Italians, together with the French, stated that they themselves, rather than their employer, contracted for the mobile phone, and did so primarily to support activities connected with private or everyday life (table 4.4).

Thus the mobile phone in Italy seems to be connected less to the world of work needs than to family and friends. In this sense it is truly a tool of domestic organization. As further, albeit indirect, evidence, we found that it was the Italians who most often paid the phone bill, either personally or through other family members, rather than their employer (71%).

The Italians have always stressed the importance of the family, which is highly cohesive. The mobile has enabled Italians to maintain or re-make their connections to the family nucleus, even from a distance. This has made it possible for Italians to locate and update everybody in the family circle with a minimum of effort. In Italy, as we have seen, those who were more likely to see their relatives were also more likely to use a mobile. Housewives were also among the groups that were heavy subscribers.

Our 1996b study demonstrated that the mobile phone was a logical step in the endogenous expansion of technology into the domestic sphere. This is because it enables women and young people to control their environment and actualize their perceived status by having their own mobile access.

We can also hypothesize that an important element in the success of the mobile in Italy is the fact that, as an individual and personal instrument, it enables people to communicate without using the public telephone. This avoidance of being on helpless public display, tethered, as it were, by the stationary means of communication, is much appreciated by the Italians.

## The mobile phone and ethical and aesthetic dimensions

I now return to and expand on my examination of the identity of the mobile, with special attention to its features of "portability" and "wearability." As mentioned above, the mobile's coming so close and intimately to the body creates very delicate ethical and aesthetic problems.

We have seen how the mobile phone is not, despite its image, very portable. Yet, with respect to other mobile technologies, it is the one item that specifically presents us with the problem of its wearability and, thus, of its relation with clothing. Various laboratories and research centers are already working on how to make the mobile more easily wearable. The risk, however, is that a design approach will be privileged that responds only to the categorical imperative of handiness and comfort on the one hand, and engineer-initiated innovation on the other. My opinion is that these criteria are insufficient to find an adequate solution, and may even be misleading.

Table 4.4 *The main reasons for having a mobile phone in Europe*

| | Country | | | | | | | | | | | | | | | | |
|---|---|---|---|---|---|---|---|---|---|---|---|---|---|---|---|---|---|
| | France n = 102 | | | Germany n = 164 | | | Italy n = 255 | | | Spain n = 81 | | | UK n = 220 | | | Europe n = 822 | |
| Reasons | No. | % of Europe | % of country | No. | % of Europe | % of country | No. | % of Europe | % of country | No. | % of Europe | % of country | No. | % of Europe | % of country | No. | % of country |
| For work | 20 | 9.5 | 19.6 | 24 | 11.4 | 14.6 | 58 | 27.5 | 22.7 | 32 | 15.2 | 39.5 | 77 | 36.5 | 35.0 | 211 | 25.7 |
| Whilst travelling | 3 | 5.1 | 2.9 | 5 | 8.5 | 3.0 | 11 | 18.6 | 4.3 | 13 | 22 | 16.0 | 27 | 45.8 | 12.3 | 59 | 7.2 |
| Only in emergency | 12 | 6.5 | 11.8 | 37 | 20.0 | 22.6 | 49 | 26.5 | 19.2 | 14 | 7.6 | 17.3 | 73 | 39.5 | 33.2 | 185 | 22.5 |
| Clubs, associations | 14 | 20.9 | 13.7 | 19 | 28.4 | 11.6 | 26 | 38.8 | 10.2 | 5 | 7.5 | 6.2 | 3 | 4.5 | 1.4 | 67 | 8.2 |
| Second home | 3 | 18.8 | 2.9 | 3 | 18.8 | 1.8 | 2 | 12.5 | 0.8 | 6 | 37.5 | 7.4 | 2 | 12.5 | 0.9 | 16 | 1.9 |
| Sport, leisure | 6 | 12.0 | 5.9 | 19 | 38.0 | 11.6 | 21 | 42.0 | 8.2 | 1 | 2.0 | 1.2 | 3 | 6.0 | 1.4 | 50 | 6.1 |
| Household purposes | 37 | 23.4 | 36.3 | 10 | 6.3 | 6.1 | 75 | 47.5 | 29.4 | 6 | 3.8 | 7.4 | 30 | 19.0 | 13.6 | 158 | 19.2 |
| No response | 7 | 9.2 | 6.9 | 47 | 61.8 | 28.7 | 13 | 17.1 | 5.1 | 4 | 5.3 | 4.9 | 5 | 6.6 | 2.3 | 76 | 9.2 |

*Note*: More than one answer was possible.

There is no doubt that handiness is relevant when we speak of the mobile; it is the most important technology as far as handiness is concerned. In the research conducted in Italy with free associations, handiness was attributed to the mobile more than to any other communicative technology, including the wireline telephone. However, at a social level, awareness has spread that handiness is often a "poisoned fruit," inasmuch as it has concealed costs, is ecologically insensitive, does not give much importance to health, and often works as an instrument of social control (Esposito, Maldonado, and Riccini, 1981). In this vein, I shall explore the ramifications of bringing communicative technologies closer to the body, that is, the other face of the mobile's portability and wearability, which re-opens the historic problem of technology's relationships with nature, art and science.

Dominion over nature, which in itself devalues imitation and therefore art, imposes a new order, one in which the creation of something dissimilar from the natural can be socially accepted, if not in many cases even desired. However, at the very moment that the artificial attempts to devalue nature, exactly the contrary happens: it is artificiality that becomes devalued, and brings upon itself a negative value judgment or perception. It is argued by some that artificiality, because of its dissonance, is perceived on the human level as worth less than naturalness. Yet artificiality holds a certain fascination for us, because the new plane on which the object is now placed is not only a plane of disharmony, but also a force that tends to be, symbolically, without boundaries. The technological object – thanks to its artificiality – is indeed able to save time, money and effort; these are precious resources for both the individual and society. But because this symbolic force is not able to compensate completely for the lack of harmony, it brings with it its intrinsic disharmonious aspects. In the case of communicative technologies, these are illusions, mystification and confusion. So what we are faced with today is a technology that is strong in its independence, not only from nature and art, but also from science, and one that is most capable of representing itself socially as a salvation myth (of progress, development, etc.).

By coming closer to the body, which is indicative of naturalness (Amsterdamski, 1980), technology, which represents artificiality *par excellence*, brandishes the specter of the machine taking over the body. By coming closer to the body, technology is in some way sucked inside the clothing, and thus fashion itself, which is such a powerful vehicle for spreading art today. Technology must therefore reconcile itself with art. Finally, by coming closer to the body, it must find a common ground of confrontation and collaboration with science.

But that is not all. By coming closer to the body, technologies disrupt the symbolical system, thus undermining fundamental and archaic dimensions of the imagination, for example the supposedly insurmountable barrier between the qualities of animate and inanimate entities. Communicative technologies introduce a perturbing element into clothing: the word. Clothing, in itself a language of "low semanticity" (Davis, 1992, p. 3), has been invaded by the mobile, a communicative means on the plane of what Ong calls "secondary orality" (Ong, 1982). So clothing, which had always been a silent language, begins to speak, with the bonding of communicative technologies. Clothing, which before belonged to the order of the inanimate, thus passes to that of the animate, typical of the voice, conversation and dialogue. This shift is significant, and must be addressed socially, because when an article of clothing, which should be inanimate, suddenly takes on the breath of life and animation, it causes tension and perhaps even alarm. This alarm is similar to what we feel when a person who is walking or sitting alone suddenly begins to speak, and it is not clear to us with whom and why this has occurred (perhaps through an earpiece on a mobile that we cannot see).

An aspect that I shall examine here, and one that is connected with the ethical problem, is the problem of aesthetics. I stated previously that, in the shift closer to the body, portable technologies are sucked into the realm of fashion clothing. How crucial is this process was demonstrated by the results of our 1996b research on free associations, where the semantic area of the mobile was described strongly as part of the category of clothing.

However, the difficulties these technologies have in forming part of the aesthetic politics of the body are obvious. Fashion, as I have already mentioned, finds it difficult to bring them together with other articles of clothing. It could be jewelry and accessories that "drag" these technologies, and especially the mobile, onto the terrain of clothing. In contrast to jewelry, which is connected with the desire to please others, technologies give value only to those who wear them. They shift the fulcrum of their effective significance from the dimension of pleasure to others to that of dynamism. The dimension of dynamism is a good description of the situation in which, when we are wearing technologies, we feel like lords or ladies of a seemingly infinite domain, where space and time seem governed according to the laws of our pleasure and where we often forget any respect for others.

Furthermore, in contrast to jewelry and accessories, which are situated in the sphere of the "superfluous" (Simmel, 1908), communicative and informational technologies are also in the sphere of necessity. On the other hand, like jewelry and accessories, technologies do not have a personal character and can in theory be worn by anyone. So, precisely because of this limited adherence to the person, they bestow the elegance that derives from this sphere of generality, as if it were an abstraction. However, technologies' capacity for attraction lies not in the preciousness of the materials, but in the heart of technological innovation, or, more precisely, the closeness to the levels reached by this innovation. What makes them more attractive is that they represent the latest development of vertical knowledge (Merton, 1949), such as scientific and technological knowledge. Continuous innovation and scientific progress make communicative technologies very quickly obsolete as consumer goods. Rapid technological aging is a primary element of disharmony and scarce sustainability in the sophisticated personal devices, a development that, as stated above, springs from the aggressive work of artificiality.

The aesthetic dimension has, therefore, in the case of the mobile, a very specific valence, one not possessed by any other technology. Through fashion, this technology will probably return to speaking the language of art, even if minor art, perhaps finding other elements of clothing (dresses, suits, jackets, watches and so on) ready to welcome and assimilate it, together with other mobile technologies.

## Conclusions

My purpose has been to delineate the mobile phone's identity in an Italian social context and to contrast it with the West European situation. The mobile is an instrument whose profile is more subtle than might have first appeared. This analysis has reduced support for what are ordinarily readily accepted hypotheses. These include that the mobile phone is an important means of communicative capacity; that it is a technology of mobility *par excellence*; that it could be considered linked to factors of metropolitan living; that it is emblematic of portability; that it is the means for guaranteeing the maximum of intimacy *tout court*. Rather, the analysis supports notions of limited attention being available during calls and the stress users place on the significance of the performance of actions and appearance. By exploring the reasons for the mobile's success in Italy, we have been able to describe other facets of this instrument that are crucial to the public's reception of it. These are its increasingly important role as a necessary "fashion accessory", its capacity of being an efficient technology of domesticity, and its tendency to become a personal instrument that enables people to communicate outside without using a public telephone.

Examination of the most relevant aspect of the mobile phone identity – its wearability – has shown how wrong it is to reduce wearability to a problem of handiness, comfort and innovation. The analysis of the mobile phone coming closer to the body in fact underlined the complexity of its social representation and of its aesthetic and ethical dimensions. The mobile phone, like all other information and communication technologies, presents itself as a "pure" technology, without subordinate roles (towards art, nature and science), prestigious, "magical," and also capable of representing itself socially as a salvation myth (such as "human progress," or Messianism). But, differently from other technologies, in coming so close to the body it acts in two directions. On the one hand, it disrupts the symbolical system, thus undermining fundamental and archaic dimensions of the imagination. Hence it raises the specter of the machine taking over the body. On the other hand, it is obliged to reconcile itself with art through fashion.

It is nevertheless evident that the mobile is developing an identity that is much more articulated and complex than that of other communicative technologies. It will be the leading mobile technology of the future, in that it is absorbing most functions of the pda and laptop (connecting with the Internet), the personal stereo (absorbing music) and the pager (always being reachable at the workplace). However, this will be less in the sense of immobilizing the other mobile technologies, which will still exist in the future, but more in the sense of selecting and taking on those of their functions that are compatible with its own coherent development.

The mobile in addition finds itself between two cross-pressures. It needs to be small and light in order to be easily handled. Yet miniaturization imposes limits in terms of the legibility of the screen. A larger screen with better resolution would doubtless improve matters.

Above all this lies the fact that the mobile's being near the human body (and tending to reside there for long periods), or even inside it, will inevitably yield new problems, especially at the existential and phenomenological levels. The human body is a complex cultural product and contains various argots and relational strategies. It also requires innumerable maintenance, utilization and strengthening procedures. The approach and even penetration of it by communicative technologies is inevitably a complex process. It cannot, and will not, be reduced to purely technical demands but rather will need to call upon the full array of social and aesthetic exigencies of the thoroughly modern human.

### References

Alberoni, F. (1998). "Conversazione con Francesco Alberoni" [Conversation with Francesco Alberoni]. In C. M. Guerci et al. (eds.), *Monopolio e concorrenza nelle telecomunicazioni. Il caso Omnitel* [Monopoly and Competition in Telecommunications. The Omnitel Case]. Milan: Il Sole 24 ore, 130–131.

Amsterdamski, S. (1980). "Naturale/artificiale." Voce dell'*Enciclopedia Einaudi* [Natural/Artificial. Entry in the *Einaudi Encyclopedia*], vol. 9. Turin: Einaudi, 792–821.

Chiaro, M., and Fortunati, L. (1999). "Nouvelles technologies et compétence des usagers." *Réseaux* 96: 147–182.

Costa, M. (1999). *L'estetica della comunicazione* [The Aesthetic of Communication]. Rome: Castelvecchi.

Davis, F. (1992). *Fashion. Culture and Identity.* Chicago: University of Chicago.

Esposito, S., Maldonado T. and Riccini R. (1981). "Condizione femminile e ideologia del comfort" [Women's Condition and Comfort Ideology]. *Casabella* 45 (467): 27–33.

Fortunati, L. (ed.) (1995). *Gli italiani al telefono* [Italians on the Telephone]. Milan: Angeli.

—— (ed.) (1998). *Telecomunicando in Europa* [Tele-communicating in Europe]. Milan: Angeli.

Fortunati, L., and Manganelli Rattazzi, A. M. (in press)."The Social Representation of Telecommunications."

Gournay, C. de (1997). "C'est personnel…La communication hors de ses murs." *Réseaux* 82–83: 21–39.

Heurtin, J. P. (1998). "La téléphonie mobile, une communication itinérante ou individuelle?." *Réseaux* 90: 37–50.

Hofstätter, P. R. (1963). Über Sprachliche Bestimmungsleistungen: das Problem des Grammatikalischen Geschlechts von Sonne und Mond." *Zeitschrift für Experimentelle und Angewandte Psychologie* 10: 91–108.

ISTAT (Italian National Institute of Statistics) (1998). *La vita quotidiana nel 1996* [Everyday Life in 1996]. Rome: ISTAT.

—— (1999). *Rapporto sull'Italia* [Report on Italy]. Bologna: Il Mulino.

Katz, J. (1999). *Connections*. New Brunswick, NJ: Transaction.

Kerkhove, D. de (1999). "L'estetica della comunicazione: per una sensibilità planetaria dell'uomo" [The Aesthetics of Communication: for a Planetary Sensibility of Human Beings]. In M. Costa, *L'estetica della comunicazione* [The Aesthetic of Communication]. Rome: Castelvecchi, 67–76.

Merton, R. K. (1949). *Social Theory and Social Structure*. New York: Free Press.

Morris, D. (1971). *Intimate Behaviour.* London: Cape.

Ong, W.J. (1982). *Orality and Literacy. The Technologizing of the Word.* London and New York: Methuen.

Simmel, G. (1901). "Zur Psychologie der Scham." *Die Zeit* 9, 11.

—— (1908). "Psychologie des Schmuckes. Morgen," *Wochenschrift fur deutsche Kultur* 2; reprinted in G. Simmel, *Schriften zur Soziologie*, ed. H.-J. Dahme and O. Rammstedt, Frankfurt am Main: Suhrkamp, 1983.

Telecom Italia (1996a). "Verso uno scenario europeo delle telecomunicazioni" [Towards a European Scenario of Telecommunications]. Research project.

—— (1996b). "La rappresentazione sociale delle telecomunicazioni" [The Social Representation of Telecommunications]. Research project.

—— (1998). "La competenza d'uso delle tecnologie comunicative" [Competence in Using Telecommunication Technologies]. Research project.

Virilio, P. (1993). *L'Art du moteur.* Paris: Ed. Galilée.

Wynn, E., and Katz, J. (2000). "Teens on the Telephone." *Info* 2(4): 401–419.

# 5    Korea: personal meanings

*Shin Dong Kim*

## Introduction

According to recent statistics, almost half of the entire South Korean population, which exceeds 40 million, use a mobile phone (see table 5.1). Considering that the expression "mobile phone," which is usually called a "hand phone" in Korea, was quite unfamiliar to most Koreans until a few years ago, the rapid diffusion of the cellular technology and its quick adoption are certainly an interesting phenomenon.

The popularity of mobile phones in Korea is most evident among young people and males (tables 5.2 and 5.3). Seven out of ten college students who are taking my courses always bring a phone to class, forcing me to continually ask them to turn it off. To enforce this rule, I even devised a penalty. The offender must sing a song in front of the class, if his or her phone rings during class.

Young people's enthusiastic adoption of cellular phones is also evident in Japan. According to a recent newspaper report entitled "Cell Phone as Teen Talisman," teenagers spend 20% of their allowance or expendable income on cellular phone bills, in a country where two out of five use mobile phones (*Yomiuri Shimbun*, 1999).

The introduction of mobile communication technology will undoubtedly affect traditional patterns of social interaction. History shows that new communication technologies, such as the telephone, television, computer, etc., have brought about social and cultural changes. It is, however, never a simple thing to understand how social interaction will change, especially when the technology is still in its initial stage of diffusion and penetration. Although the rate and speed of the mobile phone diffusion have been rapid, the changes these phones have brought to our social and cultural lives require longer observation and further exploration.

One of the difficulties in understanding the cultural impact of the mobile communication technology stems from the multiplicity and complexity of cultural behavior itself. Unlike the model of the "rational man," frequently assumed when observing the economic behavior of human

Table 5.1 *Mobile phone distribution in Korea (1999)*

|              | No.   | Percent |
|--------------|-------|---------|
| User         | 1,682 | 60.1    |
| Non-user     | 1,118 | 39.9    |
| Total sample | 2,800 | 100.0   |

*Source:* Cheil Communications (1999).

Table 5.2 *Mobile phone distribution by sex (1999)*

|                        | Male   | Female | Total  |
|------------------------|--------|--------|--------|
| *User*                 |        |        |        |
| No.                    | 1,078  | 604    | 1,682  |
| % of users             | 64.09  | 35.91  | 100.00 |
| % of male/female users | 77.00  | 43.14  | 60.07  |
| *Non-User*             |        |        |        |
| No.                    | 322    | 796    | 1,118  |
| % of non-users         | 28.80  | 71.20  | 100.00 |
| % of male/female users | 23.00  | 56.86  | 39.93  |
| *Total*                |        |        |        |
| No.                    | 1,400  | 1,400  | 2,800  |
| % of sample            | 50.00  | 50.00  | 100.00 |

*Source:* Cheil Communications (1999).

Table 5.3 *Mobile phone distribution by age group (1999)*

|                | 13–19 | 20–29 | 30–39 | 40–49 | 50–59 | Total  |
|----------------|-------|-------|-------|-------|-------|--------|
| *User*         |       |       |       |       |       |        |
| No.            | 0     | 735   | 509   | 302   | 136   | 1,682  |
| % of users     | 0     | 43.70 | 30.26 | 17.95 | 8.09  | 100.00 |
| % of age group | 0     | 70.00 | 58.17 | 57.52 | 38.86 | 60.07  |
| *Non-User*     |       |       |       |       |       |        |
| No.            | 0     | 315   | 366   | 223   | 214   | 1,118  |
| % of non-users | 0     | 28.18 | 32.74 | 19.95 | 19.14 | 100.00 |
| % of age group | 0     | 30.00 | 41.83 | 42.48 | 61.14 | 39.93  |
| *Total*        |       |       |       |       |       |        |
| No.            | 0     | 1,050 | 875   | 525   | 350   | 2,800  |
| % of sample    | 0     | 37.50 | 31.25 | 18.75 | 12.50 | 100.00 |

*Source:* Cheil Communications (1999).

beings, people's behavior in the context of culture does not necessarily follow "rational choice." Watching people use a mobile phone proves this point. It is not difficult to spot a woman on the Seoul metropolitan subway talking on her cellular phone to a friend. Anybody can easily overhear that most of her half-hour conversation has little substance. It is mostly filled with trivial aspects of her everyday life. What really annoys the people around her is hearing her final words as she hangs up: "All right. I am almost here. Let's talk about it in more detail a little later."

Filling public transportation space with her chatter, which is virtually nothing but noise to her neighboring passengers, the phone caller does not seem inclined to restrain her telephone behavior. Not long ago, it was normally considered shameful to talk about private business in public. Although many people chatted face-to-face in public on a train, bus, or in the street, people seemed to agree on "public manners," which delineated what could be said and what was inappropriate for public space. These manners seem suddenly to have evaporated in this era of perpetual contact.

Does the new technology have a magic power to make people shameless? Or has this kind of brash behavior resulted from other social factors that have nothing to do with the new technology? This, of course, is not a question to be answered yes or no. But there certainly seems to be something about the new cellular technology that makes people act in such a way.

## Thesis

Our purpose here is to explore the social and cultural meaning of the new cellular technology. It is a study more of the cultural impact on the process of cellular technology diffusion than of the technology's impact on culture and social behavior.

When a new technology enters a society, it has to face a set of cultural norms. For instance, some Korean professors consider it impolite for their students to send e-mails to them. It is not unusual to find a colleague who feels bad about receiving e-mail from a professor down the hall. He thinks it would be more appropriate for his neighbor to make a personal visit to discuss whatever. What value judgments will these people make about a particular use of a new technology?

In addition, I will discuss cellular penetration. Aside from factors that have universal implications, such as enhanced convenience and economic disposability, the rapid diffusion and adoption of cellular technology embody cultural and social realities that make this new communication medium compatible with Korean life.

While seeking answers to the question of what kind of cultural and social factors have enabled Koreans to accept cellular technology, this chapter will also show what effect cellular technology might have on the social and cultural life of Korea. For instance, we can assume that the use of mediated communication technology strongly affects the way people make appointments with one another. Making appointments is surely a form of social interaction. Just as the emergence of the telephone once changed patterns of interaction, so the cellular phone is having a similar impact. I will discuss this in a later part of this chapter.

### Remarks on data

In developing the argument of this paper, I use descriptive frequencies and some statistical evidence from the SPSS (Statistical Package for the Social Sciences) analyses of annual consumer survey data. The data were collected by Cheil Communications, a leading advertising agency in Korea. Four questions seemed most relevant for the purpose of the current study. These questions are about the social behaviors of respondents, both users and non-users of mobile phones. The main purpose of the analysis was to check if there were any significant differences between these two groups in each aspect of social behavior. Respondents were asked if they agree or disagree with the statements shown in table 5.4. Other tables are provided in the appendix at the end of this chapter.

### Conditions for fast diffusion

Several criteria are used to determine whether a new technology will be successfully diffused in a society. The criteria are: relative advantage, compatibility, complexity, possibility of experimentation and observability (Straubhaar and LaRose, 1997, pp. 39–40). Cell phone use amply satisfies all five criteria. There are also some prior conditions that affect the

Table 5.4 *Survey questions on social behavior*

| Category | Statement | Tables |
|---|---|---|
| Social gatherings | I tend to hang around with colleagues after work. | 5A.7, 5A.10 |
| Innovative | I tend to try new methods in doing work even if it involves risk. | 5A.1, 5A.7, 5A.10 |
| Drinking | To create an amicable life at work, I think one cannot avoid joining after-work social gatherings. | 5A.2, 5A.3, 5A.7, 5A.10 |
| Private life | Personal (family) life is more important than life at work. | 5A.4, 5A.5, 5A.7, 5A.10 |

diffusion of innovation: the practice or experience people have had with similar technologies, needs or problems to be solved, a willingness to be innovative, and the norms of the social system associated with the new technology. Whereas "criteria" are conditions mostly related to the generic factors of a new technology, "prior conditions" are based more on the social and cultural situation. Further elaboration of the prior social and cultural conditions is necessary to develop the main thesis of this chapter.

Let us start with one of the prior conditions mentioned above, namely, the experience of similar technologies. Unlike the moment when the telephone first appeared, the general public immediately recognized the utility of the mobile phone. Few people had difficulty understanding what the new technology was for. In the case of the telephone, however, which appeared in the USA in the last quarter of the nineteenth century and began to diffuse among the general public in the early years of the twentieth century, not many people had a clear idea what to do with the new machine. Sellers of the telephone had to "educate" people about the new technology and persuade Americans to use it (Fischer, 1992, ch. 3). Mobile telephony required no such effort in any industrialized countries when it was introduced.

Although the general public know what mobile phones are for, sellers of mobile communication services and of the instruments themselves are among the top national advertisers in Korea (KAA, 1999). Five service providers (SK Telecom, Shinsegi Telecom, Korea Telecom, Hansol PCS, and LG Telecom) are engaged in advertising wars every day on all fronts – television, newspapers, magazines, and radio. Consumers are constantly urged to buy mobile telephone services and products to live a better life and not to be forgotten by other people who are already using the service.

The second prior condition is defined as needs and problems to be solved. There were plenty of conditions in Korea that this new technology could alleviate. For example, although there were thousands of corded telephone lines, the rapidly developing Korean society has never been wired enough to satisfy the general demand. This has been particularly true in the case of the public telephone. To make a call from any crowded place using a public telephone, one needs to be lucky as well as patient – patient because the waiting lines are long and lucky because nobody knows which line will move the fastest. Luck is the god who controls the life of Koreans who form lines to use a telephone booth or washroom, to access ticket counters or teller machines. However many booths there are, lines will form in front of each one.

Some years ago, a man was killed in front of a public telephone by another who was waiting his turn outside the booth. Standing in line on a hot summer day, the assailant was extremely upset because it seemed the man in front of him would never hang up. A quarrel over the inappropriate use of the public telephone ended up an inconceivable tragedy. A combination of an unreasonable social convention – forming lines – plus hot summer weather, crowded phone booths and two hot-tempered men resulted in death. Many people who watched the news on television, however, seemed to agree that the accident was not just the result of idiotic behavior but a problem of poor infrastructure that drove people insane.

Thirdly, were Koreans "innovative enough" to be willing to pay for the mobile phone? When the mobile phone was very expensive and heavy, not many actually wanted to adopt it. However, as the cost dropped considerably and the weight and size of the phone were reduced, one did not need to be innovative any more. Technological advancement made it easy for anybody to try the new machine. And positive social impressions were associated with the new device. Rich business people were the first to use mobile phones. Whether these early adopters were actually that rich and busy was not the point. The instrument carried an aura of social status in Korean society; it was a symbol of achievement and the classy life.

According to statistics culled from a national survey, mobile phone users are more innovative than non-users. There was a significant difference between mobile phone users and non-users when asked if they agree or disagree with the statement, "I tend to try new methods in doing work even if it involves risk." The users showed a higher rate of agreement with the statement (table 5A.1 in the appendix to this chapter).

### Korean social characteristics

According to Kyong-Dong Kim, a prominent sociologist, Korean society has certain principles for organizing social life. They are hierarchical authoritarianism, crony collectivism, or cronyism, personalism, and ritualistic moralism (1993, pp. 136–146). For the purpose of this chapter, I will briefly discuss only the first three.

The Korean language reflects one of the most visible aspects of Korean social life, *hierarchical authoritarianism*. Unlike English, informal Korean speech follows an extremely complicated pecking order. (Social hierarchy itself is determined by the power ascribed to age, sex, social status, family connection, etc.) What distinguishes Korean society in terms of its fundamental dependency on hierarchical structure is one-way, top–down execution of social power. Obedience to authority is a social virtue. A common sight is a senior person speaking, surrounded by many juniors. The earth indeed revolves around the person who occupies a higher hierarchical position.

*Crony collectivism*, or cronyism, is another notable characteristic of modern Korean society. There are three types of connections through which one can achieve personal success: blood ties, regional ties and school ties. In the process of modernization, which weakened traditional forms of ties based on blood and region, the school tie survives as an indicator of crony collectivism. Making and maintaining appropriate connections are key measures of people's ability to manage their lives. It is therefore important to stay in the network of such connections. It is not enough to share the same background, such as the same school, same home town or same family name. One must *maintain* connections by meeting people and sharing information and time in order to display one's loyalty to the group. It is important to be in touch any time and any place. As the saying goes, out of sight, out of mind – and out of connections.

*Personalism*, a tendency to value personal relationships more than official ones, is closely related to the above characteristics. If two people are personally connected through associations and acquaintances, they expect better treatment when doing business. Nepotism or favoritism readily springs up in an environment where personalism is valued. And this is probably why Koreans try to define formal and informal ties.

Kim is only one of many scholars who have pointed out similar social and cultural traits in different fields of study. Related characteristics cited by political scientists include bureaucratic authoritarianism, low trust, collectivism, factionalism, formalism and political emotionalism (Yun, 1961; Lee, 1969; Kim, 1973; Hahm, 1975; Han, 1976; Choe, 1977; Kil, 1980; Paik, 1984).

Being in a group or maintaining connections means a lot in Korean society. Groups are frequently formed on some selective basis, such as home town, family name or school attended. These groups have their own rules and orders, visible or invisible, which are established according to hierarchical, authoritarian and collectivist ideas. Avoiding those groups and networks threatens one's advancement. To stay in a group, to sustain the relationships and to strengthen the ties, one should be ready to devote time and energy to the informal social life that usually begins after work. A large portion of survey respondents agreed with the statement, "I think one cannot avoid joining after-work social gatherings to make an amicable life at work" (tables 5A.2 and 5A.3). Interestingly, mobile phone users show stronger agreement with the statement than non-users (tables 5A.7 and 5A.8).

"After-work social gatherings" in this survey mean gatherings with drinks, which more often than not leads to heavy drinking and the expenditure of lots of time, energy and money. Drinking heavily, which can result in a drunken crowd making a pilgrimage from one bar to another, is certainly a burden on all the participants. Yet, in a society where establishing good relationships means drinking together and getting drunk, many get used to these drinking customs. There comes a time when it is debatable whether one drinks to maintain a good relationship or simply out of habit.

## Life after work and the use of mobile phones

There seems to be an interesting and significant difference in the way Koreans and Americans gather informally. My own limited experience with American people allowed me to observe some unique ways of gathering that my American friends take for granted. Parties, potlucks, brownbags and other types of gathering were at first quite unfamiliar to me. I had no idea what was expected at each event and that usually made me nervous. As time went by, however, I learned that these gatherings have their own shared rules and patterns. What aroused my interest was the fact that most of the occasions that involved more than three people were planned or scheduled in advance, usually a couple of weeks ahead, so that the participants would have enough time to adjust their schedules. This probably is a common social convention in an environment where one must schedule an appointment in order to have a meeting.

In Korea, however, an informal gathering tends to happen instantly or with far shorter notice. Few informal social gatherings are like US parties or potlucks. After work, people casually gather at local restaurants, coffee shops, bars, etc. Friends call each other before they leave the office to check if they can get together after work. It is frequently reported, with some cynicism, that office telephone lines are busy around 5 or 6 in the afternoon because of these calls. If a worker left the office without making any appointments, it used to be almost impossible to track a person down and bring him or her to a gathering place. With the diffusion of mobile devices, such as pagers and cellular phones, however, there has been a considerable change in the way people make appointments. Theoretically, one can contact anybody who carries such a device. It has become far easier to make and cancel appointments, and people can avoid calling their friends under the watchful eyes of peers in their office. Making appointments now has no time limits.

For those who fill up their schedule books with different appointments for the evening and night, a mobile phone is an instrument of magical power. While driving to a place where friends are waiting, one gets a call from someone at another location and immediately changes direction, calling in an excuse to the innocent friends. After a nice round of beer with these other guys, he may feel sorry for his jilted friends and call them again to make up with another round of drinks late at night. The city is all too well connected by invisible networks of two-way radios and mobile phones. This man is happily making a "nomadic" life, riding a taxi with his gun-like "handphone."

Scheduling appointments is a form of social interaction and convention based primarily on reciprocity. Appointment reciprocity assumes mutual respect for one another's time and relationships. Since Korean society is bound in deeply rooted hierarchical relationships, as I noted earlier in this chapter, reciprocal and equal exchanges of power seldom happen. To use Thompson's definition, communication is primarily a form of action, which is closely related to the power that the person possesses (Thompson, 1995, pp. 12–13). When making appointments, one considers these different levels of power. A man would not cancel his appointment with his doctor who is about to reveal a very important test result. At the same time, he would not hesitate to put off his luncheon appointment with his friend if he were informed of the sudden death of his father. But the priority of setting and changing appointments differs from person to person and from society to society.

From a series of interviews with college professors, graduate students and company employees, I found that people were accustomed to sacrifice appointments with their family members (spouses and children) in order to keep a hastily scheduled appointment with their boss. Among young people, however, this tendency is becoming weaker, and they seem to place higher value on familial and conjugal commitment. Empirical data nonetheless indirectly support the fact that many people consider their life at work more important than their private/family life. This tendency was clearer among male respondents (tables 5A.4 and 5A.10). Male and female respondents showed statistically significant differences in agreeing with the statement "Personal (family) life is more important than life at work" (table 5A.10).

Mobile phone users and non-users show significant differences in three out of four aspects of social behavior (tables 5A.7 and 5A.8). Figure 5.1 displays the differences visually. In the case of male respondents, differences were confirmed in all four aspects (tables 5A.9 and 5A.10). Users of mobile phones were more active in getting together with their colleagues, participated more in after-work drinking occasions, considered life at work more important than private/family life, and tended to be more innovative. It is far from clear whether these people are more collective and hierarchical than others. It is safe to say, however, that they certainly tend to be active in maintaining social relations at the cost of their private time. For the purpose of discussion, I would like to name them a collective group with a collective orientation. Collective orientation is acquired over a rather long time period through various stages of socialization, which means this collective orientation preceded the action

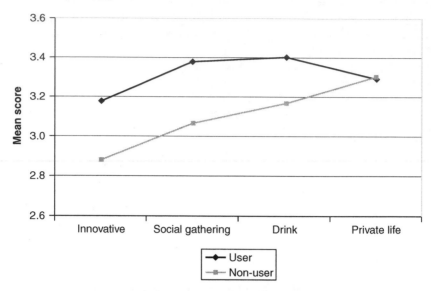

Figure 5.1 Differences in social behavior between users and non-users of mobile phones. *Source:* Survey data in table 5A.7.

of adopting a mobile phone. What then is the reason for the collective group adopting mobile phones more readily? Considering the utility of maintaining social contacts, as described earlier, this study suggests that the desire to be available any time at any place caused them to buy the instrument of nomadic life.

### Forming a new order?

The diffusion of mobile phone technology in Korean society has many factors in common with other nations. However, the purpose of this chapter was to explore if there are unique social and cultural conditions in Korea that expedite the speed and range of diffusion. Based on observations and some statistical evidence, I suggest that hierarchical and collective characteristics seem to provide conditions that are ripe for fast diffusion.

Mobile phone users can contact others more easily, and thus the patterns of getting together seem to be changing. The range of participants in after-work gatherings is becoming wider. As people move around the urban space, the meeting places tend to spread out. One of the most noticeable aspects is that the boundary of public and private space, or the perception of public and private space, is changing. I mentioned earlier the woman on the subway as an example of people who turn on a mobile phone anywhere and plunge into a private talk whether or not friends, colleagues or neighboring strangers are listening. A contract to maintain silence when using public space is being challenged. As the use of mobile phones flourishes among the young generation, they are not even aware of the gradual changes in manners that used to direct what is and what is not permitted in public.

The diffusion of mobile phones leads to the spread of nomadic life. People seem to be getting used to easy calls and easy appointments. Previously, when lovers left each other at the end of a date, they used to make an appointment for the next meeting; today, young lovers say "Call me later" instead. A wired telephone in a domestic setting was a sort of control device that made surveillance of other family members possible. Parents could monitor their youngsters' calls. They had an idea who was at the other end of the phone line. Husbands and wives could check who was calling their spouse. Mobile phones do not allow this type of mutual surveillance anymore. For many teenagers this is the technology of freedom, while for many parents it is the technology of losing control. In the case of the workplace, the reverse is happening. Managers can constantly check if their salespersons are working properly outside the company, while employees find less opportunity to slacken off.

## Appendix

Table 5A.1 *Mobile phone use and attitudes to innovation*

| "I tend to try new methods in doing work even if it involves risk" | | | | |
|---|---|---|---|---|
| Mobile phone use | Disagree | So-so | Agree | Total |
| *User* | | | | |
| No. | 453 | 525 | 704 | 1,682 |
| % of users | 26.93 | 31.21 | 41.85 | 100.00 |
| % of response | 50.78 | 59.52 | 68.62 | 60.07 |
| *Non-User* | | | | |
| No. | 439 | 357 | 322 | 1,118 |
| % of non-users | 39.27 | 31.93 | 28.80 | 100.00 |
| % of response | 49.22 | 40.48 | 31.38 | 39.93 |
| *Total* | | | | |
| No. | 892 | 882 | 1,026 | 2,800 |
| % of sample | 31.86 | 31.50 | 36.64 | 100.00 |

*Source:* Cheil Communications (1999).

Table 5A.2 *Mobile phone use and male attitudes to drinking after work*

"I think one cannot avoid joining after-work social gatherings to create an amicable life at work"

| Mobile phone use | Strongly disagree | Disagree | So-so | Agree | Strongly agree | No response/ Don't know | Total |
|---|---|---|---|---|---|---|---|
| *User* | | | | | | | |
| No. | 17 | 69 | 130 | 273 | 65 | 0 | 554 |
| % of users | 3.07 | 12.45 | 23.47 | 49.28 | 11.73 | – | 100.00 |
| % of response | 62.96 | 73.40 | 73.45 | 78.67 | 82.28 | – | 76.52 |
| *Non-User* | | | | | | | |
| No. | 10 | 25 | 47 | 74 | 14 | 0 | 170 |
| % of non-users | 5.88 | 14.71 | 27.65 | 43.53 | 8.24 | – | 100.00 |
| % of response | 37.04 | 26.60 | 26.55 | 21.33 | 17.72 | – | 23.48 |
| *Total* | | | | | | | |
| No. | 27 | 94 | 177 | 347 | 79 | 0 | 724 |
| % of sample | 3.73 | 12.98 | 24.45 | 47.93 | 10.91 | – | 100.00 |

*Source:* Cheil Communications (1999).

Table 5A.3 *Mobile phone use and female attitudes to drinking after work*

"I think one cannot avoid joining after-work social gatherings to create an amicable life at work"

| Mobile phone use | Strongly disagree | Disagree | So-so | Agree | Strongly agree | No response/ Don't know | Total |
|---|---|---|---|---|---|---|---|
| *User* | | | | | | | |
| No. | 17 | 47 | 109 | 88 | 16 | 0 | 277 |
| % of users | 6.14 | 16.97 | 39.35 | 31.77 | 5.78 | – | 100.00 |
| % of response | 62.96 | 68.12 | 72.19 | 77.88 | 88.89 | – | 73.28 |
| *Non-User* | | | | | | | |
| No. | 10 | 22 | 42 | 25 | 2 | 0 | 101 |
| % of non-users | 9.90 | 21.78 | 41.58 | 24.75 | 1.98 | – | 100.00 |
| % of response | 37.04 | 31.88 | 27.81 | 22.12 | 11.11 | – | 26.72 |
| *Total* | | | | | | | |
| No. | 27 | 69 | 151 | 113 | 18 | 0 | 378 |
| % of sample | 7.14 | 18.25 | 39.95 | 29.89 | 4.76 | – | 100.00 |

*Source:* Cheil Communications (1999).

Table 5A.4 *Mobile phone use and male attitudes to private vs. work life*

| | "Personal (family) life is more important than life at work" | | | | | | |
|---|---|---|---|---|---|---|---|
| | Strongly disagree | Disagree | So-so | Agree | Strongly agree | No response/ Don't know | Total |
| *User* | | | | | | | |
| No. | 13 | 110 | 229 | 152 | 50 | 0 | 554 |
| % of users | 2.35 | 19.86 | 41.34 | 27.44 | 9.03 | – | 100.00 |
| % of response | 81.25 | 80.88 | 74.59 | 76.00 | 76.92 | – | 76.52 |
| *Non-User* | | | | | | | |
| No. | 3 | 26 | 78 | 48 | 15 | 0 | 170 |
| % of non-users | 1.76 | 15.29 | 45.88 | 28.24 | 8.82 | – | 100.00 |
| % of response | 18.75 | 19.12 | 25.41 | 24.00 | 23.08 | – | 23.48 |
| *Total* | | | | | | | |
| No. | 16 | 136 | 307 | 200 | 65 | 0 | 724 |
| % of sample | 2.21 | 18.78 | 42.40 | 27.62 | 8.98 | – | 100.00 |

*Source:* Cheil Communications (1999).

Table 5A.5 *Mobile phone use and female attitudes to private vs. work life*

| | "Personal (family) life is more important than life at work" | | | | | | |
|---|---|---|---|---|---|---|---|
| | Strongly disagree | Disagree | So-so | Agree | Strongly agree | No response/ Don't know | Total |
| *User* | | | | | | | |
| No. | 5 | 33 | 108 | 94 | 37 | 0 | 277 |
| % of users | 1.81 | 11.91 | 38.99 | 33.94 | 13.36 | – | 100.00 |
| % of response | 83.33 | 71.74 | 71.52 | 73.44 | 78.72 | – | 73.28 |
| *Non-User* | | | | | | | |
| No. | 1 | 13 | 43 | 34 | 10 | 0 | 101 |
| % of non-users | 0.99 | 12.87 | 42.57 | 33.66 | 9.90 | – | 100.00 |
| % of response | 16.67 | 28.26 | 28.48 | 26.56 | 21.28 | – | 26.72 |
| *Total* | | | | | | | |
| No. | 6 | 46 | 151 | 128 | 47 | 0 | 378 |
| % of sample | 1.59 | 12.17 | 39.95 | 33.86 | 12.43 | – | 100.00 |

*Source:* Cheil Communications (1999).

Table 5A.6 *Statistics on total survey sample*

|  |  | Mobile phone | Social behavior | | | |
|---|---|---|---|---|---|---|
|  |  |  | Innovative | Social gathering | Drink | Private life |
| N | Valid | 2,800 | 3,500 | 1,102 | 1,102 | 1,102 |
|  | Missing | 700 | 0 | 2,398 | 2,398 | 2,398 |
| Mean |  | 1.40 | 3.11 | 3.30 | 3.35 | 3.30 |
| Minimum |  | 1 | 1 | 1 | 1 | 1 |
| Maximum |  | 2 | 5 | 5 | 5 | 5 |

Table 5A.7 *Statistics on mobile phone users' and non-users' social behavior*

| Mobile phone use | Social behavior | | | |
|---|---|---|---|---|
|  | Innovative | Social gathering | Drink | Private life |
| *User* |  |  |  |  |
| Mean | 3.18 | 3.37 | 3.41 | 3.29 |
| N | 1,682 | 831 | 831 | 831 |
| Std. deviation | 0.97 | 0.94 | 0.98 | 0.94 |
| *Non-user* |  |  |  |  |
| Mean | 2.87 | 3.07 | 3.16 | 3.31 |
| N | 1,118 | 271 | 271 | 271 |
| Std. deviation | 0.98 | 0.96 | 1.02 | 0.88 |
| *Total* |  |  |  |  |
| Mean | 3.06 | 3.30 | 3.35 | 3.30 |
| N | 2,800 | 1,102 | 1,102 | 1,102 |
| Std. deviation | 0.98 | 0.96 | 1.00 | 0.93 |

Table 5A.8 *Differences between groups on some social characteristics*

| Social behavior | Sum of squares | df | Mean square | F | Significance |
|---|---|---|---|---|---|
| *Innovative* | | | | | |
| Between groups | 62.139 | 1 | 62.139 | 65.818 | .000 |
| Within groups | 2641.604 | 2798 | 0.944 | | |
| Total | 2703.743 | 2799 | | | |
| *Social gathering* | | | | | |
| Between groups | 19.063 | 1 | 19.063 | 21.204 | .000 |
| Within groups | 988.906 | 1100 | 0.899 | | |
| Total | 1007.968 | 1101 | | | |
| *Drink* | | | | | |
| Between groups | 12.325 | 1 | 12.325 | 12.535 | .000 |
| Within groups | 1081.564 | 1100 | 0.983 | | |
| Total | 1093.888 | 1101 | | | |
| *Private life* | | | | | |
| Between groups | 0.114 | 1 | 0.114 | 0.132 | .716 |
| Within groups | 949.447 | 1100 | 0.863 | | |
| Total | 949.561 | 1101 | | | |

Table 5A.9 *Statistics on mobile phone users' and non-users' social behavior by sex*

| Sex | Social behavior | | | |
|---|---|---|---|---|
| | Innovative | Social gathering | Drink | Private life |
| *Male* | | | | |
| Mean | 3.28 | 3.38 | 3.49 | 3.22 |
| N | 1,749 | 725 | 725 | 725 |
| Std. deviation | 0.97 | 0.89 | 0.98 | 0.93 |
| *Female* | | | | |
| Mean | 2.93 | 3.14 | 3.07 | 3.43 |
| N | 1,751 | 377 | 377 | 377 |
| Std. deviation | 0.97 | 1.05 | 0.98 | 0.91 |
| *Total* | | | | |
| Mean | 3.11 | 3.30 | 3.35 | 3.30 |
| N | 3,500 | 1,102 | 1,102 | 1,102 |
| Std. deviation | 0.99 | 0.96 | 1.00 | 0.93 |

Table 5A.10 *Differences between groups on some social characteristics by sex*

| Social behavior * sex | Sum of squares | df | Mean square | F | Significance |
|---|---|---|---|---|---|
| *Innovative * sex* | | | | | |
| Between groups | 107.439 | 1 | 107.439 | 112.601 | .000 |
| Within groups | 3337.650 | 3498 | 0.954 | | |
| Total | 3445.089 | 3499 | | | |
| *Social gathering * sex* | | | | | |
| Between groups | 14.451 | 1 | 14.451 | 16.000 | .000 |
| Within groups | 993.517 | 1100 | 0.903 | | |
| Total | 1007.968 | 1101 | | | |
| *Drink * sex* | | | | | |
| Between groups | 43.630 | 1 | 43.630 | 45.697 | .000 |
| Within groups | 1050.258 | 1100 | 0.955 | | |
| Total | 1093.888 | 1101 | | | |
| *Private life * sex* | | | | | |
| Between groups | 10.682 | 1 | 10.682 | 12.516 | .000 |
| Within groups | 938.878 | 1100 | 0.854 | | |
| Total | 949.561 | 1101 | | | |

# References

Cheil Communications (1999). *Annual Consumer Report.* Seoul: Cheil Communications.

Choe, J.S. (1977). *Han'gugin ui Sahoejok Songkyuk* [Social Characteristics of Korean People]. Seoul: Kaemunsa.

Fischer, C.S. (1992). *America Calling: A Social History of the Telephone to 1940.* Berkeley, CA: University of California Press.

Hahm, P.C. (1975). "Toward a New Theory of Korean Politics: a Reexamination of Traditional Factors." In E.R. Wright (ed.), *Korean Politics in Transition.* Seattle, WA: University of Washington Press.

Han, S.J. (1976). *Han'guk Minjujuui wa Chongchi Palchon* [Democracy in Korea and Political Development]. Seoul: Popmunsa.

KAA (Korea Advertisers Association) (1999). "Top 100 Advertisers." *KAA Journal* 11: 39.

Kil, S.H. (1980). "Han'gugin ui chongchi uisik kujo pyonhwa: 1963 nyon kwa 1978 nyon" [Changes in Korean Political Consciousness: 1963 and 1978]. *Han'guk Chongchihakhoebo* 14.

Kim, H.K. (1973). Han'guk e issoso ui ilbon singmin tongchi ui yusan" [The Legacy of Japanese Colonial rule in Korea]. *Han'guk ui Chontong kwa Pyonchon* [Korean Tradition and its Change]. Seoul: Asiatic Research Center.

Kim, K.D. (1993). *Han'guk sahoe pyondongnon* [Korean Social Change: Theoretical Perspectives]. Seoul: Nanam.

Lee, Y.H. (1969). "The Political Culture of Modernizing Society: Political Attitude and Democracy in Korea." Ph.D. dissertation, Yale University.

Paik, W.K. (1984). *Han'guk ui Haengjong Munhwa* [Administrative Culture in Korea]. Korea University Press.

Straubhaar, J., and LaRose, R. (1997). *Communications Media in the Information Society* (updated edn). Belmont, CA: Wadsworth Publishing Company.

Thompson, J.B. (1995). *The Media and Modernity: A Social Theory of the Media.* Stanford, CA: Stanford University Press.

*Yomiuri Shimbun* (1999). "Cell Phone as Teen Talisman." *The Daily Yomiuri Online*, at www.yomiuri.co.jp/newse/1013so20.htm.

Yun, C.J. (1961). *Han'guk Chongchi Chegye Sosol* [Introduction to the Korean Political System]. Seoul: Munyondang.

# 6 United States: popular, pragmatic and problematic

*Kathleen A. Robbins and Martha A. Turner*

## Introduction

Despite the enormous popularity and economic success of mobile phone communication in the United States, only slight scholarly attention has been paid to its social aspects (notable exceptions have been the studies of Katz and Aspden, 1998, and Katz, 1999). Researchers can ill-afford to ignore a technology not only that has been so widely adopted around the world, but whose success seems to have soared beyond even the most enthusiastic projections of those American companies that created the technology in the first place. AT&T, which first developed cellular technology in the early 1980s, estimated that the US market would in year 2000 be 1 million users. This figure was revised in mid-1994 to 120 million mobile phone users worldwide by 1999 (*Common Carrier Week*, June 6, 1994). In fact the figure was 97 million in June 2000 in the United States alone, and in mid-2001 there were 118 million US subscribers, according to the Cellular Telephone Industry Association (CTIA, 2000, 2001). Penetration is expected to grow to 176 million or 60% in 2004 and 232 million or 76% in 2009 (Paul Kagan Associates, 1999). Although these are impressive numbers, they pale in comparison with Finland's robust 69% penetration rate (Quinn, 1999).

Allied Business Intelligence (1999) estimated that Wireless Application Protocol (WAP) equipped mobile phones would be 12% of the market in 2000 and 33% by 2005. WAP is one of protocols that are being developed to allow mobile phone access to the Internet. The Yankee Group forecast that the wireless data market would grow from US$1.8 billion in 1999 to US$13.2 billion by 2003 (*Bloomberg News*, November 8, 1999).

The impact of the Internet-enabled mobile phone will likely extend the same forces that are driving the current generation of mobile phones to over 50% penetration in the USA. David Hayden (1999) of Mobile Insights estimates that, by 2003, 75% of the 500 million mobile phones worldwide (375 million phones) will be Internet enabled.

Table 6.1 *The changing US market shares of wireless technologies (%)*

| Technology | 1999 | 2000[a] | 2004[a] | 2006[a] | 2009[a] |
|---|---|---|---|---|---|
| ESMR | 5 | 6 | 6 | 6 | 5 |
| PCS | 18 | 24 | 40 | 44 | 48 |
| Cell | 77 | 70 | 54 | 50 | 47 |

*Note:* [a] Estimate.
*Source:* Paul Kagan Associates, *Wireless Week*, October 18, 1999.

Our purpose in this chapter is to look at the demographics of mobile phone use (and non-use) in the United States, with an eye towards understanding who users and non-users are, and what their concerns might be.

### The United States mobile phone communication market

Mobile phone subscribers in the USA have a choice of four different digital technologies in two frequency ranges, 800 MHz (cellular) and 1900 MHz (PCS, or Personal Communication Service). The technologies of digital wireless[1] are TDMA (Time Division Multiple Access), CDMA (Code Division Multiple Access), GSM (Global System for Mobile Communications) and ESMR (Enhanced Specialized Mobile Radio, a variant of TDMA). There is also a large embedded base of analog customers, though this will be shrinking as customers migrate to digital technology, as seen in table 6.1.

This pattern holds in other countries, too. Worldwide, digital technology, primarily GSM and CDMA, is eclipsing analog. The rapid pace is suggested by the handset sales report in table 6.2. Despite rapid growth in the USA, the market is fragmented by the differing digital technologies. Moreover, it has a significant embedded base of analog users, accounting for about half of all such handsets in the world. Most US users do not understand the differences between analog and digital wireless technologies. The lack of a common digital standard in the USA combines with misleading phone manufacturer marketing to confuse the mobile phone consumer. (Motorola's original *analog* flip phone was marketed as the DPC 550, with DPC described on the phone as *Digital P*ersonal Communicator). Indeed, when asked, 29% of the respondents in a 1998 Nokia study said they were not sure whether they had an analog or digital wireless phone (Daniels, 1998).

[1] The term wireless includes cellular, Personal Communication Service, and Enhanced Specialised Mobile Radio, but excludes paging.

Table 6.2 *Worldwide distribution of handset sales by technology (%)*

|         | TDMA | PHS | PDC | GSM  | CDMA | Analog |
|---------|------|-----|-----|------|------|--------|
| 1999Q1  | 9.4  | 0.5 | 7.7 | 54.9 | 12.6 | 15.0   |
| 1999Q2  | 9.2  | 1.0 | 6.0 | 61.1 | 9.2  | 13.6   |

*Notes:* PHS, Personal Handyphone Service; PDC, Personal Digital Cellular
*Source:* Strategis Group, *Wireless Week*, October 18, 1999.

Another limitation to the adoption of mobile telephony in the USA is the failure of "Calling Party Pays" (CPP) to be accepted by consumers. Under CPP, the person initiating a call is billed for it (Elstrom et al., 1999). This is a primary reason for the penetration differences between the USA and Europe. In Europe, most mobile phone operators have been able to implement CPP, which expands customer usage and revenue to the mobile phone carriers. With CPP, traffic is generally balanced closer to 50/50 between incoming and outgoing calls, whereas in the USA about 75% are outbound (Rollins, 1998). Interestingly, only 20% of users in the USA have given out their mobile phone number to more than ten people (Strategis Group, press release, April 28, 1998).

The absence of CPP in the USA has been partially countered by the fact that some cellular digital carriers have adopted a "First Incoming Minute Free" pricing policy. But fear of unwanted calls for which the subscriber must pay impedes greater adoption. In November 1999, Bell Atlantic Mobile began the latest CPP trial in Delaware (*Wireless Week*, 1999). Dennis Strigl, CEO of Bell Atlantic Mobile, said he was "confident that demand for the service will bring in new subscribers from the glovebox crowd and convince them to do more of their calling wirelessly."

## Current US mobile phone users

While exploring various dimensions of wireless subscribers in the USA, it is important to recognize that, in addition to users, there are also those who have previously been users, those who plan to use the technology in the future, and those who reject the technology out of hand. Although we cannot investigate all of these categories here, it is worth bearing them in mind when thinking about potential growth rates or problems of subscribership churn.

For perspective, we start with an examination of current users of mobile phone technology in the USA. In the first national survey of the subject,

Katz and Aspden (1998) examined demographics of mobile phone users in 1993 (93) and 1995 (95). Not surprisingly, given the technology's rapid growth, subsequent polls reveal significant changes in mobile phone usage from these early surveys. We will compare Katz and Aspden's results with those of surveys in 1996 (96) and 1997 (97), two in 1998 (98a and 98b), and one in 2000 (00).

The methodologies for these surveys varied:

1. The 1995 survey (by Katz and Aspden) was a result of a 2,500 person national random telephone survey conducted in October 1995.
2. The 1996 survey, by Cellular One of East Central Illinois, was a telephone survey (Sikora, 1996) of 400 people in Illinois 7 Rural Service Area (RSA). This survey consisted of 200 randomly selected current customers of Cellular One, 100 of the competitor's (Ameritech) customers (whose names were obtained from the purchase of lists), 50 past customers of Cellular One with no current cellular service and 50 non-users who had never had cellular service. (This fourth group was identified via random dialing.)
3. Cellular One Group commissioned a survey by Roper Starch Worldwide in 1997. The methodology for data collection and the derivation of results were not given.
4. Peter D. Hart Research Associates, Inc. (1998) surveyed 1,004 wireless users in a nationwide telephone survey between January 17 and 20, 1998.
5. Nokia conducted a survey of mobile phone usage and attitudes in the USA in 1998 (Daniels, 1998). Again, the methodology for data collection and the derivation of results were not given.
6. In mid-2000, the Eagleton Institute of Rutgers University conducted a survey of nearly 793 New Jersey residents (Zukin, 2000). Although it was not a nationwide poll, we include it because of its timeliness and in the expectation that New Jersey is not greatly different from the rest of the USA. Thus, in exchange for timeliness, we may be sacrificing representativeness.

In comparing these surveys, we see that women are now the majority of mobile phone users in the USA, rising from about 40% in 1993 (table 6.3).

Mobile phone usage among women has continued to expand as costs decline – the average local monthly bill dropped from US$95.00 in June 1988 to US$45.15 in June 2000 (CTIA, 1999, 2000). The 1988 study by Rakow and Navarro (1993) reported, "more than 90% of subscribers were men." Possible reasons for this demographic change are the recognition of the benefits of mobile phones: cost effectiveness, safety

Table 6.3 *Mobile phone usage in the USA by gender* (%)

| | US population | Survey | | | | | | |
| | | 93 | 95 | 96 | 97 | 98a | 98b | 00 |
|---|---|---|---|---|---|---|---|---|
| Women | 53 | 39 | 48.5 | n.a. | 52 | 55 | 55 | 52 |
| Men | 47 | 61 | 51.5 | n.a. | 48 | 45 | 45 | 48 |

*Note:* n.a. = not available.
*Sources:* the various surveys.

(communications in an emergency is the leading reason 44% of mobile phone owners have one today; CEMA, 1998), social and convenience. (This same CEMA survey showed only 8% have a mobile phone service strictly for business; 19% combine business and personal and 27% have it for personal use only.)

The average age of the US mobile phone subscriber continues to decline. Katz and Aspden (1998) suggested that, for mobile phones, "it is middle-aged people who are the early adopters. This might be because of the cost, but we also believe the nature of one's occupation is probably even more central to the adoption decision." Recent data suggest that the mobile phone consumer wants the phone for convenience rather than business purposes.

The US mobile phone industry early on adopted stringent credit requirements that have been a significant barrier to mobile phone adoption for both young people and the "credit challenged." We believe it is this credit barrier that, more than anything else, has contributed to the "digital divide" of ethnic/race, age and educational differences (Katz and Aspden, 1998).

More recently, the industry, recognizing that a significant portion of potential users (between 30% and 40%) are denied mobile phone service because of poor or no credit history, began extensive introduction of

Table 6.4 *Pre-paid's projected share of the US mobile phone market* (%)

| | 1998 | 1999[a] | 2000[a] | 2001[a] | 2002[a] |
|---|---|---|---|---|---|
| Penetration | 7 | 12 | 17 | 23 | 30 |

*Note:* [a] Estimate.
*Source:* Donaldson, Lufkin & Jenrette (1997).

Table 6.5 *Mobile phone usage in the USA by income level (%)*

| Income (US$'000) | US population | Survey | | | | | |
|---|---|---|---|---|---|---|---|
| | | 95 | 96 | 97 | 98a | 98b | 00 |
| <15 | – | 10 | $1^d$ | $9^d$ | – | 6 | – |
| 15–24 | $25^a$ | 12 | $6^e$ | $9^e$ | $16^a$ | 23 | – |
| 25–34 | – | 11 | – | – | – | $20^h$ | 15 |
| 35–49 | $25^b$ | 12 | $40^f$ | $39^f$ | $27^b$ | $26^i$ | – |
| 50–74 | 18 | 11 | – | 11 | 19 | $12^j$ | $37^l$ |
| 75–99 | 16 | 14 | $24^g$ | 8 | $16^c$ | $15^k$ | $48^m$ |
| >100 | – | 12 | 8 | 4 | – | – | – |

*Note:* Columns do not sum to 100% owing to non-responses among survey participants concerning their income.
[a] < 30    [b] 30–50    [c] > 75    [d] < 10
[e] 10–20    [f] 20–49    [g] 50–99    [h] 25 39
[i] 40–59    [j] 60–79    [k] > 80    [l] 35 to <70    [m] 70+
*Source:* the various surveys.

pre-paid mobile phone service in 1996. Today, pre-paid mobile phones account for approximately 30% of new activations in the USA (Santos, 1998).

Other demographic changes in mobile phone usage include lowering of the mean age, income (table 6.5) and educational achievement level of owners, a trend we expect to continue.

## US mobile phone non-users

As we mentioned above, studies of mobile phone users obviously exclude significant portions of the population. By contrast, studies by both Cellular One Group in 1997 and Nokia in 1998 identify a significant difference in demographics and attitudes among three groups: current mobile phone users, those who intend to subscribe to mobile phones within the next twelve months, and the general US population (see table 6.6). Among those who expect to purchase a mobile phone within the next year, the largest group, 28%, is aged 25–34 (Roper Starch Worldwide, 1997).

Nokia research (Daniels, 1998) found that the potential user is looking to the phone to provide availability, security and contactability for close friends and family but not necessarily for work. This is in contrast to current users, who are looking for availability and contactability for both work and family. These users are comfortable using technology to help

Table 6.6 *The changing demographic profile of users, potential users and the general population in the USA*

|  | US population | Potential users | Current users |
|---|---|---|---|
| Median age | 42.4 | 35.8 | 40.2 |
| Median income | US$35,200 | US$39,200 | US$52,200 |
| Education |  |  |  |
| Some college | 44% | 54% | 63% |
| Occupation |  |  |  |
| Executive/prof. | 16% | 20% | 29% |
| White collar | 23% | 29% | 30% |
| Blue collar | 31% | 25% | 26% |
| Children < 18 | 47% | 58% | 53% |
| Spend a lot of time researching new products | 30% | 32% | 38% |
| Willing to pay for a product to make life easier | 51% | 56% | 60% |

*Source:* Roper Starch Worldwide (1997).

them achieve these goals. Table 6.7 shows how current mobile phone users have a much higher ownership of high-tech electronics than either the US public or potential users.

Table 6.7 *High-tech ownership rates among users, potential users and the general population in the USA (%)*

|  | US population | Potential users | Current users |
|---|---|---|---|
| Computers | 36 | 36 | 34 |
| Internet |  | 33 | 48 |
| CD-ROM drive | 21 | 24 | 42 |
| VCR plus | 26 | 33 | 40 |
| Pager | 21 | 29 | 36 |
| Fax machine | 10 | 11 | 25 |
| CD recorder | 14 | 24 | 22 |
| PDA | 9 | 12 | 19 |

*Source:* Roper Starch Worldwide (1997).

There is also a large segment of the US population that currently rejects the idea of owning or using a mobile phone. Roper Starch Worldwide, in its 1997 report to the Cellular One Group, noted this technology polarization. It divided the US population into three segments: "Tech Haves," "Tech Will Haves," and "Tech Nots" (also known as non-users). It defined these three segments as:

**Tech Haves**
- 45% baby boomers
- 33% executive/professional
- parents

**Tech Will Haves**
- younger than average – 39.1 years vs. 42.2 for the general population
- average income, education
- employed female

**Tech Nots**
- oldest of three groups – 47.8 years
- downscale – US$22,000 vs. US$32,000 average, low education
- not parents

Between 1995 and 1997, the "Tech Haves" increased, whereas the "Tech Nots" remained stable (table 6.8).

Table 6.8 *The changing distribution of "Tech Haves" and "Tech Nots" (%)*

|                | 1995 | 1997 |
| -------------- | ---- | ---- |
| Tech Haves     | 17   | 25   |
| Tech Will Haves| 32   | 25   |
| Tech Nots      | 51   | 50   |

*Source:* Roper Starch Worldwide (1997).

The different attitudes of these groups can be seen in their response to the statements in table 6.9. These delineate basic societal and behavioral differences that are more reflective of generational norms than right or wrong. These differences put "Tech Haves" and "Tech Will Haves" in the same group: Technology Acceptors. "Tech Nots" are here identified as Technology Rejecters. The attitudes of these two groups toward technology differ enormously.

This same polarization can be seen in the Nokia report on the differenes between users, acceptors and rejecters in their interest in accessing information (table 6.10).

This difference is especially notable in terms of accessing the Internet and having text-based services in the form of sending and receiving pages. Both of these are of course advanced services beyond simple voice conversation and voice messaging.

Table 6.9 *Attitudes to mobile phones: "Technology Acceptors" and "Technology Rejectors"*

|  | Agreement with statement (%) | |
|---|---|---|
|  | Acceptors | Rejecters |
| I am annoyed when people use wireless phones in public places | 15% | 42% |
| Everyone should have a wireless phone | 32% | 19% |
| I would like people to admire the wireless phone I have | 10% | 28% |
| I am very concerned about the cost of owning a wireless phone | 37% | 41% |
| I don't care about the style of a wireless phone so long as it works | 24% | 48% |
| People like me don't need wireless phones | 25% | 42% |
| I would find it embarrassing to use a wireless phone in public places | 29% | 42% |
| Wireless phones are just not very interesting to me | 8% | 30% |
| Once they are cheap enough, everyone will have a wireless phone | 34% | 20% |
| Owning a wireless phone means you have no time for yourself | 15% | 40% |

*Source:* Roper Starch Worldwide (1997).

Dividing the population into three groups gives us a finer-grained understanding of attitudes toward wireless technology than is possible with a binary classification of user/non-user. It is possible that further studies will enable us to understand even better the meaning of the technology by looking at subgroups divided by other factors such as gender and age.

Table 6.10 *Interest in accessing types of information: current users, Acceptors and Rejecters (%)*

|  | Current users | Acceptors | Rejecters |
|---|---|---|---|
| Internet | 18 | 25 | 7 |
| Send/receive pages | 15 | 30 | 7 |
| Corporate extranet | 8 | 15 | 6 |
| Corporate intranet | 7 | 18 | 5 |
| Electronic documents | 7 | 9 | 4 |
| Work scheduling | 5 | 15 | 4 |

*Source*: Daniels (1998).

## Security and privacy issues

The US government, through the Federal Communications Commission (FCC), has levied two requirements on the mobile phone industry that have both significant privacy risks and large potential societal benefits. The first of these is the Communications Assistance for Law Enforcement Act, which allows the FBI to "wiretap," with proper warrants, the mobile phone calls utilizing the latest digital technology. In addition to just "wiretapping," however, the FBI is requesting phone location and the ability to monitor conference calls after the person under surveillance hangs up. These rulings are being challenged in court by the US Telecom Association, the American Civil Liberty Union and the Electronic Privacy Information Center and have been modified by the courts (Schwartz, 1999, p. E03).

Phase II of the FCC's Enhanced 911 (emergency calling) requirements addresses the phone location demand. The requirements call for mobile phone providers to provide Automatic Location Identification to an emergency dispatcher by October 1, 2001. This can be accomplished either by phones that utilize the Global Positioning System or through a network-based solution. Companies were required to submit their choice for a solution to the FCC by November 9, 2000.

The impact of these combined technologies gives government agencies the ability to track the movements of these phones, in effect making them homing devices for the person carrying them. This technology also has the potential to provide consumers with increased directional information and to speed assistance response when requested. Clearly, these technologies have both benefits and disadvantages for consumers and for law enforcement.

## Issues of symbolic behavior in public space

Whereas the attitudes of current mobile phone users and of anticipated future users are similar, they differ greatly from those held by non-users – those who have no intention of ever acquiring or using mobile phone technology. However, the cause and effect of the attitudes is unclear. Are the attitudes a result of experience with the technology, or do the attitudes cause the adoption or lack of adoption of the technology?

As our demographic picture of mobile phone users grows more complex, further questions arise for the researcher. Why are these groups the ones who are adopting the technology? How do they use the technology? What does the technology mean to them as a symbol and as a tool?

Like any technology, mobile phones have both a technical capability and a socially constructed element. The mobile phone is not just a way to communicate, but also a symbol. What is it a symbol of? Some answers to this question have emerged from current research. The mobile phone can be a symbol of safety (some phones are sold on the open market that can be used only to dial 911 and other emergency numbers); the phone is also a symbol of accessibility, of others to you and of you to others.

The symbolic nature of the phone can also be seen in patterns of adoption and in the image of users. Size and other style elements seem to matter to consumers, perhaps because the look of the phone is a way to manipulate your public image. There are also larger public images about mobile phone users created by the media. For example, many youngsters need to deny dealing drugs when they have both a mobile phone and a pager – technologies that are sometimes associated with criminal activity. Within the peer groups of these young people, however, these technologies represent a hip urban image.

Some people also avoid mobile phones because of the symbolic meaning of the technology. These people either will not get mobile phones or will use them cautiously to distance themselves from the image they associate with the technology. In other words, besides economic barriers to usage, as previously mentioned, some cultural barriers (and generational barriers) still exist. The very things that attract users repel non-users.

### Questions for researchers

Although there has been much talk of globalization, the question remains: whose standards, technology and culture will be global winners? Usually America is seen as the bête noir, forcing other cultures to succumb their most precious values (social patterns and norms) to the American ethos. Interestingly, however, the development of the cell phone in America is now being driven largely by European innovations. Small countries such as Finland (and other Scandinavian countries) are creating a mobile phone technoculture that is far advanced of anything currently in America. It is important that researchers complement the American domination thesis with an understanding of this potential reverse flow of culture.

Likewise, Japan has had an enormous influence on American tastes, especially in terms of entertainment (Pokemon, "anime" cartoons and portable electronics). We are seeing the beginnings of this same influence in the mobile phone area. NTT Docomo is leading the world in wireless information access with its i-Mode service, which has been growing rapidly since its inception in February 1999. The service has proven so popular that Docomo announced an upgrade to 3G service beginning in May 2001 (*Wireless Review*, October 1, 2000) and is exploring the purchase of minority shares in several of the major US mobile phone carriers.

Left unanswered in our chapter is why the USA has fallen behind in the mobile phone communications arena. Although cellular was first developed and introduced in the USA, the transition from analog (1G) to digital (2G) service has seen the USA fall behind the rest of the world.

The slow rate of deployment of digital technology and the relatively low penetration rate of mobile phone technology are caused by multiple factors, some clear and some yet to be explained. Cost to the consumer does not seem to be the determining factor, as countries poorer than the USA have higher penetration rates. Questions of standards, infrastructure investment, wireline quality and regulation might be explanatory variables. But there may be a cultural component as well. It would be useful therefore in future research to try to isolate the cultural component relative to other drivers of adoption.

According to some of the other chapters in this book, the integration of new technology into a culture depends on how the technology relates to the social formation of the self. Nafus and Tracy (chapter 13) discuss the concept of individualism in England. According to their analysis, the individual identity in England is formed in part by regulating interactions with others (family, friends and work). In Italy, according to Fortunati (chapter 4), individuals may maintain different mobile phones to manage their connection with different social groups.

### Conclusion

Two threads tie the American case together with other cases presented in this volume. The first is that the same problems of negotiating newly defined social territory arise with the adoption of new technologies such as the mobile phone. This may be most specifically seen in the cases of manners on buses, trains, and in restaurants. However, it must surely also penetrate to the level of dyadic relationships and the privacy of the home or in negotiating communication and periodicity of contact during travel events. As Schegloff points out, in chapter 18, the interruption of a dyadic relationship by the summons of a phone and the introduction of a distant third party is highly relevant in the USA as well as in other cultural settings.

The second thread in this research is the presentation of the technology through media outlets. Besides discounts, isomorphic images are displayed in advertisements throughout the world. For instance, at the workshop, we compared Israeli, South Korean and US advertisements for mobile phone technology and found them remarkably similar in terms of the images of speediness, flexibility and social connectivity. We were struck by this congruence despite the enormous cultural and linguistic differences that characterize these countries. This of course suggests that there is a good fit between the enduring human need to communicate, regardless of cultures, and what is achievable through a given technology, in this case the mobile phone.

The question of the fit between the perceived problems of consumers and the choice of solutions is not always clear to users. In "Rethinking Residential Telecomm Usage," Dudley et al. (1996) make the point that consumers in many cases do not make the connection between what a technology might achieve for them (or at least the way that the designers of the technology envisioned its use) and adopting it for that use. Hence consumers may know about the technology and may identify a problem but may not see the technology as a solution to their problem. If this perspective is correct in terms of mobile phones, adoption may be lower than would otherwise be the case. Moreover, many advertisements for mobile phones are pitched in such a way that many consumers would not see the connection between solving their personal productivity and family connectivity problems and the mobile phone. Yet, despite the seeming disconnection between "uses" and "gratifications," the mobile phone is obviously an object of desire and usage. Hence the social and affective areas, in addition to the coordination, information-seeking and transaction-achieving domains, are important to gain a full understanding of the shifting picture of the mobile phone user in the USA.

## References

Allied Business Intelligence Inc. (1999). "Projected Growth in WAP-enabled Handsets." *Wireless Week*, November 22.

CEMA (Consumer Electronics Manufacturers Association) (1998). "Survey; Multiple Wireless Phone Families on the Rise." February 11.

CTIA (Cellular Telephone Industry Association) (1999). "Semi-Annual Wireless Industry Survey Result." June.

(2000). "Semi-Annual Wireless Industry Survey." June.

(2001). "Semi-Annual Wireless Industry Survey." June.

Daniels, Mark (1998). " '98 U.S. End User Usage & Attitude Research." Nokia Mobile Phones.

Donaldson, Lufkin & Jenrette (1997). "Wireless Communications Industry." New York.

Dudley, K., Steinfield, C., Kraut, R.E., and Katz, James E. (1996). "Rethinking Residential Telecomm Usage." Paper presented at the International Communication Association annual meeting, Miami, FL.

Elstrom, Peter, Yang, Catherine, and Baker, Stephen (1999). "A Cell Phone in Every Pocket?" *Business Week*, January 18.

Hayden, David (1999). "Hello, Half a Billion of Us Want the Net via Phone." *Internet World*, November 15.

Katz, James E. (1999). *Connections: Social and Cultural Studies of the Telephone in American Life*. New Brunswick, NJ: Transaction Publications.

Katz, James E., and Aspden, Philip (1998). "Theories, Data and Potential Impacts of Mobile Communications: A Longitudinal Analysis of U.S. National Surveys." *Technological Forecasting and Social Change* 57: 133–156.

Paul Kagan Associates, Inc. (1999). "Wireless Market Stats." October 27.

Peter D. Hart Research Associates, Inc. (1998). "The Evolving Wireless Marketplace." February.

Quinn, Kelly J. (1999). "Creating Solutions for Cellular Skeptics." *RCR Wireless News*, September 14.

Rakow, Lana F., and Navarro, Vija (1993). "Remote Mothering and the Parallel Shift: Women Meet the Cellular Telephone." *Critical Studies in Mass Communications* 10(2): 144–157.

Rollins, Michael (1998). "Wireless Voice Industry." Wireless Services Equity Research, J.P. Morgan Securities Inc., 13, October 14.

Roper Starch Worldwide, Inc. (1997). Survey for Cellular One Group.

Santos, Ivan (1998). "Do-It-Yourself Prepaid Cellular Service." Cellular One of Puerto Rico, National Marketing Forum, August 26.

Schwartz, John (1999). "New Wiretap Rules Meet Opposition." *Washington Post*, November 18, p. E03.

Sikora, Patricia (1996). "Cellular One Market Study." Cellular One of East Central Illinois, June.

*Wireless Week* (1999). "Out of the Glovebox, Onto the Air." November 22, p. 4 (Strategis Group survey results).

Zukin, Clifford (2000). "Poll of Public Attitudes." Unpublished research study, Eagleton Institute, Rutgers University, New Brunswick, NJ. Mimeo.

# 7    France: preserving the image

*Christian Licoppe and Jean-Philippe Heurtin*

### Scope and data

Our aim is to understand how trust is negotiated within the context of mobile and remote communication. To get insight into this problem, we have studied the cell phone behavior of 1,000 French users who subscribed in November and December of 1997 to OLA Itineris service, which provides one or two hours of calls for a fixed rate. These offers were aimed at first-time subscribers who tended to favor private use of the cell phone – 40% used the phone strictly for private use while 40% opted for mixed private/professional use.[1] Half of the sample came from Paris and half from the Toulouse area in southwestern France. The age distribution in the sample was as follows: 8% of the sample were below 20, 27% were in their 20s, 24% in their 30s, 22% in their 40s, and 19% were 50 or more. This age distribution was within a few percentage points of the average age distribution of OLA subscribers at the time. The sample was 55% male and 45% female.

We followed a dual methodology that analyzed quantitative calling patterns and qualitative interviews. First, we asked the users to allow us to do a statistical analysis of their usage, which we studied from June 1998 to February 1999, and then to answer questionnaires. The first set of questions was brief and generic, asked over the phone to ascertain a few socio-professional parameters. The second was given to half the sample to check on how they made themselves available on the cell phone. The last was a two-hour, in-depth, face-to-face interview with twenty participants. We thus had, on the one hand, an aggregated anonymous pattern of usage enriched with generic Personal Communication Service (PCS) and phone availability information on which we worked statistically. We also had qualitative answers that we treated separately in order to interpret the behavior of cell phone users. To commute between qualitative and quantitative data we used variables of age, gender, family situation

---

[1] The remaining 20% did not answer or did not provide a clear answer.

and working status. This was the empirical foundation upon which we built our case.

We collected data from six months after the callers subscribed to the service for a period of a year. Since we were interested in understanding the uses and dynamics of cell phone telephony, we figured that in that period of time the novelty would have worn off and, even if the use were still evolving, some patterns would have stabilized.

In that period, cell phone penetration rates in France had increased from 18% to 25%. Because of this bull market for cell phone telephony, which is still raging, and because our sample was relatively small and skewed toward use of the cell phone for private purposes rather than for professional ones, none of the figures we quote or comparisons we make are useable to build a demographic–statistical tableau of the uses of cellular phones in France. Rather than absolute quantification, we are more interested in establishing distinctive trends and patterns of use. We used the qualitative interviews to get a better grasp of the social determinants in the development of the use of cell phone telephony, and in a more general manner for all phone communications.

### The cellular phone and the management of distant phone interactions: of trust and negotiated local contexts

To an overwhelming majority of the users in our sample, all of whom continued their subscription at the end of 1997, the mobile phone is no longer an emergent technology. It is no longer owned just by showoffs, whose behavior they criticize harshly. It is not, however, so common that it is taken for granted in everyday life; its users still question its trust-worthiness.

When asked how they use a cell phone, almost all the interviewees had a story to tell about how it helped coordinate details of ordinary life. Some described routine situations gone awry, such as being caught in a traffic jam, learning that it was caused by a race in Paris, and then figuring out a better route. Or being called by your wife after you have left home in the morning, to tell you to return for some forgotten, important item. Or again, particularly with women, being able to call your children if you are unable to get to them as expected, or to be called by them if they are in trouble. Cell phones were helpful at more significant moments, such as arranging a meeting place across the border to bring a sick relative home, or scheduling holiday gatherings with relatives and friends. In each of these cases, the cell phone helped to re-establish bonds over space and time in contexts where core features of domestic life were threatened and had to be reasserted, such as coordination of home life with workplace situations, motherly devotion towards children, and kinship solidarity in the face of sickness.

### De-contextualization effects of the mobile phone

The mobile phone's use as a key resource for successful coordination over space and time lies in part in its strong impact on perceptions of space. On the one hand, it remodels the perception of the ambient space for its user. On the other hand, which is the point we will delve into more deeply here, the person who calls or is being called by the mobile phone user can no longer assign a definite location to the other person from either the geographical or the social perspective.

The cellular phone appears, within the frame of Anthony Giddens' argument, to be one of the technologies that allow for the space–time de-localization of human interactions that Giddens deemed a key feature of the institutions of modernity (Giddens, 1990). If we try to compare the use of the mobile phone with other communication technologies such as its very close parent, the fixed phone, the mobile phone appears to be a more radical institution of modernity within the framework of Giddens' argument. Indeed, though the "traditional" phone allows for the management of distant bonds and therefore some amount of de-localization in interactions, (fixed) telephone calls are still attached to places and contexts.

Before the diffusion of mobile phone technologies, whether the home or the work phone was used, it was usually plain to callers or callees where their interlocutor was (because of time schedules, for instance, and because of the absence of background noises, which ruled out public phones). They were therefore interacting with a distant correspondent, but one who could in most cases be localized in a particular spatial and social context (the home, the workplace) without any further clarification being necessary in the content of the call itself.

The use of mobile phones splits this residual localization of distant correspondents. If your correspondent uses a mobile phone, a fact that is usually made plain by the level of intrinsic and ambient noise in the communication, there is generally no ground to assume he/she is in a particular place. The mobile phone is therefore radical; it breaks apart the reference of synchronous vocal communications and the spatial contexts of the interlocutors.

By breaking any direct link between its user and geographical and social spaces, the mobile phone puts interactions at risk. A first kind of risk involves a call to a mobile phone user that threatens ongoing activities and social interactions. A second kind of risk is founded on a wrong localization, for example, where the user lies about where he/she is, initiating a potentially damaging chain of deceit, the victim being the correspondent of the mobile user.

*Social context as risk.* The first risk involves the actual material or social context of the mobile phone user. She/he is engaged in interactions whose delicate balance a sudden call (necessarily outside the framework of these ongoing interactions) may upset for two reasons: first, because the mobile phone user may get too absorbed in the call properly to handle or even distance him/herself politely from the current activity; second, because the call itself renders unsustainable the mutual framework of the ongoing interaction.

In the case of activities that do not involve the immediate presence of others, such as driving, the risk involves security issues. A public debate is raging about legally enforceable regulation and the responsibility of the user to stop the car to talk. At what point is it unethical (dangerous) behavior to accommodate the occasional call? But it does not seem a major cause of concern to our sample.

Things get slightly more heated when discussing other people in a public space being able (willingly or unwillingly) to listen in. It is important to note here that people show different levels of resistance to the occurrence of a mobile phone call, depending on the public space in question. Ordinary street contexts seem easy to handle. The most frequent source of trouble is the quality of the wireless communication (which varies with cell coverage and the sophistication of the wireless network) and the level of ambient noise that may drown the spoken utterances.

Q: Are there places from which you call more often than from others? For instance, in the street, or in a bar?
A: *No, in a bar I don't, but in the street, yes, I do.*

Patrons in restaurants, on the other hand, seem much more unforgiving about the intrusion of out-of-context phone calls. Almost all the users we interviewed said they shut off their cellular phone when dining out, some vehemently calling for some form of regulation for those who do not.

*In the restaurants I hate this, it's worse than anything. They should put up signs forbidding the use of mobile phones in restaurants. I don't know why, but it bothers me much less in bars.*

They frame the issue in terms of the superimposition of distinct spaces (our emphasis).

*I think that when one treats oneself to a restaurant, one wants quiet, between lovers for instance, or . . . We are only there, and we are not to be elsewhere.*

The public setting mentioned most often by this unwilling audience was the train, which provides an interesting middle-ground case. Adults, and particularly women and older people, in our sample testified to being embarrassed when confronted with other people's calls in which they had no interest, and which they deemed exhibitionistic (implicitly considering their own role as that of voyeur). They stressed they felt that mobile phone users were speaking louder than necessary during a call.

The train compartment is precisely the setting for that kind of civil indifference described by Erving Goffman. Using this public space for private conversations also contributes to the commodification of the train traveler, which early train users found so unpleasantly remote from the gentle salon-like sociability of coaches (Shivelbusch, 1986). Within such a setting, a sudden phone call breaks up the social order founded on civil indifference, intrudes on the personal space of surrounding travelers and may become a source of embarrassment and even a potential offense (Goffman, 1963).

The sudden mobile phone call that infringes on personal space in a public setting is particularly well illustrated in the following comment by a young professional woman in a fast-food restaurant:

*I saw people yelling at one another on the phone. It was a girl, I remember she was Asian. I was eating at the Pizza Hut; she was sitting with her mobile phone and screaming: "Who do you take me for? I know you got a wife in Africa," and so on. We could hear everything and imagine what the guy at the other end was saying. And it was, uh, everybody was staring at her. I was feeling embarrassed for her. In my head I said to myself, I will never do it. Even speaking in a normal tone on the phone, people can hear, even if everybody is eating. Oh no, I would be too embarrassed.*

When confronted with that kind of risk, mobile users develop several distinct polite tactics to handle it. A fair number of such users are accustomed to showing some sensitivity about the simultaneously ongoing interactions in which they are engaged and will seek a quieter setting. They also may speed up the phone call, for example when being called on the mobile at work,[2] with a solicitude that may be directed either towards the caller or to the surrounding people. The following female user combines both polite strategies:

> *For example, Friday we were queuing to get into a museum. I was with other people, and I got out of the queue to answer [the mobile phone]. Particularly in a queue, one is still in a public setting.*

Q: And the people who were with you didn't object?
A: *No, because they saw I ended the call quickly.*
Q: There was no embarrassment?

---

[2] For most of the users in our sample, the mobile phone is mainly dedicated to private calls, so that an incoming call on the mobile phone involves the management of private relationships within the constraints of the workplace.

A: *No, because people actually react differently to the person who doesn't care about his or her own use of the mobile phone and the person who takes the trouble to isolate herself.*

But the most complex and risky situations seem to occur when the person talking on the cell phone is simultaneously engaged in other interpersonal interactions. Indeed, even if they respect these ongoing interactions, they can be swept away by the sudden interruption of a call, getting absorbed to the point of forgetting where they are, with whom they are and what they are doing. This female user describes quite well a supermarket scenario:

*I was shopping, I was filling up [my caddie]. A girlfriend calls me, and I say, you know, well, I'm shopping. . . . And I was quite aware of people looking at me, I was feeling ill at ease and all. And then I don't know what happened, we got talking about apple jam. She said, "Go to that part of the store, you will see." And I take my caddie and my phone and we go on talking, and I did not give a damn about the people around me! It is true I was slightly embarrassed at the beginning, and then one forgets. One gets into the call. And I see other people making phone calls; they look around to see if anyone is watching, and then, well then. . . .*

A previous technology, the Walkman, led to such perceptions of the technology users insulating themselves from interpersonal interactions in public space, giving rise to a lot of public debate (du Gay et al., 1987). But this issue of self-absorption is marginal in the case of mobile phone perceptions. Adjustments are necessary. Trouble arises because mobile phone interactions are unexpected (which makes it different from the Walkman case). A private interpersonal mobile phone call can interfere with other sets of activities, impose intrusively upon an unwilling audience, and interfere with ongoing face-to-face, direct contact.

This threat to an ongoing interpersonal interaction is well exemplified in the following excerpt in which a woman working at a counter at the post office, herself a very active mobile phone user, experiences the imposition of other interactions on the one she is conducting:

*Well, they come to the post office, it rings, this gets me mad. You are talking to them and they do not listen to you. I don't like it. This really gets me steamed up. They are in front of you, they have asked you for some kind of service, and you do not exist any more. Well, this I can't stand. On the other hand, I do not pay attention to their talk unless something really strikes me.*

The dual engagement in interpersonal interactions is a threat to the smooth development of ongoing, face-to-face interactions, and thus to the social order itself.

*The spatial indeterminacy of the cellular phone user.* The second type of risk is linked to the impossibility of assigning a spatial reference to the mobile phone user. It is a risk because knowing where your correspondent is, at least approximately, constitutes background information that helps the management of the interaction:

*I always wonder a little, from the time I get a call from a mobile phone, where the caller is.*

As Giddens (1990) suggests, distant coordination requires trust on the part of participants and trust in human and material intermediaries that make the distant interaction a success. Conversely, interaction with a participant whose every activity is visible does not require explicit trust in intermediaries. Trust becomes more of an issue as contextual information disappears because of various forms of time, space and remoteness. Because mobile phone users are disconnected from their space context in the eyes of the second party, the use of the mobile phone specifically puts the interaction at risk. Mutual trust in what constitutes a proper and successful call has to be restored and explicit gauges given. Many polite solutions involve making explicit some information about where one is, i.e. describing where one is in one's own words, whether one volunteers it or because one's correspondent provided the opportunity to do so by asking. It allows one, as a participant in the mobile phone call, to frame the kind of availability one is willing to allow with respect to duration, topics or tones of the conversation yet to come.

However, the location of one of the participants entails an often irreducible intertwining of spatio-temporal localization ("going down a tunnel" or "in a restaurant" or "au café"). Or the location is developing (typically in the form "I'm on the move between A and B"). Most often it represents social contexts involving other persons:

*On the mobile one is never able to assess whether the other is alone, or surrounded by people . . . One is careful about it.*

Part of the risk involves the time dimension in a sort of Heisenbergian tradeoff. You do not know where the mobile phone user is (uncertainty in space) but you know that, notwithstanding various forms of postponed interactions (voicemail systems) or shutoff decisions, you can potentially reach him/her at some negotiated time. Certainty in time, achieved because of known schedules and experience-grounded conventions, as we will see in the next section, may be potentially damaging. This is explicit in the way couples have to negotiate subtly and sometimes uneasily between the extremes of jealousy and control on the one hand and bonding and trust on the other:

*Sometimes the mobile phone finds people in situations where they feel a bit guilty. Me, when I call my husband sometimes and when I hear the noise, I ask him "Where are you? Are you in a bar?" I feel him getting embarrassed, and I say to him that, no, it's not a problem, you shouldn't be embarrassed. But it was 2 p.m. and he is usually at work at that time. But he had started for lunch later, he was with colleagues, and he was so embarrassed.*

Conversely, a good part of our sample chose the *"I don't have anything to hide"* motto that characteristically links re-localization and trust.

Beyond that general requirement, a wide variety of context-dependent tactics are available, such as head-on dismissal ("I answer, I'm on the phone") or being purposely evasive while still providing some sketchy localization ("I just say [when reluctant to say exactly] that I'm in the street. I am in the street, that's all"). One can also lie, as in the following example (an adolescent user):

Q: Do you remember lying?
A: *Several times. Particularly with my girlfriends! It also happens often with my friends. If, for instance, I am at Parly 2 [shopping center] and I have to go elsewhere, he asks me "Where are you?" and I say "I'm home, and I can't move." That's it.*

What is negotiated here between unspecified or yet-to-be-specified contexts and the potentially unbridled reachability of the cell phone user is the traceability of people. Users can either comply with or evade the traceability requirements in a way that preserves the trust required for a satisfying interaction.

To summarize, the mobile phone creates new possibilities for coordination between callers precisely because it follows them around. However, this essential feature of the mobile phone is a two-sided coin. On the one hand, when calling or being called by a mobile phone user, one has no *a priori* indication of the spatial and social context of the mobile phone user. But some information about context is a prerequisite for the creation of the trust necessary for a proper distant interaction. Somewhat paradoxically, the de-localization, which is an essential property of wireless technologies, calls for re-localization. Mobile phone users must explicitly provide some kind of information (whether spontaneously in the course of the talk, or by answering a direct question about their whereabouts). On the other hand, mobile phone users can potentially be reached at any time. If it is necessary for them to provide some contextual elements, then the mobile phone is a potential resource to trace its owner. The management of the risk that results from mobile phone de-contextualization cannot be understood without paying attention to the time dimension that controls its other face, a potentially unlimited traceability.

### The cellular phone and the entrenchment of modernity: from trust and tracing to the construction of bonds and commitments within a flux of interactions

*Temporal synchronizations: from disclosing and anticipating bits of schedule to the tracing of mobile phone users*

If the mobile phone allows its user in principle to be reached any time (and almost anywhere), at a pragmatic level, this is not the case. It is not so because the mobile phone user can choose to block an incoming call. And though there will be variations owing to lifestyle, age, the degree of experienced mobility, and the flexibility of the activities they are engaged in, most users will choose to exercise that option at some point.

The cell phone user can choose to:

• take (or not take) the cellular phone along;
• keep it on (or off);
• if it's on, immediately answer an incoming call, or turn the phone off when it rings, or let it ring, the latter two behaviors sending the call to the voicemail system.

Of the users we interviewed, 80% said that they nearly always had their mobile phone with them, with very few intentional exceptions; 55% said they left their cellular phone switched on all the time, 25% thought they had it turned on more than off; 13% thought the reverse, and 8% almost always left it switched off. The second and third levels of availability management involved complex decisions, weighing both internally and externally the correct behavior in particular situations (that is, expressing normative opinions about others letting their mobile phones ring in specific places and situations). It would go beyond the scope of this chapter to delve into mobile phone etiquette.

Strategies can be reinforced by users explicitly stating rules of behavior to their callers, as this adolescent does:

*During the day it does not bother me, but in the evenings, I have told them that after a certain time, it is useless to call.*

The users' wishes may be made known implicitly, through grouchiness, for instance:

Q:  Did you have to make adjustments [correcting callers trying to reach him on the mobile with unimportant business]?
A:  *Never. I can be in a foul mood. They know me.*

And the users expect others to adapt:

*People who know me know quite well when they can reach me. They are sure not to get the voicemail system.*

This pattern of unavailability is neither purely random nor completely planned. It must leave some room for the unexpected or for emergencies. Here again, users set the rules, as this very active senior citizen does:

*From the time you say the mobile phone is to be used only in an emergency, then people use it only when it is, well, not exactly compelling, but at least when it is something important to them.*

Assessing importance is a delicate matter that is partly governed by expectations and conventions, and in part negotiated on the spot. The same user, when asked what qualified as an emergency, linked his definition to his sociability networks:

*Yes, but if it's family calling, the sense of emergency is in their head, and I comply with them.*

Cell phone users have a motive when they choose to dismiss incoming calls and their correspondents know that. Explicit rules, custom and experience establish an understanding between callers. This young woman is still sorting things out:

*You know, it is not because I have a mobile phone that everybody will call me on it. Moreover, it is not always on.*

When weighing the circumstances before making a call, callers are quite aware (and they may have been briefed, as we saw above) that their correspondents may be in places and situations (the home, the workplace) where they may be reached on their home or professional numbers. It is only when they move around a lot that the mobile phone comes in handy. Listen to this young woman speaking about one of her friends:

*Because he may be in at least three different places. He has got two or three places where he works and there is his home. Since I never know where he is, I prefer to call him on his mobile.*

Otherwise, the decision to call is complicated by decisions about where to call, and on which of the possible numbers.

This whole process may be simplified by clear-cut rules in clear-cut cases. This senior citizen with a predictable schedule has an established routine for the use of his cell phone:

*People that know me, well, they know that once the mobile is off, they know I am at home, necessarily. So they can always reach me.*

The rules get more complex if one takes into account personal space in the home. Some of an adolescent's friends may call her on the mobile because they do not want (or she does not want them) to talk to her parents, while others who are known to the family and are used to talking to the parents will call more easily on the family phone.

Some age differences might be relevant here. In our sample, older callers tended to try the usual phone numbers first and then the mobile. Younger users tended to do the opposite. But in all cases the potentially unlimited reachability offered by the mobile and the multiplicity of phone numbers available to the callers combine to reinforce the need for anticipatory calculations that can get quite complex and involve some fairly detailed representations and expectations about other persons' schedules. In the following excerpt, a woman in her 30s was asked whether she called her correspondents first on a fixed number or on their mobiles:

*It depends. For my husband, well, if I know it is a time when I do not know where he is, if he is coming home or still at work, well, I will first call at work, because very often he works late rather than come home. But there are times, in the morning for instance, it happened I had to reach him, someone had the wrong key or something like that, I talked to him directly on the mobile because I knew he was still in his car. At noon I call on the mobile because I know he has gone to lunch, that he is not at work. It depends on the time of day.*

But as this particular quote shows, the calculation fundamentally involves schedules, expecting someone to be in a particular place at a given time.

A simple call to a mobile phone user requires a double negotiation. The caller has to calculate and anticipate detailed schedules, and decide whether it is better to call on the mobile, using previous experience and information provided by the correspondent. The cell phone user, knowing the caller is somewhat in the dark, will have to reestablish the proper amount of trust by leaking some controlled information about his/her surroundings.

As a consequence of that double management of the interaction, the mobile phone may be used to trace persons wherever they are at any time of day. This is the rationale for various filtering and de-communication strategies (de Gournay, 1997, and chapter 12 in this volume) and as such it is rather commonplace.

Traceability becomes a more meaningful issue when looked at positively, as this middle-aged woman does:

*But from another point of view, it is so nice to be able to . . . because one can gain access to things that were unreachable. For instance, when my husband has problems with the car or he is stuck in a traffic jam, he calls me. I say to myself, this is nothing to worry about. I really do worry less. Otherwise, I would not know where he is. Sometimes he leaves at 5 in the morning. He gets back, it's already 9 in the evening. Once it took him four hours to get home – the expressway was jammed, Bois de Boulogne jammed. I am chewing my nails. And this has often happened.*

The ability for one or the other to use the husband's mobile to locate him reassures an anxious wife and becomes an act of devotion between spouses. A series of calls that are likely to be short and to the point, that in many cases just allow the resynchronization of the space and time reference points of husband and wife, have become a resource repeatedly to reassert deep emotional commitments in a very strong bonding relationship. There is a somewhat paradoxical opposition between the matter-of-factness of such mobile phone calls involving limited-scale reassurance and the importance of the long-term character and the depth of the commitment they seem to reactivate.

### *Synchronization, coordination and commitment: the building of trust and bonds in cellular phone interactions*

Our previous studies on the uses of the home phone provided evidence for a very distinctive pattern. Within networks of family and friends, phone calls were rarer and twice as long when the correspondents were farther apart. When people move, phone calls get longer and rarer in the same proportion as the distance separating them, stay the same if they do not move, and become more frequent and shorter if they move closer to some family member or friend. It is no surprise to see the phone used to maintain distant affective bonds. What is interesting to us here is the fact it is done through less frequent and longer phone calls. Maintaining strong social bonds is done more through the common management of a durable phone interaction than through the repeated act of calling.

Use of the mobile phone also shows a distinctive pattern. On the average, we observe that mobile phone calls are less than half as long as home phone calls. But the averages hide two distinct behaviors. Following our new users for one year, we saw a significant increase in lengthy calls: 75% of our users – who had a flat-rate subscription of one or two hours – made calls that lasted longer than 15 minutes; 40% of them did so once a month, and these calls represented 15% of the overall traffic of our sample.

At the other end of the spectrum, 35% of the calls in our sample lasted more than 5 seconds and less than 30. While answering systems picked up some of those calls, mobile phone users under the age of 30 use cell phones more intensively than people over 50, and they made briefer phone calls. Shorter phone calls are the essence of cell phone behavior, particularly when compared with the home phone:

*Well, the home phone, well, it is a fine tool to deepen and maintain relationships. But with the mobile phone, it is something else all together...It is much more unstable. Well, one cannot get into a conversation and have it last a long time with a mobile. So it is much less intimate, as I told you, much faster, much more information-centered.*

In a very small sample of participants who allowed us to record their actual mobile phone communications, we also observed that shorter calls were devoid of the usual opening patterns such as "Hello," "How are you?" etc., particularly when contact is made in a series of short calls. Unlike fully self-contained phone calls, mobile calls are part of a conversation pattern that continues beyond the interruptions between calls. It is therefore unnecessary to renew salutations and formal conversation openings.

We could describe these as two ideal types of phone calls: the intimate, lasting, deeply bond-nurturing home phone call, and the short, informative, goal-oriented mobile phone call. That would be wrong for two reasons. First, mobile phone users exhibit both types of behavior. So the terminal and network may be less of a constraint than is commonly thought. An adolescent in our sample said he was careful to have many short communications with his friends to keep in touch and synchronize with them without exhausting his subscription. He also had long emotional calls with his girlfriend(s).

The second reason that our above supposition is wrong is deeper and linked to the traceability property of mobile phones. Short, frequent informative calls may strengthen the formation and maintenance of deep bonds, not because of their content but because of the reassurance they bring and the amount of trust they create or reinforce. In the example quoted above, being able to call her husband and have him tell her where he is brought a sense of security and trust to the woman. The act of keeping in touch, of being able to re-synchronize spatio-temporal and contextual frames of reference for the caller and the mobile phone user, is part of an ongoing commitment. Emotional bonds are reinforced not in the content of the call but as a consequence of the trust built in a series of short mobile phone connections. The particular management of mobile phone interaction reassures both parties of their commitments, to the point where this negotiated and repeated traceability becomes part of the very fabric of the bond itself. Once again in agreement with Giddens' description of modernity, relationships appear as a reflexive project in which repeated short mobile phone calls, in which participants agree to reposition their respective context, nurture the trust feedback.

A particularly striking example of this effect, and one that is particularly reinforced by wireless technologies such as pagers and cellular phones, is the multiple calls that groups of teenagers (and not only teenagers) will make to one another on every available communication channel. We conducted a study of an arty group of non-professional party-goers in their 20s, very typical of the tribes targeted by advertisers for pagers and cell phones (Manceron, 1998). A group of them were organizing a birthday party, which meant inviting a circle of close friends and arranging for the delivery of the different parts of the necessary sound system to the flat of the host. The management of the sound system involved twenty-two calls and twelve people in the course of one evening. All these calls were short, purposeful and to the point, centered on the synchronization and coordination of delivery of the appropriate elements. The distribution of calls excluded the organizer of the party itself. For a group whose identity is tied to music, and for the organization of a party where the group will come together, this form of distributed and repeated communication along many channels and through a complex network both reasserts the bond of all those involved to the group and provides a sense of identity and commitment. The purpose of the interaction (getting the sound system together at a particular time) does not simply build upon the resources that the closely bonded network provides; it is a trial of these very bonds, which are thus reasserted in an ongoing manner along the distributed call pattern.

## Conclusion

Giddens (1990) argued that one core feature of modernity was the de-institutionalization of personal bonds, whether between spouses or among family or friends. At a personal level, trust, which asks for the opening of one individual to the other, becomes a project on which the involved parties must work. When it is not controlled by normative codes or stabilized rituals, trust must be won by providing tokens of openness, willingness, emotion and commitment. Trust is not therefore a stable category but is constructed as a process, and the bonds it supports become reflexive projects, always open to a revision of the conventions that sustain them. From the de-institutionalization of personal bonds is born the necessity repeatedly to display trust towards one another.

The cellular phone thus appears to be a potent resource of modernity. By following people around, it disconnects the automatic reference of its user to a specific context. But the proper management of phone interactions requires its users to provide at least some edited information about their context. Each instance confirms openness and trust, and establishes the relevance of the user's commitment to specific patterns of bonding.

Because the mobile phone follows people around, it makes them potentially available all the time. Along the time dimension we therefore have two separate effects: the caller must anticipate the schedule of the mobile phone user, and a wealth of possibilities for synchronizing people or activities dispersed in disjointed activities is made available.

Within the combined space and time dimensions, trust is renegotiated with each call, when the caller displays expectations and calculations about the user's activities, and the mobile phone user chooses to publicize information about his/her own context. Moreover, the increase in opportunities for reaching the mobile phone user helps to bring about interactions that are devoted only to ascertaining the respective contextual frameworks of both participants in the calls. Because it tends to be devoid of any other purpose, such a call cements the trust each has in the other, and deepens the commitments and bonds between participants.

The complex, continuous and many-faceted negotiations of traceability, trust and jealousy between husband and wife provide ample confirmation for this. The mobile phone calls create a web of short, content-poor interactions through which bonds can be built and strengthened in an ongoing process, under the guise of a reflexive project, which is the preferential mode of construction of de-institutionalization. The cell phone becomes a tool through which modernity in Giddens' sense becomes entrenched.

At the same time, the concurrent development of long relational calls on mobile phones shows that the cell phone impinges in part on more ritualized modes of expressing emotion-laden relationships. Such relationships are traditionally associated with home phone call behavior in France, which we call institutionalized bonding. The substitution issue "Will the cellular phone replace all other (fixed) phones as the personal phone?" will be answered pretty much in the way the users handle this structural tension between both uses of the mobile – to establish trust and to cement bonds and relationships.

But this also raises other aspects of the use of mobile phones, namely pricing, network quality and sound quality, which today limit the development of long, content-laden calls on mobile phones, at least in France. We also must deal with the ergonomics of terminal-embedded directories (which currently favor the use of the cellular over the fixed phone), the development of specific innovative services (for instance, Internet-based services on mobile terminals) and the particularities of given conventions and frameworks of interaction within specific contexts.

## References

Gay, P. du, S. Hall, L. Janes, H. Mackay, and K. Negus (1997). *Doing Cultural Studies*. London: Sage.

Giddens, A. (1990). *The Consequences of Modernity*. Stanford, CA: Stanford University Press.

Goffman, Erving (1963). *Behavior in Public Places*. New York: Free Press.

Gournay, C. de (1997). "C'est personnel, la communication hors de ses murs." *Réseaux* 82–83: 21–39.

Manceron, V. (1997). "Tous en ligne: usages sociaux du téléphone et modes d'interaction au sein d'un groupe de jeunes parisiens." *Réseaux* 82–83: 205–218.

Shivelbusch, Wolfgang (1986). *The Railway Journey: the Industrialization of Time and Space in the 19th Century*. Berkeley: University of California Press.

The Netherlands and the USA compared

*Enid Mante*

## Introduction

Economic globalization and the widespread use of information and communication technologies (ICTs) are blurring traditionally sharp boundaries between countries and regions, home and work, work and leisure time, and among time zones. Mobility, too, is changing the nature of the lived life: no longer simply physical, it may also be virtual. As people seek to manage these changes via their ICTs, conflicts can arise owing to misinterpretation of norms and values. At the same time, the possible rise of a universal ICT culture – with shared norms and values – might greatly reduce this problem. But what are the prospects of such a culture arising?

We can explore these questions by identifying the cultural differences that now exist and their seeming direction of change. We can do this by discussing the results of international comparative research on the use of and attitudes toward ICTs. The original purpose of the research was to identify the role cultural differences might play in the ways people use and give meaning to ICTs in their everyday lives. In turn, it allows us to reflect on how realistic it is to contemplate a general ICT culture shared by different countries. The two-pronged international research program began in early 1999 by comparing the USA and the Netherlands. A second study was conducted in late 1999 as part of an international comparison of six European countries.

## Methodology

The perceptual mapping method used by Batt and Katz (1998) underlies the main part of the American–Dutch study. We grouped diverse technological and general products and services and mapped them on the following scales: necessity – luxury; work – entertainment; intrusion on privacy – protection of privacy; time waster – time saver.

In the qualitative study, we focused on the use of ICTs (telephone, value-added services, mobile telephony and the Internet) in everyday life and repeated the above perceptual mapping scales. We also probed statements from participants on their attitudes toward ICTs, time spent using them, and opinions of acceptable behavior. We noted the age, cultural background, income and gender of the respondents and surveyed their use of ICT services, of television and, most important, of the telephone at home. In the qualitative study, we also explored attitudes and depth of feeling about these technologies. In the European study, changes in mobility, social networks and personal and social time use were the central issues that we related to how, when and where people use ICTs to cope with the vicissitudes daily life.

The interviews lasted two hours. In the American–Dutch study, participants were asked to do a short perceptual mapping exercise on diverse ICT products and services according to the above-mentioned dimensions. The answers to the perceptual mapping exercise were collected and entered on a frequency table for each dimension. These tables were discussed during the second part of the session. In the European study, participants filled out a short questionnaire to provide insight into some relevant background variables.

### The set-up of the research

For the American–Dutch research, three focus groups consisting of eight to ten middle-class residential telecom users met in each country. All groups contained both sexes; in each group there was one person with a non-standard cultural background. In both countries these users were part of an 1,800-person panel especially set up for this type of research. The six Dutch focus groups that were part of the European research had the same number of participants and were comparable in every respect to the American–Dutch study.

The members of the focus groups were selected based on their use of ICTs. One group consisted of either mobile phone or Internet users, another comprised personal computer owners and Internet users, and one was made up of non-users, i.e. people who did not use the Internet and did not have a mobile phone. Sometimes it turned out that, by the time a focus group met, a non-user had become a user of a mobile phone or the Internet. This shows how rapidly these new ICTs are proliferating.

Both in the USA and in the Netherlands a mobile phone user is often an Internet user. Quite often the Internet focus group members also had mobile phones. Interestingly, in the "both" group the use of the Internet often preceded the acquisition of the mobile phone.

## Theoretical orientation: cultural differences

Various cultures differentially imbue lifestyles and values. Two Dutch sociologists, Hofstede (1980) and Trompenaars (1993), have used a managerial perspective to study cultural norms worldwide. They found systematic differences in values and in the ways people give meaning to actions and entities they encounter in their work life.

Trompenaars proposes seven viewpoints, covering three different realms of cultural problem-solving, governing outlook on society, norms and values for behavior:

*Realm 1: human relations*

- Universalism versus particularism: all people treated equally versus differential treatment based on circumstances and personal attributes.
- Individualism versus collectivism: people seen as unique individuals with individual needs versus members of a collective group whose needs take precedence over the individual.
- Neutral versus emotional: non-affective relationships, even with kin, versus affectively charged relationships even with strangers.
- Specific versus diffuse: businesslike relationships with business partners versus personal relationships even in business dealings.
- Achieved versus ascribed status: people defined by *what* they do and know versus *who* they know and *where* they came from.

*Realm 2: attitude toward time*

- Relative importance of past, present and future.

  In some cultures, time is a straight line of events, in other cultures cyclical. For Americans, the present is most important; for the French, the past governs the present and the future. (A tangential view regards time as a reality that flows and therefore has to be caught and taken care of.[1])

*Realm 3: environment and locus of control*

- Inner-directedness versus other-directedness: values and judgments come from within a person versus taking them from others in the social environment.

Trompenaars conducted many studies around the world and concluded that there are wide differences in value orientations, not only among countries but also especially among regions in the world. An obvious example, of course, is the difference between Eastern and Western

---

[1] Although Trompenaars does not explicitly mention this aspect, I think this is a very important dimension of time experience.

lifestyles. However, we realize from our own research that one must avoid excessively simple conclusions which seems to be the situation with Trompenaars. The USA and Canada, for example, give individual freedom the highest value on a quality-of-life scale. Nevertheless, Norway, Spain, the Czech Republic and Hong Kong score almost as high on this point, whereas France and Greece find themselves almost as low as South Korea and Egypt.

Trompenaars finds a huge gap between Northern Europe (including the UK) and Southern Europe. (Oddly, the "Southern values" sometimes start as far north as Belgium). Looking at work as an individual or a collective endeavor, we find the Swedes and the Russians close to the USA as advocates of treating work as something you do together during which you are responsible for your whole team, whereas the Germans and French see it mostly as an individual activity in which you may count on the fact that others will do their job as well.

The cultural differences show up in the way people perceive their relations with others, but also in the ways they make use of artifacts, furnish their homes and spend their time. It is possible that the use of and values towards ICTs are also governed by these same cultural values, yielding different communication cultures. Thus, examining cultural differences is meaningful if we are to understand the use and adoption of ICTs.

The results from the Dutch focus groups both in the American–Dutch study and in the European study were interpreted in light of the Trompenaars dimensions. Hence we were able to develop some ideas about communication cultures and gain some insight into the way those cultures influence the use of ICTs.

## Results

### Mobility

The American–Dutch study and the European study differed in the way "mobility" was treated. In the European study, change in mobility was an explicit discussion item. In the American–Dutch study mobility was mentioned in passing as an important reason for value-added services, mobile telephones and the Internet. Nevertheless, the same issues and arguments arose in both focus group discussions.

The Dutch look at mobility both from the general societal perspective and as a personal issue. Mobility is associated with commuting, travel and going places. In general, the Dutch respondents affirmed that mobility has increased in recent decades. People live further away from their place of work, travel longer distances, participate in more activities and go on holiday more frequently. This does not mean, however, that *personal* mobility has necessarily increased. A woman with children:

*My mobility has gone down since I had children.*

One man observed:

*I am not very keen on going abroad for my holidays; I can get to a campsite in the Netherlands in one and a half hours. It's great to go cycling in the area around the campsite.*

Sometimes mobility is directly connected to virtual mobility:

*I am very mobile now, because I e-mail my relatives in the Antilles weekly; in the past we never saw each other.*

Mobility also affects social networks: children live further away from their parents; friends are scattered all over the world. This means that face-to-face contact has become more difficult and people are looking for other ways to stay in touch:

*I now e-mail my family in Australia; I have much more contact nowadays than in the past.*

Whether people perceive mobility as stressful or beneficial depends on whether they control their own mobility, whether they are mobile by choice or their mobility is directed by others. Commuting is often seen as somewhat negative, especially when commuting time is relatively long and involves traffic jams. Yet mobility is seen as something positive, if the decision to be mobile is one's own.

Mobility is also associated with time use:

*Life has become more hectic with extended working and shopping hours. You have the freedom to shop when it suits you.*

A woman says that she is able to travel during off-peak hours, which makes traveling far more agreeable.

Mobility is also associated with ferrying your children to school and other places and living an active life in one's community and clubs. Here again, the way this is perceived depends on whether it is your own choice or something you have to do.

The Americans in the American–Dutch study use the same mobility categories. It seems that business travel and day-to-day moving around are more important in American society. Distances are greater, people live further from the city centers, and the car plays a larger role than in Dutch society, where moving around may be done by car, but also by bike or on foot, especially in the large cities.

Americans did not mention the use of mobile phones on vacations. This might be due to the fact that they have far less vacation time than the Dutch and that work dominates American society far more than Dutch society, so Americans think nothing of bringing their mobile phone along on vacation. It was striking in the American focus groups that quite a few people held two jobs, one a formal "day job," the other one's own small private business.

### Reasons for the use of communication devices

Both the American–Dutch study and the European study go in depth into the need for communication devices in order to get in touch and coordinate activities when on the go. Leading a busy life demands coordination, and communication devices allow you to contact others wherever they are. The American survey shows that people who lead extremely busy lives are also heavy users of telephone and telephone services (Katz, 1999, table 4–6). Both Dutch studies also show this association.

Being reachable is the general condition that crops up in every focus group discussion. You have an answering machine, call waiting, a mobile phone, in order to be reachable. Reachability, however, does not always mean direct reachability. It also does not mean that everybody agrees on the need to be reachable. In both countries, older people in particular have the feeling that it is all right if people cannot reach them; they can always call again:

*I do not want to be a slave to my telephone.*

It seems, however, that the general norm of reachability is more internalized in the American community than in the Dutch. American respondents refer more often to the fact that their associates complain about their lack of reachability when they do not have call waiting and/or an answering device. This is probably because, in American society, devices such as answering machines and call waiting have been assimilated for a long time, whereas the Dutch have adopted these technologies only in the past few years.

Here again, control over reachability is important. Call waiting, an answering machine, voice mail and Caller ID give people the power to select whom they want to answer at what time. Busy people say more often that they want to stay in control and hence are more likely to use communication devices that enable them to have that control.

The mobile phone is growing in popularity as a means of communication when on the move. Although the Dutch respondents in the European study frequently mention reachability as a very important reason to have a cell phone, the focus group discussions revealed that this means mostly being *able to reach others* – your office, a garage, the police, your children, traveling colleagues, or friends – to say *"I am here."* Social appearance must not be neglected, though. According to Katz (1999), in the USA during the past few years the cell phone, once a rarely owned luxury item, is now practically a necessity, for both social and business reasons.

The Dutch respondents in the focus groups draw a clear distinction between use of the mobile phone for work or for security purposes:

*When my car breaks down.*
*When I am late due to a traffic jam.*
*When my daughter goes out at night.*

Chatting is also a value-laden phenomenon. Even the respondents with a mobile phone stress its functional use. Chatting is seen as undesirable, although quite a few people gave examples of this. Younger people seem to be less negative about chatting than older ones. Again, the circumstances are important. A respondent said he had a mobile phone only because he was on the move all the time. He did not mind treating it as a fixed phone for social calls.

Nevertheless, all respondents were conscious of the negative aspects of the mobile phone. Here again, control is the most important issue. People certainly do not want to be controlled by their cell phone. They want to be able to shut it off when it is not convenient to talk. Nor do they want to be confronted with mobile phones in use in public places. They feel embarrassed about being ear-witnesses to private talks. They hate the disturbing ringing.

Americans seem to have the same attitude.

Respondents who do not have a cell phone can be divided into those who do not have one but think they probably will get one in the near future, and those who very consciously do not want a mobile phone ever. People who have a mobile phone are more lenient toward those who use them just to chat than are those who do not have one. Of the have-nots, the want-nots are the most against non-functional use.

Apart from being seen as functional in certain situations, the mobile phone is seen as an enabler of mobility.

*Because I have a mobile phone, I am able, while working, to sit in the park and still be reachable.*

And a handicapped person:

*Because I have a mobile phone, I am able to go out by myself. Previously I needed someone with me.*

*Values: ICTs and bad manners*

Non-owners in particular see the mobile phone as something reprehensible. Drivers using a car phone incite a lot of aggressive feeling:

*If I see somebody in a car talking on a cell phone, I just drive up to him and hoot. ...*

A mobile phone should not be used while driving. Some respondents accept its use when the phone is hands-free; others have the opinion that even then it is dangerous.

Another sign of bad manners is talking loudly or making social calls on a mobile phone in public space. People are embarrassed to witness private conversations. On the other hand, respondents recognized that some calls are necessary, but that in such a case the caller should make the call as short and private as possible, and move to a quiet corner or leave the room. Owners differ from non-owners on this issue. Owners seem to invent compromises between the general norm and their own need. Owners do not mind a ringing phone, although they think it should be shut off in certain public places such as churches and theaters:

*I felt embarrassed when one day it rang in church.*

Owners say that they answer it as quickly as possible, use a silent signal and go outside to speak on the phone.

Non-owners more often have the feeling that ringing phones in public space are ridiculous and that their owners are showing off. In both countries they cite lots of examples of mobile phone users chitchatting in public space. One respondent in the USA witnessed a hotel evacuation at five a.m. because a fire alarm had gone off. People in their pajamas outside were calling their friends and relatives about this:

*Who would be interested in this at five a.m!*

There is not much difference of opinion among the non-users in both countries, although the deliberate non-users seem far more negative than the interested non-users.

*Cultural differences*

Respondents in the USA and in the Netherlands seem to have the same attitudes and values concerning mobile phones and value-added services. Nevertheless, there are differences, probably owing to cultural and societal background. We will compare the Katz–Batt perceptual mapping scales with some of Trompenaars' cultural dimensions.

*Necessity–luxury.* Trompenaars (1993) finds big differences among cultures in the ways people think about human relations. A person may see himself or herself as a unique individual with special needs or as a member of a group and thus obligated to assign priority to collective needs. As an example, he mentions the difference between seeing a human fault as an individual failing or as a defect that is shared by the whole team. In other words, people are inner-directed or other-directed (Tonnies, 1957). Inner-directed people follow their ingrained standards of behavior, whatever their situation. The situation, and the expectations of others, guide other-directed people. This dimension of inner-directedness versus other-directedness surfaces in the different ways people look at their responsibility to be reachable and therefore to have a mobile phone and other reachability services.

Need, or necessity, is an important dimension both in the Netherlands and in the USA. In all discussions about value-added services and mobile phones, necessity is given as a main reason to have and use such services. Lack of need is a reason not to use them. One might dislike mobile phones, call waiting, voice mail and answering machines, but they are necessary to be reachable. Business users feel this necessity more intensely. In the USA, most of the focus group participants with a mobile phone and access to the Internet had their own business, sometimes in addition to a regular paid job. In the Netherlands, quite a few mobile phone users were given the phone as part of their job.

Although reachability is an important aspect in both countries, people look at it somewhat differently. The American respondents tend to see it as an other-directed necessity: others expect you to be reachable; so it is your responsibility to be reachable. This is especially important if you have a business:

*People can call me night and day.*

Hence, taking a mobile phone call in a public space is seen as acceptable. You will have a good reason to do this, for example your boss or your family ask for it, unless, of course, it is in an inappropriate environment such as a theater or a church.

The Dutch respondents need to have personal choice in the matter. They want to be reachable, but they definitely want to stay in control – no cell phone calls in improper places and at inconvenient times. They are ambivalent about using the phone in public. They view a person who is called on a mobile phone in the street, in a shop or on public transport, not as someone with business to do but rather as somebody who wants to show off the mobile phone. The Dutch also seemed to be a little more willing to share their cell phone with a person in distress who needs to contact somebody.

These differences are less apparent for the non-owners of mobile phones. Both American and Dutch non-owners are very alike in their attitudes. They feel that, if one does not need a mobile phone for job reasons, only some other socially acceptable reasons could be offered. You could have one in case of emergency – if your car breaks down, if you are alone on the street at night, or if you are stuck in traffic and have to warn others that you will not be in time for your appointment. It is also nice to have one in order to be reachable when somebody in the family is ill. In other words, when there is no alternative.

Of course, one should use it sparingly. In both countries people who do not have a mobile phone believe that you need to have a good (i.e. acceptable) reason to have one and to use one. If you do not, you are showing off. The mobile phone is certainly not seen as a medium for social conversation. Again, take the fire alarm example:

*Imagine, there is a fire alarm and the only thing you think of is taking not your clothes, but your mobile phone!*

Or, from a Dutch respondent:

*They are already selling these mobile phones in the toy shop, ridiculous!*

*Public–private.* Trompenaars shows that there significant differences among cultures in the way the environment governs people's behavior. One area he examined is the way people want to separate their private life from their public life. For some cultures these spheres are inseparable, and the boundaries between public and private are diffuse. In other countries people tend to keep the public and private realms strictly separate. This becomes especially clear if you look at the separation of the work and private/home spheres. Trompenaars cites as an example the preparedness of workers to help their boss paint his house. In China, this is quite acceptable to a large majority of workers, whereas in the Netherlands and in Australia it is almost unacceptable.

Looking at the value people place on public and private spheres, we see that in both the USA and the Netherlands there is a feeling that the public and private realms should be separated. Nevertheless, Americans seem to be more willing to let their working life interact with their private life. Your boss and your fellow employees expect you to be reachable. It is a fact of life, so make the best of it by using signaling devices; in other words, separate the two spheres by having separate lines, or separate mobile phones, one for business and one for personal use. Call waiting is popular because business contacts can still reach you when you are using the phone for private reasons. Voice mail, answering machines and Caller ID are used as screening devices to ensure business contacts can reach you.

You find the same attitude among teenage children in the USA, where second lines for children are quite common according to the focus group interviews. Children are individuals living in the public space of the household. You have to give them a chance to separate their lives from those of their parents.

The Dutch are less prepared to let the work sphere enter the private sphere. For this reason, they are hesitant to try things such as telecommuting. Voice mail, an answering machine and Caller ID are popular as screening devices, but more to enable the called party to answer the caller at a more convenient moment. Call waiting is not popular as a screening device, although it is acceptable for business purposes. For private use, the Dutch think it is rude to put people on hold. The Americans who are not in business agree with the Dutch on this point.

Children in Holland are seen as part of a family circle and are not expected to have their own telephone lines, although quite a few respondents accept the fact that children buy their own mobile phones. Second lines are not common in Holland and certainly not so that your child can have his or her own telephone line. ISDN (Integrated Services Digital Network) allows families to have several telephone numbers to separate work and home life, or to give children their own line. But it seems that ISDN is primarily popular because it allows families to separate services – fax, fixed telephone and Internet access line – and to stay reachable while using those services.

*The time dimension.* People had to place ICT products and services on the scale of "costs time – saves time." According to Trompenaars, Americans see the future as most important, today as far less important and the past as even less of a consideration. Nevertheless, there is some relationship between past, present and future; for Americans the future is short term. You do something now in order to reap the benefits within a very short time. For the Dutch the present is more important, but the future is almost as important. The past matters very little. In contrast to Americans, however, past, present and future are separate spheres. Now is what counts; the future is something quite different. This also could explain the way people in the two countries perceive the use of time. Use time well in the present, otherwise it is wasted.

Saving time is important in both countries. Waiting in line is something people in both countries do not like. "Time is money" is a common

American slogan, but the Dutch seem to think in the same way. The telephone and telephone services are generally seen as time savers, though some respondents recognize that they also cost time, because you have to spend time learning to use them and then their use takes even more time.

An important element in this discussion seems to be the feeling of time pressure. When pressed for time, telephone calls are seen as interruptions. Time-stressed Dutch respondents especially mention the mobile phone in this context. Controlling one's own time is the touchstone factor that determines the way people look at ICTs: enablers or harassers, depending on the goal.

Many respondents in both countries see the Internet as a speedy time-saving device; information can be obtained quickly, and with e-mail one can contact others almost immediately. Somewhat surprising is the fact that spending two hours on the Net looking for travel information and ordering a vacation trip is thought to be time saving, although one might have been able to arrange the same trip with a travel agent more quickly over the telephone.

### Owners and non-owners

*The relation of perceptions to the adopter curve*

In the American–Dutch study, most of the owners were rather heavy users of ICTs, not only having a mobile phone, but quite often also using the Internet and several value-added services that enhanced their fixed phones. In the European study, there were two groups of users: early adopters who were very enthusiastic about all ICTs, and a group that used them a lot but more for specific functions. This latter group comprised the bulk of users, and they adopted the services in the middle timeframe.

The non-owners in the USA seemed to us typical middle-class conservative Americans, members of the "silent majority." They saw themselves as "dinosaurs," not adapting to the wishes of their children and surroundings. They were very pleased to find out that there were more people like them in the world. The session was almost therapeutic when they exchanged their particular views on American society and the bad behavior of people around them. Once the session was officially ended, they remained for 20 additional minutes, just talking and sharing views.

The Dutch groups of non-owners were mixed. One group was mainly the same type as their American counterparts: rather conservative people who regard ICTs as trivial or even inimical to their personal lives. They did not have the feeling, though, that they were an exception in their society. They saw themselves as rather well informed, with good reasons to reject the devices. Unlike the Americans, they were not necessarily anti-technology. Most of them thought that all the ICTs were probably inevitable in the future, and maybe they would welcome them when they were easier to use or more common. Another group was mixed and consisted of some "interested non-owners." A few had recently bought a mobile phone or were sure they would own one in the near future.

The big difference between the owners and non-owners was the perception of need. The non-owners did not need the ICTs or no longer needed them; for example, the second telephone line in the USA was disconnected when the children left home. People did not have a mobile phone or Internet access because they had no use for them, whereas owners of ICTs needed them to stay in touch, to stay reachable, to conduct their business, to save time. Non-users more often saw these products and services as luxuries. This is especially true for the Internet and the mobile phone. They interpreted luxury in two ways: necessary (the mobile phone sometimes) or nice (the Internet). We found this type of categorization in both countries.

### Changing perceptions of usefulness and necessity

The focus groups in both countries left a strong impression that the need for ICT products and services translates into usage. When people have used a service for some time, it becomes part of their daily lives and they cannot imagine life without it. This holds true for the mobile phone, but also for services such as voice mail, call waiting and Caller ID:

*When my sister-in-law got it [call waiting], I said "What the heck is this thing, why waste money?" Now it is convenient. I've gotten used to it. It's made things a lot easier.*

In this respect the Dutch do not differ greatly from the Americans:

*At first I used my mobile phone only in situations of real need. Now I find myself using it in the supermarket to ask for guidance from my wife!*

Early adopters seem to differ from the later adopters in the ways they are perceptive of novel technology and novel uses in their daily life. The late adopters in the European study seemed to have little ability to think up novel ICT uses and services. When pressed, they came up with extensions of services they already used, whereas the early adopters were more interested in the technology as such and showed far greater imagination about new and novel ways ICTs could fulfill needs.

*Situation*

Situational factors, of course, play an important role in the acquisition and use of ICTs. Personal and family circumstances dictate the feeling of need:

*I have a home phone for family and a cell phone for business.*
*A cell phone is necessary for security.*
*I work from home and have to be reachable.*
*Caller ID makes it possible to prioritize, for example, if a call is from my boss.*
*I have four daughters, so I have a second line.*
*The phone is my wife's sanity line, because her family lives far away.*

Some of these situational factors are typical for those who live in rural areas. Long distances are a bigger factor in the USA than in the Netherlands. Far more US respondents own their own businesses, in combination with second jobs. Different regulations and rates play an important role. The flat rate in the USA makes Internet access far cheaper and thus less problematic to use. In the Netherlands, people have to pay in 10 second increments, even for local calls. E-commerce is less threatening in the USA because people are already used to catalog shopping and to the use of credit cards. On the other hand, the GSM system in Europe makes it easy to use your mobile phone everywhere on the continent and also in many other parts of the world, whereas the different cell phone standards in the USA create a lot of difficulties for connections between states.

In addition, the length of time one has been exposed to technology matters. In the USA the answering machine has been a common feature for years and is accepted as a way to retrieve messages. Although not everybody likes to leave a message, it is considered good manners to do so. In the Netherlands, the answering machine was uncommon when Dutch Telecom decided to give free voice mail to each subscriber. People still feel awkward about leaving messages, and often decline to do so. The use of voice mail is also affected in both countries by how long it has been available. Because the Americans have their answering machines paid for and solidly in place, voice mail is considered unnecessary (especially as you have to pay for the service monthly) unless the answering machine breaks down.

*I have voice mail. I used to have an answering machine, but I had a lot of trouble with the tapes breaking.*

In the Netherlands, quite a few people did not have an answering machine when voice mail was introduced. The fact that voice mail is free obviously made it easier to choose voice mail over the answering machine.

*I was thinking about an answering machine, but then voice mail came, so I took that, it's free.*

## Conclusions and discussion

We have sought greater understanding of the cultural dimensions of attitudes toward ICTs by comparing use in the USA and the Netherlands. One fruitful area of inquiry was the way new ICTs were used in relationship to mobility. Both the American–Dutch and the European studies show that ICTs are used mainly for utilitarian rather than recreational purposes. There could be a life-stage bias in this though. The focus groups from which the data were drawn were adults; teens could have dramatically different attitudes. Indeed, when adult respondents disparage chatting, they often make reference to teenagers and children. Mobile phone use for social conversation seemed more acceptable to the younger members of the focus groups.

New ICTs help coordinate mobility as well as repair some of the dislocation it causes. Yet they are only partly associated with the spatial aspects of mobility. There is a strong association between their use and those who face time pressures and complex, highly interactive social networks.

The second issue we wanted to examine was the norms regulating use of ICTs in mobile situations. It turned out that there are strong, widely shared norms governing ICT use. The norms among adults are that proper conduct in public space requires that callers use the phone only in emergencies and for short messages, and that they shut the ringer off in public places where people expect to enjoy themselves, such as restaurants and theaters, or in church. If a mobile phone call is necessary, people should speak quietly and not discuss personal matters. In this respect, it is striking that the latest book on Dutch etiquette has a special chapter on unacceptable mobile phone behavior. (A Dutch newspaper columnist reviewing this book wryly suggested an addendum: "If you must discuss personal matters in public on a mobile, you should afterwards tell those forced to listen what it was all about.")

The third issue was intercultural differences between the USA and the Netherlands. Qualitative research found that respondents' expressed needs and values did not differ from country to country. This is not so surprising, given that Trompenaars' value matrices showed that the two countries are close. What differed, however, was the way people gave meaning to the value of ICTs in their own personal situations. Some of the differences might be explained by variation in cultural values. Other differences have to do with the special environment, regulations, technical standards, length of time exposed to the new technology, and price.

Looking at the work of Trompenaars, though, we would have expected more pronounced differences in attitudes and values among our Europeans of varying national cultures. So this area cries out for further investigation and reflection.

The use of the Katz dimensions and starting the focus groups with questions about the ICT products and services people owned turned out to be an excellent way to get people talking about the value of ICTs in their daily lives and to generate insight into these issues. We found it difficult to make the general part of the interviews comparable in all aspects, because the discussions were largely structured around the gadgets the respondents owned and the reasons they owned and used them. The perceptual mapping exercise structured the second half of the interview and made it possible to get insights that are more comparable.

Based on these investigations, it does seem to be the case that a universal ICT culture is emerging. That is, there is convergence among values in diverse nations despite clear variation in local values and norms in other areas. The reasons cannot be explained here, but this finding certainly invites a deeper inquiry into the nature and causes of this apparent cross-national convergence of attitudes and lifestyles around ICTs.

## References

Batt, Carl E., and J. Katz (1998). "Consumer Spending Behavior and Telecommunication Services: A Multi-method Inquiry." *Telecommunications Policy* 22(1): 23–46.

Hofstede, G. (1980). *Culture's Consequences. International Differences in Work-related Values.* Beverly Hills, CA: Sage.

Katz, James (1999). *Connections: Social and Cultural Studies of the Telephone in American Life.* New Brunswick, NJ: Transaction.

Tonnies, F. (1957). *Community and Society.* New York: Harper & Row.

Trompenaars, F. (1993). *Zakendoen over de grens/Riding the Waves of Culture.* Antwerp/Amsterdam: Economist Books.

# 9    Bulgaria: mobile phones as post-communist cultural icons

*Valentin Varbanov*

Can a nation's cell phone usage convey an accurate cultural image, in this case of a post-communist East European nation? I think so. Understanding how citizens embrace this technology can provide insight into the broader cultural configuration of a country that only recently emerged from a reality in which both its culture and its technology were directed by an often-corrupt centralized authority (that is, a communist government).

My purpose is to describe this landscape: a study of technology and culture in a poor and, until recently, oppressed nation. I am not testing any hypotheses or engaging in high-level theorizing. Rather, I have searched the newspaper archives, spoken to cell phone users, observed my fellow citizens and listened to the voices of children, young adults and seniors. I am using the mobile phone as a lens through which to view my culture. I also hope to provide an interesting snapshot that can be compared with the other nations portrayed in this volume.

Bulgaria is a poor country materially, but a generation of ambitious young people is eager to embrace what, for tradition-bound Bulgaria, are truly foreign ways. My culture will be modified as these people explore mobile phone technology, the seeming epitome of all that Western civilization can provide, the embodiment of the American society they have come to know from watching Western movies.

Bulgaria, a nation of 9 million people, was a loyal communist satellite of Russia for forty-five years. It was the very model of Leninism, with forced collectivization, political prisoners and internal spying. In late 1989, Todor Zhivkov resigned and thus ended the communist dictatorship of Bulgaria. Since then, several governments have tried to carry out reforms in all areas of social, economic and political life. Nevertheless, change has come slowly, and successful reforms still slower.

The citizens of Bulgaria have experienced new personal freedoms but there are factors that must be considered before I analyze the symbolic meaning of cell phone use. First, under Soviet direction, Bulgaria had a large communist *nomenclatura*, a hierarchical political infrastructure that was superimposed upon the society. Unlike Western or even Third World countries, post-communist Bulgaria inherited a socialist economic system, one in which the elite nomenclature continues to hold key positions in government and cultural institutions. Further, there has not always been a significant distinction between the criminal class and governmental authorities. In other words, at certain times the government – operated by the communists – resembled more a massive organized crime syndicate than a structure that reflected popular will.

Perhaps if technological change had occurred a little more quickly, the communist political elite would have had a chance to exploit cell phones for their own purposes. However, the first mobile phone system was deployed in Bulgaria only after the communists had been officially forced to step down from power.

Privatization of small, medium and large state enterprises was difficult. The Socialist Party government (former communists) was afraid to sell Bulgarian property to foreign companies, which, in turn, did not consider Bulgaria a stable country in which to start a business. Eventually the first Bulgarian mobile telecommunication company, which included the British company Cable & Wireless and the Bulgarian Ministry of Defense, opened for business as Mobikom in 1993. Today Mobikom, the leading provider of analog mobile service, has 100,000 subscribers; 95% of Bulgarian territory is covered; and roaming in ten countries in Central and Eastern Europe is available. As of 2001, seven more companies had followed in Mobikom's footsteps, and the overall penetration rate is about 4%.

Not surprisingly, keeping indigenous control over these eight cell phone service companies has been an important consideration. However, nationalism is not the sole motive for this concern. Former communists who remain in various positions of influence want to keep substantial control, as well as profits, from this growth industry.

In 1994, the first Bulgarian GSM (Global System for Mobile Communications) corporation, called Mobiltel, was established. Its goal was to build a GSM digital cellular mobile communication network in the territory of Bulgaria. Shareholders in the corporation were the Tron Company, First Financial, Eastern Market Telecom and BulSim EOOD. Two central offices with a capacity for 270,000 subscribers and 300 cell sites offer a service to the 140,000 subscribers. The services of Mobiltel cover 67% of the country and 85% of the population. The company signed roaming service contracts with 146 GSM operators in 71 countries from five continents and with the (now defunct) satellite operator Iridium.

Mobiltel, recording a 159% rate of growth for 1998, now ranks seventh among Central European companies and second among GSM operators.

In January 1999, it reported 320% growth in the number of subscribers, although at 63,000 the total is still small.

On March 20, 1995, the Post and Long Distance Communication Committee announced that it would award a second license to build another digital cellular phone network. (In order to foster competition the European Union requires at least two GSM operators.) The Bulgarian Telecommunication Company applied for the license and sought reliable business partners.

One of the most furious battles in the telecommunication business will take place in Bulgaria in the near future. Experts predict an apocalyptic price war between the giant Mobiltel and its European competitor KPN. Mobile service prices in Bulgaria are among the highest in the world. KPN intends to cover the whole country with a digital network, replacing ordinary analog telephones with digital ones and offering lower prices than those offered by Mobiltel – the first and only GSM operator so far.

Over the past few years, Mobikom and Mobiltel have used various strategies to promote their service.

Mobikom's first published advertisements date back to February 1994. At the very beginning advertising was not as pervasive as it is today. Single ads appeared once a month on average in some of the newspapers and magazines. But Bulgarian people were well informed about the existence of this exceptionally convenient means of communication. Mobile phones were introduced in 1993, but a lot of people knew about the invention of mobile phones much earlier. Information invaded the country via films and the Internet and because Bulgarians were now freely traveling abroad. Children knew about mobile phones from films and toys. Students were able to read about the small, light, comfortable, portable, wireless telephones that one could use everywhere – in the car, in the office, at home, outside, in an airplane. The Internet was another source of information, a marvel after so many years of restricted information.

From July 19 to 26, 1999, Mobiltel introduced an advertising campaign in anticipation of its 100,000th subscriber. Every day on the pages of the most popular newspapers it announced the latest number of customers. It promised a Motorola 3688 cell phone as a prize for its 100,000th client. The prize included a free business subscription for a year.

Mobikom's advertising campaign, dedicated to its 100,000th client, distinguished itself by its originality. This campaign took place on May 3, 1999. Its slogan was "We are at every kilometer." This title was borrowed from a television series that aired thirty years ago on Bulgaria's one television channel. The program depicted the communist partisans who struggled against the then Nazi-allied Bulgarian government in the summer of 1944. The main characters in this serial were determined communists. However, a lot of Bulgarians had a negative attitude towards this programming in light of the communists' abuses once they had seized power from the Nazi sympathizers. Nevertheless, the organizers of the campaign chose the slogan for a reason. They divided the area of Bulgaria, which is 111,000 km$^2$, by the number of subscribers, which was almost 100,000, and came up with approximately one Mobikom subscriber per km$^2$. So they claimed: "We, Mobikom, are at every single kilometer, even if it is square."

Then they staged a grand event. The chosen day was May 3, which was the start of the International Technical Fair in the town of Plovdiv. The fashion agency Vissage provided 130 beautiful girls, who boarded buses in the center of Sofia, bound for Plovdiv. They traveled along the Trakia highway. The temperature was about 30°C. The girls were dressed in white T-shirts, blue jeans and hats, and they carried mock Benefon Spica phones that were as big as themselves.

The bus stopped every kilometer and dropped a girl off on the highway. She attracted a lot of attention as she tried to sign drivers up for a trial service. The drivers were very interested. Some of them stopped and asked the prices of the mobile phones and the cost of service. Others offered mineral water or Coca-Cola to the girls, who were suffering owing to the intolerable heat. In addition, some men made indecent proposals to the girls. (Bulgarian highways are notorious nowadays for roadside prostitution, or "outdoor brothels." Pimps distribute girls, most of them gypsies, along a highway in the morning and pick them up in the evening. When driving on such highways, it does in fact appear that some prostitutes do have mobile phones.) Mobikom's girls had a totally different task and they were vigilantly guarded by officials posted near-by.

The idea and the execution of the campaign were new experiences for my country. Most of the people who witnessed this event were interested in mobile phones; they got a lot of information about the prices, the services and the company itself. The campaign gave the necessary information and enticed a lot of people to purchase a mobile phone. Witnesses of the event will remember the models in white T-shirts and hats emblazoned with the emblem of Mobikom, carrying big mobile phone dummies.

Mobile phones are very often given as corporate prizes. The Kraft Jacobs Suchard Company arranged a contest for wholesale dealers. The contestants had to send fourteen labels from the boxes of two types of wafers to the manufacturer. The winning entries were drawn in the presence of a notary. The more entries a dealer sent, the greater opportunity to win. One hundred mobile phones were given away.

The Mobikom company sponsors the weekly TV program *Oh, These Wry Faces*. The guests on this long-running show are awarded a mobile phone at the end of the program. The guests are usually famous Bulgarian intellectuals – actors, artists, scientists, politicians, doctors and singers. The company then ran ads containing the photo, the name and the profession of these famous people who use mobile phones.

Mobiltel is famous for its sponsorship of one of the most popular football teams in Bulgaria – Levski. Mr. Grashnov, the president of Mobiltel, is chairman of the board of directors of the Levski football club. On November 12, 1999, Mobiltel announced that it would become the general sponsors of another football team, called Botev, from the town of Vratza.

The bosses of Mobikom and Mobiltel can often be seen at various social events, some of which they sponsor. On October 12, 1999, there was a party honoring Stefka Kostadinova, a winner of seven world records, an Olympic record and a European record for the high jump. Although she was not chosen, she was one of the ten nominees for the title "sportsperson of the year." Mr. Grashnov was at this party, accompanied by Michael Chorney. According to a report in a Bulgarian newspaper (*24 Hours*, October 12, 1999), Mr. Chorney was suspected of being involved in a Russian Mafia money-laundering scheme. The newspaper also said that the presence of Mr. Chorney in Bulgaria and his public appearance in the company of Mr. Grashnov were the reasons Prime Minister Ivan Kostov had advised his ministers to avoid contact with Mr. Chorney and even to replace their GSM phones with mobile phones from Mobikom.

John Munury, the CEO of Mobikom, is the head of the Foreign Investors Organization. He is an admirer of Stefka Kostadinova and says that she is his favorite sportswoman. Mobikom sponsors a lot of parties organized by A Twenty-First Century Mission, a foundation boasting the motto "significant persons with significant presence."

The name of the Mobiltel corporation – the first Bulgarian GSM operator – will remain memorable both for contemporary Bulgarians and for future generations because of its generosity. An Orthodox Church was built near the winter resort of Pamporovo in the Rhodope, a mountainous region in southern Bulgaria. Money for the building was raised with the help of the weekly TV political program, *Panorama*. The names of 6,724 firms and individuals who contributed were written in a special book which will be kept in the church forever. These donors gave between US$5 and US$70,000, the largest contribution being given by Mobiltel. Mr. Grashnov made a personal gift, too. In addition, he announced that US$10,000 in proceeds from the football match between Levski and the Central Sport Army Club would be offered as a gift to buy mural paintings.

Despite all these creative promotional efforts, only 2.5% of the Bulgarian population has a mobile phone. The prices are too high for ordinary people. For example, only a few teachers in Rousse possess mobile phones. The average monthly teacher's salary is US$80. A Mobifon plus a Mobilik card good for 40 minutes of talking costs US$125. University lecturers, assistants and professors, unable to afford a mobile phone, sometimes have a negative attitude towards students who possess one. Once an absent-minded student forgot to turn off his mobile phone in class and the professor became furious. None of the 360 dressmakers in Rousse, who make US$100 a month, has a mobile phone.

Doctors have a greater need than most for a mobile phone, but the state can afford neither to provide them nor to pay doctors according to European standards. The average monthly salary of state doctors is DM 200. One such doctor, who works only in a state hospital, received a mobile phone as a present from relatives who work abroad. But he is not able to cover the running costs, so he has not connected it. He hopes one day to establish a private practice and, when his income is sufficient to pay his bills, he will use it. The wealthy doctors in Bulgaria are mostly gynecologists and dentists who set up a private practice. Many gynecologists have mobile phones.

People in Sofia have better opportunities to work and study, and 40% of Bulgaria's mobile phone subscribers live there. When foreign tourists or businesspeople visit Sofia for the first time, they are amazed by the number of men and women driving expensive cars such as a Mercedes or a BMW. And all of them have mobile phones. It is not surprising or unusual to see children and their grandmothers talking on their mobile phones in the street. Early in the morning a lot of young businessmen on their way to work talk on their mobile phones as they walk into their luxurious offices.

Sofia is the Bulgarian business center. It seems all the foreign companies that invest in Bulgaria, or just do business there, settle in Sofia. Imports and exports are centralized in Sofia. Certainly the major Bulgarian companies are headquartered in Sofia.

How did Sofia become the business nexus? Sofia was the political capital of Bulgaria before the communists were displaced, so former state employees and government officials quickly set up private businesses after the fall. They possessed strategic information about the state's economy and took advantage of this. The people who began to carry on trade – retail or wholesale, domestic or foreign – succeeded in making a lot of money. Some of them became millionaires almost overnight. The state enterprises were still producing quality goods with established stable markets abroad. Instead of the state, a select few benefited from the new situation. They were able to get millions of dollars in credit from the banks, and became rich. We call these people credit millionaires. A lot of them took the money and left the country. Those who remain continue their businesses and are creating a new social class – the "nouveau riche."

A lot of uneducated people of low intelligence have become "important persons." To show off their new social status, they got a mobile phone as a symbol of their "significance," even though they did not need one. Such people talk loudly when walking in the street, shopping in the supermarket, dining in a restaurant, even at parents' meetings at school.

Unique to Bulgaria is another interesting group of mobile phone users – the large number of famous former boxers, weight lifters and wrestlers now in private employment. They form an impressive group, many of them having won European, Olympic or world titles. These tough, vigorous men, retired from sport, found a new vocation as bodyguards in banks, private firms, insurance companies, exchange offices and security companies. Mobile phones became the tools of their trade.

We call all these former sportsmen "wrestlers" because the majority of them were wrestlers. In Bulgarian, the word is "*boretz*," which has another meaning of "fighter." This second meaning prevailed as time passed because their activities were often connected with applying force. Most of these owners of mobile phones can be classified as of lower than average intelligence. They were treated very cruelly by their trainers and were forced to spend most of their time in the gymnasium, where they worked hard to become champions. When they give television or press interviews, they show their lack of education. These people were among the first to create the image of a man with a mobile phone. This image was a comical one. On the one hand, they were uneducated and most of them did not know how to use all of the functions. On the other hand, they possessed one of the world's newest and most sought-after technological inventions.

When mobile phones appeared on the Bulgarian market for the first time, some criminals succeeded in getting them. On January 24, 1994, newspapers reported that armed hooded policemen had broken into the Mobikom office in Sofia. The previous night, criminals had exchanged gunfire in front of the Sevastopol cinema. A mobile phone was found near the site. The policemen received an anonymous message that one of the criminals was hiding in the Mobikom office. But the policemen did not find him. The next day a high-ranking official from the Ministry of Internal Affairs apologized to John Munury, CEO of Mobikom, who accepted the apology and considered the case closed.

On March 3, 1995, a leader of a criminal group was killed near the town of Kustendil. Some newspapers reported that the two hostile gangs used mobile phones to give instructions. After the shooting, the killers called the police and let them know that there was a man dead, and they described the exact place where the body could be found.

On March 9, 1995, ten masked gangsters broke into an apartment in the Nadejda building complex in Sofia. They stole US$5,600, 300 grams of gold, jewelry, a mobile phone and a Nissan car worth US$16,000.

In another instance, the police arrested three thieves who had broken into the hotel rooms of the Health Minister, three Members of Parliament, the Parliamentary Secretary of the Health Ministry and two policemen while they were attending a summer workshop in the Borovetz resort. The thieves pinched gold jewelry, two mobile phones, a watch and two Astra pistols. Some of the stolen goods were found in the flats of the thieves, but they succeeded in selling some jewelry abroad. Police suspect the gang had stolen from other hotels throughout the country.

Former prisoners were employed in the same way the "fighters" were. They got mobile phones from their employers. These people created a negative image of the man with a mobile phone. So intelligent people used their mobile phones surreptitiously. That is why at the beginning it seemed only the fighters and criminals were using mobile phones.

But, as time went on, various groups of people were successful in setting up businesses. And, logically, they became mobile phone subscribers. So over time people changed their attitude toward the person with a mobile phone. In the past, fighters, pimps, criminals, and other unsavory people created the image of the mobile phone user. These people used to wear shiny training suits and sneakers made in Turkey – a fashionable way to show their business affiliations. Today people who use mobile phones are well-dressed men and women. Even some students from secondary schools and universities, mostly businessmen's children, have them.

In 1999, 1,500 Bulgarians committed suicide. This is the first time in a generation that more of my people killed themselves than were killed in car accidents. The Psychology Center at the General Staff of the Army reported that in 1989 there were 16 suicides per 100,000 people; in 1998, there were 18.3 per 100,000 people. Of these, 44% were pensioners, but middle-aged people, teenagers and drug-addicts are now committing this desperate act. Family conflict is the most common reason for these tragic incidents.

The reason I bring this up is because, in November 1999, I had a very troubling experience. I was on my way home at 8 o'clock in the evening and I saw a man fall from his seventh-floor apartment window. The man smashed into the pavement a mere 10 meters away from me. It was dark and the streets were deserted. My first impression was that a large black coat had fallen to the ground. However, several young people who work in the small shops on the ground floor of the apartment block rushed into the street and quickly realized what had happened. A young shopkeeper who had a mobile telephone was able to call for an ambulance. Within three minutes, the ambulance arrived, but it was too late. The man had already died. Still, it was impressive to see the mobile phone used so quickly and efficiently.

However, a mobile phone does not guarantee that a citizen in Bulgaria will receive quick emergency care because the emergency telephone number, 150, is often busy and it takes a long time to get connected to a dispatcher. Once a rich businessman who had a mobile phone could not reach 150 and, when he got his wife to the hospital, it was too late. He had found his wife at home half-dead. She had been stabbed repeatedly by someone who had broken into their home. The businessman said that if an ambulance had arrived in time, the medics could have saved her life. The man was upset and rich enough to offer, for the first time in the history of Bulgaria, a reward of US$1 million for the capture of the murderer. (It is unclear why the businessman did not call other potential sources of assistance if he had a mobile telephone at his disposal.)

In small towns and villages people prefer to take people to the hospital themselves rather than call the emergency number and wait for the arrival of an ambulance. In Sofia an ambulance can reach a given address within 20 minutes, if the ambulance is not out of service, which occurs about half the time. Three minutes after a call is received, the ambulance is on its way to the address. A medical emergency team is responsible for only 150,000 people (in Europe, it is 250,000), but radio station LOTOS (which operates within a 40 kilometer radius) is used to transmit the calls and these connections are not reliable. If there were mobile communications, the connections would improve significantly.

A lot of people, mainly businessmen, were able to travel abroad and some of them even bought mobile phones before being able to use them in Bulgaria (because the network had not yet been built). Many Bulgarians from the southeastern part of the country frequently travel to Greece and they were the first Bulgarians to buy mobile phones. They became customers of the Greek telecommunication companies. Many continue to use the services of the Greek companies because of their competitive tariffs.

The Communist Party outlawed television sets made by nations other than Bulgaria or Russia. Foreign brands were available only in duty-free shops, frequented by a small group of people. These included doctors, nurses, drivers, sailors and builders who had worked abroad and been paid in foreign currency, and, of course, the ruling class, which was allowed to acquire foreign currency at special rates.

The situation in Bulgaria is different now. Anyone with the necessary resources can go to an exchange office or a bank and buy currency. Anyone can go to the offices of the mobile communication companies and choose a cellular phone from the great variety available. Nobody will ask you the source of your money. It might be savings from a state salary, an inheritance, an illegal business or bribes, or it could be stolen, a lottery prize or laundered money.

Mobile phones are starting to appear in Bulgarian popular culture – in jokes, songs and symbols.

Have you heard the one about the fighter who was driving his new BMW while speaking on his mobile Nokia, when he had an accident? Luckily he survived and only lost his hand. His car was a write-off. When the police arrived, the fighter was crying, "Oh, my God, I lost my BMW." The policeman noticed the missing hand and offered to take him to the hospital immediately. The fighter, who was distraught because of the ruined car, heard the policeman and began crying even louder, "Oh, my God, where is my Rolex? Where is my Nokia?"

A lot of songs have been written recently in which mobile phones are mentioned. A very famous Bulgarian actor, Slavi Trifonov, who is also a great singer, had a hit called "A Ferrari in Red." For years, this song was everywhere – in discos, cafés, buses, taxis. Even toddlers sang this song in the playground in front of my housing block. The lyrics include the line: "If I only had the mobile phone number of God, we would make a deal with him."

Many songs feature a man with a mobile phone. He is generally a prosperous figure – rich, good looking and well dressed. Girls are very attracted to this man. They admire him as a symbol of power, glory and success. For instance, one popular song reminds a man carrying a cell phone: "Oh, tiger, tiger, if you have money, you will have young girls, if not – old ladies." Another song includes the refrain: "You are wearing sunglasses / You are driving a nice car / You are calling my telephone number / From your mobile phone. / You are staring at girls' eyes, / I can see – you are nice / You rely on your charm every day / You were born to be a liar."

The lyrics of a *chalga* song (a mix of Bulgarian folk music, Oriental motifs and silly lyrics popular with young people) include the following refrain: "Today money conquers the world. Those who don't have it, they hardly live. He who has money will buy sweets, chocolates, croissants, jam. He who has money will buy GSMs, mobile phones and Toblerone chocolate."

The Bulgarian National Assembly has had trouble coming up with a new national symbol. They have discussed it for many years, with no result. Making fun of this situation, a famous Bulgarian actor,

Pavel Popandov, suggested that the National Assembly should alter the national emblem. Instead of a lion wearing a crown, the emblem should depict Khan Asparuh, the legendary hero who established the Bulgarian state in 681, riding a white horse and talking on a mobile phone.

On November 4, 1999, the Bulgarian government adopted a national strategy for the development of high-technology industries. Ministers approved a draft program for high-tech parks and activities open to both Bulgarian and foreign businesses. The state, municipalities, universities and the Bulgarian Science Academy will be able to establish such parks as well. Undoubtedly they will pay close attention to new telecommunication technologies. All Bulgarians are looking forward to the day when their country no longer lags behind in adopting innovations, and will perhaps take part in creating some of them.

However, mobile phones are not currently a top priority for most Bulgarians who have to cope with many hardships, which will not be solved by mobile phones. People are faced with more important decisions than whether or not to have a mobile phone. Nonetheless, its status as a national icon seems assured, and its symbolic and phenomenological prominence speaks volumes for the nature of culture and hierarchy in Bulgarian society at the start of a new millennium.

*Part II*

# Private talk: interpersonal relations and micro-behavior

The chapters in part I examined mobile communication from the perspective of national cultures. The chapters in this part examine how the mobile phone is enrolled in the detailed choreography of daily life and the communication problematics that arise when integrating mobile communication into everyday life. We see in these chapters the micro-practices and practical theories of personal technology use that must emerge for the technology to be usable. Although each chapter is drawn from a particular cultural context for understandable reasons, these chapters highlight fundamental problematics in managing perpetual contact as mobile communication is made an aspect of everyday life. The phenomena dealt with in this part, if not universal, may at least be pandemic among the industrialized countries, independently of their "East–West" orientation or other particularistic dimensions.

Drawing on Norwegian research, *Richard Ling and Birgitte Yttri* outline the concept of micro- and hyper-coordination. Their data come primarily from ten small-group interviews in Norway conducted during the fall of 1999. They found that micro-coordination – largely an instrumental activity – was common for two-career parents. They found that teens, in addition to instrumental uses, have adopted many expressive uses. Compared with adults, teens rely heavily on mobile phones to control and affect their social presentations of self. The confluence of these factors leads to something original that Ling and Yttri call hyper-coordination. The teens' adoption of technology follows from their specific life stage when they desire access to peers and wish to distance themselves, to a certain degree, from their parents. Other advantages are that mobile phones allow them new ways with which to develop intimate relationships and to remain abreast of social life. Hence, while the mobile telephone is a logical tool for both teenagers and adults to manage their private sphere, the teens have developed a more elaborate sense and sensibility of perpetual contact.

*Eija-Liisa Kasesniemi and Pirjo Rautiainen* examine how teens use the short messaging service (SMS) available with their mobile phone subscription. They interviewed Finnish teens (aged 13–18) who own a mobile phone, as well as their parents and teachers. They describe how text messaging has become part of teenage culture in Finland. Teens gather around their mobiles to read and compose messages and they collect messages and share them among their cliques. SMS is having, we believe, a substantial impact on their lived experience. It is an important part of dynamically fine-tuning social relationships and self-image construction. It is also noteworthy how the mobile phone, which is often presented as an individual's communication tool, is used to perform distributed, collaborative relational work. The Finnish teens use this tool in a manner that would inspire awe in the computer-supported cooperative work community. The teens have also developed practices to make a clumsy interface work, an interface, we might note, that would probably not be a successful technology had it been introduced solely as a text service. Like the Norwegian teens, the Finns have shown tremendous dedication and ingenuity in achieving communication bliss with their peers and, in so doing, have elaborated the ways and means of perpetual contact.

*Chantal de Gournay* explores micro-behavior on the cellular mobile phone in France; in particular, how the mobile phone expands informal conversation at the expense of formal conversation. The material is primarily drawn from a survey carried out for EURESCOM P 903 in Paris and Montpellier between September and November 1999. The survey consisted of six focus groups composed of ten people. Her argument is quite different from conventional criticism that media reduce face-to-face contact and thus create social distance. The crisis is about not the loss of intimacy but the ascendancy of the private sphere over the public sphere and subsequent loss of formal conversation, which is an important form of expression and sociability. Her findings reveal another side to the innovations identified in the studies of Scandinavian teenagers and the consequences of improved opportunity for private talk.

*Dawn Nafus and Karina Tracey* think of mobile phones in terms of the dialectic between continuity and change. They examine how household members in England talk about the role of the mobile phone in their households. They show how the "novel" mobile phone reaffirms old cultural notions about individuality. The primary site of changed continuity seems to be in the social construction of the individual person, and thus this chapter examines the ways in which the mobile phone is implicated in the production of individuality and personhood. By working through several moral economies of the object, they explore how the meanings evoked in processes of individuation may change while "attitudes" might remain manifestly conservative.

# 10 Hyper-coordination via mobile phones in Norway

*Richard Ling and Birgitte Yttri*

## Introduction

*The mobile telephone is a big part of my life.*

*A mobile telephone is actually an expression of your personality.*

These words of two teenaged female informants describe their relationship to the mobile telephone. Yet their use of the device is a recent phenomenon. None of the teens included in this analysis had had a mobile telephone for more than four years. What is surprising is the degree to which the mobile telephone has been integrated into their lives. It is not simply a security device, nor is it used only to coordinate everyday events spontaneously. It is used for a range of interaction and is also important as a symbol.

Our chapter looks at how the mobile telephone's adoption has yielded new forms of interaction and especially coordination. We call these micro-coordination and hyper-coordination. In Norway, where the analysis has taken place, the mobile telephone is well entrenched. With more than half the population armed with at least one mobile phone, no other country, save Finland, has a higher per capita consumption. The penetration is even higher among certain groups. In one of the focus groups, five of nine boys had two mobile telephones. For example, as of May 2001, as many as 94% of the oldest teens have a mobile telephone (Ling, forthcoming).

Owing to the recent yet explosive growth of mobiles, it is quite noticeable as a cultural phenomenon. All the informants, even the youngest ones, remember life before its popularization. This recency effect provides rich material for study.

One of the impacts of mobile telephony is the opportunity for nuanced instrumental coordination. This forms the core of micro-coordination. With the use of mobile communication systems, one need not take an agreement to meet at a specific time and place as immutable. Rather, those meeting have the ability to adjust the agreement as the need arises. In addition, mobile communication systems allow for the redirection of transportation to meet the needs of social groups. This is largely a functional and instrumental activity.

Moving beyond this, "hyper-coordination" encompasses instrumental coordination and adds two other dimensions. The first is the expressive use of the mobile telephone. That is, in addition to the simple coordination of where and when, the device is employed for emotional and social communication. People chat with each other. The short messaging service (SMS)[1] function is used to send chain letters, and personal messages that range all the way from innocent and saccharine greetings to vulgar pornographic images. One sees the integration of the group via the use of the mobile telephone. The second aspect of hyper-coordination is in-group discussion and agreement about the proper forms of self-presentation vis-à-vis the mobile telephone – that is, the type of mobile telephone that is appropriate, the way in which it is carried on the body and the places in which it is used. Thus, hyper-coordination encompasses instrumental and expressive use of the mobile telephone as well as strictures regarding the presentation of self. One can see that the mobile telephone provides a type of integration or "coordination" that permeates several dimensions of social life.

This is important to teens because they consider that with one's peers the style of contact and presentation is pre-eminent. Thus, hyper-coordination is not simply the use of the device to coordinate activities. It involves social and emotional interaction and includes strictures as to the type of terminal one should use and its proper uses.

## Method and general framework

### Method

From earlier work we have come to understand that several themes are important when considering mobile telephony. These include security, coordination and accessibility. Further, we have begun to find that each of these three themes is of importance to different age groups. Earlier analysis has pointed to the possibility that accessibility is important for youth, that coordination is an important theme for career parents, and finally that security and safety are important for elderly users.

To examine this we selected four age groups and planned a series of ten group interviews. All the informants were mobile telephone users.

---

[1] This system allows for messages of up to 160 characters in length to be sent between GSM telephones. In addition, some graphics can be sent via this system. Text messaging is generally cheaper than voice calls and so is quite popular among cost-conscious teens who pay for their own mobile telephone use.

The informants in four of these groups were teens between the ages of 14 and 18. Another two groups consisted of informants aged 19–27. A third pair of groups was composed of parents in two-career families. The last two groups comprised older mobile telephone users. The youngest group received extra attention because their adoption and use patterns seemed quite different from those of the other groups.

The transcripts of the group interviews form the core of the material examined here. During the group interviews, the participants were asked to discuss their ownership and use of mobile telephones. In addition, they were asked about various problem areas and future developments surrounding mobile telephony.

Group interviews were transcribed and analyzed using a flat database program that allowed for the identification and sorting of themes and core concepts at several levels of specificity. (We translated the quotes used here from Norwegian into English).

### Framework for the analysis

The results of the group interviews can be partially represented by the matrix in table 10.1. The table has two axes. The vertical axis is the movement from instrumental to expressive types of interaction, that is the movement from communications that have to do with security and coordination to those that are more focused on the exchanging of feelings and emotions. The horizontal axis is an adaptation of Calhoun's taxonomy of social interaction (1987, 1992). Based on Cooley's distinction between primary and secondary relationships, Calhoun expands this to include four levels, three of which are included here. The first level, primary relationships, is characterized as being directly interpersonal and involving "the whole person." Secondary relationships are direct too but might also include "relationships that require the mediation of a complex communication system." Calhoun specifies tertiary relationships as those in which one never meets the other face-to-face but rather the relationship is mediated through a communication system. An example is

Table 10.1 *Forms of interaction via the mobile telephone*

|              | Intimate/primary   | Secondary          | Remote       |
|--------------|--------------------|--------------------|--------------|
| Instrumental | Security           |                    | Security     |
|              | Coordination       | Coordination       | Coordination |
| Expressive   | Social interaction | Social interaction |              |

bureaucracy – for instance, sending in an application that is handled by people functioning in a formal position. For our work, this has been changed to people with whom one has only remote interaction via the mobile telephone. One can think of various information services such as the person one calls to get a bus schedule or to reserve tickets to the movies. In these cases, there is real interaction, but, like Calhoun's tertiary form of interaction, there is no long-lasting form of engagement.[2]

The cells have been filled in with three types of activities: security, coordination and social interaction. The mobile telephone, it seems, is often bought with the notion that it will be a device to increase one's security. However, as the mobile telephone becomes increasingly embedded in one's everyday life it gains other attributes and is used in other ways. Instead of simply being a lifeline, it is also used to coordinate various everyday activities. In addition, for some, it crosses over the divide into more expressive forms of interaction. If one applies a somewhat broader reading to the expressive dimension of the table, it also includes issues of display and the presentation of self.

One can see a type of adoption cycle at a social level. In its most basic form, the adoption is to solve a specific problem, i.e. security in the case of accidents. In this situation the interaction is directed towards the intimate sphere and perhaps the representatives of institutions such as emergency services. As the use and ownership become more routine interaction moves to various types of coordination. Finally, there is the development of expressive interaction. In this way, the table describes the embedding of the technology in everyday situations, through the movement from the extraordinary and unexpected to the expected and the mundane. This dynamic has also been described, using other terms, by Silverstone (1994, pp. 122–131) and Douglas and Isherwood (1979).

## Micro-coordination

Beyond security, one of the primary functions of the mobile telephone is mundane coordination, or perhaps the micro-coordination of everyday life. When introducing this concept, it is worthwhile describing the context into which it is being introduced.

The need to coordinate activities is a basic social function. Many of the large social institutions include the coordination of interaction as part of their activities. Coordination is a vital dimension to transportation,

---

[2] Calhoun describes quaternary relationships in which individuals are not even aware that they are the subject of interest. Situations in which there is wire-tapping or other forms of eavesdropping fit into this group. This form of "interaction" will not be considered here.

particularly in modern urban settings. This, in turn, is affected by changes in the efficiency of communication such as that seen in the development of the mobile telephone.

### Transportation, telecommunication and the development of the cities

Hägerstrand asserts that "to avoid transportation humanity invented the city" (Hägerstrand, 1982). It is obvious, however, that cities have not eliminated the need either for transportation or for coordination. Indeed, they may have had the opposite effect. Until the development of tele-graphy, transportation and communication were, in effect, synonymous. The speed of transport was also the speed of communication. With the development of Morse telegraphy and other systems of telecommunication, transport and communication were separated from each other (Giddens, 1984, p. 123; Standage, 1998). Until recently there was a relatively strong barrier between the two, in that a person in transit was *incommunicado*.

With the rise of the mobile telephone, the communication and coordinating potential of telephony has entered a new era. Previously, coordination involved the direction and control of transport from geographically fixed terminals or nodes. Mobile telephony means that these stations are becoming less necessary. It is this notion that has given rise to the idea of micro-coordination, which is the coordination of interaction without the need for larger nodes or centralized bases of operation.

### Mobile communication and micro-coordination

This gives rise to several different types of coordination (Haddon, 1999; Katz, 1999; Ling, 2000a). The first, basic logistics, relates to the redirection of trips that have already started; for example, one partner calling the other and asking them to stop in at the store on the way home. This might extend all the way into the store – the husband calls the wife while standing inside the store because he needs to know if it was whole or skim milk that was on the shopping list (which he left on the kitchen table). Another version is the "softening" of time; for example, sitting in a traffic jam and calling ahead to the meeting to let them know that you will be late.[3] A third variation is the progressively exact arrangement

---

[3] This type of coordination plays on the notion that time is a system used for the coordination of social activity. The modern era is characterized by the use of the mechanical clock to coordinate interaction (Beniger, 1986; Dohrn-van Rossum, 1992; Kahlert, Mühe and Brunner, 1986; Landes, 1983; Sobel, 1996; Zerubavel, 1985). The development of mechanical time keeping and standard units of time allowed people to make agreements

of a meeting. Two parties, for example, might generally agree to meet somewhere at an approximate time. As the two are in transit they might call each other to confirm the timing and the location. Finally, if the two cannot locate each other at the agreed place at the agreed time, there can be a third round of calls for the final location of each other. Thus mobile communication allows for the structuring and rationalization of interaction, particularly among distributed participants (Lange, 1993, p. 204). These types of coordination form the core of our idea of micro-coordination.

The material describing the use of the mobile telephone to coordinate one's activities comes from the group interviews with two-career parents and, to a lesser degree, from the older informants. The informants described the various dimensions of micro-coordination in their comments, such as the arrangement and rearrangement of various logistical details on the fly.

IDA: I have to get in touch with my husband because he is out and about a lot and that is why I am glad that he has a mobile telephone. So when we are out and about, both of us, then we can talk with each other while we are out and about.

INTERVIEWER: What is it that you talk about when you are out?

IDA: All about practical, everyday things.

INTERVIEWER: Does it happen very often that both of you are out?

IDA: Yeah, as a matter of fact.

INTERVIEWER: On the average?

IDA: Over the past day I have only called him once and that is not too bad only that. Often it is three or four times during the day.

INTERVIEWER: Yeah, but the topics, is it...?

IDA: "Can you drive the youngest one to music lessons?" "Can you get him?" "Can you go to the store and buy milk?" It is that sort of thing. And someone has called and needs keys to this or that house.... He works for the city and he has keys to a lot of buildings and there is always an alarm going off some place or another and [he] needs the keys....

We see some of the same issues in Anne's comments.

ANNE: That is pretty nice if you are away from home and cannot reach somebody via the regular telephone then you can call and leave a [SMS] message. So we use a lot of messages.

INTERVIEWER: What kind of messages do you send?

by reference to an external system. As time keeping became more portable, this system of social coordination became quite standardized (Landes, 1983). As transportation expanded there was a need for better navigation based on extremely accurate time keeping (Sobel, 1996). Further, as the speed of transportation increased there was a need for far more coordinated scheduling (Beniger, 1986).

ANNE: It is if somebody is late, it can be if we need to buy something, if there is something important that he needs to bring home, if he needs to call somebody or if he has been home and has to give me a message. It is not like "Hi, I am doing fine, etc." It is something that we need.

Anne's final comment, "It is something that we need," is a key theme in many of the comments. It points to the idea that the interaction over the mobile telephone is often instrumental in nature for these informants. It is also often used in the intimate sphere outlined in table 10.1 above. The calls involve exchanging information that allows for the ongoing but mundane maintenance of everyday life. Tom takes up the same theme when he says, "There are always a lot of short messages, like children who need to be picked up at day-care, and things that come up, meetings...." One also sees this use of the mobile telephone for micro-coordination in Ida's comments.

The need to be available for children's activities was a theme that several of the informants brought up. The mobile telephone helped the parents manage the logistics of driving the children and it also helped them manage their common role as volunteers in various free-time activities.

OLE JOHAN: It is very nice to be available when you know that you have kids in the marching band and the soccer team, you know. And there are always messages regarding picking-up and driving and not the least with the marching band. There can be driving to pick up things for the flea market and things like that. And it is nice to be available, that you can get messages and so on. It is things like that. People plan in the afternoon what they will do and so that they don't start to double book themselves with a lot of things and you come home and find out that there are other things to do because you have not gotten a message and cannot plan your free time.

The fact that these activities need to be done while one is either in transit or away from a traditional telephone means that the mobile telephone is well suited for this need.

We also came across material that confirms the notion of "remote care-giving" described by Rakow and Nivarro (1993). Although the notion of care-giving may seem to have an expressive ring to it, the way it is practiced here shows that it also has an instrumental aspect. The mobile telephone is used not to exchange emotional content, rather to make concrete arrangements and deal with practical issues.

KARI: I call very little, very short, very short conversations actually. But I say that I will be late if something happens on the way home. Then I can call the kids and tell them that I am coming, that I am on the way. Before, I had to stop at a gas station to telephone if there was something. And for practical things, I call my husband and ask him to do something on the way home or at work. Then I send a text message to him because he refuses to take a mobile telephone call on the subway.

This is both micro-coordination and the discussion of the "proper" use of the mobile telephone. It also foreshadows the discussion of concealed use among youth in that it describes the context-sensitive and discreet use of the mobile telephone.

The two-career parents described very active lives. They had demanding jobs as well as demanding free-time activities. For some of these people the mobile telephone has become a necessary part of their everyday lives.

OLA: It is very important for me at any rate, but I don't like having a mobile telephone. I work with building stores you know, and we are always behind schedule and things are late and a lot of that. And when I am in one of those periods I know that when it rings between 7 in the morning and 7 in the evening something is wrong. And in the summer I work as a soccer coach for some 14 year olds. And when you have fifty of them with all that that entails of this and that. Like yesterday, it started to rain a little and so you get fifteen to twenty [calls] in the space of a very short time asking if there is going to be practice and a lot of things like that. So I could do without it but I have to have it you know.

Tom described the use of the mobile telephone to coordinate portions of both his work and his private life. His description, however, indicated that the two are relatively independent. Other informants related how the mobile telephone allows the tighter integration of their work and private lives. Nikolas works in the marketing department of a large company:

NIKOLAS: Let's say that I am out shopping and suddenly remember that I have to buy something, let's say toilet paper or light bulbs. I park the car near the store. Then I might get a [job-related] telephone call there. It is like, I can go out of the store and talk with the person there, and you can take a message and be available even though you are doing something in your private life, and that is very nice because working hours are quite long anyway and you can sneak in things that you need privately during working hours. You are more free.

This section has described the instrumental use of the mobile telephone in the micro-coordination of everyday life. Many of the comments have focused attention on the need for coordination among members of the intimate sphere. In addition, we have seen the mobile telephone used for the coordination of more remote groups, for example soccer teams and in work situations. Next we look at more expressive uses among teenage users.

### Hyper-coordination

In the section describing the general framework we noted that the group interviews were designed to examine three general uses of mobile telephony. First, the oldest users frequently focused on issues of safety and security when discussing mobile telephony. The middle-aged users focused on the coordination potentials of the system. The youngest users – those in their mid-teens – had perhaps the most distinct profile. Beyond the instrumental uses of safety and logistical coordination, their use was often expressive in nature. There were also strictures regarding the style and modes of use. For this group the importance of the system was far more central than for the older groups. Even the young adults were much less focused on the technology than the mid-teens.

In the section that follows, we will examine the role of adolescence in contemporary society to contextualize the subsequent analysis of hyper-coordination.

#### *Adolescence, contemporary society and accessibility*

*The concept of adolescence in contemporary society.* There is a well-established discussion of adolescence in the anthropological literature. Much of this focuses on the transition from childhood into adulthood, rites of passage and the issue of sexual maturation (Gennep,1960). This analysis divorces the notion of physical maturation from that of the social definition of the individual as an adult. The wide variation in the age at which one undergoes a rite of passage in pre-literate societies underscores the social nature of this transition.

The idea that the transition from childhood to adult life has a social component is also important when describing adolescence. In industrialized societies the specific rite of passage is largely replaced by a more or less extended apprentice adulthood. During this period the individual learns the skills needed in order to function as an adult. Unlike less differentiated societies, however, the teenager cannot often expect to perform exactly the same type of work in the same location as their parents. The need for workers with specific skills in industrialized society has also resulted in the expansion of the educational system. This in turn has meant that the period of youth is extended and that there is age sorting in order to make teaching more effective. This age sorting has the effect of spawning a peer culture wherein individuals acquire some of their orientation to the world via friends of the same age (Hogan, 1985).

Thus, adolescence is the period when the individual masters various types of social and technical knowledge in addition to filling in the outlines of the role they will fulfill later in life. As noted in earlier work:

Specific knowledge can include an understanding of personal economy, strategies for negotiation with various groups and individuals who have alternative cultures, the role of gender and sex in one's life, how one secures a job and the expectations of the working world, a sense of personal style and integrity, and recently, an understanding of how one interacts and uses information and communication technologies (ICT). (Ling, 2000a, p. 103)

Many of the intergenerational differences in life experience are a result of rapid developments in technology. The speed of change in the material culture is often far greater than that of attitudes and expectations (Ogburn, 1950). Children's experiences of and attitudes towards technology are likely to be different from those of their parents and perhaps even their older siblings. Thus, one must select that information that is relevant rather than accept it uncritically. In this way socialization is not simply received but rather the individual is active in the process. Glaser and Strauss have spoken of this as "shaping" transitions (1971, pp. 57–88). Here we can see the role of the peer group, which can assist (perhaps misguidedly) in the transition from childhood to adult life. This does not mean that the differences in experiences are always accepted without comment. They can be and sometimes are seen as significant moral issues.

In contemporary society, the peer group gains significance during adolescence. It is during this period of life that friends are most central to the individual. Before this point, one's parents are in focus and, later, one's partner and children gain a central role. According to Rubin, "[t]his is perhaps the only time in our lives when friends come fully to center stage, transcending all other relationships in immediate importance as they engage us on a daily basis around every aspect of living." The interaction with peers takes over significant portions of the teen's time and energy. Rubin also notes that relations with one's family are often "fraught with the conflict of the struggle for independence" (1985, p. 110). To this end, various devices, styles, ruses and other social props are used to demarcate the boundary between the teens and their parents. As we will see below, the mobile telephone and the jargon surrounding its use have become tools used for marking the boundary.

Turning now to the other major element in the discussion here, information and communication technologies (ICTs) have had a significant impact on society at all levels. Transport, administration, health and a whole set of social functions have been and are being affected by the development of these technologies.

Examination of ICTs' integration into pre-existing social structures is important too (Bijker, 1992; Bijker, Hughes, and Pinch, 1987; Haddon, 1992; Haddon and Skinner, 1991; Silverstone 1993, 1994).

It is necessary to be aware of their meaning to both the user and the context in which they find themselves. This perspective is of particular relevance because the fashion and status significance of the various ICTs have incisive but quickly shifting meanings. Their symbolic meaning and the ways in which they are perceived have themselves become the impetus of social institutions in Berger and Luckmann's sense of the word (Berger and Luckmann, 1967).

Bringing ICTs and adolescence together, the simple functional understanding of ICT is important for their future life. In addition, ICTs can be a factor in the need to establish identity vis-à-vis older generations. This is nothing new, as many forms of differentiation have been brought into this arena. "Outlandish" clothing, seemingly atonal music, various plays on vamping and sexual display, forms of talk and argot are all available as ways to define and enforce the boundary. More recently, the use and display of various forms of ICT have also come onto the scene in this context.

Looking specifically at telephony, a dominant issue in the work that has been done up to this point deals with the time spent using the traditional fixed telephone (Aronsen, 1977, p. 31; Claisse and Rowe, 1987; Kellner, 1977, p. 292; Lohan, 1997; Mayer, 1977, pp. 228–231). Mayer's work is useful in that he traces the extended use of the telephone to teens who had recently moved within an urban area. This introduces the notion of the individual trying to maintain a social network, a theme that is brought up below.

One could almost use the metaphor of a car with its engine revving and the clutch in. In many ways, youth find themselves in this situation. They have not yet begun the work of hauling themselves through life. In addition they have the luxury of a disengaged period before the serious matters of establishing themselves and caring for others have begun in any serious way.

*Adolescence, access and the role of the mobile telephone.* Turning now to the role of the mobile telephone for adolescents, the widespread adoption of the device points to the importance of availability for teens. Unlike the adults, who can feel stressed by the mobile telephone, the teens thrive on access and interaction. To receive a message is a confirmation of one's membership in the group (Stuedahl, 1999). Thus, it is an occasion that receives extra attention. One sees this in the comments of Bente (18) when she says: "If I get a text message I am curious. I want to be included, so, like if I am in the shower and I get a message, I, you know, have to read it. If I write a message and don't get a response immediately then it is like, you know, ehhh . . . "

The teens feel that accessibility is an important aspect of their social life. To be available to friends and to know what one's peers are doing is central.

Accessibility is an expression of their status and it is cultivated and developed.

To understand the background to teens' adoption of the mobile telephone we must also consider the economic issues of mobile telephone ownership. The pre-paid card system has greatly fostered mobile telephony use among youth.[4] It eliminates an oft-cited concern of parents that the teens will abuse their telephone privileges and run up unexpectedly large bills that the parents will have to pay. Often, but not always, the teens themselves are responsible for buying their own pre-paid cards.[5]

The marginal economic situation of the teens means that they must be frugal in their telephone use. When asked what she considered the biggest social problem with mobile telephony, Erika (17) responded simply, "It is way too expensive."

Teens' straitened circumstances also make them acutely aware of costs and alternatives. Hence there is some attraction to the notion of having a standard subscription, since the need constantly to buy pre-paid cards is circumvented.

ODA (18):  I have a standard subscription because I use the telephone a lot both for calling and for text messages, so I would use up three pre-paid cards a month. It is a lot easier, and cheaper, for me to have a normal subscription.[6]

This thriftiness has, in turn, supported the popularization of SMS text messages because they are unit priced and in many situations are cheaper than a telephone call, particularly since a conversation often gets prolonged.[7] This is reflected in the comments of Nora (18), "a little message is a lot cheaper to send," and Rita (18), "it is so expensive to call

---

[4] In this system one pays beforehand for telephone access. When the allotted sum has been consumed, one cannot call out to other (non-emergency) numbers. One can, however, continue to receive calls and text messages for a certain period, which varies by operator. The "card" refers to the card upon which the access number is printed. This is the physical object that is purchased, which in turn activates the individual's account.

[5] This is quite age determined, in that younger teens often receive support from their parents whereas older teens must pay for their own telephone use (Ling, 2000a).

[6] With a standard subscription one pays a fixed rate per month in exchange for a lower per minute price.

[7] Originally the system was free. However, when it suddenly gained popularity in September 1998 the traffic threatened to overwhelm the normal mobile voice system. It was at this point that the tariffing system was established. Currently an SMS message costs slightly less than US$0.20. By contrast a standard telephone call from a mobile telephone with a pre-paid card costs between US$0.25 and US$0.90 per minute depending on the time of day and the type of telephone being called.

with a mobile telephone, it is not worth doing it." The same theme arises in the comments of another informant.

ARNE (17): I start using SMS when I have only a little money left on my card. When I have a lot of money on my card, I call. When it is down to 7 kroner (US$1.00) then I start using messages.

As indicated, pricing would seem to be a great spur to SMS in mobile-to-mobile interaction. It is about two to three times more expensive to call a traditional fixed telephone from one's mobile telephone than to call another mobile in the same network. Thus, teens' growing access to mobile telephones along with the high price associated with calling a fixed telephone have served to establish the mobile telephone as a parallel communication system.[8]

MOBILE "HAVES" AND MOBILE "HAVE NOTS" Ownership of a mobile telephone is very much related to being in contact with one's friends and knowing what is happening at a given moment. In the words of one boy, "It is stressful not to have my mobile telephone because I don't know what is happening" (Arne, 17). A girl said, "When you are going to meet somebody you have to get hold of them and most people do not just sit at home every single day so it pays to have a mobile telephone" (Erika, 17). Yet another noted:

NORA (18): It is practical to be available because you do not miss anything. It is also practical that others are available; at any rate it is irritating not to be able reach people when you want to reach them and get them involved in something. It is very irritating.

The opposite side of this issue is those who are without mobile communication.

ODA (18): I have a friend [without a mobile telephone] who lives an hour and a half away, so you cannot get in touch with her either at home or at work you know. If you want to get a message to her then it is a big problem. It is the same with me if I don't have a telephone with me.

It also emerged that Oda did not have a valid pre-paid card and was unable to send SMS messages. Thus, she had fallen out of circulation.

---

[8] It is also more expensive to call from a mobile telephone to another that is in a competing operator's network. This prompted one respondent to note that he has "Telenor" friends and "Netcom" friends, that is, friends determined by the mobile telephone operator with which they have a subscription.

She noted, "Nobody bothers sending me text messages because my card is empty and I cannot answer."

ACCESS AND THE TRADITIONAL TELEPHONE    One might answer that the traditional fixed telephone can also be seen as a way to manage accessibility. This suggestion is out-moded, at least in the eyes of some informants. According to one girl, "Nobody sits at home and waits for the [fixed] phone to ring" (Ida, 18). Another noted, "To get in touch you have to call their mobile phone" (Erika, 17). To a certain degree, the teens had replaced the system of fixed telephony with that of a mobile system of interaction. There was even the suggestion that one is unreachable via the traditional fixed telephony system. One girl said, "A lot of my friends only have my mobile telephone number.... Generally you have more control if you have a mobile telephone because your friends can call you all the time. You are more accessible then" (Oda, 18). Another noted:

ERIKA (17): I think that the mobile telephone is most important in relation to my friendship network because I have the memory full of phone numbers and that is only mobile phone numbers. I could not get in touch with my friends at their home phones.

COMMUNICATION OUTSIDE THE PURVIEW OF PARENTS    We have noted that adolescence is a period of life when one is perhaps least focused on relations with family and most concerned with one's peers. The mobile telephone taps into this in that it provides adolescents with their personal communication channel. As we have seen, the mobile telephone produces a communication network that is parallel to that of the traditional telephone but has the advantage of being outside the purview of authority figures. For some this was seen as a way to interact without bothering others in the house. It is also ubiquitous. One boy said, "If somebody wants to get in touch with me at night then they should be allowed to get in touch at night without disturbing my parents" (Erik, 14). The mobile telephone enables continual access. It is little wonder then that the technology has been so readily adopted.

This parallel communication enables teens to start to establish a life that is separate and removed from that of their parents. Although they are still seen as socially immature – that is, not completely competent at the tasks demanded of an adult – they are nonetheless in the process of establishing themselves in that world. The mobile telephone allows for that development in that the child controls the interaction and the messages that are sent and received without any monitoring by parents.

RITA (18): It is ok if somebody leaves a message on the answering machine on my mobile phone instead of the family's machine. I can call people who call; it is a little more private.

ERIKA (17): If I am not home and if I didn't have a mobile telephone then my parents would be clear about all the people I hang out with and if they [the friends] wanted to leave me a message when I am not home but instead put it on the telephone answering machine then they would have to be fast on their feet when thinking about what they want to say. When you have a mobile telephone then you have a private answering machine and a private telephone.

The mobile telephone also offers the ability to communicate while physically in another situation. For example, the informants were asked if they had turned off their mobile telephones when participating in the group interview. A common response was that they had turned off the sound but the telephone was still on. Thus, they were still available to their social network even when participating in another social event. A similar attitude was shown towards the use of the mobile telephone in school. Erika, whom we have cited before, said:

I have a lot of friends who work at night and at other times outside of school time. If they want to get in touch with me when I am at school then it is fine with me because it is boring there anyhow.

When members of the social network are gathered together face-to-face, however, they take precedence over the use of the mobile telephone and SMS.

ERIKA: If we are sitting together and somebody gets out their phone, then you are a little irritated. That is something you do at school and on the bus.
INTERVIEWER: Ok, so it is not normal to sit down at a party and write [SMS messages]?
ERIKA: Then you might say that they have low social standards.

Finally, the nuances of communication have advanced such that one can even exclude and snub potential interlocutors when using the mobile telephone.

ERIKA (17): If somebody I don't like calls me then I just press "no" and then they get the busy signal and then they know that it rang first and then they got the busy signal.

Here is the mobile telephone being used to snub people that one wants to avoid.

MANAGING ACCESSIBILITY AND THE MOBILIZATION OF THE SOCIAL NETWORK    The adoption of mobile communication can outstrip the teen's ability to manage social life (Ogburn, 1950). The high premium placed on accessibility can, in some cases, lead to an uncontrolled situation. This is seen in the suggestion that one can quickly mobilize help when in a threatening situation from a large social network via the mobile telephone.

RITA (18): If, for example there is some trouble, then it is a bigger problem; for example, if there is trouble then somebody calls all their friends and then it can be dangerous.

ERIK (14): It doesn't have to be dangerous.

RITA: No, you're wrong because then they call others and so it just gets bigger, you know. It has to be if there are a hundred involved instead of just two.

ERIK: Yeah, but it is good if twenty people are going to beat you up.

RITA: But the problem just gets bigger you know.

The suggestion here that the mobile telephone can mobilize broader forces is somewhat similar to that of Lien and Haaland (1998). Their work indicates that the efficiency of the system means that the social friction of traditional face-to-face mobilization serves to reduce the severity of such violence. By contrast, the fragmentary and point-to-point nature of the mobile telephone means that rumor can more easily spread (Shibutani, 1966). On the negative side, however, face-to-face communication affords a certain broadcasting efficiency, in that one can announce the event in a location where a group is assembled and thereby involve all possible participants.

Parties arranged in the homes of the teens are another type of social event that can spin out of control. The mobile telephone enables individuals to gain access to parties and exciting social events.

INTERVIEWER: We have the sense that the mobile telephone expands the area that you move in and the number of people that you are in contact with . . .

HELEN (15): That's true.

INTERVIEWER: . . . that you will be in contact with others who you would not normally be in contact with.

ANNIKA (17): For example, if you are at a family party and you were going to go to a party afterwards but that party is canceled and you sit there and say "What shall I do now?" So instead of just sitting there you send text messages to others and eventually you find a place you can go or a party or something. Or sometimes you go someplace and there is nothing happening and you find out that something is happening in another place.

CHARLOTTE (15): Last week I was at a party at my best friend's house and suddenly there were people who I had never seen before and it was like "Hi, how did they find out about this?" But that was surely the mobile phone because somebody heard about it and they called somebody they half knew and when they came, I had never seen them you know.

The informants saw the mobile telephone as the technology that enabled this to happen. Although potential partygoers benefit from the ability to locate exciting happenings more easily, the host can be faced with an invading horde.

GEIR: I don't see why people have parties any more because it takes off, there are tons of people who come and break things you know.

IVAR: It is just because everybody has a mobile telephone.

INTERVIEWER: But do you have rules, in your group do you make rules about how you will deal with this?

GEIR: If I wanted to have a party then I would have talked with my friends and said, like, invite just friends and get them to not tell everybody and not to really play it up so that everybody comes.

INTERVIEWER: How do you organize your social life then if you cannot have parties?

GEIR: You can have parties, but you risk that a gang will come and begin to steal things.

INTERVIEWER: Does it get out of hand because of the mobile telephone?

IVAR: Yeah, because there was somebody who called a lot of others, it is just people who call others they know.

This is the same dynamic described by Manceron (1997) in relation to the nomadic search for parties and happenings among youth in Paris. In that case the traditional telephone was used, but the emphasis on rapid updating among a social group is the same. Thus, there may be a type of social lag where the adoption of the technology has gone faster than the development of methods for controlling its consequences.

Having set the stage by reviewing the role of adolescence in society and having examined the impact of the mobile telephone on the desire for accessibility, we now turn to the three aspects of hyper-coordination. In particular we look at the functional use of the mobile telephone among teens, its expressive use and finally the role of the mobile telephone in the display of self.

### Instrumental use of the mobile telephone

The functional issues described here are the use of the mobile telephone in interaction with one's parents and the use of the mobile telephone in coordinating – perhaps micro-coordinating – with peers.

*Interaction with parents.* Informants among the "parents" group had several disparate ideas regarding the use of mobile telephones among teens. On the one hand, it was seen as a synthetic need, but others saw the device in terms of the security that it provided.

One mother doubted the need for the mobile telephone among teens. "I don't think that [my son] needs one. I believe that it is a demand that has simply been created. That is why I am doubtful. Is it really necessary for them all to talk with each other all the time?" Others differed. Echoing the outline presented in table 10.1, a common theme for these parents was the security that the mobile telephone provided.

ANNE: I have a boy who is 17 and is in high school and he has not gotten [a mobile telephone] yet but he can borrow one sometimes. But now I am thinking about a cheap one that suits his needs. Because he is beginning to go out occasionally now. He goes downtown and, it is not that he needs to call me or that I need to call him, because it doesn't matter if he has the mobile telephone with him, *but if something should happen.* He was someplace this summer, at a conference at the university, and he missed the last subway train from there or something. And then he could have called so that we could go and get him. We had planned that he would go with some others on the subway but they didn't make it. And they stood there. In those kinds of situations I think it is good to have a mobile telephone . . .

MARTA: I have a 17 year old and the worst thing I know is when she goes downtown. I am so afraid but I just have to accept this you know. But it helps that she has a mobile telephone because she can call if anything happens. It is not to control my daughter that she should take her mobile telephone when she goes out, but it is, ahh . . .

INTERVIEWER: For her safety?

MARTA: "If something happens, call home and we will come immediately!" you know. Because she needs to go out and experience Oslo. She has to learn about the world.

The teens had a somewhat different perspective. Still, much of the teens' discussion of mobile telephones vis-à-vis their parents revolved around the issue of safety and security. The adolescents recognized the convenience of the mobile telephone when it came to arranging transport and so on with one's family. There was, however, a certain ambivalence about the potential for one's parents to control them via the mobile telephone.

NINA (18): There are telephones where you can set it up so that, if a certain number calls, it goes straight to the telephone answering machine, for example if parents call then it goes straight to the answering machine.

ARNE (17): I do that.

INTERVIEWER: You do that?

ARNE: Yeah, when I am out on the weekend I do that.

INTERVIEWER: Who do you exclude?

ARNE: The family.

Another boy (Morten, 14) said, "I usually block my parent's number...
but then there is a lot of fuss when I get home."

When the teens see that it is the family telephone number, they refrain
from answering and make some excuse such as that "I didn't hear it
ring." This is a well-recognized strategy. It follows from the notion that
peer groups are important during this phase of life and that there is a
need to distance oneself from the older generation.

It is clear that the issue of control is in the background here. In some
cases the mobile telephone was used more clearly to maintain an overview
of the activities of children. This was usually the case with younger children. The teens knew of children who were still in elementary school who
had received mobile telephones from their parents. In one case, a 9- or
10-year-old neighbor was reported to have a mobile telephone. "She uses
it so that her mother can call her to come home and eat dinner. But you
could agree on that beforehand" (Marianne, 17).

There was a feeling among the teens, however, that this was not necessary. They felt that so long as one has a relatively small circle of friends and
small radius of interaction there is little need for mobile communication.
"[When I was younger] I was more in the neighborhood, I was together
with a few friends you know. My parents could just call the parents of my
best friend and we were playing there" (Rita, 18). The implication is that
as one's social life becomes more complex and the range of interaction
grows there is an increasing justification for owning a mobile telephone.

*Coordinating activities with peers.* As with the two-career parents
and as shown in table 10.1, the mobile telephone was used by the teens in
the micro-coordination of their affairs. In response to the question about
how often they call friends to coordinate, Arne (17) said, "I imagine that
75% [of my calls] are like that. You just wonder about where they are
or if they are coming or what they are doing or things like that. They
just call to hear what is happening. We call before school to find out if
they have left home or after school to find out what they are doing after
school."

The need for coordination is heightened during periods set aside for
social interaction. According to one informant, "On a Friday there are a
lot more text messages than on the Thursday because people are out and
need to find out what is going on" (Erika, 17).

This is the use of the mobile telephone for normal micro-coordination
of their nightlife. Since they do not have their own home telephone or
an office telephone it is the simplest way for them to get in touch with
each other. Both voice and SMS are used in this activity.

INGER (17): If you have a mobile telephone, you can change plans along the way. You do not need to agree to meet either; you can just call whenever you want actually.

INTERVIEWER: But how do you make agreements?

INGER: I don't know, you agree where and when you are going to meet and if there is a change you say that you will meet in another place for example, if that is easier.

ARNE (17): I usually just make plans by calling [on the mobile telephone]. "What are you doing tonight?" "I don't know yet." "Ok, I'll call you later."

INTERVIEWER: Do you call and ask if you can do something together?

ARNE: Yeah, for example today, when I am here, I can just agree with my friends that I will call them when I am done. It is easier than planning what you are going to do [beforehand].

This sequence echoes the logistical micro-coordination noted among the parents' group.


### Expressive use of the mobile telephone

Although the mobile telephone has an undeniable instrumental function, one thing that sets apart use among the teens is its expressive function, that is, as a device to communicate emotional preferences as opposed to more task-oriented information. The expressive side of social interaction via the mobile telephone is summarized by Nora (18) when she says, "[with] friends it is chatting, parents . . . call for something."

The expressive interaction can include things such as "chain" SMS messages, notes indicating expression of interest in potential boy/girl friends, various types of jokes and even a type of haiku where the message has to have exactly the maximum 160 characters. The teens report that the jokes often deal with sexual matters.[9] Again this follows from the teens' immersion in peer group culture where they develop knowledge about "adult" issues and the strategies they need to deal with them.

At a more abstract level, these expressive messages are confirmation of a relationship. It is a type of social interaction in which the sender and receiver share a common, though asynchronous, experience. Sending a message refreshes the contact between the two.

The experience has a concrete content such as a joke or a picture. In addition there is a meta-content; that is, the receiver is in the thoughts of the sender and when they next meet they will be able to base a certain portion of their further interaction on the exchange of messages.

---

[9] During the focus groups, for example, informants showed items such as "About one million are having sex right now and what are you doing?" Another girl displayed a graphic showing an erect penis with drops of semen coming out of the end.

The messages serve to tie the group together through the development of a common history or narrative. As one teen noted, "If you get a good message or one that is cool you often send it on." Thus, the sharing of messages is a type of gifting and it is a part of the relationship's objectification (Berger and Kellner, 1964).

There is also a sense in which the sending and receiving of messages is an objectification of popularity. The more popular one is, the more people one can send to and receive from. In the case of SMS, these friends also need to be mobile telephone users. Thus, those who do not have a mobile telephone are by definition outside the group.

In many ways, SMS is an updated version of passing notes. The use of SMS to exchange sexual images and descriptions (content) combines with the intrigue of who might have sent the message and to whom it might be sent (social network) to give the technology a strong attraction. It also highlights an important aspect of teens' life – the exploration of sexuality and the development of social interaction skills.[10] SMS messages can deal with areas of life that the teens are in the process of learning. Thus, they are an extension of the peer group, which is often where one learns how to manage quasi-illicit activities and where one finds help in defining the boundary between what is proper and improper.

*The social use of asynchronous discourse.* On an interpersonal level, SMS is an important medium for filtering communications; it also allows one to reflect while composing a message. In Goffman's terms, the indirect nature of text messages allows one to arrange "face," that is, it allows one to consider the effect that is desired in the message. One sees this in Ida's comments.

IDA (18): Then you do not have to use your voice, which can shout or break up. *You have to have time to think* . . . . You always use [text messaging] in situations like this because it gives the other person the chance to think about it and answer "no." If the person is on the phone, it is not always so easy to answer no. (Emphasis added)

Another respondent commented on the situation described by Ida as follows.

ERIKA (17): I got an SMS message just now. I had asked him if he could come and get me [after the group interview] but I wouldn't have dared to call and ask because that would have been a little . . . then I would have known that he would not have dared to say "no" even though he meant no, because he is

[10] The element of intrigue can be seen in the following message reported by one of the informants. "Hi, you don't know who I am but if you want to know follow the instructions carefully."

very shy and kind. So, instead, I sent an SMS message and that way I know
that he will say no if he doesn't want to do it.

Somewhat later Erika supplemented this interaction by saying that the
boy had an ulterior motive in driving her home.

[He] is, yeah, a little interested in me and he would not have dared say this to me,
I know that. I am with him every day and he hasn't said anything, but he dared
to send a message. That way he avoids confronting me.

Here we see the unfolding of a parallel interaction. On the one hand,
the rather irrepressible and post-modern Erika is sitting in the group
interview, but, on the other hand, she is negotiating both a ride home
and, in a larger sense, perhaps the initiation of a relationship with another
person. There are two points to be made here. First, SMS is being used
to manage the establishment of a potential relationship. Second, a point
to which we will return below when discussing parallel front stages, this
is literally taking place during the group interview.

Focusing for the moment on the establishment of relationships, the
informants provided the following comments:

INTERVIEWER: You said that when you meet people when you are out on the
    town you send text messages because it is easier than talking together. Is this
    when you are out in town?
RITA (18): No, this is the day after or something. If you have exchanged tele-
    phone numbers then it is a lot easier to send a text message than to talk
    together.
ERIKA (17): If you meet a nice guy when you are out and he gives you his
    number, then you don't know if he is a jerk and that is why he did it or if he
    is serious. So, you send him a message and then at least you know that. He
    also has the opportunity to say no.
IDA (18): Or if you regret it, then you just don't take the call or send a
    message.
INTERVIEWER: Don't send it back?
RITA: Then you avoid a situation where you have to sit and talk with a person
    that you really don't want to talk with.

The informants point out the advantages of SMS for exploring a potential
new friend. The initial contact is face-to-face. A part of this ritual includes
exchanging mobile (not fixed) telephone numbers, which are entered into
their mobile telephones on the spot for later reference. During the next
few days, one may contact the other using an SMS message.

There are many strategic advantages to this approach. It couches the
situation in a more careful and controllable context, allowing "time to
think," as noted by Ida. Noncommittal questions such as "How are you

doing?" or "Did you think that the music was good on Saturday?" mark the contact, are a signal of interest and test the other's sincerity. The informants indicated that it is important to ask a question during this initiation phase since it displays interest and identification. The next step is some form of access display, which either is an opening for further interaction or closes off its potential (Schiffrin, 1977).

An SMS message allows one to compose the text deliberately and perhaps confer with a jury of one's friends about the content. The message goes directly to the individual, meaning that there is no need to broadcast one's interest to the other person's parents by using the family's telephone. Another point is that one avoids having to deal with the fluster and embarrassment of a face-to-face interaction and awkward small talk with either the object of one's interest or his/her parents. Finally, the logistics of delivery are quite simple. Since the SMS message is not a physical object, unlike a written note, there is no need to see the other person, nor is it possible for the object to be intercepted by other friends or, for example, one's teacher. Thus, the interaction is much more careful and considered, which allows one to handle the situation with a *savoir-faire* that is unavailable in face-to-face situations.

If the other person responds positively, then one can take the opportunity to respond and perhaps move into more synchronous modes of interaction. The stately pace of the interaction also allows one to avoid "giving off" the wrong signals during the critical early stage of the interaction.

*The quantification of popularity.* The teen group was remarkable in that almost all the participants had between 100 and 150 names in the automatic dialing registers of their telephones. Many of the names were infrequently used but it was nonetheless usual to note the name and number of new acquaintances in this manner. It was important to the teens for the register to be full. It was far less common for participants in the older groups to have full name registers. This is an indication of their social currency. Like receiving a lot of SMS messages or a lot of messages on their answering machine, a full name register demonstrates one's social popularity.

ERIKA (17): I have received seven or eight messages from him today and so I have answered seven or eight messages, but that is not how it is every day you know. When I come home I often have a pile of text messages from the day, but it varies in relation to who you are in contact with and what day it is.

A participant in one of the older groups, who was a coach for a soccer team, described another variation of this. He said, "I had a team in the

Norway cup [a week-long soccer tournament] and there were four boys and they had an internal competition. They erased everything [from their mobile telephone name registers], and the one who got the most girls' numbers ... " Again, one sees the device being used as a way to quantify popularity.

*In-group definition and control of group boundaries.* The data show that the mobile telephone is one of the strategies used in the development and control of group boundaries, and that language helps to define a sense of group membership, particularly vis-à-vis the older generation. At the same time, the extraordinary networking potentials in mobile communication mean that it can be difficult for a specific peer group to maintain the boundaries of in and out groups.

The use of slang, that is newly created words used by a limited group, denotes the group as unique and separate from other social groupings. It provides the group with a sense of intimacy and in-group solidarity. Those who are outside the group either will not understand the meaning of the slang or will be clumsy and imprecise in its use. The use of slang among adolescents is particularly common because it allows them to establish an identity separate from that of parents, teachers and other adults.

When considering the use of the mobile telephone and in particular SMS there is an emphasis on homophones, cognates and abbreviations. This has part of its genesis in the somewhat difficult process of entering letters into a message,[11] along with the limitations on the length of a message. The messages also mark group boundaries. Since there is a certain illicit tinge to SMS messages, particularly those sent and received in school and those having to do with, for example, sexual topics, it is advantageous to camouflage the contents. Thus, those who are outside the group may not immediately recognize the sequence "CUL8R" as meaning "See you later."

*The mobile telephone as an element in the presentation of the self*

The final dimension of hyper-coordination is the use of the mobile telephone in the presentation of the self. The analysis based on table 10.1 does not specifically touch on this dimension since much of it has to do

---

[11] The alphabet is arranged on the standard telephone keypad with, for example, A, B and C on the #2 key. Thus to type "C" one must first be in text mode and then press the #2 key three times.

with direct unmediated interaction. In this dimension we are more concerned with the physical aspects of the terminals, the style of use within the context of various social situations and the culture that has arisen around these issues.

*Issues surrounding style and display.* The physical aspects of the mobile telephone were important for the informants. Having the correct style and type of device was vital in one's presentation of self. It was telling that, when asked about which type of telephone they had, several of the respondents were unwilling to show their handsets because they were too old, too big or unfashionable. One respondent, Ida (18), noted that she "was not exactly proud" of her telephone. A mother in one of the older group interviews said that her daughter refused to use her mobile telephone because of its size and vintage.

MIA: My 13 year old is allowed to use her father's, but she refuses. It belongs in a museum. It is two years old and one cannot be seen with it. I was on the ferry from Denmark with my two daughters last weekend. I said to one of them that she could call home and say that we would be landing at such and such time. "With that telephone? Are you crazy?" It was a point-blank refusal. She had to change the [SIM] card over to her own telephone. She would not touch the other one in public. She would have to hide to do that.

The informants were quite well informed about the newer models on the market. It was clear that they knew the models and their capacities and possibilities, though it must be said that the design and visual impact of the handset were important.

The size of the device is important in determining its desirability. It was common to describe the ideal device as being small. As noted by one informant, "It depends on what looks like and also the size. It is often the small, very nice mobile telephones that have the highest status" (Nina, 18). If the telephone is small, it means that it is not visible. "It is important that it fits in your pocket, that it doesn't stick up so that when it rings they know; that is not too good" Erik (14). Big unfashionable telephones are often referred to as "bricks" or "refrigerators." One can also see the emphasis on size in Inger's comments.

INGER (17): I have a real ugly Bosch telephone.
INTERVIEWER: Why is it ugly?
INGER: Because it is big and ugly.

Functionality is only a secondary consideration. One informant for example noted that he was interested in buying a new handset. Its technical specifications enable it to access Internet content via the Wireless Application Protocol (WAP).[12] His comments, however, seem to be more focused on the physical aspects of the device.

ARNE (17): I could imagine getting the [Nokia] 7110.
INTERVIEWER: What is that?
ARNE: It's the one that is coming soon; it has the roller on it.
INTERVIEWER: Roller?
ARNE: Yeah, you can page down, it's real smart.

This striving to have the smallest or best device could however tip over the edge and become vulgar. Having the most exclusive devices was seen as simply showing off.

Beyond having the correct device, there is a well-prescribed style of use and display. The placement on the body indicates one's *savoir-faire*.

INTERVIEWER: Where do you carry your mobile telephone, on your belt?
ARNE (17): Covered up as much as possible.
INTERVIEWER: Covered up as much as possible?
ODA (18): It is tacky to have your mobile telephone on your belt. It is not very cool to show off your mobile telephone.
INTERVIEWER: It is not cool to show it off?
NINA (18): I think that it looks dumb.
INTERVIEWER: Where should it be?
INGER (17): In either your purse or your bag.
ARNE: Or in your pocket.
INTERVIEWER: Why shouldn't you show it?
ODA: It's not that you shouldn't show it off but you look like the village idiot if you have it on your belt.

Thus, there is a fine balance to be struck. One must be savvy in terms of the appropriate models and styles. Further, one needs to know the appropriate way to carry the device and where to include it in one's dress. Finally, one needs to know the line beyond which expensive devices are seen as being conspicuous display.

*The culture of concealed use.* Another issue here is the facility with which one uses the mobile telephone in other social situations. Apart from social activities where one is focusing on the face-to-face interaction, i.e. intimate discussions with friends, it was acceptable to use the mobile telephone in most social situations. In some situations, such as in the theater or on other more formal occasions, it was felt that it was more discreet to turn off the sound.

---

[12] This technology allows for the more efficient downloading of material from the Internet, including e-mail.

School is another place where it was felt that one could use the mobile telephone so long as the sound was turned off and one was not observed using the device. However, given the slightly illicit nature of the mobile telephone in school, it is not surprising that the informants described a set of methods with which to conceal the use of the mobile telephone. Informants equated the use of the mobile telephone to pass notes, pool information and other quasi-illicit activities.

During school the informants noted that they used text messages because the sound for the handset could be turned off and thus not arouse suspicion. The mobile telephone was seen as being a better medium than traditional paper-based notes. "It is no use passing notes because they see it immediately. However, they cannot see if you have your mobile telephone in your pocket for example" (Ola, 14).

There is, however, a type of judgment involved in deciding how much attention to pay to "front-stage" activities. Use of the mobile telephone in the context of other situations is not something that is done only by teens. This aspect of the mobile telephone has been a part of its profile from the very beginning of its popularization (Ling, 1998).

We have already reported on Erika's management of two parallel activities: participation in the group interview and interaction with her potential new boy friend. In Goffman's argot, she was operating on parallel front stages that were to some extent mutually exclusive (Goffman, 1959, p. 139; Ling, 1998). When she was involved in situation A, those in situation B were not active. Here, via SMS, this girl was hopping in and out of the face-to-face interaction occasionally in order to negotiate the second interaction.

This situation underscores the difference between the use of voice mobile telephony and SMS. With synchronous voice telephony, one must pay attention as the event unfolds. One can only with difficulty and with the forbearance of others have a telephone conversation "on the front stage" (Goffman, 1971).[13]

By contrast, SMS enables one to operate on the front stage although one must also be conscious of the small-scale boundaries between the front and the back stage. Thus, in situations where it is illicit to use a mobile telephone, such as during school, the areas that are out of the direct sight of the teacher become, in effect, the back stage, or perhaps even a parallel front stage. These small spaces under the desk, in one's pocket or in one's purse allow for the manipulation of the mobile telephone. This in turn allows for parallel communication, be it instrumental or expressive.

---

[13] In addition to the exchange of SMS messages during the group interview, Erika even managed a short telephone call with her potential paramour. In this case she asked permission of the others to accept a call from him.

One's street credibility is threatened if one is so clumsy as to be caught. In fact, friends who are not in class report that they call others sitting in class in order to make their telephones ring, resulting at worst in the confiscation of the individual's telephone until his or her parents come to school to retrieve it. This in effect enforces the rule that one must turn off the ringer for one's mobile telephone while in school. It also describes the covert nature of the device.

## Conclusion

Table 10.1 showed a general framework for analysis and highlighted our interest in examining the role of instrumental and expressive communication among various social groups. At the most basic level the mobile telephone was used for security. This was often an issue for elderly respondents. Coordination was a more common theme for active adults, especially two-career parents. We have called this type of interaction micro-coordination.

We also found a major shift among teens and their use of the telephone. In this case, in addition to instrumental use, they have adopted the expressive use of the device and used it in the social presentation of self. This leads us to call their use hyper-coordination. This adoption of technology follows from their specific life stage. The telephone is a logical tool for teens because they are in a situation in which they desire access to peers and yet wish to distance themselves, to a certain degree, from their parents. Other advantages are that it offers them new ways to develop intimate relationships and to remain abreast of social life.

Regarding future developments, table 10.2 extends table 10.1 to include the potential ability to access information from third-party sources, for example databases with relatively fixed information as opposed to persons. This potential lies in the development of systems such as WAP and the third-generation mobile telephones now being developed. It follows that various coordination functions can be carried over to

Table 10.2 *Future forms of interaction via the mobile telephone*

|  | Intimate/primary | Secondary | Remote | Third-party information |
|---|---|---|---|---|
| Instrumental | Security | | Security | |
| | Coordination | Coordination | Coordination | Coordination |
| Expressive | Social interaction | Social interaction | Social interaction | |
| | Gaming | Gaming | Gaming | Gaming |

mobile interaction with, for example, bus schedules and other types of databases.

In addition, the technology will likely support real-time chat and many types of games that are currently (or soon will be) available on the Internet. Thus, social interaction will be carried out via various servers that allow one to establish friendships and engage in social interaction with others outside one's immediate geographical peer group (Ling, 2000b). Gaming is also likely to be popular with virtual opponents, especially among friendship circles (co-located or remote) and possibly even with strangers.

In summary, we see among Norway's teens a remarkable move from the instrumental to the expressive. It is likely that they will take this approach to mobile telephony with them as they age and as consuming interest in peer groups wanes. As they move into young adulthood they will continue to be heavier users of the mobile telephone than prior generations, though the intense use of youth will be left behind.

## References

Aronson, S.H. (1977). "Bell's Electrical Toy: What's the Use? The Sociology of Early Telephone Use." In I. de Sola Pool (ed.), *The Social Impact of the Telephone*. Cambridge, MA: MIT Press, 13–39.

Beniger, J.R. (1986). *The Control Revolution: Technological and Economic Origins of the Information Society*. Cambridge, MA: Harvard University Press.

Berger, P., and Luckmann, H. (1967). *The Social Construction of Reality: A Treatise in the Sociology of Knowledge*. New York: Anchor.

Berger, P.L., and Kellner, H. (1964). "Marriage and the Construction of Reality." *Diogenes* 45: 1–25.

Bijker, W.E. (1992). *Of Bicycles, Bakelites and Bulbs: Toward a Theory of Sociotechnical Change*. Cambridge, MA: MIT Press.

Bijker, W.E., Hughes, T.P., and Pinch, T. (1987). *The Social Construction of Technological Systems: New Directions in the Sociology and Technology of History*. Cambridge, MA: MIT Press.

Calhoun, C. (1987). "Computer Technology, Large Scale Social Integration and the Local Community." *Urban Affairs Quarterly* 22(2): 329–349.

—— (1992). "The Infrastructure of Modernity: Indirect Social Relationships, Information Technology and Social Integration." In H. Haferkamp and N. Smelser (eds.), *Social Change and Modernity*. Berkeley, CA: University of California Press, 205–236.

Claisse, G., and Rowe, F. (1987). "The Telephone in Question: Questions on Communication." *Computer Networks and ISDN Systems* 14: 207–219.

Dohrn-van Rossum, G.D. (1992). *History of the Hour: Clocks and Modern Temporal Orders*. Chicago: University of Chicago Press.

Douglas, M., and Isherwood, B. (1979). *The World of Goods: Towards an Anthropology of Consumption of Goods*. London: Routledge.

Gennep, A. v. (1960). *Passage Rites.* London: Routledge & Kegan Paul.

Giddens, A. (1984). *The Constitution of Society: Outline of the Theory of Structuration.* Berkeley, CA: University of California Press.

Glaser, A., and Strauss, B. (1971). *Status Passage.* London: Routledge & Kegan Paul.

Goffman, E. (1959). *The Presentation of Self in Everyday Life.* New York: Doubleday.

——— (1971). *Relation in Public: Microstudies of the Public Order.* New York: Harper.

Haddon, L. (1992). "Explaining ICT Consumption: The Case of the Home Computer." In E. Silverstone and E. Hirsch (eds.), *Consuming Technologies: Media and Information in Domestic Spaces.* London: Routledge, 82–96.

——— (1999). Personal correspondence, October.

Haddon, L., and Skinner, D. (1991). "The Enigma of the Micro: Lessons from the British Home Computer Boom." *Social Science Computer Review* 9(3): 435–449.

Hägerstrand, T. (1982). "The Impact of Social Organization and Environment upon the Time-use of Individuals and Households." In L.S. Bourne (ed.), *Internal Structure of the City: Readings from Urban Form, Growth and Policy.* Oxford: Oxford University Press, 118–123.

Hogan, D.P. (1985). "Parental Influences on the Timing of Early Life Transitions." *Current Perspectives on Aging and Lifecycle* 1: 1–59.

Kahlert, H., Mühe, R., and Brunner, G.L. (1986). *Wristwatches: History of a Century's Development.* West Chester, PA: Schiffer.

Katz, J. (1999). *Connections: Social and Cultural Studies of the Telephone in American Life.* New Brunswick, NJ: Transaction.

Kellner, S. (1977). "Telephone in New (and Old) Communities." In I. de Sola Pool (ed.), *The Social Impact of the Telephone.* Cambridge, MA: MIT Press, 281–298.

Landes, D.S. (1983). *Revolution in Time: Clocks and the Making of the Modern World.* Cambridge, MA: Belknap.

Lange, K. (1993). "Some Concerns about the Future of Mobile Communications in Residential Markets." In M. Christofferson (ed.), *Telecommunication: Limits to Deregulation?* Amsterdam: IOS Press, 197–210.

Lien, I.L., and Haaland, T. (1998). *Vold og gjengatferd: En pilotstudie av et ungdomsmiljø.* Oslo: NIBR.

Ling, R. (1998). " 'One Can Speak of Common Manners': The Use of Mobile Telephones in Inappropriate Situations." *Telektronikk* 98(2): 65–76.

——— (2000a). " 'We Will be Reached': The Use of Mobile Telephony among Norwegian Youth." *Information Technology and People* 13(2): 102–120.

——— (2000b). "Direct and Mediated Interaction in the Maintenance of Social Relationships." In A. Sloane and F. van Rijn (eds.), *Home Informatics and Telematics: Information, Technology and Society.* Boston: Kluwer, 61–86.

——— (forthcoming). "Teen Girls and Young Adult Men: Two Cultures of the Mobile Phone."

Lohan, M. (1997). "No Parents Allowed! Telecomms in the Individualist Household." In A. Kant and E. Mante-Meijer (eds.), *Blurring Boundaries. When Are Information and Communication Technologies Coming Home?* Stockholm: Norstedts, 131–144.

Manceron, V. (1997). "Get Connected!: Social Uses of the Telephone and Modes of Interaction in a Peer Group of Young Parisians." In A. Kant and E. Mante-Meijer (eds.), *Blurring Boundaries. When Are Information and Communication Technologies Coming Home?* Stockholm: Norstedts, 171–182.

Mayer, M. (1977). "The Telephone and the Uses of Time." In I. de Sola Pool (ed.), *The Social Impact of the Telephone*. Cambridge, MA: MIT Press, 225–245.

Ogburn, W.F. (1950). *Social Change*. New York: Viking.

Rubin, L. (1985). *Just Friends: The Role of Friendship in Our Lives*. New York: Harper.

Schiffrin, D. (1977). "Opening Encounters." *American Sociological Review* 42: 679–691.

Shibutani, T. (1966). *Improvised News: A Sociological Study of Rumor*. Indianapolis, IN: Bobbs Merrill.

Silverstone, R. (1993). "Time, Information and Communication Technologies in the Household." *Time and Society* 2(3): 283–311.

—— (1994). *Television and Everyday Life*. London: Routledge.

Sobel, D. (1996). *Longitude*. London: Fourth Estate.

Standage, T. (1998). *The Victorian Internet*. London: Weidenfeld & Nicolson.

Stuedahl, D. (1999). "Virklige fantasier: Kibermedia og Goa Kyberia." In K. Braa, P. Hetland and G. Leistøl (eds.), *Netts@mfunn*. Oslo: Tano Aschehoug, 219–232.

Zerubavel, E. (1985). *Hidden Rhythms: Schedules and Calendars in Social Life*. Berkeley: University of California Press.

# 11 Mobile culture of children and teenagers in Finland

*Eija-Liisa Kasesniemi and Pirjo Rautiainen*

## Introduction

It took me exactly two weeks to collect these hundred messages. And that wasn't even all of them!!...I didn't really censor them. There are arguments and clearing up misunderstandings, stuff like that. But a lot of it is just "pointless" messaging, when the person you're sending messages to may be nearby or you've just been writing about something totally unnecessary just for fun. On the other hand, there is a lot of agreeing on when and where to meet and stuff like that. What can I say about them?! Your basic everyday messaging. Boring really. There, another hundred messages up. I didn't remember to write down nearly all of them. (This month I sent 283 messages and received about the same number.) The most important reason for messaging is us getting to know the boys next door and short messaging with them. Most of the messages are pretty unnecessary, but fun – I've really enjoyed reading them!!

Girl, 15, northern Finland, in a letter to a researcher[1]

It was 1995 when private individuals in Finland first sent short text messages with their mobile telephones. A text message is a short message sent from one mobile phone to another or from an operator to a mobile phone subscription via the short messaging service (SMS). The SMS, developed as a side product to other mobile communication services, was expected to remain overshadowed by mobile calls. The use of SMS, however, has surpassed all expectations. The 5 million inhabitants of Finland sent nearly 1 billion text messages in 2000 (Ministry of Transport and Communications, 2001, p. 8). SMS has quickly become a means to deal with everyday life, rather than a service for special user groups. A variety of value-added services are now available via SMS to manage everyday concerns. These include news headlines, TV and movie listings, horoscopes, directory and address inquiries, the weather, sports scores and dictionaries (Ministry of Transport and Communications, 2001,

---

[1] All citations in the article are direct quotations from the interviews, letters and text messages of teenagers participating in the research project.

pp. 22–24). In addition, official use in the form of transaction and information services, such as banking and flight or train schedule inquiries, is developing alongside entertainment and personal communication.

The SMS phenomenon, however, is not simply a story about an information technology solving information needs. It is a story about how an information technology becomes a communication device. Nowhere is this story clearer than in the way text messaging has become part of the everyday lives of Finnish teenagers. Text messaging captured the interest of the youngest generation of Finns in 1998, and it is now common for teens to have more SMS messages than calls on their invoices (Ministry of Transport and Communications, 2000, p. 27). Text messaging, like TV and the Internet, has established itself as part of the adolescents' everyday life as a teenager. Indeed, the use of SMS by Finnish teens is one important realization of a form of mobile communication culture. The study reported here explores this unique form of life in two ways. First, it documents practices of text messaging as it relates to the life of teenagers. Second, it identifies some unanticipated consequences of the formation of text messaging culture.

### Purpose

Our focus is text messaging by adolescents of 13–18 years of age with other adolescents. Teenagers exchange messages mostly with other teens even though they remain members of family households. The popularity of SMS in this age group does not seem to be affected by the apparent limitations of text messaging as a mode of expression. A text message contains only text, and the maximum length of a message is 160 characters. The messages do sometimes incorporate pictures or little animations, but they too are based on characters included on the keypad of the mobile handset. Despite its limited scope, a text message finds its way to times and places where a call would be impossible or at least unsuitable. Teenagers send messages during class in school, a text message unites two young lovers in the middle of the night, and a message sent by mom discreetly instructs the teen to come home from a party. Teens use short messaging to express the entire spectrum of human emotions. Through SMS, teens hate, love, gossip, mediate and express longing, even when the writer lacks the courage to call or in situations where other communication channels are inappropriate. The text message is the back door of communication.

I have to say that SMS is absolutely super! It saved a friendship of mine. A friend got mad at me and wouldn't answer the phone anymore (saw the number) and wouldn't answer the door. I sent her a message (and you always read your messages...). So we're still friends. (Girl, 16, eastern Finland)

Teenagers' communication with other teens stands in contrast to their communication with family. Teenagers send messages to family, parents and siblings to organize everyday life, such as agreeing on schedules or informing the others about a change of plans. The tone of teens' family messages is frequently practical: "I'm at football practice. Pick me up at 7:30," or "I'm going to a friend's house straight from school. I'll eat at McDonalds. Won't be home till late." The use of text messaging in families by teens is similar to the use of text messaging between parents and young children. The average age of text message users, in fact, is constantly decreasing as SMS becomes an important part of the everyday lives of Finnish families. Children primarily send text messages to immediate family and close relatives, such as grandparents. The function of children's messages is mostly communication for the sake of keeping in touch, and the messages are used to organize day-to-day life and to reinforce the family unit. The "nice device" and the "exciting messages" provide the motivation to write "important things" via SMS in the middle of a parent's workday.

RESEARCHER: How did it make you feel, getting messages during the day at work?
INTERVIEWEE: Well, it felt great of course, when your daughter sends you a message saying mommy, I love you, I took out the garbage. (Mother of 11-year-old girl, eastern Finland)

There are significant differences between the SMS communication of teenagers and children. These differences are in part due to the fact that children do not organize their daily life independently in the way adolescents do. The focus here is on the use of SMS in the life of the adolescent as a teenager.

### Data

The data are collected as part of research conducted at the Information Society Research Center (INSOC), which is a multidisciplinary unit aiming to create opportunities for information society research and teaching at the University of Tampere. INSOC has studied the text messaging of Finnish teenagers since 1998. The research on text messaging is part of more extensive research into the mobile culture of Finnish children and teenagers, launched in 1997. In the spring of 1998, a significant change took place in the research field. Suddenly, instead of talking about calling and changing color covers on their mobiles, all teenagers wanted to give their views on text messaging. The number of text messages sent quickly surpassed the number of calls made. It is important to talk about the messages in research interviews, but it is the messages themselves that shed light most effectively on the phenomenon. The research on teen mobile culture was expanded to include the collection of text messages. The text message research bank now has nearly 8,000 collected messages.

Six different types of material were collected between 1997 and 2000: tapes of the interviews and word-for-word transcripts of them; field notes by the researchers and documents of free-form contacts with interviewees; mobile communication journals by teenagers; short messages collected by teenagers; two surveys; and picture material consisting of photographs and children's drawings.

### Informants

Since the launch of the project in 1997, researchers have interviewed nearly 1,000 children, youths and adults from all areas of Finland. The interviews take place with individual teens and with friends and family. The duration of the individual interviews is one to six hours. The interviewees are recruited through several different channels: advertising in newspapers, the Internet, teachers at schools, day-care centers, directly from families, and the snowball technique (i.e. young people telling their friends about the research). Most of the teens offer to continue their participation in the research after the initial interview.

The qualitative research conducted at INSOC aims to diminish the gap between the researcher and the researched. The researchers treat the teenagers and adults involved in the research as *informants*, who are experts about their own lives, rather than as passive *subjects* or *respondents*. The young have the right to ask and get answers. The informant is seen as a co-researcher, as someone who interprets the material in cooperation with the researcher. The negotiation between the researcher and the informant helps manage unforeseen demands of the research context and fosters trust between the researcher and the informant.

The mobile telephones used by the teenagers are their own, not borrowed from parents or shared by the whole family. The mobile is a personal communication device, not jointly used by the family like the traditional fixed-line phone.

The data are based on material collected in the field, in cooperation with the informants. The researcher enters the everyday life of the interviewees: home, school, work or free time. The fieldwork consists of participant observation and thematic interviews. The research also utilizes material collected by the informants before or during the research period. It incorporates the following types of popular writing material produced by the young: observation journals, collected short messages with cover letters, and e-mails and short messages sent to the researchers. The informants took their role seriously:

Collecting messages has become part of my daily rhythm. It's been an interesting experience! I've written down every single message, I'm pretty conscientious! (Girl, 17, eastern Finland)

The adolescents over 13 collect messages by copying both sent and received messages character by character on special forms. The methods vary individually.

First I wrote the messages down right after I had got them and read them, but later I started to write them down the same night. In the end I would write them down when there was no more space for them [in the memory]. (Girl, 17, western Finland)

The textual material of the research is wide, rich – and indirect. Looked at from the point of view of source criticism, we are examining paper copies of digital text messages, their non-digital variants. The possibility of error is always present when messages are collected in this manner. SMS users cannot save text messages like e-mail, thus the current method is almost the only conceivable one. We considered videoing the messages directly from the display of the mobile, forwarding the messages to the researcher, and dictating the messages onto tape, but currently these methods are too laborious and too inexact.

The research group has developed a network of teenagers, parents and teachers who also contact the researchers on their own initiative. These teenagers talk about changes in the mobile phenomena, or send the researcher the latest chain message going around the circle of friends. This enables the researchers to keep up with current trends, particularly with regard to social innovations. The network guarantees that the research is up to date and flexible. Continuity in research relationships minimizes the number of misinterpretations: the researchers can verify if they have interpreted the teens' lives correctly.

Contacts between teenage informants and adult researchers pose challenges to the research process. During the research, the young have talked about using mobiles to supply alcohol to the under aged, for selling stolen goods, and for shoplifting. They also describe how they avoid phone bills and difficult situations caused by large phone bills. The child–adult or teenager–adult research relationship always contains the juxtaposition of *us* against the outsiders, *them*. In spite of this, some teenagers see the interviews as an opportunity to relate their problems: the researchers hear of mental violence within the families, of bullying in schools, and of the pressures of being different. Indeed, the contacts with teenagers can deepen into friendship. The researchers must regularly reflect on their loyalties; for instance, should they be loyal to the young, whose trust they have gained, or to the norms and regulations of Finnish society.

Some may see the depth of these research relationships as a problem in data gathering, but in fact it provided for a richer experience for the researcher and deeper understanding of teenage life. The research relationship, however, is based on mutual trust. On the part of the researcher, qualitative research requires a capacity for empathy. This does not mean that researchers should accept everything they discover, only that they should understand it.

The analysis is conducted from an *emic* perspective, using the informants' own classifications. The analysis is based on their set of values, while continually checking how researcher presuppositions may influence analytic interpretations. The qualitative approach to research emphasizes the relationship between the researcher and the researched. This relationship is not exhausted in a single communication and thus stands in contrast to conventional market and usability research.

## Background on the social context of Finnish teenagers

The everyday life of Finnish teenagers is characterized here in terms of the basic paradox of their social position: Finnish adolescents usually have a strong voice in matters concerning their life, yet they are financially dependent on their parents. Even after leaving school, many Finnish teenagers continue to live with their parents during their first years as a student. We briefly describe four cultural scenes important to Finnish teenagers, their mobility and mobile telephones: school/hobbies, income, religion and leisure. These scenes provide a glimpse into the social and economic conditions surrounding mobile phone use. The upshot is that Finnish teenagers' lifestyle is comparable to the hectic communication routines in the tightly scheduled lives of business executives.

### School and hobbies

Compulsory education for Finns ends at the age of 16, at which time adolescents can move to general upper secondary school or to vocational school. More than half continue in general upper secondary school, which takes two to four years to complete. From there, the student moves to a university or a polytechnic. The educational system is free of charge for Finnish children and teenagers under 16. The state, not the family, is responsible for most of the cost. Consequently, parental and child consumption is able to focus outside of school toward products such as hobbies and mobile communication (see Haven, 1999).

Teenagers commute extensively in their everyday lives because of their hobbies. During one day, the teen may have to travel, sometimes long distances, from home to school, back home, then to football practice or a dance studio, then perhaps to a friend's house and, finally, back home again. In Finland, the minimum age for acquiring a driver's license is 18, so transportation involves the use of public transport or the family car driven by a parent. Discussing rides to sports practice or other hobby groups is a frequent subject in teens' text messages and mobile calls to parents. Dealing with mobile communication during a piano lesson or in a dance class is clearly impossible but, even when the owner may be occupied elsewhere, the devices are on constant standby to register possible calls and text messages.

### Income

Finnish teenagers have significant disposable income deriving from part-time work, government support and a weekly or monthly allowance from parents. The government grants a monthly family allowance for families with children under the age of 17, most teens receive an allowance at home, and many have part-time jobs. Teens use their money for personal consumption on mobile phone services, clothes and hobbies. Finns' mobile bills amount to US$36 on average.

### Religious confirmation

The mobile communication of Finnish youth is linked to the institution of confirmation in Finland. Some 85 percent of Finns are members of the Evangelical Lutheran Church. The year that Finnish teenagers turn 15, they take part in religious courses leading to confirmation. As late as 1997, many parents held the opinion that teenagers had no need for a mobile, at least not before confirmation. A year later, the mobile had become a typical confirmation present.

### Leisure

Finnish teenagers' independence and control over their own lives are particularly apparent in their use of alcohol. It is illegal for anyone under 18 to consume alcohol. Yet most Finnish 16 year olds use alcohol at least occasionally. Although illegal, teen alcohol consumption is tacitly condoned by adults.

As Finnish bars and pubs admit only people over 18, popular meeting places for teenagers include youth discos, cafés, rock festivals and, above all, city streets and shopping malls, where thousands of teenagers may gather on a Friday or Saturday night. Some sit outside buildings, while others wander around looking for friends, or drive around the block in their cars. The people gathering on the streets and in the discos are typically over 13 but, especially in larger towns, late-night street life appeals to children younger than this.

The phenomenon of dating does not really exist in Finland. Girls go out in pairs and groups of friends, and boys go out with boys. Frequently, these girl and boy groups consume alcohol amongst themselves before the actual party. As the night progresses, girl and boy groups gradually mix. Girl–boy couples are likely already to be involved in a relationship, or at least aspiring to be: asking a person out is usually a sign of a willingness to begin a long-term romantic relationship. Girls make the first move as frequently as boys do.

## Text messaging culture: the case of Finnish adolescents

A culture of text messaging has developed among Finnish adolescents. The SMS phenomenon has generated its own terminology, customs and social norms. Finnish adolescents have developed their own vocabulary that marks the unique aspects of text messaging culture. They do not speak of sending text messages or short messages; instead, they use words such as *tekstata* or *viestailla*, verbs derived from the equivalents for the nouns "text" and "message". It is a culture, however, that grows out of the unique circumstance of teenage life. The contents of the messages exchanged by teenagers range from contraception to death. Teens send messages on weekdays to ask for help with homework, and on Fridays they use SMS to locate friends, find dates or purchase alcohol. In this section, we first describe three cultural practices: message collecting, chain message circulating and collective reading and composing. These practices demonstrate how text messaging culture is a collective experience that expresses adolescents' identification with other teenagers. We then explore how the incorporation of SMS into everyday life is an occasion for unanticipated shifts in the grounding of teen communication behavior. We describe changes in teen social networks, language use and communication formats.

### Message collecting culture

A text message is a digital group of characters that exist in a mobile phone for a short time, ranging from a couple of minutes to a few weeks. Because teens send and receive a significant number of messages, there is not enough memory on the SIM card or in the memory of the mobile handset to store even the most interesting of messages. Yet many teens manage to keep their most personally important messages in their mobile phones. These may be messages from the initiation of the current romantic relationship, anniversaries related to it, or messages to do with a significant friendship. Most commonly, messages retained in this way are the "first-ever" messages sent or received via SMS.

Like the oral tradition, text messages are difficult to capture: today's message will not exist tomorrow. This is a problem for the teens as well as the researchers. While some teens retain the most important messages on their mobiles, others have begun a movement to counter the perishable quality of text messages. Many teens copy their messages into calendars, diaries or special notebooks designed for collecting SMS messages. This practice of message collecting is an important part of text messaging culture.

Collecting practices vary individually. Some collect every message. Others opt for collecting messages that are personally significant in some way: messages sent by a boyfriend or girlfriend, or messages from best friends. Collected messages help the person to remember and reminisce, and thus return to the past.

RESEARCHER: Do you ever write down messages when you have to delete them, in a calendar or anywhere like that?

GIRL: In this notebook I have all the messages Aaro's written to me since we got together.

RESEARCHER: How did you come up with the idea?

GIRL: The phone couldn't fit any more and I wanted to keep them to read later. (Girl, 16, eastern Finland)

Text messages are also collectable items that teens actively compare and trade with friends. The text message collecting behavior of girls is much more visible and more organized than that of boys. Collectors, almost without exception, are girls.

I started collecting messages almost immediately I had got my mobile and my friends started bombing me with them. First I wrote them on whatever pieces of paper I could lay my hands on, but then I needed to get a notebook and write them all in there. My friends have been a big help in collecting messages, they often call me just to give me a few. You can also find them on the Internet. (Girl, 14, eastern Finland)

Boys have not developed collecting into a hobby as girls have. Their copying is an occasional activity influenced by message content that is personally significant. Girls, by contrast, reflect more diversified interests in collecting messages and more readily offer relational importance as a reason for collecting a message.

RESEARCHER: Have you ever written them down, if you've had to delete them for some reason?

BOY: Well at some point Emma sent me these poems. If I've had to delete them, I think I've had to delete one or two of them, I've written them down on paper then, the poems.

RESEARCHER: What kind of poems were they?

BOY: What were they now... there was one that went "When you look at me you seem distant, when you look at the clouds you seem close." Stuff like that.

RESEARCHER: Why were they so important you felt you had to write them down?

BOY: They just sounded so good somehow, so I thought I'd keep them.

RESEARCHER: Where do you have them now?

BOY: They're on a piece of paper in a drawer. (Boy, 17, southern Finland)

Another type of text message teens collect are "chain messages" circulated through their network of friends and acquaintances. These will be described in the next section.

### Circulating chain messages

Chain messages are fixed, unchanging text messages that circulate from one mobile phone to another. These messages are the most crystallized form of collective text messaging behavior. Chain messages are the successors to chain letters. Like chain letters, chain messages derive from other forms of folklore. Teens circulate short poems, song lyrics, jokes and wishes as chain messages. These messages often become the fad of the week until people get bored with it. In the tradition of chain letters, some messages promise the sender money or luck in love.

```
When love loves love, love's love doesn't know how much love's love
is loved by love. Send this message to five others and you'll be lucky
in love![2]
```

Some chain messages clearly are meant for mobile telephone owners. The content of such messages relates directly to the handset or use of the mobile. There is a teasing tradition that mocks any operator or device manufacturer not used by the sender. These messages also play on pan-Scandinavian humor themes.

```
I-am-GSM-virus "sweden" if-you-do-not-pass-me-on-within-an-hour-
then-your-phone-will-turn-into-a-pitiful-eerikson-----
```

---

[2] In the original Finnish, the examples are word-for-word copies of actual messages. Typing errors and fluctuation in the use of capitals and lower-case lettering have been reproduced in the translation. The number of characters utilized varies between the original messages and their translations.

At regular intervals, a wave of messages connected to operator folklore washes through Finland. The messages, composed in official style, "inform" the user about their subscription being disconnected and advise them to contact the operator's customer service.

```
Your subscription will be disconnected due to unpaid bills and its
detected misuse. For further information please call 98009491 Yours
NMT GSM invoicing
```

The most active chain message enthusiasts are 13–15 year olds. Older teens claim to be bored with chain messages. A "good" chain message among teenagers is one with "adults only" content, which typically has something to do with alcohol, sex or cigarettes.

```
YOU CAME TO MY HOUSE. I HAD A TREAT FOR YOU. AT FIRST YOU DIDN'T WANT
IT, BUT THEN YOU PUT IT IN YOUR MOUTH. YOU COULD FEEL THE FOAM RUNNING
DOWN FROM THE CORNERS OF YOUR MOUTH. AH, THE TASTE OF BEER.
```

Chain messages are a means to signal a break with childhood. The messages often mock childhood heroes such as Disney characters, Santa Claus and fairy-tale characters. Mobile communication covers the whole of teenage life, even the less polished areas.

```
You let me have it between my lips,I felt I could have all of it. I
gagged and blushed and almost choked. How strange yet sweet was my
first smoke
```

```
HAVE I GOT A POEM FOR YOU: fuck is fun,fuck is funny. some people fuck
for money. so fuck yourself and save the money [In original English]
```

```
Ain't got the muscles of Arnold Schwarzenegger Nor the body hair of
Mel Gibson nor the looks of Brad Pitt...but I lick like Lassie!
```

Popular operator logos – small graphics used to personalize the screen of a mobile – can serve the same purpose. Daring chain messages and logos are a hidden aspect of teen text messaging culture. They are not meant for adults to see.

There is no significant difference between girls and boys in reading chain messages, forwarding them, or storing them. The chain message does not seem to avoid the "nice girls" or the "quiet boys." Alarmed parents have occasionally expressed their horror at texts they have seen on the mobiles of the teenagers. Messages that may sound nasty or crude are part of the process of growing up. The messages are similar to stories and jokes told in schoolyards without the intermediary mobile. Teens use the messages to test their limits and step outside the role of child.

*Collective reading and composing of messages*

The most surprising feature in the text messaging of Finnish teenagers is the extent to which it incorporates collective behavior. Teens share SMS material in both concrete and symbolic ways. Text messages are circulated among friends, composed together and read together, and fitting expressions or entire messages are borrowed from others. This behavior stands in contrast to the property of mobile communication perhaps most frequently mentioned in advertising: its private, personal nature. With a mobile terminal device, one can be reached by others whenever it is convenient. The developers of new services describe these services in terms of customization and personalization. The developers' visions, however, concentrate on the needs of the individual rather than on the idea of a mobile community. The aim is differentiation, not unification.

Text messaging goes against this image of mobile communication as an individualistic communication channel. This is due, in part, to the way teens read messages to each other. Teens keep their messages in mobile phones and special notebooks, so that the message recipient can return to it repeatedly. Many of the messages are by no means disposable. The reader of the message may be the mobile owner or the owner's friends. They read messages to each other in bars and cafés, at parties and at school. The messages are read as a sign of confidence, out of curiosity, and simply to pass the time.

When we first came here we were sitting in the living room, and Liisa and Timo were fiddling with each other's mobiles. They were reading each other's messages and I don't know what else. It looked really cute. (Girl, 16, western Finland)

Lovers often indicate trust in a romantic relationship by allowing the other to read their messages. Friends also tend to go through each other's SMS communication. The content of an individual message often raises discussion: Why does it read like this here? Cross-reading is also an instrument of silent control, because the messages indicate what is happening in one's life and with whom one has contact. Many couples describe the reading of messages as returning to the good and bad moments of their time together. Rereading the messages serves to build and maintain the relationship.

RESEARCHER: Do you think your boyfriend and other people also keep the messages?
GIRL: Yeah, Kai's kept all of my messages. It's fun to read them, when you read your own messages first and then Kai's. (Girl, 16, western Finland)

The messages are also written together. Despite its seemingly intimate tone, girls' communication in particular is not always one-on-one. An invisible but significant "SMS consultant" exists between the sender and the recipient of the message. The consultant is either a close friend of the sender or a verbally talented and socially sensitive member of the group of friends, a veritable SMS virtuoso. These teens are consulted most commonly when the relationship is just beginning or in a crisis. The skillful writer helps the sender to compress the expression of their most significant emotions into 160 characters. This consists of editing the text and suggesting suitable words. Some girls report that the use of these consultants is common even in a quiet phase of a relationship with no current problems or high points. "I've shown my message and asked if it's right," states a 15-year-old girl. The consultant improves the quality of the message and, by working together, enhances the girls' group solidarity. Text messaging is a way to share relationships. Because the message is usually sent under the sender's name only, the recipient of the message is generally unaware of the number of people involved in composing the message and the time spent in formulating it.

The three practices described here, message collecting, circulating chain messages and collective reading and composing, are means by which teens enact their text messaging culture. Through SMS, teens collectively engage each other and sustain their teenage relations. The practices also reveal some otherwise unnoticed or unanticipated changes in the basic grounding for communication.

### Relationships

The communicative style teens enact in SMS may clash with their communicative style when they are not using SMS. This can have consequences for initiating and maintaining relationships. It may seem that an individual has two different personalities: a brave SMS self and a more reserved real-life self. A good example of this was a 15-year-old girl who, for a period of two weeks, kept sending text messages to the researchers prompting them to come and interview her as she had so much to say. The messages were clear and reflected self-confidence. At the time of the interview the researcher discovered a girl, quiet as a mouse, who locked herself in her room and looked suspiciously at the researcher, not wanting to answer most of the questions. The SMS persona and the real self did not meet. The girl had developed a habit of doing via SMS what she lacked the courage for in real life.

In another case, a couple meet daily in school, but professing love, or even admitting that they know each other, is limited to nightly SMS messages exchanged over the GSM network.

BOY:  But like every time we'd see each other, once we got the thing going again,
we'd never talk about it in school. In fact everything happened by SMS.
RESEARCHER:  Why would you not talk about the messages in school?
BOY:  Well, they were so, you know. I tried to avoid it too, especially face to face,
I didn't want to say it to her straight out in school or anywhere like that.
RESEARCHER:  Do you think you two had like different personas, like a school
persona and an SMS persona?
BOY:  Yeah, you could say that, yeah. (Boy, 17, southern Finland)

The boy never tells a girl that he loves her, but late at night the girl receives
emotionally laden messages filled with tenderness.

Finnish teenagers do not marvel at the technology permeating their relationships. They frequently acknowledge the mobile as an intermediary
member. Relationships often start with a text message, are maintained via
SMS, and can be terminated by sending a message. Some of the relationships end owing to lack of actual encounters or disappointment brought
on by reality. As some of the girls put it, the smooth-talking prince of
SMS turned out to be a frog.

### Language

The wider the phenomenon has spread, the more discussion it has evoked
in the Finnish media about the influence on the language and written expression of teenagers. Similar questions have been raised about the influence of e-mail. Opinions differ. Finnish teachers have been worried about
the negative effects that the free-from, often quickly written text messages
may have on the teenagers' capacity for written expression. SMS communication does not rely on traditional grammar or punctuation required
in texts written for school. Teens write messages in all lower case or all
capitals. Words are shortened. Inflectional endings characteristic of the
Finnish language are left out. If the message is difficult to get across in
160 characters, word spacing can be left out. With the spaces omitted,
each word may be capitalized for clarity.

We have been sending them with Kristo so that whatever you write you write
without spaces so that you can work them out for yourself later. Or if you have
to say something and 160 letters is just enough, then you just write it all together
and don't put in any punctuation or anything. (Girl, 16, western Finland)

Messages often bear more resemblance to code than to standard language. A text filled with code language expressions is not necessarily
accessible to an outsider.

The unique writing style provides opportunities for creativity. A mistake in one letter, a typing error, can produce a new term of endearment,

which may remain in the SMS language either for a short time or permanently.

RESEARCHER: Have you developed some kind of special language for your messages? If an outsider reads them, will he understand what you mean?

BOY: Ever since the beginning we've always had this thing that we don't put any spaces between words and we write every other word in capitals and every other in lower case, so you can see where one word ends and another one begins. That way you save spaces and punctuation marks. Now there's also this German u with two dots [ü], that's become kind of a mini smiley. It's only one character, so you don't always need to use two for it. And we abbreviate words quite a lot.

RESEARCHER: What words are they?

BOY: One that's really common is "gn" for good night and things like that. (Boy, 17, southern Finland)

Teachers presume that these elements will be transferred from text messages to more formal texts. They are partly right. More than girls, Finnish, boys have a tendency to resent official teaching of Finnish, and their texts are short and less expressive. So the negative transfer from SMS communication to essays written once or twice a month is possible. Our research suggests a benefit. Boys describe how they will spend 15 to 30 minutes composing a single message if they consider it significant. Boys' messages are not produced without forethought. They look for suitable words to encapsulate what they want to say, and they reflect on whether the recipient will interpret the content correctly. These concerns and activity suggest that their writing is not simply mechanical and device oriented but is purposeful and emotional. Indeed, boys would write even less than they do now without SMS and e-mail.

Teenagers' SMS messages frequently use foreign languages, apparently reflecting an interest in languages. The use of languages other than Finnish serves a pragmatic purpose. The teens substitute concise expressions from other languages for long Finnish words, thus saving space. The teens find it easier to express strong emotions in a foreign language, so they often use English terms of endearment and declarations of love. In addition, frequently used abbreviations, such as "C U 2MORROW @9," often derive from English.

*Personal text message repertoires*

Many expect adolescents' SMS communication to be performed according to a fixed formula. This interpretation of the text messaging culture of the young, however, is mistaken. The text messages collected by the research project reveal the variety of repertoires of SMS expression and teens' creativity in adapting their messages to circumstances. The violin teacher, for instance, receives a formal message whereas the mother receives an excuse that imitates spoken language. Best friends and acquaintances, however, receive messages laced with slang, plays on local dialects, puns and insider vocabulary. Girls and boys with romantic interests exchange messages full of vocabulary and expressions culled from romantic short stories published in magazines. Text messages are not uniform but instead divide into a variety of styles according to their content and form. Even so, the SMS communication of adolescents is evolving at the community level.

When we compare messages written recently by a teenager with ones written a few years earlier, the difference is apparent. The early messages are similar in style to letters and postcards or telegraphic language. The message begins with a greeting and ends with a signature identifying the sender. In its purest form the "postcard message" is a congratulatory message, a greeting that replaces the traditional birthday card, or a reminder that in its brevity resembles text on a small note card.

```
IWISHYOUGOODFORTUNEINLIFE,ANDCONGRATULATIONSONYOURSPECIALDAY!
LOVE,PETE
```

```
CONGRATULATIONS! THE CARD IS ON THE WAY BUT STUPID AS I AM I FORGOT TO
SEND IT YESTERDAY SO IT'LL PROBABLY BE THERE TOMORROW! SORRY.
```

```
remember the sprite
```

The descriptions "brief," "informative" and "pragmatic" constitute the core of the stereotypes regarding boys' text messaging culture. Boys have a tendency to state the essentials in a near laconic tone: "We're playing tomorrow at 12:00 pm!" "I DONT KNOW!" or "02:00 pm."

Teens make different use of the 160-character space. Girls' messages are full of social softening, extra words and emotional sharing of experiences. Boys tend to write only about what has happened, and where and how it has happened, whereas girls contemplate the reasons behind incidents and include descriptions of how the matter has affected them. Girls' language is nuanced and meandering. Boys typically do not utilize the entire 160 characters, opting instead for messages of about 40–50 characters. Girls, for their part, emphasize the fact that the space fills up easily. They speak of "padding material" that is used to fill up the message after the main point has been made. It can consist of chat, gossip or telling your friends how much you love them. Girls also criticize boys' competence to interpret SMS messages. Girls say they must write their messages to boys in "plain language" without too many compressed expressions, references and suggestions.

GIRL: Well, me at least, when I write to boys...they always need an entire sentence (laughs)...'cause they're like "What does this mean?"

RESEARCHER: Is that really the only way they'll get them?

GIRL: Yeah, they don't get them otherwise and then it's like...you have to write really properly, for them to get it.

RESEARCHER: What about when boys send you messages, are they different to what girls send? Are they as long or the same...?

GIRL: No they're short, really short. They're like "I was at home, didn't do anything." Period. They're like stupid, something that you might as well not send at all.

RESEARCHER: Why don't boys use all 160 characters to get their money's worth?

GIRL: I don't know. Maybe...maybe they can't be bothered or...

RESEARCHER: Do you ever get really long ones from boys?

GIRL: No.

RESEARCHER: Never?

GIRL: Well, maybe sometimes...but they don't use any padding, like we do. (Girl, 15, eastern Finland)

Text messaging, however, is much more interactive than memos and letters. SMS culture is engaged in adapting written text into a type of conversational interaction. This is evident in the extensive use of question–answer dialogue, which is a format that motivates response. A distinct custom has emerged around the answering of messages. Leaving an SMS message unanswered is almost without exception interpreted as rudeness. Teens assume that everyone carries their mobile phone with them at all times. The message sender expects a reason from the message recipient for failing to reply in time. The most often stated time limit for an acceptable delay for a reply is 15–30 minutes.

```
I'M REALLY STRESSED OUTAFTER SENDING TONI THE MESSAGE. I REALLY
SHOULDN'T HAVE!HE HASN'T SENT ANYTHING BACK. MAYBEIT'S OVER NOW. ARE
YOU ANXIOUSABOUT TOMORROW?

PatiencePatienceMyFriend! Maybe he's getting back from the fun fair
and hasn't had time to answer yet. But should I be stressed if you
are?:)I'm not.
```

Teens have devised a means to reply without incurring a charge. A text message costs about US$0.15. Since many messages require acknowledgment but not necessarily a full response, the message can be acknowledged by making a short free-of-charge signal call by calling and hanging up after the phone has rung once or twice. Since the caller's number will appear on the screen, the sender will know that the text message has been received. These acknowledgment calls have different names in different parts of Finland. The names translate as "prank," "alarm," "bomb" and "killer," to mention but a few.

Like other communication, text messaging is constantly changing. Dialogue-style text messaging is common, but it too has developed a number of variants. Sometimes messages expand into lengthy conversations or begin to use language similar to chat on the Internet. Reaction speed is important when messages comprise one or two words like chat room language. A Line in a chat conversation is like a sign-off for a speedy exchange in the corridor: "OK! It's a date! See you then!" Conversational SMS communication imitates natural discussion. It is contemplative, impulsive and meandering.

```
05:54 pm
How's your summer been so far? we had confirmation this morning.
Great time in the church uh-huh!!
05:55 pm
It's been ok. the bands getting a shitload of gigs this summer.
check HTTP://XXXXXX.XXX.NET
06:00 pm
Where do you have the gigs?
06:01 pm
Parties, Outdoors everywhere and in this club.
06:05 pm
Do you play your own songs
06:05 pm
Yea.that's all we do play.
06:09 pm
Well, don't break any legs or anything
```

The conversational quality of text messaging can be seen in the following example where a 17-year-old girl is asking her friend for a favor.

```
09:52 pm
COULD YOU DO ME A FAVOR THAT'S LARGER THAN LIFE: BRING ME ONE OF THEM
BEADED HEADDANDS? IF NOT, THAT'S OK, JUST SAY SO. DON'T FRET OVER IT?
09:55 pm
IF IT'S EXPENSIVE, SMS ME, OK? YOU'LL GET THE MONEY RIGHT AWAY, OR IF
YOU DON'T GOT ANY, BEFORE YOU GO. PLEASE GET ONE WITH WHITE BEADS NOT
YELLOW. THAAANKS!!!
10:02 pm
I DON'T KNOW, DO YOU THINK THE YELLOW ONE WOULD LOOK MORE LIKE REAL
PEARLS?
```

### New cultural artifacts

Text messaging has spawned new cultural artifacts that help individuals make the mobile handset and SMS part of their regular lives. These innovations reflect the practices and consequences described above. One operator offers a special SMS notebook with space for each message.[3] The notebook enables SMS enthusiasts to retain otherwise perishable material. Another example of how thoroughly Finnish society has been penetrated by the phenomenon of SMS can be seen in a guidebook offering ready-made short messages. It contains 160-character aphorisms for every conceivable situation. The paperback can be used to find an expression for feelings of love or disappointment, for example: "Sorry, I've got a feeling my keypad's locked today. See you around," or "Too many interruptions with you. I switched operators. This one listens without interrupting, offers free calls and favors nightly conversations. Sleep tight"(Laaksonen et al., 2000).[4] Finally, because text messaging is often used as a form of conversational interaction, with a strong expectation of a reply, a series of innovations in keyboards has taken place. A separate miniature keyboard that can be snapped onto the mobile introduces the touch-typing system familiar from computer keyboards to the mobile phone and thus enhances the speed of message writing.[5] Some companies have developed and implemented predictive text input systems. These systems guess the content of the message and offer ready-made words for the writer to accept or edit. The predictive text input system does not accept slang or dialect unless taught by the user.[6] The mobile of a lazy user "speaks" only standard language with no personal tones. Will these writing systems have an effect on the development of the Finnish language or perhaps influence the personal style of their users? Is it the device or the user that will adapt?

### Teens, text and mobile phones

Our research explores the extent to which mobile phone users and the use of mobile communication services shape existing culture and even generate new lifestyles. This study reveals how the mobile phone, and SMS in particular, serves communicative purposes. The data presented here strongly suggest that the mobile phone and SMS are not the primary motivation for SMS use. The most significant factor in teen text messaging culture is the content of the messages. This is most evident in the practices of

---

[3] See, for example, http://www.sonera.com.
[4] Examples from the book have been translated. See http://www.gummerus.fi/kustannus/.
[5] See for example, the ChatBoard keyboard at http://www.ericsson.com/.
[6] For further information on predictive text input, see, for example, http://www.nokia.com/phones/7110/phone/new/predictive.html. For information on T9 Text Input, see www.tegic.com.

message collecting, circulating chain messages and collective writing and reading. Each of these practices is organized around the production and exchange of messages that enable adolescents to be teenagers and to manage their unique social position between childhood and adulthood. Text messaging culture, however, is possible because of mobile technology, and the way teens work the technology into their everyday life has consequences for the quality and manner of their teenage communication. This is most evident in the shifts in social relationships, language and communication formats. These changes realize further innovative behavior, which may be contested, within the larger culture. This is evident in the development of SMS and mobile telephone accessories and the redesign of mobile telephone keypads.

The results of this study are bounded in important ways. These boundaries give the project scope but also leave many aspects of mobile life unexamined. The data are derived from a sample that is broad but not exhaustive. The results describe the main features of teen text messaging culture, but it remains to be seen how these practices generalize to the entire population of Finnish adolescents and adolescents on an international scale.

The findings reported here suggest lines for further research. Since teen text messaging culture has its own unique format, which has evolved with the introduction of the mobile phone and SMS, it is worth considering how this culture compares and contrasts with other cultural niches. In particular, the research looks into how the fact that communication centers on a single terminal device affects the everyday lives of people. There are numerous questions in this regard:

• Is telecommunication affecting the unity of families in a negative way?
• Does the new communication channel create a new sense of community?
• What is the relation between the individual and the collective?
• How is mobile communication integrated into the way people manage their lives?
• What type of mobile content do they use to add sense to their lives?
• Will a new mobile lifestyle create a new reality and environment alongside the old ones?

Generating new and interesting questions is only one factor in understanding mobile culture. Another problem is drawing attention to mobile culture from a research perspective. For instance, mobile culture has been studied very little in Finland. This should be odd, considering the high penetration rate of mobile telephones and the speed of its growth.

There is no single reason for this but many contributing factors. We conclude by considering why mobile phenomena have garnered so little social scientific attention in Finland.

First, the phenomenon is probably over-familiar and thus easy to overlook. It may be difficult to see what there is to research in everyone possessing a mobile, considering that at some point everyone in Finland also had a regular phone.

Second, the mobile phenomenon fosters contempt. There is more interest in belittling and poking fun at the phenomenon than in serious discussion of its consequences. Mass media stories offer rather shallow treatment of the topic. For example, they generally focus on how mobiles in trains and public spaces disturb other people. Every Finn by now *knows* that other people make "Hi-I'm-here-now-I'll-be-there-soon" calls. What has attracted less attention, however, is the real use of mobile phones. In public discussion, mobile use is frequently perceived negatively. For instance, unlike computers and information networks, the mobile has not been thought of as a device for the intelligentsia. In early 1990s, the mobile phone was perceived as an adult toy for the better off, a teddy bear for yuppies, as it was called. Though basic models have since become accepted as part of Finnish streetscape, many Finns now see the use of WAP phones, which give access to the mobile Internet, as a negative culmination of the consumption culture of the new decade.

Third, researchers are only now beginning to grasp the actual complexity of the field. Mobile communication intertwines with customs, the management of individual and community life, and repertoires of oral language and written expression, such as we have documented here. The phenomenon is primarily a reflection not of consumption culture but of the more basic communicative aspects of human existence. There is significant material to be developed that addresses the varieties of human communication and shifts in human existence. These are found in the subcultures of different age and social groups and the mobile cultures of different countries.

Fourth, mobile communication phenomena are hidden aspects of society in part because the content is short-lived and difficult to capture. Owing to wide media coverage, *every* Finn is aware of the fact that adolescents are heavy users of SMS. Yet, even most of the parents of teenagers are unable to say what it is the teens actually send each other via SMS. This study shows how this hidden aspect of life can be documented and examined, thus contributing evidence to larger societal discussion of mobile life.

Fifth, the phenomenon is unquestionably connected with consumption and industry. The data necessary to elevate the discussion about mobile life is not only private to the individuals but also embedded in the proprietary concerns of an industry. This presents numerous challenges for conducting research and the types of relationships into which researchers may enter. Our research is an example of a cooperative effort between academic researchers and business partners. The research conducted at INSOC is part of the National Technology Agency's "Telecommunications – Creating a Global Village" program. It is also a cooperative effort with the terminal device manufacturer **Nokia Mobile Phones** and the telecommunications operator Sonera Mobile Operations. The researchers' position between the academic world and the world of business has generated some ethical questions that the research group has dealt with by developing a simple code of conduct based on the general principles of academic research. First, the researcher should always have respect for the informant (maxim I: Explain the purpose of the research to the interviewees, and tell them what the results will be used for). Second, the results should be published as the researcher sees them, independently of outside influences (maxim II: Do not hesitate to report and publicize results that might be considered unfavorable by the financing companies). Seemingly negative results reveal important aspects of culture that everyone should be aware of.

In closing, it is worth mentioning that the phenomenon of mobile life has been expected to blow over like other fashion trends. The professional journal of Finnish teachers, for instance, warned schoolteachers about teenagers' mobile phones and other technical toys considered to be whims of fashion. The chief editor, Hannu Laaksola, asserted that "portable telephones and virtual pets are devices that simply do not belong in the classroom. Many schools have thus taken an inimical attitude towards them. If they are not banned completely now, their use will get out of hand and there will be more technological playthings on the way" (Laaksola, 1997). In the year 2000, it is difficult to find anyone fighting this losing battle. The mobile has found a permanent place in children's school bags and teens' pockets – in some regions, the mobile communication penetration level among Finnish teenagers has surpassed that of adults. Yet the role of mobile phones, text messaging and a mobile way of life are only just beginning to be understood. This study contributes by closely examining how people actually use mobile devices and services in their everyday life.

### References

Haven, Heikki (ed.) (1999). *Education in Finland*. Official Statistics of Finland, Education 1999:4. Helsinki: Statistics Finland.

Laaksola, Hannu (1997). Editorial in *Opettaja*, August 26.

Laaksonen, Annukka, Koivulahti, Janne, Mallon, Mark, and Polvinen, Tatu (2000). *Tekstiviestejä sinulle* [Text messages for you]. Helsinki: Gummerus.

Ministry of Transport and Communications (2000). *Case Mobile Finland.* Publications of the Ministry of Transport and Communications, 16/2000. Helsinki.

   (2001). *Tekstiviestimarkkinat 1999–2002* [The Short Messaging Service Market 1999–2000]. Publications of the Ministry of Transport and Communications, 20/2001. Helsinki.

# 12    Pretense of intimacy in France

*Chantal de Gournay*

## Introduction

In France the mobile phone, launched in 1987, developed slowly at first, before suddenly taking off in 1997. Since then its annual growth rate has been 120%, with the number of subscribers rising to 14 million in 2000, a little under 30% of the population. This success needs to be analyzed not only in light of the exceptional speed of diffusion but also because of the mass phenomenon (quantitative threshold) it expresses. For once, sociologists of technology are not asking the question: "What is curbing the adoption and use of the tool?" On the contrary, they are wondering: "What are the limits of growth?" of a tool that no one doubts, least of all non-subscribers, is destined for universal ownership. In many surveys non-subscribers mention a prevailing pressure to acquire a tool that they do not need but that they will eventually purchase.[1]

Excluding the corded telephone and, to a lesser extent, television, no other medium has had the same potential for universal use. Under pressure from other industrialized countries, the telephone became ubiquitous in France only in the 1970s, nearly a century after its invention. Unlike the corded phone and television, the mobile phone is neither revolutionary nor the harbinger of a new technological capacity. It merely reproduces existing properties of the telephone but shifts them onto new ground and into previously inaccessible situations. In contrast, diffusion of other, more revolutionary systems such as the fax and the Internet has been mediocre in France, despite the fact that they enhance the transmission of written communication and data that are more fundamentally

---

[1] Two focus groups, each composed of ten non-subscribers, were formed in France in September 1999 for EURESCOM. Even though they did not use mobile phones themselves, they were fully aware of all the possibilities offered by the tool because the people around them were subscribers. The majority said they intended to acquire one in the near future because "everybody's got one." "It's difficult to fight against the cell phone. You're old-fashioned if you haven't got one." "It'll be a must for everyone. It's like the Minitel for students: you can't register at university anymore without using the Minitel."

important to the economy and society. There are more mobile phones than computers in French homes.

Three properties of the mobile phone are noteworthy: reachability, immediacy (direct contact combined with voice interaction) and mobility. Immediacy is an advantage common to both the mobile and the corded telephone. Reachability is an advantage of the mobile phone but it depends on the cooperation of its owner because, if he or she is unavailable, the result is the same as with a corded phone. Mobility is unquestionably the distinguishing characteristic.

### Mobility

We should view mobility as a secondary attribute of the mobile phone. The extremely rapid development of this tool in the past two years – way beyond the group of initial users, professionals who traveled a lot – coincided with young people and women, a mobile segment of the population, identifying the mobile phone as a valuable tool for private use.

At this point I wish to point out that my earlier analysis of mobile phones needs to be revised. At that time I perceived "the emergence of nomadic trends in society" (de Gournay, 1994). However, current statistics on users' actual mobility show that the daily distance traveled has barely increased but the trips occur more evenly throughout the day. There is little difference now between peak hours and the rest of the day – people move about all the time, including the evening, for leisure and especially for shopping.

The success of the mobile phone cannot be explained by structural factors of economic or social change because the organization of labour, family structure, the transportation infrastructure and urban life have undergone no objective changes that coincide with the introduction of mobile phones. Paradoxically, for the first time in France, the trend towards national centralization and urban concentration (constant since the industrial revolution) has reversed. The probable consequence will be shorter daily trips because jobs, leisure activities and cultural sites are closer to home, even if French men and women are using air transport more for holidays, tourism and professional trips. We therefore need to look for explanations elsewhere.

### Thesis

We have learned that most mobile phones are used to coordinate daily interaction with family, friends and co-workers. Therefore, we will not examine the mobile phone from the point of view of its functions (its properties or the technical network) but we will compare the forms of communication and interpersonal relations it allows, promotes or dis-qualifies with the social norms, codes and conventions established for earlier media. The aim of this chapter is to describe the evolution of tele-phone customs that control use of the mobile phone, and to show how this evolution is likely to corrupt the goals, rationale and performance of the tool.

I assume that the mobile phone has enjoyed a favorable social context for its expansion, and that this context reflects a change in social behavior, not a change in the way social interaction, work or the domestic sphere are organized. Although the mobile phone may not be a technological innova-tion as such, it does offer a *format* that enables users to transgress codes of human interaction and to redefine, or at least individually to renego-tiate, the collective norms governing social and emotional relationships (courtesy, reciprocity, publicity/confidentiality of interaction, etc.). That is why the success of the mobile phone is based on its ideological rather than its practical opportunities.

This type of assertion is obviously valid only if one discounts a more convincing explanatory factor, the drop in prices, which propelled the mobile phone into the orbit of regular consumer products. But should not sociologists go further than the price argument (Carmagnat and Robson, 1999, p. 87)?

The normative redefinition is characterized by:

- circumvention of institutional authority in order to obtain direct access to people, in both professional and family relations;
- expansion of the private sphere and the occupation of collective spaces by forms of communication and rituals formerly reserved for intimacy;
- simplification of the formal structure of language when speaking on a mobile phone;
- reduction of the public sphere, combined with fewer possibilities for mediation and circulation of speech, owing to the generalization of an exclusive form of two-way (dyadic) communication, excluding third parties.

## Accessibility: a harbinger of the deregulation of civil coexistence

The mobile phone both revealed and triggered a revolution in commu-nication practices – similar to a "guerrilla" war – with everyone trying to convince those around them of the validity of his or her own ways. It would be futile to try to find any coherence in the expectations and prac-tices of mobile phone users; many studies on the subject show that they frequently contradict themselves, depending on whether they are talking about making or receiving calls. In particular, there is a contrast between the desire for omnipotence (attained through personal and immediate accessibility) fulfilled by the mobile phone and the refusal of reciprocal accessibility, becoming unreachable either by keeping the number secret or by systematically channeling calls to the voicemail box.

Parents give their children mobile phones in the hope of controlling them at all times, even in places that were hitherto inaccessible (school, the street, while traveling). However, those same parents, while traveling or on business appointments, refuse to be available to their colleagues or clients. Previously legitimate rules guiding individual conduct in interaction with others, such as the minimal obligation to be accessible to the public when engaged in contractual relationships, have become obsolete because of mobile phones. For example, a firm or public organization in France does not have the right to keep its telephone number secret (i.e. unlisted), yet mobile phone numbers are de facto secret because their listing in the directory is voluntary rather than automatic. As a result, whole categories of professionals have become inaccessible to the public because they are reachable only on their mobile phones. Deontologically this is unacceptable.

This insidious deregulation of public life reflects the increasing multiplicity of roles that everyone is obliged to assume in situations of communication. We can find an analogy in modern transportation. Today, most individuals are motorists, pedestrians and train passengers, and sometimes cyclists or motorcyclists as well. These different modes represent irreconcilable interests and incompatible attitudes. Individual motorists, if they were on foot or cycling, would consider themselves in the guise of motorists as their own worst enemy.

Similarly, the communicating individual adopts strategic behavior in the competitive world of communication. Take the corded telephone users who refuse to contact people on their mobile phones because they know that they are subsidizing the mobile phone users. (It's analogous to taxpayers who do not drive paying for toll-free motorways.) Conversely, owners of mobile phones, especially business men and women, who systematically reroute incoming calls to their voicemail box, are fully aware that they have obtained relevant information at the caller's expense.

The recent development of the strategic use of the telephone, in both private and professional contexts, has resulted in an increase in asymmetrical communication relationships. This asymmetry is significant because it does not relate to the symbolic sphere of personal relations only. The cost of a service or access to it obviously controls the relationship between service provider and customers. But a new challenge to the relationship between governor and governed arises if businesses can no longer be assured of unconditional access to staff during working hours, and if those same staff consider it illegal for their phone number to be publicly known (which is the case for the majority of mobile phone users). Then we are in full civic regression.

The fantasy of absolute individual freedom of access to communication masks the need for regulation, without which that freedom would be nothing but a theory. Such regulation exists in the transportation field, where a driver's license is required and the same traffic rules apply to everyone. With the current rapid expansion of communication systems, what is the acceptable code of communicational interaction? Not only has no such code been defined, the code that gradually evolved for the use of the corded telephone is being destroyed by chaotic and divergent uses of the mobile phone.

## The primacy of private life

In support of the argument that the popularity of the mobile phone stems from factors outside its actual usefulness, we note that, of the sixty individuals questioned in the focus groups, nobody mentioned the social or professional utility of the device. In almost all cases they spoke of its relevance to personal life, highlighting its advantages in terms of "ease" of use (compared mainly with the Internet) and the part it plays in interpersonal communication. Other tools were classified in terms of their "informative" value, clearly distinguished from communication:

*The cell phone is reassuring, it's to reassure parents.*

*It's so my parents' phone isn't busy all the time.*

*The mobile phone's not a communication tool. Lots of young people have one just for the image.*

*It's spread so quickly because it's easy.*

*I don't give my cell number to anyone at work. Elsewhere, I give it to everyone.*

*My parents [who live in the country] feel better about my having a cell phone. When there's a bomb blast in Paris, they immediately check.*

*The cell phone is easier [than the corded phone] to control [i.e. one can switch it off or screen calls]; the disadvantage is that one doesn't know where the other person is.*

*What is bad is we have the feeling they use it for anything. It should be kept for emergencies only.*

*In supermarkets it's a kind of tyranny.*

*Mobiles get on my nerves. It's a form of pollution. It's an escape from being alone. They're scared of being bored.*

Mobile phones were originally used to communicate during emergencies or to firm up appointments between people whose schedules were fluid and therefore required last-minute coordination. Today the mobile phone is used for routine communicating, mainly with spouses or other family members, just to "keep in touch." This shift in the role of the mobile phone – from a tool used in professional and emergency situations to a family coordinator – would not have been possible in France without an underlying change in social relations and a challenge to the legitimacy of boundaries between the private, professional and public spheres.

To be sure, the blending of the public and private spheres has, for a long time, been deemed an inevitable result of the proliferation of technological networks in the home. Futurology has, however, analyzed this phenomenon mainly from the viewpoint that the outside world would invade the home. Thanks to television and the Internet, the home would have "a window open onto the world."

Because of the mobile phone, this point of view has been reversed. It is a bit of their intimacy that people are taking outside the home, so that the public is put into the position of a "voyeur," involved whether it likes it or not in the secrets of households or couples, accidentally overhearing private conversations in public places.

We will analyze the blending of the two spheres as an ideological phenomenon, which is not reducible to technological developments but, more profoundly, challenges the legitimacy of social norms and institutions. The confusion of time–space references stems from a slow maturing of individualism, reflecting a transformation of the meaning and values attributed to social success. This happened independently of technological mastery.

### Criteria of social success

Traditionally, at least since the bourgeois revolution of 1789, the criteria of social success have been divided into four categories, at least two of which are found in the current paradigm of individualism:

- a professional career;
- cultural and intellectual qualifications ("cultural capital," according to Bourdieu);
- personal social network ("society life" to the Enlightenment thinkers, "social capital" to Bourdieu, "social networking" to citizens of the USA);
- family structure, reduced to its main purpose of transmitting a heritage (goods and moral values), which occurs only through parenthood.

Using these four criteria, an ambitious individual could climb the social scale without having to prove any personal growth, either emotional (love), spiritual (religion) or physical (health, sexuality, etc.). This point exemplifies the profound cultural difference between France and North America (cf. the Clinton Affair). Now, it is on this very ground of intimacy (the association of social success with personal fulfillment) that the change in behavior is taking place. Private life and professional life are entangled, and their values are cumulative on social and individual levels. In reality, both demand the same degree of personal investment and organization, without which the deterioration of one results in failure of the other. Psychoanalysts and psychiatrists are witnesses to this, for most of the cases of psychological distress they treat today stem from this interaction of professional stress and family tension.

Of the four criteria of social success mentioned above, two have become obsolete: cultural capital and social capital. It is precisely in the void left by these two values that the dialectic of intimacy has found its new legitimacy. In France, the waning of these two categories of social competition is related to the proliferation of communication media, which have undermined the role of those institutions that formerly guaranteed the transmission of knowledge and culture. Schools and universities have to compete with television and now also with the Internet.

These media have similarly weakened the role of the group in the control and legitimization of sociability. In the Proustian sense, social order is based on elaborate codes governing the cooptation of individuals by the circle that they are supposed to "frequent," that is, the places in which they are supposed to "be seen." Modern sociability, by making it possible to maintain social relations "from a distance," primarily by means of the telephone, has abolished the protocols of public life and thereby eliminated criteria for the evaluation of "social capital" (good manners, verbal skills, signs of refinement in dress, level of education, and so on). Using a screen or telephone, nobody is required to display the slightest social competence. This is an egalitarian result of distance communication which disqualifies the concept of "social capital," if not that of a "social network," for the former cannot be controlled by any outside judgment and classification of competence (such as taste or good manners).

One's place in society life is an exceptionally strong determining factor in the legitimization of social status (or class) in France (see Habermas, 1979, and Agulhon, 1970, particularly on the role of the public sphere: parlor, theater, opera, etc.). The current return of a lifestyle centered more around intimate circles is an unquestionable sign of the ideological decline of the bourgeoisie and its values. Like a pendulum, the decline of society life is offset, symbolically, by greater visibility of private life, necessary to fill a public sphere emptied of its substance. Not only has work become the only legitimate occupation of society, but the rest of the day has to be devoted to the accomplishment of emotional success at home, leaving no place for socialized activities.

Personal fulfillment is the only value as legitimate as work, and it demands the same attention and is displayed in a way that is visible to all. That is why the intrusion of personal communication in workplaces is now not only tolerated but even promoted as an indicator of the worker's balance and therefore of his or her performance. From this point of view the mobile phone acts as a medium for the "publicization" of emotional fulfillment. At work, in town, while traveling – every call on the mobile phone secretly expresses a message to the public: "Look how much I'm in demand, how full my life is." The phenomenon is, moreover, confirmed by statements denouncing the apparent absence of significant content in, necessity for, or urgency of most mobile phone conversations.

*The content of communication hasn't improved with the cell phone. It's always a little muddled, it's skin-deep contact via satellite, it's merely a fuse between us.*

*One feels uncomfortable* [listening to telephone conversations in public places] *especially when it's not for work and it's not urgent. It's just to say: Hi.*

*It's a way of multiplying contacts even if the conversation is shorter.*

### Mobile phone conversations: from formal to informal

Bourgeois (formerly aristocratic) society life externalized personality in two ways: through the body (appearances, clothing, gestures) and through speech (conversation skills, rhetoric of seduction and argumentation). In modern social relations, owing particularly to the predominance of reduced, distance communication between two speakers, not only has the obligation to "appear" become superfluous, but the content of communication is devoid of the formal attributes previously required in verbal exchange with the outside world. In other words, the constituent formality of verbal competence (sequential organization of speech, logical sequence typical of argumentation, virtuosity of eloquence and seduction) disappears with the decline of society life. We are witnessing the dwindling of bourgeois ethics and aesthetics of communication, both of which defined precisely, if not the very concept of conversation, then at least its art.

It is therefore not surprising that it is the content of mobile telephone conversation that is harshly judged by its detractors. In reality, it is the absence of "formality" in the conversation that they perceive. For this type of talk is hardly different from what one says at home where people are so used to each other that they no longer have to "converse" but only affirm an emotional presence (Pass the salt, please. Are you cold? What did you do today? I missed you. I love you.) But such intimate talk (between close friends, between "us two") carried on in public via the mobile phone seems emptied of its substance, it is the zero degree of conversation, the phatic proliferation of communication.

We are witnessing a "fetishization" of communication insofar as the mobile phone, through its personalization, is used not for interaction but rather for a "fusional" relationship[2] with someone the user is close to. One takes a part of the other person with one, sure of his or her availability for permanent and total possession. Women in Italy possess several private mobile phones, each devoted to pre-identified correspondents: husband and children, lover, friends (see Fortunati, 1998). Fetish-object rather than medium, the mobile phone has the ability to fulfill all fantasies of power and exclusive possession of the person close to one, such as one's mother. Whereas the corded telephone has often been compared to an umbilical cord, the most appropriate image for the mobile phone might be a child's teddy-bear, seen almost as part of the body, intended to reassure and compensate for all emotional wants.

This evolution is simply the continuation of a trend observed by Sennett (1974), who sees contemporary narcissism as a symptom of a society unable to cope with symbolic transitions or mediations between internal life and external life. This trend, which in France began at the end of the nineteenth century, is strengthened by the media, and above all by television, which has become a space for the exhibition of intimate dramas (psy-shows and reality-shows). Through public talk, this space allows us to redefine the status of the *obscene* (literally, that which cannot be shown on the public scene, but which is finally revealed by television). By publicly exhibiting personal problems, individuals demand that the community take charge of them (as witnesses). Through this act they identify their solitude by highlighting the inadequacy of their social connections to fulfill the role of mutual aid and listening – which brings us back to the problem of interpersonal communication.

This problem relates to a loss we can blame on the telephonic form of interpersonal communication, of which the mobile phone is the ultimate embodiment. How can one talk of oneself – and, above all, how can personal drama have meaning – if one is unable to use the language resources required for a narrative? When Habermas (1979) talks of the "subjective emancipation of bourgeois society" in the eighteenth century, he is referring precisely to the rapid growth of intimate revelations,

[2] This desire for fusion was expressed remarkably well by a user (quoted above) in the following spontaneous metaphor: "it's merely a *fuse* that we've put between us."

achieved through letters, private diaries and parlor conversations (Mme. de Stael asked her guests to think up scenarios as a game).

Using the telephone "format," subjects are limited to a discontinuous sequential organization of talk, requiring alternating dialogue in the form of questions and answers. This deprives them of the possibility of recounting their story. In other words, the telephone is a device ill suited to listening (and reserved for the *mise en scène* of talk, where one of the protagonists must accept a passive position); it is more appropriate for exchanging information. The poor sound quality on the mobile phone, constantly muddled by ambient noise, exacerbates the problem. Paradoxically, the place where subjects can find a substitute for listening is not with the intimate friends and family with whom they communicate, but on television where they are granted only a limited time to speak!

### Telephone sociability: from the dispersed social network to the inner circle

Areas of sociability in the modern world have been reconfigured by means of distance communication and withdrawal into the nuclear family. It would be foolish to think that the quality and perpetuity of social networks have not been affected by these dual realities. The sociological and anthropological theories that have governed the complexity of social links are insufficient for explaining these new dynamics, especially when they are based on the metaphor of a *network* borrowed from science and technology.

The current configuration of social relations (excluding functional and organizational relations) can no longer be likened to the image of a network because these relations are no longer maintained by encounters situated in physical and social space. They depend primarily on the use of telephony, which confirms a form of exclusive and bilateral relation. As soon as relations are partitioned into segments functioning as pairs, they cannot form a network because they are intransitive, that is, they cannot be switched to a third party who is contiguous. (Contiguity is spatial; therefore, except for functional relations, one cannot form a relationship without initial face-to-face interaction.) Transitive or intransitive: that is the qualifier that distinguishes social from intimate relations. I can be the friend of my friend's friend, but I cannot be the lover of my friend's lover, just as the relationship between mother and child is unique.

We also know that sociability conditions change when individuals move in together to live as a couple. The intransitive nature of these relations becomes evident because, if the couple splits up, common friends generally have to choose between the partners. By contrast, in traditional societies, the perpetuity of social relations withstands the rupture of intimate relations because the social group (whether a caste, class or clan) ensures mediation between those concerned, in keeping with the concept of a network.

*When friends divorce, it's complicated, you can't invite everyone at the same time.*

*We tried to keep our friends* [after divorce] *and in fact we lost them.*

*Everyone has his own life. We see each other less. We do not have this idea of a clan any more.*

*Nowadays ICT helps you to have a clear conscience: people keep in touch with family and friends with quick, brief phone calls, but this means there is an unfortunate tendency to avoid face-to-face contact.*

Use of a mobile telephone requires that telephone relations be exclusive, in the fusional mode of couples or the umbilical cord (mother–child). We are seeing a desire for closure of the relational network, reduced to a few close friends and the family core.

First, users wish to control the availability of their phone number and thus limit random connections with other people not recognized as special relations. This practice is out of keeping with the very aim of the telephone, which, through the directory, promoted "democratic accessibility," and violates the rules of the social hierarchy as defined by personal rank and status.

*It's better if there's no mobile directory because a cell phone is personal, it's more intimate.*

*Mobiles generate groups, they introduce social differences.*

Secondly, by wishing to eliminate intermediaries who occasionally latch onto interpersonal relations when they are in a shared space, the "chain reaction" effect of chance relationships is reduced. The best example of this is parents who remain in constant contact with their children even when they are outside the home. Claiming to care about their children's *safety* (another leitmotif in the success of mobile phones), parents develop a "paranoiac" vision of the community, reflecting a lack of trust in social institutions and in any environment other than the family. Teachers are suspected of no longer being attentive to or understanding children's needs. Children in the neighborhood have to be avoided because they are seen as "a bad influence."

*It's a prison* [of the mobile]. *I'm scared people will shut up and have no more contact with others.*

*What annoys me is that people speak loudly on their cell phone. They do not talk to their neighbor on the train, they use their mobile instead.*

The desire to control the exclusivity of parent–child relations, through the possession of a mobile, results in feelings of inequality in public institutions, which have always taken care to equalize individual possessions within them. How do children from poor families, who do not own mobile phones, feel when their fellow pupils exhibit their telephones? Formerly, the school imposed uniforms to limit social inequalities symbolically. And what about the discrepancy between pupils and teaching staff who, in carrying out their functions, do not have personal access to the school's telephone lines? (The same can be said of hospitals, where the medical staff share one telephone per ward whereas patients who can afford it have a private telephone.)

## Conclusion

The examples cited in this chapter enable us to assess the excesses of a medium that has conquered its market not by meeting the structural needs of economic and social organization, but rather by adopting a symbol appropriate to the modern individualist in civil society. The reader should not, however, see this critique of the mobile phone as an implicit warning of a crisis in face-to-face sociability, of a degeneration into "distance" sociability. Thorough research has highlighted how telephone and face-to-face sociability complement one another (Smoreda and Licoppe, 1998; Rivière, 1999). It even seems as if the mobile phone, by leaving room for improvisation, sometimes supports meetings or group outings because it makes it easier to contact and set up a meeting with an individual at the last minute.

More precisely, the critique expands upon a recent definition of sociability that diminishes the role of conversation as a fundamental form of social expression. Since conversation remains the form through which any disinterested face-to-face encounter has to operate, the lack of *formal* conversation in mobile phone calls prevents us from confusing the two types of relation. We cannot claim that these two types of sociability can be cumulative or even substitutive; they do not fulfill the same relational function.

Interpretation of social networks in recent or current sociological studies tends to reduce sociability to a theory of resources – systems of mutual help, trading of services, mechanisms of solidarity (Granovetter, 1982; Wellman and Wellman, 1992) – based on an updated model of the archaic community and described in the image of family solidarity. There nevertheless remains a disinterested dimension of public life, of a profoundly non-utilitarian nature that is not convertible into service delivery, which defies this interpretation of social relations. Conversation, like the series of images that people give of themselves, constitutes the very substance of this disinterested sociability at the root of modern societies. It would be regrettable if sociologists failed to question the evolution of this dimension when studying human interactions via the mobile phone and Internet.

## References

Agulhon, Maurice (1970). *La République au village*. Paris: Seuil.

Carmagnat, Fanny, and Robson, Elisabeth (1999). "L'Évolution des usages du téléphone portable." *Usages et services des télécommunications*, Actes du colloque d'Arcachon.

Fortunati, Leopoldina (1998). "Revêtir des technologies." *Réseaux 2, Quelques aperçus sur le téléphone mobile*.

Gournay, Chantal de (1994). "En attendant les nomades. Téléphonie mobile et mode de vie." *Réseaux 65*.

Granovetter Mark (1982). "The Strength of Weak Ties: a Network Theory Revisited." In P. Marsden and N. Lin (eds.), *Social Structure and Network Analysis*. Beverly Hills, CA: Sage.

Habermas, Jurgen (1979). *L'Espace public*. Paris: Payot.

Rivière, Carole-Anne (1999). "La Spécificité de la sociabilité téléphonique (dans son rapport au face à face)." In *La sociabilité téléphonique, contribution à l'étude des réseaux de relations personnelles et du changement social*, doctoral thesis. Paris: IEP.

Sennett, Richard (1974). *The Fall of Public Man*. New York: Norton. In French: *Les tyrannies de l'intimité*. Paris: Seuil, 1979.

Smoreda, Zbigniew, and Licoppe, Christian (1998). "Effets du cycle de vie et des réseaux de sociabilité sur la téléphonie: Etude sur le trafic résidentiel." CNET report no. 5518.

Wellman, Beverly, and Wellman, Barry (1992). "Domestic Affairs and Network Relations." *Journal of Social and Personal Relationships* 9 (August): 385–409.

# 13    Mobile phone consumption and concepts of personhood

*Dawn Nafus and Karina Tracey*

Contemplation of a mobile telephone,[1] or, in general, technology, evokes ideas about change or the social consequences of change. The implicit understanding in societal and academic terms is that technological innovation engenders a number of social ramifications. This thesis is not necessarily deterministic, defined as the notion that the nature of an object necessitates a given set of social relations (Latour, 1993). Sociologists and anthropologists alike have devoted themselves to working past the problem of technological determinism (Ormond, 1995; Bloch and Parry, 1989) in arguing that mere materiality plays no role in social constructions. In exploring a middle ground, we ask how mobile phones can be rationalized in concepts of continuity and change. This chapter theorizes how society's concepts of old and new, on the one hand, and individuality and community-relatedness, on the other, are pertinent to everyday use of material objects. We argue that all four components of these dichotomies rely on people to create and negotiate meanings for themselves. Our central claim is that the mobile phone acts as a means of providing material characteristics for these often conflicting societal concepts.

We focus on the social construction of individuality through mobile phone consumption. In fact, it might be better said that the English strongly associate the mobile with the perpetual reinvention of the individual.[2] The meaning of mobile phones can be correlated to Hirsch and Silverstone's (1992) conception of a "moral economy," whereby members of a household compare and contrast themselves with one another as well as with other households, thereby developing identities and moralities by

---

[1] We use the British terminology of "mobile phone" to refer to the wireless telephone.

[2] Our interview sample comprised an English population. We did not extend the study to the British population in order to reduce complexity rather modestly by eliminating some ethnic differences. This is not to deny the salience of a state-based community, but to avoid the pretence of shared linear history based around citizenship. Of course one could make the same case for "the English," because it too is in every way unbounded and contested like any social construct. We do not assume the practices of English people to be in any way about some reified English-*ness*.

way of distanced relatedness. Although relatedness is emphasized, distancing provides the space for rendering notions novel. Because we cannot assume the existence of individuality *a priori*, we argue not only that individuality contains ideas whose significance fails to be shared outside a particular milieu, but that it is socially crucial within that context.

By exploring social continuity, we do not argue that the uses of the mobile phone can be surprisingly conservative, utilitarian or "old-fashioned," or that our informants place social limits on mobile phone use to conservative ends. Rather our argument hinges on the reverse – that new uses of mobiles are being realized and, in the very act of exploring technological possibilities, old notions are made new again. This distinction is one of preservation and reproduction. In researching the problem of what constitutes novelty, we consider the terms upon which consumption decisions are based, and how those terms might change while conclusions about mobile phones may remain, on the surface, quite similar.

Our data are from two years of work on a three-year qualitative and quantitative study aimed at understanding how information technologies fit into the lives of British households. The research was conducted by British Telecommunications (BT). We draw upon thirty-nine semi-structured interviews conducted throughout the country.[3] Our concern with the problem of individuality was prompted by an impasse in our research. We detected a generational gap in how persons understand mobiles. Whereas one might expect a generational divide in the reception of a new technology, with young people more likely to be adaptive, the divide, in fact, works in reverse. Apart from teenagers (who are the only group to express real enthusiasm), feelings toward mobiles range from indifference to outright hatred of them, their owners and everything they represent. Indifference tends to be expressed by middle-aged and older persons, while fierce invective comes almost exclusively from the under-30 group. Actual ownership of a mobile mitigates these feelings only slightly. Most owners speak about mobiles only in terms of utility, but many under-30 owners will talk in terms of both utility as well as their unsavory social capital. In doing so, every effort is made to distance themselves from the latter aspect. Clearly, the mobile phone is not a technology that can be rationalized simply in light of its social ramifications.

This puzzle prompted us to look more broadly at patterns of consumption of other technologies and commodities, and the process of consumption itself. By considering the process of consumption – that is, how goods become a part of people – rather than how goods are utilized by consumers, we are able to see how "old-fashioned" approaches to

---

[3] The study is indeed UK wide; however, we draw on interviews conducted in English households.

technology in fact have everything to do with new, post-modern modes of consumption.

In discussing the "social life" of an object (Appadurai, 1986) such as a mobile phone, it is tempting to talk about it as if it is a primary locus of social relationships. Yet we cannot assume that the population focuses on the mobile phone as a distinct and unique object of technology. Our informants largely discussed mobiles as yet another object of consumption, not separable from the consumption of other technologies. They compared and contrasted different technologies and made implicit comparisons between things such as the mobile phone and the laptop computer, among other technological goods. If these goods represent modes of communication (here in its double sense), then each object is only a piece of a whole (Douglas and Isherwood, 1979). Therefore, we draw on informants' discourses concerning technologies other than the mobile phone.

Our cultural perspective is largely shifted by the contradictory ways informants frequently talk about technology. For instance, one of the striking perceptions of mobile phone use is that while, ideologically, mobiles are associated with particular classes of people, the practice of using them is construed as classless. The class associations depend greatly on the speaker – for some, mobiles are for businessmen; for others, they are for young flashy "ladies' men," and conceivably, although we have no data to support this, mobiles may be used for criminality and drug trafficking. In fact, the informants' expression that "they are everywhere now" and "everyone has them" could be interpreted not so much as a statement of their ubiquity or classlessness, but as evidence that they have been appropriated by the middle classes. These statements imply a vast range of ideology in addition to issues of economic hierarchy. In general, each class perceives a cultural dominance over other classes. Ubiquitous mobile phone usage is explained as practical and useful, while simultaneously, upper-class mobile phone usage is described as ostentatious and tautologous. Lower-class users might be described in terms of vulgarity. In describing persons in between the extremes, talk tends to turn to utility and their mass presence, particularly when talking about oneself. "It's useful for safety in emergencies," claim many middle-class women, even though they use it primarily for non-emergencies, i.e., to ring a waiting party warning they will be late.

There is an enormous conceptual gap between the kinds of people who actually use mobiles and the kinds of people informants *think* use mobiles, as well as a gap in how people say they use them and actual practice. These gaps, which are created ironically through constructs to protect selfhood, warrant close examination of the cultural meanings rather than emphasis on social divides. One of the few consistencies found is that mobile consumption is tied to selfhood, which is based on the diverse and fluid meanings engendered by mobiles in terms of class, generation, political stance, and gender.

The chapter is structured as follows. We first situate our informants in a theoretical framework. We then examine the moral economies of mobiles more closely, and outline some of the relationships made between persons. We raise disparate issues, from concepts of time to notions of kinship. We also emphasize that individuality is eclectic, and that commodities, such as mobiles, are linked in very different ways and affect the personality of the individual. Finally, we re-examine the generational discrepancy by arguing that the process of evolving into an individual vis-à-vis consumption has affected many, but in a way that follows closely how the individual has typically always transformed.

### Half full and half empty

As Hirsch and Silverstone (1992) argue, information technology poses unique challenges because it is both a set of artifacts to be consumed as well as a medium within which social relations are conducted. There is a rich body of literature on English kinship and social networks (Finch, 1989; Strathern, 1981; Firth, Hubert and Forge, 1969), which considers information technology's capacity as a social medium in depth, but we are more concerned with its direct relationship to consumption as objects. We find Marilyn Strathern's (1992) approach to the issue of continuity and renegotiation in the context of English kinship useful in looking at consumption. Strathern examines the process whereby persons elaborate various concepts such as "the individual" vs. "the family," and "natural" vs. "artificial," which are deployed in negotiations of kin responsibilities and identities. Rather than using dualities or either/or categories, Strathern defines opposites as two sides of the same coin. This extends to her view of social change. Change is constant and continuity is perpetually renewed; "the stable and the transient coexist in such a way that makes it possible to ask how much change there is" (1992, p. 10). Dualities and analogies may endure while their interpretations are constantly changing. For example, anthropologists might trace the English love of nature back to medieval times. Professed love of nature has a connection to the practice of gardening and pet ownership, equally ancient traditions. An interest in pets and gardening suggests ways of thinking about nature and the individual, but how those concepts are interpreted changes through history. MacFarlane (1978) demonstrates continuity and cultural roots; however, Thomas (1984), with equal rigor, shows radical change in the concept of nature. Consider that the analogy garden :: nature :: individual :: mankind

suggests only possibilities for interpretation; what lies within the colons is subject to historical construction.

Strathern's view of English kinship demonstrates how structure can generate conflicting notions of personhood:

> The particular relationship between parent and child generates the image not just of a son or daughter but an individual. The child that comes from its parents is not its parents, and this provides an image for thinking about the contrast between tradition and novelty, relationships and individuals. That the child comes from its parents prompts a counter interpretation – tradition innovates; relationships produce individuals. (1992, p. 14)

Strathern does the critical task of de-naturalizing the very notion of discrete persons. The fact that in English life there exists such a concept as an individual – a person who can be separated at some level from his or her kin – is not automatically self-evident. In Strathern's main field site, Mt. Hagen of Papua New Guinea, there is no such thing as an individual. There is no concept with which to separate one person from another; rather, persons are an amalgamation of different kin and trade relations. Although the English recognize that they act in different roles and capacities with reference to others, there remains a sense that somehow underneath it all lies a core person – an individual. In Hagen, however, there are only "dividuals." We mention this not as an exotic tidbit but to emphasize that, if the concept of the individual need not exist, then it and its cousin "relatedness" are concepts that are subject to change where they do exist. What is at stake here is not individual*ism*, or its North American cousin "rugged individualism," but the "fact" of individuality. Strathern places individuality as the "first fact of English kinship." Because kin relationships are deeply caught up in domestic technologies, the production of individuality itself must also be implicated in these objects.

Strathern's work helps us see that reworking of "the facts" is possible because each component of ideologies or objects is always multi-sided. It is up to the individual to choose the piece that warrants elaboration. As silent objects, communications technologies can be seen as breaking or enabling the building of kin relations. Because "the household" and "the individual" are multifaceted concepts, and the mobile phone does not directly demand a particular understanding of these concepts, the English are able to talk about the mobile as doing both the breaking and the enabling. Electronic access might be seen as "invading" the home, as in the common sentiment from mothers who do not want to have phone calls disturb their children's bedtime. This is echoed in talk of mobiles as a "metaphor for vulgarity" (Ling, 1999), in that they break up one kind of sociability by singling out an individual with a ring, demanding the introduction of a second context. At the same time, technology might expand the home by bridging communication between family members. This is best exemplified by the community of Saudis we interviewed who use e-mail and the phone to maintain the integrity of the wider household, consisting of people in many houses. Or it might be used to slow change in the household structure and keep it together for as long as possible; for example, the practice of giving children charge cards so that they would be completely unhindered in ringing home.

Mobile phones are more strongly implicated than fixed lines, in individuation for the mechanical reason that they are worn on the body; but this fact is not culturally significant. In the case of the community of Saudis, mobiles seem to be used to maintain collectivity. Their concern is to ensure that shared practices continue,[4] rather than to create personal distinctions – only certain persons may make arrangements for meetings between and within households. Nor does "individuality" necessarily have to be an exercise in freedom, as evoked by the term "individualism." In the case of English teenagers, individuality is itself a kind of collectivity, much more so than in the rather mild way we might talk about the "social construction of individuality." Individuality here is at its most coercive: mobile use stems from the pressure to be conspicuously social, just like everyone else. Peer pressure and coolness certainly have their place, but to be seen as a follower is equally a *faux pas*. Some teens aspiring or successful in conspicuous sociality might enthusiastically embrace mobiles, whereas others, sensing its coercive implications, talk of poseurs or insincere people. In all of these cases, different aspects of distinctiveness or relatedness are called upon, yet the notion of homes and individuals as bounded units is maintained. In order to account for how these become bounded, we need to examine the context in which these kinds of juxtapositions are made.

### Individuation and selfhood

In this section, we trace the use of mobiles through their moral economies. However, it is worth first considering whether primarily the individual per se or the household should be explored in our study of the reinvention of individuals. Households constitute an intensely shared material world within which persons individuate themselves; therefore we must discuss "the individual" in relationship to the household. Often this process takes place through juxtaposition of identities within the house, or

---

[4] As far as we know; we have not studied this community in any depth.

by contrasting one's own household with others. In one interview, an informant states: "I've got a friend that's quite willing for her four year old to swear because it's quite common knowledge in that house that that's what you do; I wouldn't allow mine to do it but then again mine will sit up and play with a computer until late at night." Hirsch and Silverstone suggest that it is households, rather than individuals, that provide the center for consumptive meanings because they constitute a moral economy. Silverstone is very specific about the notion of moral economy:

The moral economy of the household is therefore both an economy of meanings and a meaningful economy. The household is a moral *economy* because it is both an economic unit... in the public economy and at the same time a complex economic unit on its own terms. It is a *moral* economy because its various activities... are informed by sets of cognitions, evaluations and aesthetics internal to the household. These are expressed in the specific and various cosmologies and rituals that define or fail to define the household's integrity as a social and cultural unit. At stake then is the capacity to display, create, sustain autonomies and identities within it. (Hirsch and Silverstone, 1992, p. 18)

Mobile phones, then, are situated within the context of a moral economy. One of the striking aspect of mobiles is that, with the exception of cases of economic hardship,[5] they are almost always construed as under the ownership of a single person, whereas fixed-line phones are considered a "public" utility, even if the "publicness" is with respect to the "private" home. In the English case, the majority of mobile phone owners purchased them for their own use. This does not mean, however, that they escape the exchange of moral meanings. Mobile phones are actually exchanged between parents and adult or teenage children, and are nearly always used to help the latter establish their own independence. Mothers give teenagers mobiles as a kind of "digital leash" (Ling, 1999). However, this exchange also can be interpreted as a means through which parents enable their children to establish public personhoods, particularly since teenagers assign enormous weight to their social networks outside the home. The English consider development of a public persona independent of the house as inevitable.[6] Mobiles enable parents and children to check in with each other as the children explore new spaces. Parents claim that their teenagers' mobile use is based on a need for contingency or contact should an emergency arise, and the fact that they give them

[5] *The Economist* (1999) reports that, in South Africa, either the poor pool resources to acquire one or private individual ownership is in effect rendered public by hiring it out to others as if it were a payphone. University students in the UK practice similar types of economies.

[6] For comparison see Pine (1996): in rural Poland, the household rather than the individual establishes public personhood.

only to teens rather than to young children means there is an element of public development at stake. Just as it is possible in this context to be too young to wear cosmetics, so it is possible to be too young to own a mobile, according to our informants. This point was made clear for us when talking to a mother of three daughters, who would not purchase a mobile for her youngest two, but would for her eldest as soon as she started driving: "I'd like her to have one in case the car breaks down."

Similarly, in exchanges of mobiles between adult children and their parents, the negotiation of "help" works to maintain personal integrity and independence. These exchanges are still ultimately aimed at the establishment of new, separate households. Steve and Svetlana, a retired working-class couple, purchased a mobile phone from their son, who was no longer able to afford calling on it. The act of purchasing the mobile rather than receiving it as a gift preserved the integrity of all parties, but the underlying concern was the perpetuation of the son's distance from the family household. Through this exchange, they simultaneously create both distinct and related households. The son is not in the household, but only by virtue of the fact that he is part of the household.

In another example of how household exchange of a mobile phone promotes independence, one informant gave his mobile phone to his brother at university, having found it to be annoying. This informant decided his brother had more use for it, despite not having a fixed dwelling; in order to be socially independent, the brother needed a fixed phone number, rather than using resources that belong to parents or friends. With full adulthood, and thus individuality, comes discrete ownership over things. As these exchanges of mobiles imply, with independence also comes the establishment of a discrete identity, even if it is simply an electronic one. Therefore, it is important to note that, in cases where mobiles are circulated, it is usually to help establish that individuality. As MacFarlane puts it, the English are enacting their habitual "denial" of kin obligations. This denial is in fact a half-denial, originating in the medieval period and cycled throughout history – in the reconceptualization of man's relationship with God during the Reformation; in Enlightenment notions of rights and contracts; and in the production of nuclear families during the industrial revolution (MacFarlane, 1978; Thomas, 1984; Allan, 1996). The seemingly innocuous question of who is in and who is out of the household becomes increasingly difficult to answer when household exchange of the mobile phone takes place. The exchange between family members makes it possible to be in the household and out of the household at the same time. Thus, the category of "household" is losing its explanatory power because membership in a "household" presumes one is either in the household or outside of it.

In the absence of physical exchange, moral juxtapositions may take place with respect to calling others out of moral obligation. For example, a spouse who uses the mobile to ring home to inquire whether the other party needs something, or to warn of lateness, is not just being efficient but constructing him- or herself as a proper spouse. Mobiles can make one more aware of moral obligations, particularly when the option of calling is presented by owning a mobile but then thwarted by malfunction, as this woman expressed to one of our informants: "This [pointing to her mobile]! I am going to step on it – I have run out of call time an hour ago. I need to let my family know that I will be late and I have been trying to refresh my number for the past hour and I can't get through." In this case, the moral question is not only "What is the polite thing to do?" but also "What kind of a person am I?" This daily practice of maintaining moral relationships is incorporated into the idea of individuality.

Mobility itself can serve as blocks in the building of identity. For example, Steve and Svetlana use their mobile phone to bridge a gap between private or public identity. Although they have otherwise conservative notions of gender roles, Svetlana is considered the more public of the two, because she is taking courses at a local university and is active in their grandchildren's school. On the one hand, both see Svetlana primarily within the domestic realm; both claim that Steve "helps" her with the cooking and tidying. On the other hand, the mobile builds a bridge whereby Svetlana is able to maintain her ideological role "inside" while her practical role is "outside," because she can check in with others in the household at whim. Outside and inside, and public and private, are not zero-sum constructs: Svetlana thinks of herself as both out and about as well as central to her home. She told us she would never consider buying a pager, "especially if it was Steve who called and I couldn't get to a phone. I'd panic!" Rather than bridging the two worlds, a pager would make the distinctions between public and private more apparent. The reverse could equally be the case. Svetlana could consider "public" mobility as being in the "private realm," and that having a mobile could place her activities into the "public" realm by communicating her whereabouts and activity details. This is an extremely complex issue, however, which is subtly examined by Licoppe and Heurtin in chapter 7 in this volume.

We explored some of the types of negotiations that take place with mobiles. Notions of public and private, the meanings of kin obligations and the building of new households are all predictable spheres of mobile phones in connection with morality. However, there are some unexpected spheres, which suggest to us the sheer complexity of personhood as well as the multivocality of mobiles. For example, emotional attachment to the conspicuous busyness of mobile users can have as much to do with moral personhood as with social mobility. One teenage girl from a working-class family said that she was desperate to own a mobile so that she might become an upper-middle-class professional "like Ally McBeal." In the absence of owning one, she would ring her father's friend on his mobile for the sheer association with it. On a subconscious level, she is reproducing the wider cultural premium on gentrification. For her, aspiring to become a professional is a way of separating herself from her working-class family. It is also a way for her to think of herself as a moral person, and that she should strive for something "better." The mobile phone makes a statement about her identity and her relationship to her family by embodying the contrast. Her family is not necessarily denigrated in her making this contrast, since the ability to make things better for one's children is a powerful and legitimate ideology. Should she succeed in becoming a higher-class professional, conflicts no doubt will arise; her family accordingly may use the specter of the mobile phone as a lightning rod for contempt.

People construct themselves as moral persons in a broad and conceptual sense related to time. Some of the sociological literature implies that individuals would want to make their social lives efficient (Katz, 1999). Efficiency and the constructions of time that accompany capitalist societies are not notions shared cross-culturally. Rather, we argue that the mobile phone is a tool that enables one to be efficient by working through a (capitalist) conceptualization of time as malleable – spendable, wasteable, stretchable and contractible. In the example of the spouse ringing home to see what needs to be purchased, the concepts of morality and efficiency come into play. Morality, in the case of making arrangements, invokes a sense of "utility." In ensuring that time is "managed," the integrity of the discrete individual is reinforced. This social construction prompts one to believe one can control time; in fact, the possibility of incoming calls is a source of owners' realization that they are not fully the "manager" and that their newly expanded autonomy might backfire.

We suggest that the mobile phone is implicated in all of these negotiations in different ways: morality, efficiency and productivity, independence, and a desire to aspire to the upper-middle class. All of these constructs are moral constructs and, in the English case, morality is understood in terms of a core of self. Traits such as independence and productivity emanating from the core of the self, in fact, exist in relation to ideas external to the physical self. In a sense, the practice of expressing the essence of oneself should be considered as a Western social fact and not as an academic *faux pas*. The core of selfhood is made apparent primarily in the creation of new households. "He is on his own now; he's his own person," parents say. This core, however, cannot be built in a vacuum of abstract ideas, but needs physical, aesthetic and mythological embodiment. The mobile phone serves this purpose in its discursive and physical use, paralleling the multifaceted constructs of the self, and mediating between notions that constitute individuality itself.

Further, individuality contains a notion of discreteness and separability, but also an element of relatedness, which is particularly seen in practices of kin claims. The constellation of persons communicating via the mobile phone is significant in defining the self. Decisions about what kinds of person are allowed to witness its use and in what context further selfhood. The two elements of "self" and "related," although in practice born from one another, ironically threaten to counteract one another. Whereas contactability (relatedness) both impedes and enhances personal effectiveness (autonomy), mobility contributes to self-freedom and social breakdown. These issues come from notions of what personhood is, rather than from *a priori* mechanics of technology.

We have broken down the Euro-American understanding that individuals exist as bounded units distinct from one another, and emphasized the individual qualities of mobile ownership rather than treating mobile phone technology as a collective utility. We suggested the English are constantly working on building different kinds of individualities through moral economies, and that new households retain their continuity within the context of old households in the act of becoming distinct. This neither explains why those who are strongly anti-mobile are nearly exclusively under the age of 30, nor does it fully explain what is new and what is old about mobile consumption or about individuality. In order to answer these questions, we need to expand our view to informants' consumption of general information technologies.

### Multiple ways of consuming?

Daniel Miller (1987, 1988a, 1998b) maintains the theme throughout his work that individuals appropriate mass-produced goods to identity and create their selfhood. By translating goods from the sphere of alienated commodities into the domestic realm, individuals make statements about their identities and individualities and overcome the alienation of capitalist economies. However, this social patterning must be viewed historically rather than in ideological terms.

Two families in particular have managed to articulate their consuming process, and so we will compare them in some detail. They represent a shift in understanding how goods are related to the self. This shift echoes the broad changes in the shift from modernism to post-modernism.

The first household, the Steins, is a middle-class household and includes three adult children and multiple grandchildren living in their own households. Penny and Jim Stein are extremely methodical and deliberate when it comes to purchasing. One can trace how this premium on explicitness and rational decision-making itself transforms the types of decision made. The value placed on using old knowledge to generate new knowledge renders them extremely adaptive. They have no fear about new technologies, only reserved judgment. Their explicitness also gives them a reflexive awareness of how this process generates meaning and personhood: "You have to have some sort of forward planning otherwise it's just a day-to-day living, and if you do that, then you're finished. Our son is the opposite way round – children are different obviously."

One would think that the Steins would be perpetually trying new things, seduced by labels of "new and improved." Yet they are extremely brand loyal: "It's like washing powder – you use the same washing powder for years and years and years and then you think, 'Oh maybe I'll try something new.' But nine times out of ten you end up going back to the original product."

The Steins are not simply older people set in their ways, resistant to change. If their mobile phone provider were to change the quality of their services, they would not hesitate to switch, and they are vigilant in seeing if that happens. Their manifest conservatism has to do with the value they see in deepened knowledge of a particular product over time. In being smart consumers, they base the value of a trusted brand not only on how well it works, but also on the packaging and bundling of services. Jim Stein emphasized throughout the interview that he needed to have a better handle on where his checks were going: "It is more sensible for me to have one bill for everything rather than half a dozen things going to half a dozen companies – the mobile, the house phone, the TV. It makes no sense!"

In this context it makes sense that the Steins are relatively nonchalant about mobile phones. They own one, and use it primarily to call kin while traveling. For them, the mobile is simply an object that fits into household needs, rather than a social implement. The Steins perceive the mobile phone as an informational product that lacks materiality because it does not possess the contours or aesthetics associated with objects such as a jumper or a painting. The mobile is understood primarily as an object or utility, and its object "nature" is what renders it relatively innocuous. Similar households, usually with older or adult children, whether middle class or not, tend to perceive the mobile phone as a non-threatening object as well. Although people might recognize the social use of the mobile, for older generations approval of the social aspects is given easily. Another couple demonstrated this rather well:

Q:  Do you have a mobile phone?
DONNA:  Next week I'm getting one.
Q:  Why are you getting one?
LARS (BOTH DONNA AND LARS ARE LAUGHING):  Well because her daughter has one and her son's got one and Pauline down the road has one and Carolyn has one. She's going to find some reasons now why she must have a mobile phone.
DONNA:  Well, we go up and down motorways...
LARS:  We've been going up and down motorways for how many years?

Some see the mobile phone as merely useful, but, for many, mobiles are emblematic of older ways of consuming.

In contrast to the Steins, the Brennans use different goods, perceive them differently and use them in different ways. Melissa and Daniel, aged 26 and 31, respectively, are a couple who live together in London and have no intention of having children. They are urbane, involved in the culture industries and upper middle class.

What makes them interesting is that they are part of a growing legion of information workers, which distinguishes them from other interviewees in their approach to technologies. The problem Melissa and Dan face in negotiating technologies is not the relationship between the tangible material aspects and the conceptual aspects. Whereas the Steins incorporate information technologies as a necessary backdrop to consuming other things, where all the features are known, Dan and Melissa focus on the hollowness and meaninglessness of commodities themselves. For example, Dan's claim that the Internet is *more* trustworthy because it is "less motivated by publishers' eye" (that is, regard for marketplace success) stands in stark contrast to Steve and Svetlana's concern that information appearing on the Web is "rubbish" because anyone can put something up on the Internet.

Dan and Melissa clearly present problems of cynicism and the crisis in creativity brought about by greater reflexivity and deliberateness in consumption. Their cynicism is far from unique. Not only do others repeatedly echo their sentiments but, on a different level, it is suggested that there is an explosion of cultural reflexivity (Lash and Urry, 1994). The difference between Dan and Melissa's cynicism and the equally active discernment of Penny and Jim might also be compared to the difference between a modernist stance and a post-modernist one. Dan and Melissa have taken Penny and Jim's deliberateness a stage further by trying to perceive the subtleties behind technological objects. They provide evidence of a loss of certainty and a sense that the production of technological commodities has gone too far, or rendered the world alienated and hollow. They have to be much more active in *making* technologies fit with their identities by producing sensible meanings. This half-production extends to their perceptions of the Internet, to their interest in exotic, hard-to-find objects, and to their insistence that their holiday-making habits are "travel" rather than "tourism."

This shift in the process of consumption, from fitting objects into a construct of requirements to contributing actively to the production of their meanings, explains the disdain Melissa and Dan, as well as countless others, have for mobile phones. In the words of Carl, another information worker: "Mobiles are like a cheaper version of a laptop for a yuppie. Though I do think laptops are different from mobile phones because mobile phones are personal, a laptop you can actually use, it has a function, you can word process on it; you can play games if you want to. If you've got a laptop, then you need a laptop really; any moron can have a mobile phone and make it go doo da doo..." Carl, who was looking for a job in computer programming at the time of the interview, was far more fervently critical of social concepts of the mobile phone. His comments powerfully portray his attitude to technologies of the future: "Having things like e-mail phones is just defeating the purpose of the whole thing; I think you should just make people learn." His statements are somewhat extreme, but these younger groups of people nevertheless base much of their identity on reflexively creating their consumptive worlds. Without this creation, their individuality is called into question, coming dangerously close to "any moron." The existence of other people's mobiles, their moronic "doo da doo" ringing, presents the possibility of a selfhood mediated by someone else, and is therefore, along with the breaking of Ling's social space, an implicit threat to individuality itself.

It seems odd, then, that both these households, which express such strong feelings against mobile phones, actually own them. Indeed, their attitude is that they are a "necessary evil." When asked why they purchased one, talk turns to utility, particularly in the context of safety. Melissa told us: "The mobile is the bane of his life; I certainly don't want one." Yet she uses Dan's mobile just as often as he does! Carl, who is extremely keen on new technologies, gave his mobile phone away to his brother at university. He claims that he got rid of it because he would be in public places and see others on one, and think: "You shouldn't be on the phone! I don't think I'm that self-important to warrant needing to communicate no matter where I am really, so I didn't really turn it on that much." It is significant, though, that he gave it to a brother at university, who is just establishing himself in the public world, rather than giving it to parents or friends. Although he distances himself from the object, at the same time he subscribes to wider notions about what mobiles are "for."

## Conclusion

One conclusion is that mobiles do not fit neatly into a simple hierarchy of technology. The future convergence of data transfer and mobile phones as the crowning moment of technological wizardry circumnavigates this practice of post-modern consumption. Another conclusion is that the mobile phone is associated with meanings and contributes to historically based social processes in ways that all objects do; it should not be looked at solely in terms of what makes it unique or novel. The old concern for individuality is in every way made new again, as demonstrated through similar technological objects. The desire for difference cannot be seen outside its relationship with a centuries-old tradition of difference. We leave it to the other authors in this volume to further explore practices that do constitute novelty in a direct way. It is compelling that the social production of individuality is not self-defeating, although the tension between relatedness and distinctiveness is often cause for humor, as the following "headline" from the satirical magazine *The Onion* suggests: "Study Finds Peer Pressure for Non-Conformity Skyrockets." It is true that the individual is a social construct, but we have seen how people use the mobile to set themselves off from each other at a micro-level rather than in opposition to the state or "society." It is these micro-differences – who dominates public space among households, who is courteous enough to ring home, and who depends on whom – that are critical in everyday life.

## References

Allan, G. (1996). *Kinship and Friendship in Modern Britain*. Oxford: Oxford University Press.

Appadurai, A. (1986). *The Social Life of Things*. Cambridge: Cambridge University Press.

Bloch, M., and Parry, J. (1989). "Introduction." In J. Parry and M. Bloch (eds.), *Money and the Morality of Exchange*. Cambridge: Cambridge University Press.

Douglas, M. and Isherwood, B. (1979). *The World of Goods*. London: Allen Lane.

Finch, J. (1989). *Family Obligation and Social Change*. Cambridge: Polity.

Firth, R., Hubert, J., and Forge, A. (1969). *Families and Their Relatives: Kinship in a Middle-Class Sector of London*. London: Routledge & Kegan Paul.

Hirsch, E., and Silverstone, R. (eds.) (1992). *Consuming Technologies: Media and Information in Domestic Spaces*. London: Routledge.

Katz, J. (1999). *Connections: Social and Cultural Studies of the Telephone in American Life*. New Brunswick, NJ: Transaction.

Lash, S., and Urry, J. (1994). *Economies of Sign and Space*. London: Sage.

Latour, B. (1993). *We Have Never Been Modern*. London: Harvester Wheatsheaf.

Ling, R. (1999). "Restaurants, Mobile Telephones and Bad Manners: New Technology and the Shifting of Social Boundaries." Paper presented at the

Human Factors in Telecommunication 17th International Symposium in Copenhagen, Denmark, May 4–7.

MacFarlane, A. (1978). *The Origins of English Individualism*. Oxford: Blackwell.

Miller, D. (1987). *Material Culture and Mass Consumption*. Oxford: Blackwell.

(1988a). "Appropriating the State on the Council Estate." *Man* 23: 353–372.

(1998b). *A Theory of Shopping*. London: Polity Press.

Ormond, S. (1995). "Feminist Sociology and Methodology: Leaky Black Boxes in Gender/Technology Relations." In K. Grint and R. Gill (eds.), *The Gender–Technology Relation*. London: Taylor & Francis.

Pine, F. (1996). "Naming the House and Naming the Land: Kinship and Social Groups in Highland Poland." *Journal of the Royal Anthropological Institute* 2 (September): 443–459.

Strathern, Marilyn (1981). *Kinship at the Core: An Anthropology of Elmdon a Village in North-West Essex in the Nineteen-Sixties*. Foreword by Audrey Richards and Epilogue by Frances Oxford. Cambridge: Cambridge University Press.

(1992). *After Nature: English Kinship in the Late Twentieth Century*. Cambridge: Cambridge University Press.

*The Economist* (1999). "Special Survey on the Telecommunications Sector," October 15.

Thomas, K. (1984). *Man and the Natural World: Changing Attitudes in England 1500–1800*. London: Penguin.

*Part III*

# Public performance: social groups and structures

In this part we probe how mobile communication technologies are affecting social groups and structures. Parts I and II were largely cross-sectional in their nature. Here, we seek to take a longitudinal perspective on the relationship between mobile technology and social structural processes. In a sense, the earlier essays focused on agency whereas these chapters place stress on structure.

In his usual broad and urbane approach to vital matters, *Kenneth J. Gergen* elaborates the concept of "absent presence" to tackle the major developments in communication technology of the twentieth century. He argues that increasingly such technologies transport a geographically distant, but engaging world of meaning into the immediate context of living. In certain respects, the expanding dimension of the absent presence has been destructive. The capacities of face-to-face communities to sustain values, coherence and solidarity are undermined. The ability of the individual to sustain a sense of centered identity or a compelling code of values is eroded. These processes have been intensified with the advent of the Internet. The entry of the mobile phone into cultural life, however, serves as a major exception. It stands as perhaps the most significant technological support of the face-to-face community. He concludes that there are also inherent potentials for the mobile phone to act as a bridging device across disparate enclaves of meaning. This intriguing argument places personal communication and information technologies in historical perspective while sharpening our understanding of how technology and sociality interpenetrate.

Along parallel lines, sociologist *James B. Rule* explores the span of the twentieth century. He notes that social scientists have often characterized the world's advanced societies as "mass societies." Durable as this characterization has been, computing and communication technologies have of late done much to undermine it. Instead of "mass" society, computing has helped precipitate what might be called "particularizing" society, in which individuals are linked to major social institutions through exchange of extremely detailed and constantly emergent data specific to each individual citizen. Technologies and practices of perpetual contact further sharpen some of these particularizing qualities. The result is a new set of both ethical and political questions that are inadequately addressed from the standpoint of "mass society" assumptions about media influence. Rule proposes contrasting models to help make sense of how the media of perpetual contact may impinge on key social values.

*Berit Skog* explores a sample of Norwegian teens in terms of their media consumption, social backgrounds and attitudes and outlooks. We are fortunate to have such a comprehensive and large dataset. She concludes that girls prefer the symbolic and social aspects of the mobile phone, whereas boys are attracted to the features and functions of the device. Yet, although there are differences that are statistically and substantively significant, in proportional terms these are not dramatic differences: both genders are concerned about both domains. She also notes the class-reproductive characteristics of the technology, which, along with Internet, lead working-class youth to confirm and strengthen the more modest educational aims of their parents. This is a statistically independent effect. The popularity of the mobile phone among teenagers may involve even more than its iconic representation of a youth ideal. The results of the surveys of Norwegian teens reveal how the mobile phone is implicated in the identity project youths must master under the conditions of modernity.

*Georg Strøm* presents a valuable cross-cultural comparison that shows how revolutionary telephone technology is, and the mobile phone in particular. Not all countries superimpose their cellular telephone technology on a pre-existing telephone infrastructure. In other words, the telephone exists on a plane where the ordinary assumptions of industrial society do not apply. This is the case, for instance, in a *barangay*, or rural Filipino village. In contrast to Europe or the USA, where people tend to use the telephone whenever possible, people in the *barangay* go personally or send a message whenever possible and use the telephone only when there is no alternative. Villagers accept the fact that, instead of making a telephone call, they must go in person to a public office when they wish to conduct official business. Likewise, it is unexceptional to travel three days to inquire whether a job is available. Thus there is value in focusing on the substantial efforts devoted to providing emotional support for the physical demands of effecting communication, including keeping contact with far-flung members of the family. The consequences of this substantial social group commitment to communicating via physical rather than electronic means are discussed in detail. Obviously, the coming of the mobile phone will have enormous consequences for the *barangay* social structure that will extend far beyond the economic efficiencies provided to its possessors. This has already been seen at the political level by the pivotal role the mobile phone played in the 2001 ouster of Philippine president Joseph Estrada (mentioned in chapter 1). The use of mobile phones can reconfigure activities at every level, ranging from the social micro-structure to the political macro-structure.

*Emanuel A. Schegloff* gave the opening keynote address to our workshop on perpetual contact. Hence, it gives us a sense of symmetry and balance to allow him the final word among our authors and, via a framing statement to his historically and substantively important appendix, the final word to the entire volume. In his keynote address, modified for presentation here, he draws attention to the intersection between his early research on telephone interaction and issues of mobile communication. He does this by noting that perpetual contact may be better characterized as a state of continuing incipient talk. This is a stretch of talk structured by topic or by some course of action that can come to a close and have silence set in. It is undoubtedly useful to anchor our understanding of the mobile telephone, and indeed the telephone conversation itself, by recalling that incipient talk has been with humans for millennia. In fact, as demonstrated in this chapter, new communication technology highlights, among other things, not only the problem of perpetual contact itself, but also the possibility of making contact. One interesting consequence of this focus lies in how it reframes technological innovation. Rather than seeing the developmental trajectory of the telephone and associated services as simply an outgrowth of a technological imperative, Schegloff shows how innovations are analyzable in terms of perpetual contact and incipient talk – the possibility of making contact. Indeed, much of the negotiation of interaction described in the chapters on private talk and the social change described in the chapters on public performance reflect the interactional demands involved in managing a continuing state of incipient talk.

# 14   The challenge of absent presence

*Kenneth J. Gergen*

"Let your home know where your heart is."
(Billboard advertisement for cellular phone)

The setting is a retirement home for the elderly. Wilfred enters the veranda in search of two close friends. He is in luck, they are both present. But alas, one is lost to her Walkman and the other is engrossed in his book. Neither notices Wilfred's presence. Frustrated, Wilfred is left to stare silently into space. Such is the beginning of Ronald Harwood's London play, *Quartet*. Young or old, we instantly identify with the scene. How often do we enter a room to find family, friends or colleagues absorbed by their computer screen, television, CDs, telephone, newspaper, or even a book? Perhaps they welcome us without hesitation; but sometimes there is a pause, accompanied even by a look of slight irritation. And at times our presence may go completely unacknowledged. We are present but simultaneously rendered absent; we have been erased by an absent presence.

It is the twentieth-century expansion of absent presence that I wish to explore in what follows. My concern is with the growing domain of diverted or divided consciousness invited by communication technology, and most particularly the mobile telephone. One is physically present but is absorbed by a technologically mediated world of elsewhere. Typically it is a world of relationships, both active and vicarious, within which domains of meaning are being created or sustained. Increasingly, these domains of alterior meaning insinuate themselves into the world of full presence – the world in which one is otherwise absorbed and constituted by the immediacy of concrete, face-to-face relationships. In what follows I wish first to explore the development of absent presence and to consider its broad consequences for cultural life. As we shall find, these consequences are both significant and multidimensional. Inasmuch as they also disrupt broadly valued traditions, they are effects about which one can scarcely be neutral. I will then take up the entry of the cellular phone into cultural life. In certain respects the cell phone extends the domain of absent presence. Yet, because of its particular technological configuration,

227

it stands to subvert or reverse the major effects of other communication technologies. Finally, I shall turn briefly to the future. Although cellular phone technology is currently generating interesting and significant cultural formations, it is unclear whether the trajectory can be sustained.

## The expansion and implications of absent presence

Walter Ong's (1982) classic treatment of orality and literacy was chiefly concerned with the effects of print technology on mental life, including the structure of memory, rational analysis and forms of understanding. Little attention was devoted, however, to the implications of print technology for social life, to the ways in which print relations impinge, for example, on patterns of trust, intimacy, family life and community relationship. Yet in terms of social life there is an important sense in which print technology is one of the most significant revolutionary forces of the past 2,000 years.

To appreciate this possibility it is useful to consider the social genesis and function of language. Language comes into being – into meaning – through coordinated relationships among persons. It is through language that persons acquire their ways of understanding the world and themselves. Within communities, both an ontology of everyday life and a moral code are typically established in language, and these languages play an integral role in both constituting and rationalizing communal traditions and institutions (Gergen, 1994). Thus, as we come to generate languages of justice, freedom and knowledge, for example, and as these languages come to play a constitutive role within our institutions (for example, law, governance, education), so does a group gain the possibility of mutual understanding and the recognition of themselves as an identifiable community.

Lacking outside interference, local ontologies and moralities can be sustained with relative ease. Lacking dissenting voices, there is little with which to compare and little grounds for question. Thus, so long as all voices join in the assertion of a flat world, there is little reason to cry out that the world is round! Such a claim, in itself, might seem nonsense – without meaning. It is thus that the development of print technology harbors the potential for pandemic revolution: myriad voices from far-flung locales may enter without detection at any time to challenge the cherished realities of one's immediate community. Print technology functions much like a Trojan horse; once inside the walls a veritable army of discontent can spring forth. In print, the absent voices are now present and, as they are absorbed, the claims of local community are diminished. Of course, as censorship, newspaper closings and book burnings all suggest, virtually every traditionalist and tyrant has come to realize the unsettling potentials of print technology. The creation of home town newspapers, Bible study groups and the academic canon are but a few manifestations of the same technology pressed into protecting the established realities and moralities.

Yet, despite its significance, print technology must be seen as but a first force in the historical emergence of absent presence. Technological developments of the twentieth century have dramatically expanded the domain. I am not speaking here merely of the development of lighting systems that enable people to read on a round-the-clock basis. Nor is it simply the massive increment in published works – newspapers, novels, professional books, and the like. It is said that approximately 90% of the published works of the Western world were produced in the preceding century alone. Rather, we must consider as powerful contributors to absent presence virtually all communications technologies that enabled people to communicate at a distance.

There are first of all what may be considered the technologies of *monological presence*. Here we may include most prominently the emergence of radio, electronic recording devices (e.g. phonograph, cassette and compact disk recordings), film and television. In each case the technologies are populist – with radio and television now reaching virtually every household in the United States – and sustained by major industrial investments. In their contribution to an absent presence, however, there are two noteworthy factors.

First, in certain respects there is a relatively low degree of dislodgement potential, that is, the capacity to unseat local commitments to the real and the good. Although, as monologic technologies, they may provide information or stimulation, in doing so they speak but are not directly spoken to. They insert alterior voices into daily life circumstances but there is little means (save, for example, by talk radio) by which one can respond. One cannot ask for clarification, elaboration or examples, nor can one raise questions. In effect, there is little potential for the kind of dialogic engagement from which more profound transformations in understanding and commitment are born. Nor do the monological speakers typically have knowledge of the personal lives of their audiences. The messages of radio, television and film are in this sense impersonal. As a result the voices carried by such monologic technologies typically remain one step removed from the life of the audience.[1] They may be heeded or not,

---

[1] It is interesting to consider print technology in this regard. Although it is a monologic technology, print often carries a transformative capacity far exceeding that of radio or television. In part this difference may be traced to the fact that the act of reading borders on the dialogic. That is, because one can pace one's reading – pausing to deliberate and

relegated to the status of "background noise" or terminated at the flick of a switch.

The second important feature of these monologic technologies is their progressive privatization. At their inception such technologies facilitated collective reception. Families might gather round the radio and then the television. Recorded music was typically played on a family unit, and thus available to all. The cinema served as an invitation for an outing – with friends, a date or family. The incoming voices were thus made available to all. In these circumstances an audience could deliberate on what it had heard or seen. There might be broad differences in opinion that would work against the disruptive capacities of the medium. As many communication studies demonstrate, there are numerous instances of an audience appropriating the meaning of the incoming material for its own purposes. For example, Brown's (1994) study of soap opera audiences suggests that, contrary to the common view that the "soaps" sustain a patriarchal value structure, women negotiate the meanings of the materials in ways that galvanize resistance against the patriarchy. Through their conversations, women use these materials in empowering ways. However, as the cost of monologic communications technologies has declined and miniaturization has progressed, so have they been progressively removed from collective deliberation. Many households now have several television sets, so that different family members may indulge their independent preferences. On many jet planes each traveler has a private screen with multiple channel choices. Video cassettes now invite film viewing in the privacy of one's room; devices such as the Walkman allow people to indulge their musical tastes in private. Further, with the multiplication of radio stations and television channels, there is a diminishing chance that others will have been exposed to the same materials. In sum, in the case of monologic technologies we find a relatively low degree of transformative power, but an increasing potential for immersing people in private as opposed to collective worlds.

A useful contrast can be made between monologic and *dialogic communication technologies*. In this latter category we may include the telephone, video and computer games and, most prominently, the Internet. All such technologies facilitate the flow of interactive movement in meaning. I shall postpone consideration of the telephone until we take up the development of the cellular phone. In the case of video and computer games, although dialogic, they are also relatively barren in terms of content relevant to a world outside themselves. We worry about the reverberations

silently to act out the part of the author – reading facilitates a higher degree of engagement. To put it another way, in reading one often creates a vision of the author along with a private relationship with him/her.

of violence in such games, but the analogy between space warfare, for example, and the challenges of everyday life is thin. Far more important in terms of transforming our constructions of the world is the Internet. In terms of absent presence the Internet promises to be much more profound in its consequences than the development of print. Here we have a technology that enables instantaneous connections to be made among persons throughout the world. Alien voices from any locale and around the clock may instantaneously insert themselves into one's consciousness. Further, e-mail communication invites a high degree of dialogic engagement. In contrast to monologic technologies, one participates in the construction of the world, and this construction can be uniquely tailored to, and expressive of, one's individual circumstances. Unlike many monological technologies, e-mail is also fully privatized. In effect, the present is *virtually* eradicated by a dominating absence.

## Cultural reverberations of absent presence

The Internet is profoundly disrespectful of tradition, established order and hierarchy. (Fareek Zakaria, editor, *Foreign Affairs*)

Given the surging expansion of absent presence – through both monological and dialogical technologies – it is important to consider more fully the impact on cultural life. This account is pivotal, inasmuch as we shall find telephone technology functions in such a way as to deflect or alter these tendencies in significant ways. I consider, briefly, four significant changes in cultural life.

### Dangerous liaisons

In Laclos' eighteenth-century novel *Les Liaisons Dangereuses*, the major protagonists and lovers, Valmont and Merteuil, develop a pact that will enable them to compete in the seduction of others. Their intimacy will be reinforced by their ability to reveal their desires and manipulative intentions to each other, and to rely on each other to help in consummating these desires. Yet, in each seduction they risk the possibility that their own intimate bond will be broken. Either might fall in love with the object of desire. The result of this delicate play of desire and trust is catastrophe. In an important sense the emerging domain of the absent present renders daily life a landscape of dangerous liaisons. As radio, television, magazines, books and film consume our fantasies, ignite our desire and offer new ideas and directions, so the realities embedded in what we often call our "primary bonds" are placed under potential threat. One's interests and enthusiasms may be directed elsewhere. The dialogic development of local meanings may also be curtailed; when we are listening to voices from afar we are no longer building the realities and moralities of the local together. As Internet interaction increasingly absorbs our attention, new clusters of meaning emerge. Although these may be compatible with the primary domains of reality and morality, they may also function independently, tangentially or antagonistically.

Herein we find the dark side of what cyber-gurus such as Howard Rheingold (1994) hail as the coming of cyber-community. It is when the local ceases to hold sway, when it becomes irrelevant or alien, that the essential bonds of communal trust are frayed. Friendship, intimacy, family and neighbors cease to be the primary sources of meaning, and become the objects of deliberation from yet another domain of reality. More dramatically, when the command of the local is destroyed, the stage is set for flagrant violations of its moral standards – for indulgence in child pornography, the mass suicide of the Heaven's Gate movement, or the massacre at Columbine High. It is important here not to overstate the case. The conditions under which cyber-communal processes can captivate the user remain quite unclear, and many critics are highly skeptical of the forces of cyber-mediated relationships.[2] For example, as the volume of e-mail continues to expand, so is there an inflation of the word. Individual communiqués can become lost in a sea of competing contenders. And when one is responding to a large volume of electronic mail, one's replies may shift in definition from "personal expressions" to "utilitarian" or "obligatory" acts. The personal may become pragmatic. At the same time, there are populations for whom cyber-communities may be a fruitful or indeed essential option. For the aged, the infirm or the isolated, cyber-connections may be an invaluable source of support; for the prison inmate, the cyber-community may be a useful link to the culture at large; for those who need support and empathy, a cyber-community may provide far more resources than one's family and friends.[3] In whatever fashion, as the domain of the absent present is enlarged so the importance of face-to-face relations is likely to be diminished.

### Horizontal relationships

It is common in Western culture to think of relationships in terms of their degree of centrality; in the academic world, for example, we theorize extensively on the impact of "significant others" in our lives. Further, strong value is traditionally placed on close relationships. We commonly

---

[2] See, for example, Jones (1998), Kiesler (1997) and Porter (1997).
[3] See, for example, Miller and Gergen (1998).

count lives the richer when they achieve depth or intimacy in relationship. The value placed on depth can be contrasted with yet another ideal, that of breadth of acquaintance. We are wary of the social isolate and pity the outcast, and we speak of the enrichment, opportunity and substantial support to be derived from having an array of friends, colleagues and acquaintances. For analytic purposes let us frame the former ideal in terms of *vertical* and the latter in terms of *horizontal* relationships. In these terms it is also clear that these ideals tend toward antagonism. Relating in the vertical register typically requires dedicated attention, effort, commitment and sacrifice. When one is successfully engaged in the vertical register one frequently finds there is no need of others or little interest in them. By the same token, to have many friends, colleagues and the like is also demanding of time and effort. The adolescent who thrives on popularity carries a heavy burden; the young man who seeks out his chums every evening may have difficulty with serious relations; and the adult who relies on "networking" dwells in a labyrinth without end.

In this context we may see the expansion of absent presence as essentially favoring a cultural shift from the vertical to the horizontal register of relationship. As the technologies of absent presence divert and redirect attention, so they expand the range of relationships (either actual or imagined) in which the person is engaged. To become enamored of the works of a given author, film director, composer, dancer or jazz musician, for example, is essentially to broaden the network of relationships in which one is engaged. For many men, televised sports, for example, serve as surrogate companions; during Sunday afternoon football a young man does not require either a spouse or those "buddies" with whom he once attended the games. The Internet expands the horizontal network exponentially. Surfing the web functions much like saying "hello" to a vast brigade of acquaintances – some superficial, others arresting. In significant degree we may be witnessing a wholesale devaluation of depth in relationship. This is surely suggested by the fact that the average age at which people marry has increased, and the likelihood of remaining married continuously declines. As census data indicate, Americans will soon live in a country in which the majority of people live alone. But, it should be added, these people are not likely to be living without television, radio, CDs, a video-cassette recorder or a computer.

### Humans without qualities

In Robert Musil's volume *The Man without Qualities* we confront the possibility of a culture in which individuals have little in the way of identifiable character. It is not only Ulric, the major protagonist, who feels that he is "equally close to and equally far from all qualities and that they are all, whether [my] own or not, strangely a matter of indifference" (1954 [1930], p. 151). Rather, Musil sees the society as moving in this direction. Although prophetic in certain respects, Musil had yet to encounter the dramatic expansion of absent presence. In certain respects the communication technologies in question may be considered self-eviscerating. For what is required in order to achieve a quality of character, a personality trait or a moral posture, or indeed any personal manner of thought or feeling that we might typically identify as "myself?" In important degree, the possession of an identifiable self requires a community of persons who recognize one as a certain kind of a person, who affirm this recognition over time and situation, and who hold one responsible for sustaining this manner of being. As Alasdair McIntyre has put it, to be a moral self is "to be accountable for the actions and experiences which compose a narratable life within a community"(1984, p. 202).

Yet, as the domain of absent presence expands, so the scaffolding for a recognizable self is eroded. With each new enclave of meaning, whether vicariously or interactively constituted, there are new selves in the making. To view a film depicting war, romantic love, heroism, sexuality and the like is silently to play out the possibility of a different self. The horizons of being are challenged; the local may slowly seem parochial. The Walter Mitty, Frank Harris or Thomas Ripley within may yearn for escape. With video and computer games these yearnings may gain in clarity and potency. Such games indeed seemed to have fueled the actions of the Columbine High assassins. In the case of the Internet, to form an e-mail relationship, to join a listserv, to participate in a chat room or to explore a virtual religion or a pornography site is to expand on the possibilities of "who I am." At the same time, however, as the communal sources for an identifiable self are diminished, it becomes increasingly difficult to answer the question of "who am I?" We move then into a cultural condition in which our identities are increasingly situated, conditional and optional.[4]

### The new floating world

In late-nineteenth-century Tokyo, a new way of life sprang up among the merchant class, a way of life that centered on transient pleasure, and revolved around entertainment, sensual indulgence and prostitution. Because of its corrosive effects on social tradition, it was also a world decried by people of rank. In the twentieth-century West we confronted the emergence of a new form of floating world, one ushered into being by the

---

[4] For further discussion of technology and the loss of self, see Gergen (1996, 2000).

technologies of absent presence. My concern here is with the emergence of a world of meaning cut away from the pragmatics of everyday life.

To appreciate the point, return to the earlier argument for the social basis of language. As proposed, language comes into meaning through relationships as people coordinate themselves around various activities. Consider then a *primary level of coordination* in which the activity takes place within material circumstances and in which the language is essential to effective action. For the surgeon who calls for a scalpel, the pilot who calls for a flight plan, or the builder who calls for a quick-drying mortar, it is essential that the recipient's referential use of the language is identical. Although not always so precise, the everyday use of language in face-to-face relationships is often of the primary variety. Comments such as "Please pass the sugar," "Have you seen my car keys?" and "The assignment for Monday is . . ." are closely wedded to pragmatic outcomes. Contrast this with a *secondary level* of coordination in which the actions at stake are those of speaking or writing. Here, for example, we might discuss our conflicting ideas about the president, the values embedded in the curriculum or our impressions of a film or book. In such communication our talk may ultimately impinge on our conduct in material conditions of interdependency, but not always and necessarily. But then consider third- and fourth-order levels of coordination, where we discuss, for example, the dynamics of our conversation about abortion, or the values of poetry or how history books have treated various minorities. Here we move toward what might be viewed as a floating world of signification, that is, a world in which the relationship of the language to ongoing practical activity is ambiguous if not irrelevant.

It is this new floating world that is facilitated by the expansion of absent presence. To read a novel, see a film or watch televised sports is to engage in a world of representation – what Debord (1983) might call the "world of the spectacle" and Baudrillard (1994) would term the "hyperreal." Similarly, when e-mail exchanges create their own realm of "conversational objects," they can float free from their moorings in everyday life. But, we may ask, what are the reverberations of floating realities in everyday life? Here we should consider, for example, their suppressing effects on the first-level languages. Simply put, as our attentions are poured into floating realms, so the skills, the repertoires and the creative developments required for effective exchange in daily relations diminish. The philosophical literature on ethics continues to feed upon itself, while the ethical dilemmas of daily life are cast aside; the endless discussions on electronic listservs often have little function other than ensuring their own continuation. At worst, to live in floating worlds of absent presence may mean the devaluation of mere day-to-day activity. Compared with the glories of space wars, the academy awards and championship chess, having a full-time job, going to the market, paying taxes and raising children may seem exercises in ennui.

Again, I border on overstatement. To an important extent it is the language of the un-real that furnishes the source of enchantment in cultural life. In the pragmatic language of the real, things simply are what they are – a man, a woman, the sun, the moon, earth, water, and so on. It is when languages are imported from another realm that the everyday realities are transformed, when the humdrum turns wondrous. It is by virtue of the non-practical realm of meaning that what we call idealization or romanticizing occurs – woman becomes "the woman!" sunsets evoke rituals of worship, "moonlight becomes you" and water becomes holy. And there will always be a need for languages not so embedded in "the real" that we cannot turn in critical reflection; in an important sense, liberation from convention requires that we look beyond the practically embedded languages of the culture.

## Retrenchment and reconfiguration: the cellular phone

"Without my cell phone my emotional life would be in ruins." (Sarah, from Willow Grove, PA)

The erosion of face-to-face community, a coherent and centered sense of self, moral bearings, depth of relationship, and the uprooting of meaning from material context: such are the repercussions of absent presence. Such are the results of the development and proliferation of our major communication technologies of the past century. Yet, curiously enough, the telephone was not included in the preceding discussion of absent presence. We must now make amends. It is also when we begin to consider the function of the telephone that we begin to appreciate the profound potentials of the cellular phone. This is not to say that the effects of the cell phone are univocal. Clearly there are differing forms of usage, each of which modifies what I shall here consider its central thrust in cultural life. Consideration of these matters must await discussion of the telephone.

When the telephone entered cultural life early in the twentieth century, it primarily served as an extension of face-to-face relations. Neighbors and business colleagues could communicate with each other without the inconvenience of transporting themselves bodily. Neighbors had instant access to each other and, with the help of an operator, could reach those outside the immediate vicinity. (I recall here my attempt at the age of 5 to "run away from home," only to find that my parents were able to trace my every move as they talked by phone with observant neighbors.) To be sure, we find here the expansion of absent presence, but far different in kind from that previously considered. The telephone does indeed demand that participants divorce their attention from their immediate surroundings. However, it is essential to distinguish between absent presence arising from what might be called *endogenous* sources as opposed to *exogenous* sources. Unlike radio, mass publication, film, sound recordings and television – all of which originate from outside the community – telephone conversation in the early years was largely endogenous. It originated within and extended the potentials of face-to-face relationships.

In many respects the telephone has lost its capacity as a resource for endogenous relationship. In part this is owing to the public dissemination of telephone numbers and the falling costs of long-distance transmission. There is, for one, a standing invitation for the distantly known suddenly to enter into our immediate lives ("We met last year at...;" "I am calling because your daughter is my daughter's best friend at school..."). More significantly, the world of commerce is increasingly seizing on "the cold call" or telemarketer to generate business. The answering machine, originally used to ensure that the messages of intimates would not be lost, is now as often used for defense against the distant and the commerciant. It is not a recording instrument that is desired, so much as a screening device to select among calls one will choose to answer. (Many have even abandoned their answering machines in order to reduce the flow of messages for which an answer is anticipated.) Further, because the automobile (along with mass transit and jet transportation) invites a high degree of mobility, and because dual-income families are becoming the norm, few denizens of the face-to-face community are present on a round-the-clock basis. Most suburban communities stand relatively empty during the day. In effect, there are only remnants of the face-to-face community remaining for which the telephone may serve as a prosthesis.

It is at this juncture that the drama of the cell phone becomes most fully apparent. The cell phone now serves as an instrument *par excellence* for endogenous strengthening. The realities and moralities of the face-to-face relationship are revitalized. This is not only because of the perpetual connection that a mobile phone allows. But the very fact that the user is rendered vulnerable to calls at any time of day or night invites careful selection of those who will be granted access to one's number. Such access is typically limited to those who are otherwise "close" in the traditional sense: family, intimate friends, close colleagues and the like. It is thus that the nuclear circle can be perpetually sustained. Yes, the domain of the absent presence is broadened,[5] but this time it is typically the casual relationship that is disrupted as opposed to the nuclear. The dialogical nature of the communication serves as a further source of vitality. Examples of such nuclear strengthening are everywhere available. On an hour's rail journey from New York to Philadelphia the man in the seat behind me called his "Maria" no fewer than four times to share the fruits of his ruminations. Sandra from Willow Grove uses her 45-minute journey to work to spend time with her intimate friends each day. Neighbors supply their growing adolescents with cell phones to insure close and safe watch.

The efficacy of the cell phone in extending the power of endogenous realities is partially reflected in the resentment many feel toward those using them in their presence. It is not simply that one's reverie may be interrupted by a nearby conversation; it is the fact that such conversation actively excludes one from participation. Cell phone conversation typically establishes an "inside space" ("we who are conversing") vs. an "outside space" constituted by those within earshot but prevented from participating. The fact that "it doesn't matter whether you listen or not" underscores the impotent insignificance of the outsider. If one happens to be closely related to the cell phone user (and relatively equal in status), resentment at the other's engagement may become acute. In the manifest structure of privilege, one is defined as secondary, not significant after all. The efficacy of the cell phone in sustaining endogenous ties is further revealed in the complaint voiced by many that "my cell phone is like a prison." Here we find a backlash against the continuous intrusion of obligations, standards and expectations of one's circle of intimates. In a world in which one is often and increasingly engaged in a multiplicity of relationships, the continuous enforcement of a single perspective may seem restrictive and oppressive.

This revitalizing of face-to-face relationships also has broad-scale cultural reverberations. Consider the consequences of absent presence as earlier discussed. Rather than the leveling of significance in relationships, the cell phone lends itself to a retrenchment of verticality. Given the privilege granted by the cell phone to a select few, there is less tendency to move laterally and superficially across relationships. Rather, one's communication time is increasingly spent in the presence of "those who matter." By the same token, brakes are placed on the concatenating tendency toward self-fragmentation and diffusion. With the cell phone, one's community of intimates more effectively sustains one's identity as a singular and coherent being. One is continuously, if sometimes painfully, reminded of one's

---

[5] Between 1985 and 1999, the number of people subscribing to wireless phone services in the USA increased exponentially, from some 200,000 to almost 80 million.

place in the flux of social life. Here too lie the resources for refurbishing the moral compass. By revitalizing the singular identity, a singular pattern of rights, wrongs, duties and obligations is made clear. The contours of conscience are clarified.

With respect to the floating worlds encouraged by preceding technologies of absent presence, a more complicated picture emerges. On the one hand, the cell phone does invite an expansion of a symbolic world that may be little related to the immediate, practical surroundings of either speaker. When the pedestrian, the diner or the passenger on the train are locked in cell phone conversation they cease to be full participants in the immediate context. It is the fatal impact of such distraction that has led many countries and US states to outlaw the use of cell phones while driving. (An Israeli driver was recently arrested because he was driving with his knees as he occupied himself with two cell phones.)

At the same time, the cell phone facilitates new integrations of the absent and the present in more subtle ways. Consider a story related by a colleague. At a family dinner table the parents are putting the brakes on their teenage daughter's social plans for Saturday night. She simply must be home by midnight, they argue, and her friends' parents would all agree with them. Rather than yielding to the demands of the far superior forces, the daughter pulls her cell phone from her pocket and proceeds to call her friends. When one after the other the friends inform her that their parents agree to the late hours, the dialogue takes a different direction. Slowly a compromise plan evolves. The worlds of adolescents and adults, families and distant neighbors are interwoven. In another instance, I listened as a customer in the checkout line of a local store called a friend. As we all became aware, she was shocked to hear that an acquaintance had died. After the call was over, a customer whose purchases were being tallied at the cash register turned to say that she too had known the man and was sorry to hear the news. At this, the merchant joined in to say that, yes, the news had appeared in the morning paper – which he then produced for all to read. Again, the cell phone helped otherwise disparate worlds to be knitted. In effect, because of its flexible insinuation into wide-ranging social contexts, and the semi-public character of the communication, the cell phone is virtually unique in its capacity to link otherwise absent worlds to the immediate circumstance.

## Perils of prophecy

Quicker than a click. Mind-blowingly diverse. Internetcentric, synergistic and digital. In the extreme. [In twenty years] the trends grabbing hold now [will] become just another part of our rapidly evolving and distraction-rich lifestyle landscape. (USA Today, Millennial edition)

A case has been made for the emergence within the twentieth century of a pervasive state of absent presence. Yet, although the form of absent presence favored by most of the century's major communication technologies is inimical to community, relations in depth, the sense of self, moral character and functional linkages between realms of meaning and action, the cell phone serves as a potentially powerful device for impeding the cultural drift. In many respects we might thus welcome the continuous development and proliferation of cell phone technology. At the same time, there is reason for significant pause before drawing such a conclusion. Two lines of argument are especially pertinent.

On the one hand, we can anticipate significant resistance to the proliferation of the cell phone of present construction. There is good reason to suspect that the lives of substantial segments of the population are so intimately entwined with technologies of television, video, recorded music and the Internet that the kind of localism favored by the cell phone would operate as a hindrance to a valued way of life. From their standpoint, the very outcomes favored by the cell phone may have negative connotations. Cell phone technology not only favors a kind of parochialism, but also stands as a wedge against the kind of polyvocal participation required in an increasingly multicultural world. A singular and coherent sense of self or a commitment to a single moral order or to a single community may seem arbitrarily limiting. Participation in the full global flow of signification means staying loose, traveling light and seeing issues from all sides. From this standpoint, a new form of cellular phone technology is desired, one that indeed is far more consistent with the other communication technologies described above.

Such resistance and desire will feed the fires of technological change, and specifically transformations in the cellular phone that will undermine its present functioning. That is, while having doubts about around-the-clock accessibility to a small group of intimates, there is much to be gained from a small mobile instrument with the capabilities to extend outward into the social and material world. Already there are cell phones that contain calculators, calendars and other offerings of the palm secretary. We can anticipate the development of a cell phone that will function like a small computer, enabling access to the Internet and the world wide web. One will be able to exchange e-mail, listen to music or read the latest zine. With this inevitable tendency toward expanding the functions of the instrument, absent presence of the exogenous variety will only be intensified. There is good reason to hope, however, that investment in traditional cultural values will stimulate further innovation that will insure that a tension remains between stable and nurturing traditions and the forces of unfettered change.

## References

Baudrillard, J. (1994). *Simulacra and Simulation*. Ann Arbor, MI: University of Michigan Press; originally published in 1981.

Brown, M.E. (1994). *Soap Opera and Women's Talk*. Thousand Oaks, CA: Sage.

Debord, G. (1983). *The Society of the Spectacle*. Detroit: Black and Red; originally published in 1967.

Gergen, K. J. (1994). *Realities and Relationships: Soundings in Social Construction.* Cambridge, MA: Harvard University Press.

(1996). "Technology and the Self: From the Essential to The Sublime." In D. Grodin and T. Lindlof (eds.), *Constructing the Self in a Mediated Age*. Beverly Hills, CA: Sage, 127–140.

(2000). *The Saturated Self*, 2nd edn. New York: Perseus.

Jones, S.G. (ed.) (1998). *Cybersociety 2.0*. Thousand Oaks, CA: Sage.

Kiesler, S. (ed.) (1997). *Culture of the Internet*. Mahwah, NJ: Erlbaum.

Laclos, C. de (1940). *Dangerous Acquaintances: Les liaisons dangereuses*. Trans. E. Dawson. London: Nonesuch.

MacIntyre, A. (1984). *After Virtue*, 2nd edn. Notre Dame, IN: University of Notre Dame Press.

Miller, J.K., and Gergen, K.J. (1998). "Life on the Line: The Therapeutic Potentials of Computer Mediated Conversation." *Journal of Marriage and Family Therapy* 24: 189–202.

Musil, R. (1954). *The Man without Qualities*. London: Secker & Warburg. Original publication in German, 1930.

Ong, W.J. (1982). *Orality and Literacy. The Technologizing of the Word.* London: Methuen.

Porter, D. (ed.) (1997). *Internet Culture.* New York: Routledge.

Rheingold, H. (1994). *The Virtual Community*. London: Minerva.

# 15 From mass society to perpetual contact: models of communication technologies in social context

*James B. Rule*

My subject here is partly technology and partly the history of ideas. It has to do, on the one hand, with the characteristics and possibilities of the technologies of perpetual contact. It also has to do with the succession of theoretical models that have shaped understanding of communications technologies in the past, and promise to do so in the future. If we are to grasp the role of technology in changing the social world, it helps to take stock of where the concepts for understanding that role come from. And if we can get a grip on the uses and failures of models that shaped the thinking of earlier decades, perhaps we will have a shrewder approach to modeling the technologies of the future.

The first model from the past that I want to evoke is that of mass society. From the end of the nineteenth century to roughly the 1960s, social critics held it axiomatic that the world's "advanced" societies were dominated by mass processes. In this view, populations of these societies were constantly at risk of manipulation from remote, powerful government and corporate organizations. The medium of this overbearing influence was mass communication, understood as the large-scale transmission of standardized, over-simplified, emotion-charged stimuli. Citizens were seen as likely to be subjected to mind-deadening, manipulative messages via the press, broadcasting and mass political parties. Such dynamics were seen as favoring authoritarian movements, whose leaders could thus work their will over populations deprived of their critical faculties by exposure to mass communications.

By the end of the twentieth century, such models had come to seem far less threatening, and less salient. Engaging our attentions by then instead were a new set of images or concerns – those surrounding what I term "particularizing communications." These are not standardized, one-way transmissions, but exchanges of highly specific, interactive data between individuals and organizations. These exchanges enable organizations to make and carry out discriminating decision-making concerning individuals. In various writings (for example, Rule, 1973; Rule et al., 1980), I have described the results of these exchanges as relations of mass surveillance.

The technologies and practices of perpetual contact represent a striking exemplification and extension of the logic of mass surveillance.

In this chapter, I consider a series of models that may help assess the prospects for the technologies of perpetual contact – either in their convergence with empirically documented characteristics of those technologies, or by divergence from them. These discussions begin with notions of mass society and mass surveillance. I then go on to consider other models of the possible future social roles to be played by mobile telephony and its kindred technologies.

## Mass society

For decades, from roughly the 1920s to the 1960s, mass society thinking was the indispensable lens for viewing certain essential aspects of the world's "advanced" societies. Above all, mass society provided a master model of linkages between ordinary citizens and the major institutions of those societies – both government institutions and private sector organizations. When long-standing ties of community and locality broke down, mass society thinking posited, citizens tended to become unmoored and psychologically defenseless, potential prey to emotional, standardized signals from remote sources. As William Kornhauser put it in *The Politics of Mass Society*,

People are available for mass behavior when they lack attachments to proximate objects. When people are divorced from their community or work, they are free to unite in new ways. (1959, p. 60)

It is in this vulnerable state, Kornhauser believes, that people are most susceptible to manipulation via mass communication. The forms taken by such communications might range from the "yellow" journalism of the early twentieth century, to authoritarian political movements or charismatic agitators whose appeals are propagated via broadcasting.

In its earliest inspirations, mass society thinking was evidently a conservative, indeed reactionary, mind-set. But by the middle decades of the twentieth century, mass society ideas were taken up by liberal and left-of-center commentators as a kind of intellectual shield against totalitarian movements of both the right and the left, including Nazism and Stalinism in Europe and McCarthyism in the United States. Among its best-known proponents in this later phase were Hannah Arendt, Emil Lederer and C. Wright Mills.

In terms of political values, mass society thinking conveyed concern over the possibility of meaningful democratic deliberation and pluralism in the face of overbearing, intolerant social influences. It reacted against what it saw as anonymizing, de-individuating trends in citizen participation in larger social institutions. Its nightmare image was one of citizens no longer engaged in reasoned deliberations with neighbors, fellow community members and others immediately at hand; instead, citizens of mass society had their political decisions made for them, and their mind-sets transformed, by propagandistic, standardized, repetitive messages from distant manipulators.

Mass society thinking abruptly crashed as an intellectual movement in the 1960s; it simply ceased to engage the imaginations of sociologists and other social commentators. The reasons for this striking theoretical eclipse would repay considerable attention. One element of the explanation surely lies in various research efforts that found that mass influences – for example, in electoral campaigns – were mediated by personal contacts and other intimate social ties. Another element has to do with the fact that, by the 1960s, many social scientists came to support the sorts of revolutionary movements theoretically decried by mass society thinking.

But another reason, I believe, has to do with the technologies shaping relations between citizens and major institutions having altered. Displacing mass communications technologies from center stage were a new set of technologies based on computing and involving fundamentally different patterns of information flow. Instead of unidirectional, uniform transmissions from remote institutions to millions of people, the new technologies made it possible both to send and to receive data in fine detail on this same mass scale.

## Particularizing technologies and mass surveillance

These particularizing technologies and practices share with mass communications the fact that they involve large organizations' addressing vast numbers of individuals at a time. In other respects, however, the sociological content of the relationship is utterly different. For particularizing relations involve organizations' monitoring of the fine detail of individuals' affairs, and responding with discriminating organizational decision-making and action. They thus combine the impersonality and distance of mass communications with the often invasive attentions characteristic of the most intimate communities and relationships.

Whether the organization in question is a national system of income taxation, a system of driver licensing, a credit card company or a direct marketing operation, the underlying logic of the relationship is the same. The organization must monitor the unfolding realities of each individual's life-situation, and respond with the precise action warranted by all the recorded "facts" about "the case." Whether the organization seeks to assess and collect taxes, allocate consumer credit, set terms for insurance coverage or deliver effective advertising appeals, the broad pattern of the relationship is the same.

The term I use for the social processes that support such particularizing relationships on a large scale is "mass surveillance" – that is, the systematic monitoring by organizations of large numbers of individuals' affairs. This term is not intended to carry any one value connotation. Surveillance, as I conceive it, is a basic and ubiquitous social relationship. Its manifestations range from the benign to the malevolent: from the attentions of parents to their children's actions and associates, to those of intensive-care ward staff to their patients, to those of counter-espionage agents to suspected spies. Surveillance, in this sense, has been with us as long as human beings have been social animals. What is noteworthy about mass surveillance is the juxtaposition of content and context – the fact that large, highly rationalized, otherwise "impersonal" organizations manifest the ability to maintain close, interactive monitoring of literally millions of individual subjects.

Computing is not an absolute *sine qua non* for mass surveillance. One can discern origins of these practices in early state-sponsored social insurance programs or credit-granting practices that were clearly in place well before the middle of the twentieth century. But obviously the rise of computing has vastly abetted tendencies of large organizations to maintain finely detailed records of individual affairs, and to predicate their dealings with those individuals on the content of those records. These relationships, I would argue, were as basic to the social structures of "advanced" societies at the end of the twentieth century as were the institutions of mass society to earlier social structures.

Note that such particularizing relationships have, in just a few decades, come to support social arrangements of great importance. The best example here comes from consumer credit. It is difficult to imagine now what retail trade and a variety of other activities would be like in the absence of nearly universal credit card use. But when the original creators of the predecessors to today's Visa cards sought, in the 1950s, to extend credit card services to middle- and low-income consumers, they faced a nettlesome sociological problem – to wit, to whom to allocate the cards they sought to offer. Their first attempts along these lines nearly bankrupted their operations, after they issued credit cards nearly at random. Only after grasping the need to fine-tune their surveillance over access to, and use of, the cards were they able to turn mass market credit card issuance into the hugely profitable business that it is today.

It would be wrong to imagine that particularizing relationships between large bureaucracies and ordinary citizens are necessarily imposed by the former on the latter. In fact, our expectation that such organizations will take precise account of our affairs and circumstances is a key feature driving the development of particularizing technologies and processes. As citizens of the early twenty-first century's "advanced" societies, we expect, perhaps even demand, that insurance companies will tailor the terms and availability of insurance to the particular details of our "records." We have much the same expectation about our tax liabilities, our consumer credit opportunities and our driving records. Indeed, we are so accustomed to a world in which huge, otherwise "impersonal" bureaucracies take exact account of such details about us that we may find it hard to imagine what life would be like if the detailed personal data that support such attentions were unavailable to such organizations.

## Creating the infrastructure of mass surveilance

Particularizing social relationships are in no sense the direct and simple results of computerization. Like all techno-systems, computing requires "embedding" in specific social relationships. Mass surveillance, more specifically, requires both technologies for mastering vast, finely grained detail on citizens' lives and social structures for generating, transmitting and using such data. The creation of these structures is not automatic. Indeed, in historical perspective, their development is initially halting and incremental.

Thus, at the beginning of the twenty-first century, we take it for granted that authoritative personal data on most citizens will be generated as a matter of course at many important (and, increasingly, unimportant) life junctures. But, as recently as the beginning of the twentieth century, even births and deaths were not universally recorded in many statess. Credit reporting, in its early-twentieth-century infancy, was limited to simple exchanges of lists of bad debts among local retailers. Income taxation was problematic when first introduced, given the sparseness of authoritative documentation of people's financial affairs. The evolution from these situations of haphazard and rudimentary availability of personal data to today's world of automatic and proliferating data production is a historical development of some consequence.

Notice something of great import about the generation of data for use in systems of mass surveillance. Given the endemic conflicts of interest over determinations to be made on the basis of such data, the most valuable personal data are those generated by sources independent of the individual concerned. Consumers, for example, generally prefer to provide only the most favorable items of their credit histories on credit applications; the data most sought by credit grantors, by contrast, will be from sources not selected by applicants. Similarly, the US Internal Revenue Service (IRS) would find its efforts to enforce compliance stymied if its only source of data on taxpayers' affairs were the taxpayers themselves. Or, again, auto insurance providers will hardly be content with applicants' own accounts of past claims and accident histories; they will insist, wherever possible, on direct access to independent information on these matters, preferably from strong state systems of recording.

The middle and latter decades of the twentieth century saw a gradual but relentless process by which such institutional sources of surveillance-relevant data have grown up. As recently as the mid-twentieth century in the USA, the only way of obtaining all sorts of relevant personal data was from the individual concerned – a situation that certainly favored privacy interests but undercut the efficiencies of mass surveillance. Since then, however, the list of points at which bureaucratically usable personal data are routinely generated has grown impressively. Credit and automatic teller machine or cash cards create detailed records of movements and activities. Third-party payment of medical bills requires far more precise and extensive documentation of one's medical care usage. The rise of cyberspace, needless to say, has created a vast array of junctures, from website visits to e-mail transmissions, that document people's interests, social networks and buying habits – again, quite independently of individuals' wishes in these matters.

As organizational sources of surveillance information proliferate, they become increasingly symbiotic. Government organizations increasingly exploit personal data from private sector institutions; corporations seek to use government-generated data in the same ways. The IRS, for example, seeks to supplement tax return data with reports from consumer credit agencies, in order to weigh the credibility of taxpayers' own accounts of their financial situation. Credit grantors, by contrast, often require copies of tax returns to substantiate data provided by consumers themselves on credit applications. Similar observations can be made of personal data exchanges in insurance, driver licensing, employment screening, direct marketing and a variety of other junctures.

Perhaps now I should make explicit the relevance of these trends to the emerging technologies and practices of perpetual contact. The latter manifestly work to extend the realm of "private" life that is subject to monitoring by organizations independent of the individuals concerned. Indeed, they mark a significant new step in the movement toward what I have called "total surveillance" – that is, a world in which every fact and every moment of every individual's life registers with a single, centralized agency of surveillance.

## From mass society to perpetual contact

Mass society thinking embodied a characteristic set of value concerns. These included sensitivity to the dangers posed to deliberative democracy from potent, standardized sources of mass communications, with their supposed ability to deaden citizens' critical faculties and redirect their public behavior. Some of these concerns seem valid in retrospect, some overblown.

In any case, the period of their salience is past. In its place, we have a new set of images and concerns – those associated with particularizing policies and attentions of large organizations. Here the perceived value issues have to do not with impersonal influence processes that undermine the individuality of respondents, but with the invasion of privacy. In contrast to mass communications, the particularizing practices of mass surveillance threaten to go too deeply in the detail of our lives, to become too personal, too closely tailored to our specific circumstances and biographies. And if the dynamics of mass surveillance are in some respects the opposite of those of mass society, the dynamics of perpetual contact carry that contrast one step farther.

Since the 1960s, concern about the privacy-invading qualities of particularizing systems has spawned a considerable literature. There is every reason to expect perpetual contact systems to provide further inspiration for that literature, as commentators seek to assess the dangers that may be posed by these new practices.

Some will no doubt minimize the dangers involved. After all, one argument will go, perpetual contact systems are not being imposed on anyone. One can always turn off one's mobile phone, or simply never use a mobile phone in the first place. So long as the principle of individual choice in these matters is respected, this view would go, any such innovation can only leave everyone better off than before.

But if the history of mass surveillance, and its contrasts to mass society, have anything to teach us on this point, it should be caution. The appeal of the kinds of information generated by perpetual contact systems – real-time logs of people's movements and activities – is predictable. We ought to act on the assumption that, when data are this widely desirable, all sorts of pressures will come to bear, over the course of social change, to compel its production and appropriation.

Once data of this kind are known to exist, strong inducements inevitably come into play to make such data available. Thus the logs of perpetual contact data will be as much subject to legal process as any other personal records. Law enforcement agencies, from the IRS to the FBI to state and local bodies, will want to enjoy the same easy access that they now enjoy to bank and credit card records, which are potent sources of data in their surveillance efforts.

Then there are questions about how long participation in systems of perpetual contact will remain authentically voluntary. The history of other junctures that generate authoritative personal data should be instructive here. When bank checking accounts and mass market credit cards first appeared, no one thought of them as anything other than an attractive option – something that anyone could take or leave. Today, obviously, things are much different. For certain ordinary transactions – booking a hotel or a rental car, for example – a credit card is all but indispensable. Similarly, anyone who applies for a consumer loan and claims not to have a checking account will surely attract skepticism, if not suspicion. The forces at work are much the same as those mentioned above in the case of income tax returns. The fact that everyone can be assumed to submit income tax returns – under pain of government sanction should they be proven false – makes it possible for other interested agencies to demand the production of those documents, whether the individual concerned wishes to accede to such demands, or not.

The day may come when it becomes essential, in order to initiate certain relationships, to make available the logs of one's mobile phone use. Under certain scenarios, one could imagine that submission of such logs could become a requirement in applications for positions as law enforcement officers – so that applicants with a history of spending time in high-crime areas could be brought under heightened scrutiny. Or one could imagine that parole might be predicated on the parolee's keeping his or her mobile phone on at all times, so that his or her movements could be monitored. One could imagine that court restraining orders requiring persons to stay away from certain places might be implemented similarly.

To some, these possibilities may appear fantastical, the stuff of science fiction. But they do not strike me as any further removed from current realities than these realities are from the informational environment of a generation ago. Who, at that point, could have predicted the rise of today's active markets in personal data, let alone envisaged legislation or policy that might have constrained their growth? Who could have predicted that personal data so marketed would be collected, without our knowledge or consent, from electronic "sites" that we would be "visiting" by computer?

The predictive power of social science is widely disparaged, and often for good reason. We should be frank in admitting that many important social developments such as those just noted were not accurately anticipated, even by those who had most to do with bringing them about. But other things are predictable – if not in terms of specific events, in terms of broad trends and forces. We can predict with some confidence that, as the practices of perpetual contact unfold, contest over access to the data concerned will grow more acute, along the lines anticipated above. We can take it for granted that, the more detailed and continuous the personal information generated by such systems, the sharper will be disputes over who may appropriate it and how it may be used. The world has come a long way since the trunk lines of data flow were dominated by mass communications. The rise of systems of perpetual contact takes us a significant step further in that evolution.

## Models of things to come

Mobile telephony is obviously well on its way to becoming a major force in reshaping social arrangements. For students of technology, it is proper, and in fact irresistible, to seek to anticipate what larger social role these new technologies will assume. All that we know for sure is that this role will resemble that of other emergent technologies in certain respects, and that in other ways past experience will provide no guidance whatsoever.

At this early stage, it can be hard even to take adequate stock of the range of possibilities. Here, again, models help – models that at least identify how the technologies of mobile telephony may or may not impinge on key social values. Consider three salient models in the form of paired opposites or ideal-typical contrasts in the roles that these technologies may assume.

### *Appendectomy vs. drug addiction*

One classic, Enlightenment-inspired model pictures technological change as a series of "solutions" to pre-existing "problems." In this view, new technologies arise as responses to "needs," sources of discomfort or disadvantage that weigh against human interests, whether publicly recognized or not. Thus the history of technological innovation is essentially a history of progress, as a greater and greater array of needs is incrementally fulfilled by innovative human response to felt necessity.

Contrasting with this model is a vision picturing technological innovation not as a response to "problems" that are objectively given, but in fact as created by the same processes that generate the "problems" in the first place. The basic logic of this position was first formulated by Jacques Ellul (1964). "Needs" for technological intervention are proclaimed, Ellul argued, by a pervasive mind-set that sees in every technologically shaped social setting the origins of further "needs" that require further technological interventions. The very world-view that produces the "solutions" generates the "needs."

Thus the first of these models might picture mobile telephony as resembling an appendectomy – a solution for a problem whose existence is hard to deny, even for those who do not understand how it comes about. In the contrasting model, the technology is more like a "fix" of an addictive drug than a life-saving operation. Desperate though the addict may be for a fix, the underlying craving the drug satisfies would never arise unless first incited by taking the drug. The fix may alleviate the craving temporarily, but it only makes future cravings of the same kind more intractable.

Does the demand for mobile phones – as currently documented, and as it may unfold in the future – more closely resemble the "need" for an appendectomy or that for a drug "fix"? Clearly it makes little sense to treat this question as a matter for binary choice. Instead, we should regard it as the basis for a research program. To what extent do the "needs" for which people use mobile phones appear to have pre-dated the technology? Some such "needs" appear clearly identifiable; for example, the need to summon help in situations of imminent danger. For other ranges of use, the addiction model may come closer to the mark. To the extent that one could show that use profiles serve purposes of social display or conspicuous consumption, for example, one would have to take Ellul's thinking as a more informative model.

### Embryo vs. a random walk

The second pair of polar models reflects the tension between determinate and indeterminate visions of the future of mobile telephony. To what extent are the future social roles to be taken by this technology pre-ordained? How much is it reasonable to assume in advance about who will use the technology, how widely, for what purposes and with what repercussions for other social arrangements?

Many commentators, for example, speak of the anticipated "trajectory" of this technology, invoking a metaphor that implies a powerful model of determinacy. Like the image of the life-cycle of a plant or animal, or of the collapse of exhausted stars into black holes, or Pareto's rise and decline of social elites, this notion of technology as embryo carries with it the notion of a fixed and foreseeable sequence. Part of that sequential character has to do with matters such as the curve described by increasing "saturation" of the technology, that is, the speed at which it can be expected to reach its maximum usage (however that may be understood). Other aspects have to do with the forms it may take: the sorts of "needs" served, the social contexts of its use, the new relationships and activities expected to arise from it, and so on. This complex succession of qualitatively distinct states, like those in the development of embryos, can theoretically be understood and anticipated.

The opposite model is the random walk – the notion that the steps in the development of this technology are loosely coupled, perhaps totally indeterminate, like the course of a whimsical stroller heading in no particular direction. In this view, the completion of any one "stage" in the development of mobile telephony would give no grounds for any conclusion about what might happen next.

Here, too, there is no point in treating these contending models as either–or possibilities. Some aspects of the future of these technologies are undoubtedly predictable, and some are not. But which is which? Is it reasonable to anticipate a set "trajectory" for the diffusion of mobile telephones? Is such a trajectory bound to approach the levels of saturation achieved by the use of television, wired phones or other near-universal technologies? And if one is confident enough to take such quantitative trajectories for granted, what about qualitative developments? To what extent are the forms, the functions and the social contexts of mobile telephony knowable in advance?

If there is a hazard built into such judgments, it lies in the too-easy comparison of this technology to other established, highly consequential technologies. It is not easy to recall the "non-events" of promising technologies that looked at one time as though they would assume the importance of radio, the automobile and the Internet. And we recall the wildly inaccurate assumptions about how those technologies would be assimilated, even on the part of those who helped launch them. Any attempts to project the future of mobile telephony must give careful account of the relative admixture of embryo-like elements, as against the qualities of randomness that creep into most complex social processes.

### Niche-dweller vs. weed

Ecologists warn of an insidious effect of human intervention in the environment – the proliferation of "weeds." By this they mean something more specific than things that grow where not invited in your garden. "Weeds" in this context are a sizable category of natural species whose environmental adaptations are so broad as to permit them to inhabit and thrive in very diverse environments. Familiar examples range from raccoons to crab grass to grey squirrels to the common house fly. Some of these we regard as noxious, others not, but what they share is not their appeal or lack of it. It is their knack for making themselves at home in the widest variety of settings – from urban to rural, tropical to arctic, moist to dry – and for out-competing species adapted to distinctively local environments. Encouraged by worldwide movements of persons and goods, weeds of this kind seem to go more or less wherever humans go, and when they get there they often predominate among the local fauna.

"Weeds" in this sense have an exact social analog in the standardized practices and institutions that proliferate in the wake of globalization. Perhaps everyone has noticed how artifacts and practices of American mass culture seem to be turning up in the most distant corners of the world: Nike shoes in Africa, American university sweatshirts in France, memorabilia from Michael Jackson and Michael Jordan adorning cafés in Thailand, and so on. These practices have their institutional analogs in the proliferation of franchise businesses: McDonald's, Pizza Hut, amazon.com, and so on. Like weedy species, these weedy institutions give us reliability and predictability at the cost of moving us toward a uniform world-wide environment.

Mobile telephony could prove to be a "weedy" technology in its own right, by destroying the distinctive qualities of milieux constrained by the physical presence of participants. Everyone has noticed the irritation of restaurant diners on being subjected to conversations carried on via mobile phone by other diners. Objections to these technologically abetted additions to restaurant dining, it seems to me, go well beyond the contributions of the conversations to sound levels. Instead, they have to do with the breakdown of the boundaries that mark the restaurant dining room as a distinct and protected milieu. One of the things that people seek in going "out to dinner" is the experience of being "out," that is, in a setting where people are removed from workaday concerns, where they are concentrating on food and their immediate company.

This same kind of "weediness" could clearly characterize the social role of mobile telephony quite generally. If perpetual contact comes to be defined as normative in any and all social settings, then clearly all sorts of relationships, milieux and institutions will lose their distinctive character. Experiences from walking in the wilderness to worshipping to museum-going could be transformed through the loss of boundaries with the rest of participants' lives – just as "foreign" countries come to look less different from the United States, the more the weedy influences of American culture and commerce project themselves around the world.

Or perhaps not. Norms could grow up that would confine reliance on perpetual contact to circumscribed times and settings. Should this occur, mobile telephone use might come occupy its special niche in social ecology, something that one does on very specific occasions, rather than crop up everywhere, invited or not, like an invasive plant.

## Concluding thoughts

"All historical events are inevitable," a noted historian once insisted to me; "but some are more inevitable than others." Such mind-expanding but scarcely simplifying advice should certainly apply to efforts to foresee the future of perpetual contact technologies. We know that not all social roles for these technologies are equally likely. Some are barely feasible, under any conditions; others seem highly probable. Yet the fund of experience of other thinkers confronting other technologies aborning ought to be useful for us. Some models that have seemed absolutely persuasive in the past have lost their luster. Elsewhere, the social evolution of specific technologies has taken directions that no one seems to have anticipated at their launching.

So, certainty is a utopian aspiration in efforts such as these. Anyone who promises to foretell the detailed "trajectory" of mobile telephony should probably be disregarded out of hand. Still, our disciplines do provide us with some tools to separate the more probable futures from the less. And, among such tools, models such as those considered here surely deserve a special place.

## References

Ellul, Jacques (1964). *The Technological Society*. New York: Knopf.
Kornhauser, William (1959). *The Politics of Mass Society*. Glencoe, IL: Free Press.
Rule, James B. (1973). *Private Lives and Public Surveillance*. London: Allen Lane.
Rule, James, McAdam, Douglas, Stearns, Linda, and Uglow, David (1980). *The Politics of Privacy: Planning for Personal Data Systems as Powerful Technologies*. New York: Elsevier.

# 16    Mobiles and the Norwegian teen: identity, gender and class

*Berit Skog*

### The mobile phone in teen identity and subculture

In Norway two-thirds of teens own or have access to mobile phones, so how they are used and viewed by teens is an important issue. Through two surveys of mobile phone use among Norwegian teenagers, we gain insight into this technology's role in young people's lives. Clearly, though, a large role is occupied by the short messaging service (SMS), which allows transmission of text messages via mobile phone. Though messages are limited to 160 characters, they are quite economical (Ling, 2000). SMS has spurred teens to create an anglicized clique-based abbreviated language. The mobile phones also have various technical facilities including the ability to download ring tones ("hit" pop music), logos, pictures and games; mobiles are available in various brands, designs and colors. The newest ones, WAP (Wireless Application Protocol) phones, access the Internet and e-mail. Hence teen users are not only consumers but producers as well since they are free to create an individual phone by combining the above elements. The flexibility and social contact allowed by the technology mean that it has become harnessed as part of many a teen's identity project.

Identity itself is the process by which social actors use cultural attributes to recognize themselves and construct meaning (Castells, 1996). For teens, three processes are formative in constructing their identities: reflexivity, makeability and individualization (Ziehe, 1989). *Reflexivity* is a cultural way of mirroring (individual, subjective, social or cultural) selves or identities through symbolic images in media, verbal language or face-to-face interaction (Grodin and Lindlof, 1996). *Makeability* is the perspective that sees personality and lifestyle factors as being open to influence. Individuals make choices about their content rather than simply accept tradition passively. *Individualization* means that, as industrial society develops, the significance of social background decreases while the subjective importance of the inner world increases. Giddens (1991) attributes the rise in other-directedness to one's need for confirmation from others of a stable identity. Thus, identity becomes more multifaceted, personal, self-reflexive and subject to innovation (Kellner, 1992). The mobile phone objectifies a technological device that allows young people to create and negotiate their gendered and social class-based identities. The process by which this is done can be understood as an identity project.

Our study's central objective was to see the way girls and boys use mobile phones. Although we found only small differences between girls and boys in mobile telephone ownership, which was to be expected (Ling, 2000), their relationships to the mobile phone varied widely. This may be seen in light of the status of the mobile phone as a technological object. The social concept of technology emphasizes its maleness and masculine nature (Wajcman, 1991). For instance, Turkle (1984) found that boys and girls tended to use two different styles of computing, which she calls "hard" and "soft" mastery. Hard masters are mainly boys, imposing their will over the machine by implementing a structured plan, and aiming to control the machine. Girls tend to be soft masters, having a more "interactive," "negotiating" or "relational" style. Hence it is reasonable to believe that girls would prefer the social and qualitative aspects of the mobile phone, whereas the boys would stress its brand image and the technical capabilities.

In addition to the practical and functional utility of the mobile phone, it is laden with cultural meanings and images. It may be used to project a desirable image to others, to express social status and to make visible personal characteristics (Dittmar, 1991). In his study of material possession according to social class, Rosenlund (1992) showed that mobile phone ownership was higher among working-class than among service-class men. Middle- and upper-class people want possessions that serve prestige, status and self-expressive needs. According to Bourdieu (1984), those with higher education or cultural capital have the legitimate culture and will tend to appreciate traits such as cultural sophistication, "good taste," refinement and eloquence. They are the first to use new kinds of food, clothes and material possessions, using trend-setting as a way to distinguish themselves. This implies that the status image of the mobile phone may have an impact on the class division of mobile phone ownership among teenagers. Thus, the second question addressed here is whether social class origin has an impact on teenagers' ownership of mobile phones.

This study will further look into the possible effects of mobile phone use, for example on self-esteem. This refers to a child's relationship with parents, siblings and peers, whereas academic self-esteem is a factor on entering school when children receive feedback about themselves in relation to other classmates (Tapscott, 1998). It may be expected that different cultural capital factors will influence academic self-esteem, such as parents' class position and parents' interest in school work (Skog, 1994), time spent on homework and the number of books at home (Knudsen, 1978; Bourdieu, 1984). Self-esteem may also be affected by the use of interactive digital devices such as the Internet, where users act on their environment. Using a mobile phone implies assessing, composing sentences, and interacting with others. Thus, we will explore whether or not the ownership of a mobile phone affects academic self-esteem.

Tapscott (1998), among others, argues that today's young people are very fluent in digital media. Although folk wisdom bolsters such arguments, it is nonetheless useful to explore empirically whether or not the use of mobile phones is connected with the use of other types of interactive technology, such as computers, the Internet, CD-ROM and e-mail.

## Data and measures

Our data are drawn primarily from a survey, "Analogue and digital learning material: pupils and teachers in the information society" (the ADL study) (Skog et al., 1999), whose purpose was to describe the information and communication technology (ICT) situation in the Norwegian compulsory ("public" in American usage) school, focusing on pupil and teacher use and views of ICT (e.g. computers, the Internet, CD-ROM). The data are based on a representative sample of students in the ninth grade. The sample was drawn by a two-stage stratified sampling procedure. In the first stage, schools were divided into four strata according to language type (Norwegian/New Norwegian) and size of school (small/large). In the second stage, schools within each stratum were se lected by a random probability procedure, and all pupils in the ninth grade at the selected schools were included. The questionnaires were administered by the school authorities in the spring 1999 term. The sample studied consisted of seventy schools including 2,979 pupils. Among the pupils sampled, 84% responded.

In addition, we use data from an October 2000 self-selection sample survey, "Mobile phone and youth" (MPY). Here sixty-seven teen girls and fifty-three boys answered questions concerning the importance of and their use of mobile phones. We did this not to make statistical generalizations but to be able to better analyze patterns of behavior between girls and boys in relation to mobile telephony (Aaberge and Laake, 1984).

### Independent variables

*Father's and mother's occupation.* Information on the main occupation and employment status of the father and the mother is taken from the survey. Three social classes were distinguished based on this information (Erikson and Goldthorpe, 1992): service class (highest), middle class and working class (lowest).

> *Parent interest.* This is an additive index based on pupils' answers on a five-point Likert scale ("strongly agree," "agree," "don't know," "disagree," "strongly disagree") to statements concerning parents' interest in their school work: "My parents read my school books," "My parents help me with my school work" and "My parents are interested in my school work."
>
> *School attitudes.* The school attitude measure was based on pupils' answers to the following statements (again using a five-point Likert scale): "It is important to get good grades," "I feel content at school" and "Education is important for my future."
>
> *Number of books.* This variable is based on the question "How many books do you think you have at home?" ("fewer than 20," "20–50," "50–100," "100–500," "500–1,000," "more than 1,000"). This variable may indicate the level of cultural capital in pupils' homes (Bourdieu, 1984; Skog, 1994).
>
> *Time on lessons.* This variable shows the average time spent on homework on a daily basis. The pupils chose among the following categories: "I never do any homework," "less than 15 minutes," "15–30 minutes," "30–60 minutes," "1–2 hours" and "more than 2 hours."
>
> *Use of technology in homework.* The technology use measure is an additive index, and shows how often the pupils use different types of technology (such as the Internet, PC, CD-ROM) in their homework. The pupils gave their answers on a five-point scale ("very often," "often," "sometimes," "seldom" and "never").
>
> *Education plans.* This variable covers the students' plans for further education and work. A list of possible education was presented, and the students were asked to place themselves on this list. A dichotomy was created between "University or higher education" and "No higher education."
>
> *Future plans and job priorities.* The variables were factors determining students' plans for further education and work. A list of job motives was presented, such as "to get a high income," "to get a managerial position," "to combine with having children," "to help other people" and "to be in contact with other people." The subjects were asked to the rate the importance of each motive ("important" and "not important").

*Dependent variables*

The dependent variables used in the analyses conducted here are:

*Mobile phone ownership.* The subjects were asked whether they owned a mobile phone.

*Academic self-esteem.* The self-esteem measure was constructed by asking the pupils to evaluate their school performance compared with that of their classmates (Imsen, 1996) (worst group, second-worst group, second-best group, best group).

*Use of computer* and *Use of the Internet.* The pupils were given a list of possible functions of computers (such as games, CD-ROM, the Internet) as well as of the Internet (such as e-mail, homework, games). They were asked to rate each function on the five-point scale for frequency of use described above.

*Mobile phone functions.* Functions supposed to be important for the use of mobile phones were listed, such as calls, friends, easy to reach, SMS, time consumption, WAP.

*Mobile phone characteristics.* Factors supposed to be important for the choice of mobile were listed, such as color, design, performance, ring tones, ease of use, logo, brand.

The subjects were asked to rate the importance of each mobile phone function and characteristic ("very important," "fairly important" and "not important").

## Results

Table 16.1 presents the ownership of mobile phones with respect to gender and social class as well as other factors.

*Mobile phones and social class*

A striking result is that more teens from a working-class background own mobiles than do those of higher classes ($p < .01$). This finding suggests that the mobile phone may be more of a status symbol among working-class teenagers. Teenagers planning university studies or higher education were less likely to own a mobile compared with those with lower educational aims. This finding supports a class based interpretation because teens from working-class homes have lower educational aims than those with a more academic background (Skog, 1994).

Another interesting finding is that a higher proportion of the teenagers who give priority to obtaining a high income and a managerial position in a future job have a mobile phone, compared with teenagers who are

Table 16.1 *Mobile phone ownership: results of the ADL study*

| Independent variable | Mobile phone ownership (%) | | |
|---|---|---|---|
| | Yes | No | *N* |
| Gender** | | | |
| Girls | 41 | 59 | 1,408 |
| Boys | 45 | 55 | 1,466 |
| Father's occupation*** | | | |
| Service class | 39 | 61 | 968 |
| Middle class | 43 | 57 | 485 |
| Working class | 46 | 54 | 743 |
| Mother's occupation*** | | | |
| Service class | 39 | 61 | 1,190 |
| Middle class | 44 | 56 | 826 |
| Working class | 49 | 51 | 254 |
| Education plans*** | | | |
| University/higher education | 39 | 61 | 2,174 |
| No higher education | 44 | 56 | 732 |
| Dyslexic*** | | | |
| Yes | 60 | 40 | 109 |
| No | 41 | 59 | 2,633 |
| Deaf** | | | |
| Yes | 65 | 35 | 174 |
| No | 42 | 58 | 2,569 |
| Help other people | | | |
| Important | 42 | 58 | 1,878 |
| Not important | 42 | 58 | 821 |
| Combine with children | | | |
| Important | 42 | 58 | 1,825 |
| Not important | 43 | 57 | 872 |
| High income** | | | |
| Important | 43 | 57 | 2,639 |
| Not important | 33 | 67 | 158 |
| Managerial function*** | | | |
| Important | 54 | 46 | 556 |
| Not important | 40 | 60 | 2,133 |
| Contact with other people* | | | |
| Important | 42 | 58 | 2,458 |
| Not important | 47 | 53 | 283 |

Statistical significance: $^{*}p < .10$, $^{**}p < .05$, $^{***}p < .01$

other-oriented or who want to combine work with having children or a job where they can get in touch with other people. Thus, the young mobile phone users may be said to stress instrumental motives, whereas the non-users stress socially oriented motives in their preferences for a future job.

## Mobile phones and gender

Although more boys than girls have a mobile phone, the differences are small (45% vs. 41%). The teenagers were presented with a list of possible factors of importance in the choice of a mobile phone, each to be judged on a three-point scale. In order to make the results clear, figure 16.1 shows the proportion of girls and boys who answered that a factor is "important."

Both girls and boys prefer a mobile phone that is easy to use: 79% of both sexes stress this factor. However, there were gender differences.

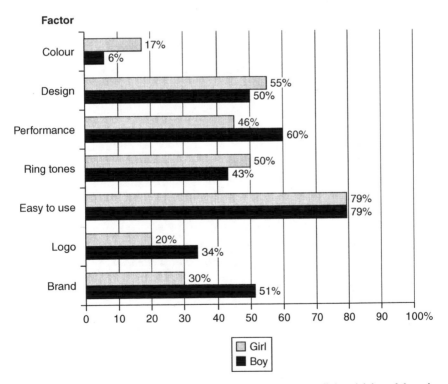

Figure 16.1 Factors considered "very important" in girls' and boys' choice of a mobile phone. *Source:* Table 16A.1.

**Factor**

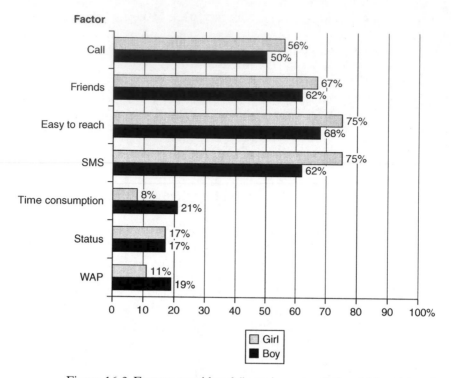

Figure 16.2 Factors considered "very important" for girls' and boys' use of mobile phones. *Source:* Table 16A.2.

Higher proportions of girls than boys found the design and ring tones of the mobile phone important: 55% of girls and 50% of boys stressed the design of the phone, whereas 50% and 43%, respectively, stressed the ring tone. Color evaluations too differed by gender: 17% of girls found the mobile phone color important, compared with 6% of boys. The boys emphasized other aspects of mobile phone use: 51% of boys found brand to be important, compared with 30% of girls. These results suggest that the boys focus on the technical facilities of the phone whereas girls stress the performance facilities, though both genders do care about both domains.

Figure 16.2 presents girls' and boys' evaluations of functions that are considered to be "important" for the use of a mobile phone. To be accessible is regarded as the strongest motive for the use of a mobile phone, stressed by 72% of the teenagers. Sending text messages (SMS) is another important factor, stressed by 75% of girls and 62% of boys. However, pastime and WAP facilities are more important for boys than for girls.

Thus, some interesting gender differences are revealed. Girls are more oriented towards the social aspects of mobile phone use, whereas boys stress the technical functions. However, both groups strongly underline the social and communicative functions of the mobile phone.

These functions are especially important for young people with disabilities. Table 16.1 shows that higher proportions of youth with dyslexia or hearing problems own a mobile phone relative to other youth. (Hearing-impaired youths are able to communicate with their friends by means of SMS.) Thus, the mobile phone may represent a way to compensate for these deficiencies, by what I would call "digital competence."

### Mobile phones and academic self-esteem

Table 16.2 shows the results of the regression analysis for the effects of various variables on self-esteem. Model 1 represents an analysis of variation in academic self-esteem by gender and class. Model 2 controls for the possible impact of various cultural capital factors. Model 3 controls for the Internet at home, and Model 4 for a PlayStation. Model 5 controls for mobile phone ownership.

Model 1 indicates that social class explains some of the variation in self-esteem, with mother's and father's occupation significant at the .01 level. The significance of mother's occupation disappears when the cultural capital factors and the technological equipment are introduced (Models 2–5). This indicates that father's class position is a strong explanatory factor in this analysis.

The cultural capital factors explain some of the variation in self-esteem, school satisfaction and number of books at home, as well as time used on lessons. Use of technology in homework is significant at the .05 level. Internet at home also influences self-confidence ($p < .01$), whereas a PlayStation has no impact. In Model 5, all variables are controlled. School satisfaction, number of books at home and father's occupation are all associated with self-esteem (all significant at the .01 level). The effects of the cultural capital variables as well as of father's occupation, which were stable when the Internet and PlayStation variables were introduced (Models 3 and 4), are reduced when the mobile phone is introduced into the model. The introduction of the mobile phone adds to the explanation of self-esteem. However, having a mobile phone is negatively associated with self-confidence, and the effect is significant at the .01 level. The mobile phone is negatively correlated with time spent on homework and cultural capital, but not with the Internet at home.

These results show that having a mobile phone is negatively correlated with academic self-esteem as well as with the cultural capital factors,

Table 16.2 Determinants of academic self-esteem (four-item scale)

| Variable | Model 1 B | Model 1 Beta | Model 2 B | Model 2 Beta | Model 3 B | Model 3 Beta | Model 4 B | Model 4 Beta | Model 5 B | Model 5 Beta |
|---|---|---|---|---|---|---|---|---|---|---|
| Constant | 3.49 | ** | 1.69 | ** | 1.65 | ** | 1.69 | ** | 1.77 | ** |
| Gender | −.05 | −.03 | −.02 | −.01 | −.02 | −.01 | −.01 | −.01 | −.01 | −.01 |
| Father's occupation | .14 | .15 ** | .11 | .12 ** | .10 | .11 ** | .10 | .11 ** | .09 | .10 ** |
| Mother's occupation | .10 | .09 ** | .05 | .04 | .05 | .04 | .05 | .04 | .04 | .04 |
| Use of technology | | | .02 | .05 * | .01 | .03 | .01 | .04 | .02 | .04 |
| Parents' interest | | | −.03 | −.03 | −.03 | −.03 | −.03 | −.03 | −.02 | −.03 |
| Lessons | | | .06 | .09 ** | .07 | .10 ** | .06 | .10 ** | .06 | .09 ** |
| School attitudes | | | .26 | .21 ** | .26 | .21 ** | .26 | .21 ** | .25 | .20 ** |
| Number of books | | | .11 | .16 ** | .11 | .16 ** | .11 | .16 ** | .10 | .15 ** |
| Internet at home | | | | | .11 | .07 ** | .10 | .07 ** | .11 | .07 ** |
| PlayStation | | | | | | | −.06 | −.04 | −.04 | −.02 |
| Mobile phone | | | | | | | | | −.17 | −.10 ** |
| ($N = 1,707$) | $R^2$ .038 | Adj. $R^2$ .036 | $R^2$ .127 | Adj. $R^2$ .123 | $R^2$ .131 | Adj. $R^2$ .126 | $R^2$ .132 | Adj. $R^2$ .127 | $R^2$ .142 | Adj. $R^2$ .137 |

$* p < .05; ** p < .01$

**Use of computer**

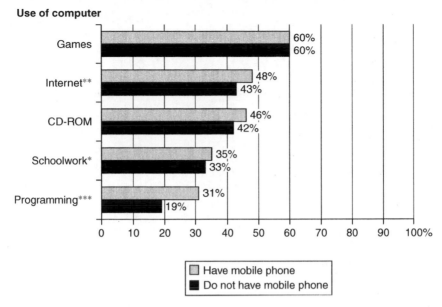

Figure 16.3 Teenagers who use the computer "often," by mobile phone ownership. *Note:* statistical significance: $*p < .10; **p < .05; ***p < .01.$

but positively correlated with Internet use. This suggests that the mobile phone is not used as a status symbol among the upper-class teenagers. The mobile phone may rather be regarded as a part of a digital project among working-class teenagers.

### Mobile phones and digital competence

Based on the ADL data, figure 16.3 shows the percentage of mobile phone owners and non-owners who often use a computer at home, and what they use it for. Having a mobile phone increases use of the Internet: 48% of mobile phone owners use the Internet often, compared with 43% of the non-owners ($p < .05$). Furthermore, a significant difference between the two groups is found in programming: 31% of the mobile phone group vs. 19% of non-owners. Mobile phone owners also use the PC for schoolwork more often than the non-owners. In games and CD-ROM no significant differences were found.

The differences between the two groups are further stressed in figure 16.4 (based on the ADL data), which shows the use of the Internet at home according to mobile phone ownership. The mobile phone owners use all the Internet functions more often than the non-owners. This

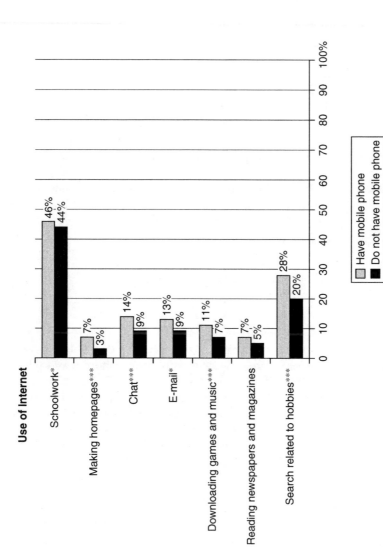

Figure 16.4 Teenagers who use the Internet "often," by mobile phone ownership. *Note:* statistical significance: \*$p < .10$; \*\*$p < .05$; \*\*\*$p < .01$.

applies particularly to search related to hobbies, downloading of games and music, making homepages and chatting (all significant at the .01 level). There are also significant differences between the mobile phone group and the other group with respect to use of the Internet for e-mail and homework ($p < .10$).

These results show that mobile phone owners are more likely than other teenagers to use digital technology. This indicates that the mobile phone group may be identified with digital capital instead of traditional school-oriented capital.

## Discussion

### *The mobile phone as a class phenomenon*

Our finding that a higher proportion of youth with working-class parents than service-class parents have a mobile phone (table 16.1) coincides with Rosenlund (1992). This is interesting because the latter group might be said to have the economic resources to buy a mobile phone. This suggests the mobile phone is not considered to be a distinction project among upper-class youth in Norway. They seem to have an ideological resistance to the adoption of the mobile phone. The class pattern in this study suggests that upper-class teens use a conscious singling-out process, and that this group has interests, hobbies and a lifestyle in which the mobile phone is not a "must." When everyone has got a mobile phone, it is no longer a status symbol, and a potential trend-setter has to find other ways to signal her/his exclusivity. A possible strategy may be to buy a new and more expensive phone, e.g. a WAP phone. These results conceal an interesting in-gender group difference: A closer examination of the data reveals that a significantly higher proportion of working-class boys than service-class boys own a mobile phone ($p < .01$), whereas there were no differences between girls according to class position (Skog, 2000). This finding may reflect the fact that the mobile phone functions as a status agent among working-class boys. This may be seen in light of Turkle's description of hackers: mastery over this type of technology may bestow some power on these boys; in relation to the symbolic rewards of a mobile phone, being "heroes" in pushing forward the frontiers of technological progress (Turkle, 1996). Thus, the mobile telephone may serve as symbolic capital for working-class teenagers, bringing status and honor to the owner (Bourdieu, 1984).

The class aspect in this study is further demonstrated by the fact that a smaller proportion of the mobile phone group than the other group were planning a university education (table 16.1). The mobile phone may be regarded as an expression of social–material position and membership in different social groups, as well as of gender.

### Gendering of mobile phones

A high proportion of girls have a mobile phone, which is shown by Ling (2000). This is an interesting finding, because a smaller proportion of girls than boys use other types of technology, such as computers, the Internet or CD-ROM (Skog et al., 1999).

Traditionally, technology has been designed to match technological skills, with men in mind (Wajcman, 1991). Girls have increasingly become users of technical artifacts, some of which were previously in male domains, such as computers. However, the mobile phone, like the computer, is not a type of technology associated with muscle, manual skill or all-male environments. Girls have acquired competence and knowledge of the type of technology that the mobile phone represents, which may convey a change in stereotypic female interests.

In factors considered to influence the choice of a mobile phone, some interesting gender differences were found. Girls' responses tend strongly towards the symbolic pole (color, design) and boys' towards the functional pole (technological performance, logo, brand) (table 16A.1). In terms of reasons for the use of mobile phones (table 16A.2), a higher proportion of girls than boys underline the SMS function. Boys are more inclined to emphasize the mobile phone as a leisure activity and its WAP function (Internet and e-mail access). Thus, for boys the importance of the mobile phone relates to its functional, practical and instrumental qualities, whereas girls stress the symbolic and expressive aspects, particularly in terms of social relationships and interpersonal ties. This corresponds to Dittmar (1991), who documents that men and women emphasize their possessions differently.

It could be said that the gendered relationships to the mobile phone reflect traditional gender roles by underlining the central aspects in girl and boy cultures. Girls seem to symbolize "soft" mastery, whereas boys may be identified as "hard" masters of the mobile phone. This may be seen in light of Turkle (1984). Nevertheless, many girls stress the importance of the technological facilities, and boys too emphasize the contact possibilities of mobile phone use. Thus, girls' use of and relationships to mobile phones may be regarded as the female acquisition of technology, and may transcend the gender determinism that has characterized the digital field.

The gendering of mobile phones may be described via the use of mobile phones, as well as in how gender leaves its imprint on mobile phones. The mobile phone companies seem to design phones to match the traditional female and the male cultures: the phones combine technological facilities with a rich selection of colors, designs, ring tones and logos. In female magazines, the color, design and social dimensions of mobile phones are addressed, whereas in male magazines the mobile phone advertisements have a technical and sporty profile.

### The mobile phone as digital capital

This study reveals that a higher proportion of teenagers who own a mobile phone also use other types of technology. They more often program (31% vs. 19%), use the Internet (48% vs. 43%) and use the CD-ROM (46% vs. 42%). These results taken together with other findings (table 16.2) indicate that young mobile phone owners have a general digital interest and competence, whereas non-owners may be described in terms of traditional school-oriented competence.

This pattern reflects central developments in the labour market. A digital job arena has emerged, employing persons mainly because of their technological digital competence rather than their formal education. The results in table 16.1 support this argument. In their future plans, significantly higher proportions of the young mobile phone owners stress a short education, a managerial position and a high income, compared with non-owners. This picture reflects the hacker or nerd phenomenon. Young men are being "head-hunted" to design web pages, program machines or act as computer consultants. The informal training that is taking place in these subcultures is extremely important in equipping people with transferable skills and enabling them to obtain employment in the field of digital media (Cunningham, 1998). Thus, the mobile phone may be seen as a symbol of a technological culture that generates job arenas with special strategies, rules and demands for qualifications.

For girls, the mobile phone may offer the motivation and the opportunity to use other types of technology. Girls are the majors users of the SMS system, which symbolizes the creative potential of the mobile phone, allowing text to be combined with graphics. Thus the mobile phone may represent an arena to train them for jobs in digital media, for example as web designers. This is in line with Sefton-Green (1998), who argues that girls' use of technology may be regarded as educative in the vocational sense, because many kinds of employment are presumed to require familiarity with electronic technology. Further empirical research is needed to explore this question fully.

*The mobile phone as an icon in youth culture*

Like previous research on the use of mobile phones among teenagers, this study highlights socio-environmental and gender factors. It also highlights the usefulness of the mobile phone to deaf and dyslexic people.

The mobile phone may reflect a digital culture, a consumer–producer system and a learning arena. The mobile phone may be regarded as a metaphor for modernity, in which the pull between the local and the global, reconfiguration of the consumer/user and changing power relations between teacher and taught are key parameters of the conditions in which young people are growing up (Sefton-Green, 1998).

A mobile phone appears to be the perfect tool for mastering modernity. It is simultaneously a way to master digital technology and, by sending text messages and communicating, an important way of processing modernity on social, cultural and psychological levels (Nissen, 1998).

The popularity of the mobile phone among teenagers may be seen in the light of central trends in modernity: reflexivity, makeability and individualization of youth cultures (Ziehe, 1989). Young people create their identities by means of factors such as language, clothes and symbols (Giddens, 1991). The mobile phone seems to be used as a personal style concept among teenagers. A special color, design and brand may be chosen to personify the mobile phone, as well as a special logo or ringing sound. A girl may choose a color that matches her clothes, thus giving the mobile phone an ornament status in a dressing project. With the mobile phone teenagers can position themselves in relation to a number of time-typical trends: being easily accessible, flexible, communicative, informed and up to date. Furthermore, they can simultaneously have an overview of and control different types of arenas: school, home and leisure time. Thus, the mobile phone symbolizes a lifestyle and the dynamic youth ideal in modernity.

### Acknowledgment

This chapter is partly based on data from the project "Analogue and digital learning material: Pupils and teachers in the information society" (Skog et al., 1999). This project is supported by the National Learning Centre, and is carried out at ALLFORSK and at the Department of Sociology and Political Science, Norwegian University of Science and Technology, Trondheim.

## Appendix

Table 16A.1 *Girls' and boys' evaluations of factors considered important in the choice of mobile phone*

| Factor | Importance (%) | | | N |
|---|---|---|---|---|
| | Very important | Fairly important | Not important | |
| Color | | | | |
| Girls | 17 | 9 | 73 | 64 |
| Boys | 6 | 40 | 55 | 53 |
| Total | 12 | 23 | 65 | 117 |
| Design | | | | |
| Girls | 55 | 45 | 0 | 60 |
| Boys | 50 | 50 | 0 | 48 |
| Total | 53 | 47 | 0 | 108 |
| Performance | | | | |
| Girls | 46 | 47 | 8 | 66 |
| Boys | 60 | 36 | 4 | 53 |
| Total | 52 | 42 | 6 | 119 |
| Ring tones | | | | |
| Girls | 50 | 36 | 14 | 66 |
| Boys | 43 | 25 | 32 | 53 |
| Total | 47 | 31 | 22 | 119 |
| Easy to use | | | | |
| Girls | 79 | 18 | 3 | 67 |
| Boys | 79 | 19 | 2 | 53 |
| Total | 79 | 18 | 3 | 120 |
| Logo | | | | |
| Girls | 20 | 41 | 39 | 66 |
| Boys | 34 | 26 | 40 | 53 |
| Total | 26 | 35 | 40 | 119 |
| Brand | | | | |
| Girls | 30 | 50 | 20 | 60 |
| Boys | 51 | 30 | 19 | 53 |
| Total | 40 | 41 | 20 | 113 |

*Source:* MPY data.

Table 16A.2 *Girls' and boys' evaluation of functions considered important for their use of mobile phones*

| | Importance (%) | | | |
|---|---|---|---|---|
| Factor | Very important | Fairly important | Not important | N |
| Calls | | | | |
| Girl | 56 | 3 | 41 | 64 |
| Boy | 50 | 4 | 46 | 54 |
| Total | 53 | 3 | 43 | 118 |
| Friends | | | | |
| Girl | 67 | 33 | – | 64 |
| Boy | 62 | 38 | – | 50 |
| Total | 65 | 35 | – | 114 |
| Easy to reach | | | | |
| Girl | 75 | 22 | 3 | 65 |
| Boy | 68 | 21 | 11 | 53 |
| Total | 72 | 21 | 7 | 118 |
| SMS | | | | |
| Girl | 75 | 16 | 9 | 64 |
| Boy | 62 | 19 | 19 | 53 |
| Total | 69 | 17 | 14 | 117 |
| Time consumption | | | | |
| Girl | 8 | 50 | 42 | 64 |
| Boy | 21 | 38 | 42 | 53 |
| Total | 14 | 44 | 42 | 117 |
| Status | | | | |
| Girl | 17 | 25 | 58 | 64 |
| Boy | 17 | 45 | 38 | 53 |
| Total | 17 | 34 | 49 | 117 |
| WAP | | | | |
| Girl | 11 | 17 | 72 | 64 |
| Boy | 19 | 32 | 49 | 53 |
| Total | 15 | 24 | 62 | 117 |

*Source:* MPY data.

# References

Aaberge, R., and Laake, P. (1984). "Om statistiske teorier for tolking av data" [Statistical Theories and the Interpretation of Data]. *Tidsskrift for samfunnsforskning* 25: 165–186.

Bourdieu, P. (1984). *Distinction. A Social Critique of the Judgment of Taste.* London and New York: Routledge & Kegan Paul.

Castells, M. (1996). *The Rise of the Network Society*, vol. I. Oxford: Blackwell.

Cunningham, H. (1998). "Digital Culture – the View from the Dance Floor." In J. Sefton-Green (ed.), *Digital Diversions. Youth Culture in the Age of Multimedia*. London: UCL Press.

Dittmar, H. (1991). *The Social Psychology of Material Possessions*. New York: St. Martin's Press.

Erikson, R., and Goldthorpe, J. (1992). *The Constant Flux. A Study of Class Mobility in Industrial Societies*. Oxford: Clarendon Press.

Giddens, A. (1991). *Modernity and Self-Identity. Self and Society in the Late Modern Age*. Cambridge: Polity Press.

Grodin, D., and Lindlof, T.R. (eds.) (1996). *Constructing the Self in a Mediated World*. Thousand Oaks, CA: Sage.

Imsen, G. (1996). *Increasing Equality*. Report No. 11, Department of Education, NTNU.

Kellner, D. (1992). "Popular Culture and the Construction of Postmodern Identities." In S. Lash and J. Friedman (eds.), *Modernity and Identity*. Oxford: Basil Blackwell.

Knudsen, K. (1978). *Inequality in the Primary School*. Institute of Sociology, University of Bergen, Norway.

Ling, R. (ed.) (2000). "Norwegian Teens, Mobile Telephony and Text Messages." Technical Newsletter from Telenor Research and Development, No. 2–2000.

Nissen, J. (1998). "Hackers: Masters of Modernity and Modern Technology." In J. Sefton-Green (ed.), *Digital Diversions: Youth Culture in the Age of Multimedia*. London: UCL Press.

Rosenlund, L. (1992). *Taste. An Introduction to Pierre Bourdieu's Sociology*. Report 4, Rogalandsforskning, Stavanger, Norway.

Sefton-Green, J. (ed.) (1998). *Digital Diversions. Youth Culture in the Age of Multimedia*. London: UCL Press.

Skog, B. (1994). "Culture and Class in the Academy." ISS Report No. 40, University of Trondheim, Norway.

  (2000). "Mobile Phones as a Symbolic Capital in the Youth Culture." In R. Ling and K. Thrane (eds.), *The Social Consequences of Mobile Telephony: The Proceedings from a Seminar about Society, Mobile Telephony and Children*. Telenor Research and Development, No. 38/2000.

Skog, B. et al. (1999). "Pupils' Use of Analogue and Digital Learning Material." Report No. 4, ALLFORSK.

Tapscott, D. (1998). *Growing up Digital. The Rise of the Net Generation*. New York: McGraw-Hill.

Turkle, S. (1984). *The Second Self: Computers and the Human Spirit*. London: Granada.

  (1996). *Life on the Screen: Identity in the Age of the Internet*. London: Weidenfeld & Nicolson.

Wajcman, J. (1991). *Feminism Confronts Technology*. Cambridge: Polity Press.

Ziehe, T. (1989). *Ambivalence and Manifold*. Copenhagen: Politisk revy.

# 17    The telephone comes to a Filipino village

*Georg Strøm*

When satisfying the communication needs of a country, it is necessary to understand the culture and economic preconditions. In particular it is necessary to be aware of areas where assumptions made in other parts of the world do not fit the local realities. This chapter focuses on the micro-aspects of providing telecommunication in a low-income rural area – on the conditions of the individual user, not on the more general economic or organizational aspects. I have used my own observations during visits to the Philippines between 1997 and 2000 and those of my wife, who grew up close to the *barangay* (Philippine village) featured in this chapter.

## Main results

In the *barangay*, communication, even by telephone, is generally not instantaneous: it takes between a few hours and several days to get a message to someone or to get him or her to the phone. In addition, the costs of calls are almost prohibitively high.

In contrast to Europe or the USA, where people tend to use the telephone whenever possible or convenient, people in the *barangay* go personally or send a message as the norm, using the phone only when there is no alternative. People may travel two hours to visit someone, who turns out not to be at home, and then either go back or wait hours, in the hopeful expectation of the occupant's return. It is accepted practice that one appears in person at a public office rather than making a phone call; likewise it is common for people to travel for three days simply to inquire whether a job is available.

Yet there is a different view when local communication is contrasted with distant communication. Despite the high costs, the phone is often crucial for providing emotional support to and keeping in contact with members of the family working in other parts of the country or abroad.

274

## Briefly about the Philippines

The Philippines has a population of 74 million people and an area of 300,000 km$^2$. It is about three-quarters the size of California, but with more than twice its population. The Philippines is a low-income country (mean family income of US$3,000 per year) with a high level of education (mean years of school are a little over eight).

## Telephones in the Philippines

In the Philippines there are only about 90 fixed phones and 50 mobile phones for every 1,000 people, most of them in offices or owned by the middle and upper classes. Among the majority it may be as few as 2 fixed phones per 1,000 people. However, the number of mobile phones is growing explosively, especially in urban areas.[1]

It is possible to get cellular phones with cards for pre-paid calls and no subscription fee, cellular phones with different types of subscription and of course ordinary subscriptions for fixed phones. In addition, as in Europe or the USA, there are different tariffs for calls at different times, between different telecommunication companies and for automatic and operator-assisted calls.

## Description of the *barangay*

The *barangay* featured here is situated in the Zamboanga Del Norte region, on Mindanao, which is the largest southern island of the Philippines, approximately 700 km from Manila. In March 1999 it comprised 254 families or 1,320 people with an average of 5.2 people in each family.[2] It is 4 km from Polanco, the center of the area, which has the high school, municipal administration, post office and police station, and it is 11 km from the nearest larger city, Dipolog, which has some 100,000 inhabitants. Income in the *barangay* is mainly from farming, though a few people work as teachers or in offices in Polanco or Dipolog. There is an elementary school in the *barangay*, a high school in Polanco and a college in Dipolog.

The *barangay* is an administrative unit governed by an elected *barangay* captain. Being a *barangay* captain is considered a part-time job, salaried by the regional government.

---

[1] Figures from the National Statistics Coordination Board (www.nscb.gov.ph) and *Philippine Daily Inquirer*, July 7, 2000 (www.inquirer.net).

[2] Number of families in the *barangay* supplied by the *barangay* captain; the average number of people in each family from National Statistics Office, *Philippines: QuickStat*, August 1999 (although the latest available figure is for 1995) (www.census.gov.ph).

### Access to phones

When the local congressman, Romeo Jalosjos, campaigned for re-election in 1996, all *barangay* captains in the area received a cellular phone, including the one in this *barangay*. That is today the only phone in the *barangay*. It is a low-cost GSM (Global System for Mobile Communications) handheld cellular phone with no field strength indicator, only a built-in antenna and no access to an elevated external antenna, which might improve the coverage.

Apparently the cellular system is designed mainly to cover the city of Dipolog, 11 km away, and the highway passing through it; the *barangay* is on the margins of this coverage area. The area is hilly, with ridges covered by coconut trees and banana palms. Traditional houses are built of bamboo and coconut wood, but houses in the center of the *barangay* are increasingly built of reinforced concrete, whose iron rods partly block the radio signals. In particular, the house of the *barangay* captain is built of reinforced concrete. A consequence of these modern building practices is patchy coverage. For instance, the phone cannot receive calls when in certain positions in or around the house.

In the Polanco area, which has 17,000 inhabitants, there is one public phone in the post office. However, the phone is frequently unavailable because of technical or other problems. In Dipolog, there are about ten unattended payphones and a PT&T (Philippine Telegraph and Telephone Company) staffed phone shop with eight phones and a fax machine for use against payment.

In addition, people who work in an office can use the phone there. They may receive and pass on messages, or they may use the phone to make calls of their own. It is in general accepted that persons working in an office may receive private calls for themselves or members of their family. It is likely that the phones are blocked such that national or international calls require some sort of approval, but I have no precise information on the specific procedures employed.

### Comparative prices of phone use

The monthly subscription cost of a fixed-line phone is 400 pesos (US$10). This is more than a schoolteacher can earn in one day or a manual worker in two days, and is equivalent to the price of 25 kg of rice or 6 kg of dried fish, both staples of the local diet.[3] The cost of a 3-minute

---

[3] Based on a teacher's monthly salary of 8,000 pesos and a six-day workweek, on a manual worker's daily salary of 70–150 pesos, on the typical price of a 50 kg sack of rice, and on a price of 50–100 pesos/kg, depending on the type, for dried fish.

daytime (7 am to 10 pm) national call from a fixed phone is 16.5 pesos (US$0.41),[4] equivalent to the cost of 1 kg of rice, 0.25 kg of dried fish or a half-bottle of rum.[5] A schoolteacher has to work for 27 minutes to pay for the call, whereas a manual worker has to work for 1–2 hours.[6]

The cost of a 3-minute daytime call from a cellular phone[7] is about 30 pesos, or 50 minutes of work for a schoolteacher, 2–4 hours of work for a manual worker, or enough to buy 2 kg of rice or two half bottles of rum. The cheapest cellular phone with a starter kit for pre-paid calls costs 3,000 pesos (US$75), or which is seven and a half days' salary for a schoolteacher or at least twenty days' salary for a manual worker.[8] In comparison, a Danish schoolteacher has to work for little more than half a day to pay for a phone with a starter kit for use with pre-paid calls, and for about 3 minutes to pay for a 3-minute daytime call.[9]

These prices are constantly changing because of competition and general economic conditions, but phone services remain expensive compared with other local prices and salaries.


### Use of phones

The use of phones is determined by a combination of limited access, high prices and a number of cultural and practical aspects.

The concept of a phone is not familiar, so phone calls are less useful. People who are not used to planning and making calls find it difficult to get everything talked over and concluded within the comparatively short time available, and the call may be wholly or partially wasted. They may run out of money before they have finished asking how every single member of the family is, and before they have had a chance to discuss the actual reason for the call.

The concept of a cellular phone and a normal quality of service is also unfamiliar. It is accepted that the connection sometimes is bad, but this is not attributed to the patchy coverage. In fact, it caused some surprise when I demonstrated how the quality of the connection (and the chance of receiving a call) could be improved by moving the cellular phone a small distance to the side.

---

[4] Philippines Long Distance Telephone, press release, December 24, 1998 (www.pldt.ph).
[5] A 375 ml bottle of Tanduay rum, 65° proof, costs 15 pesos.
[6] Based on an 8-hour workday for a schoolteacher and a 9-hour day for a manual worker.
[7] Price from *Smart*, November 1999 (www.smart.com). The price is for pre-paid calls to another cellular phone with the same telecommunication provider.
[8] *Philippine Daily Inquirer*, July 7, 2000 (www.inquirer.net).
[9] Because of the Danish liquor taxes, a Danish teacher can talk for 40 minutes for the cost of a half-bottle of rum.

An additional problem is lack of access to the full phone number. Phone numbers are often given without area codes, making it difficult for even a skilled phone user to place a national call without operator assistance.

For most people in the *barangay*, the phone does not support instantaneous communication. It takes from a few hours to a couple of days from when they want to transmit a message until they can get a reply.

When trying to contact someone in the *barangay*, it is normally necessary to call at least twice. If a sales lady[10] working in Manila wants to talk with her mother, for example, she may make the first call to the *barangay* captain or his wife on a Saturday afternoon. She will say that she wants to speak with her mother the next Monday at 4 in the afternoon. The captain or his wife may then give a message to the sales lady's mother when they meet her, or they may send a child with the message. The mother will then come early to the house, maybe by 2.30 or 3 o'clock, and wait for the call. If the phone has been left in a bad location in or near the house, it may not receive the call from the daughter. After waiting for a couple of hours the mother will then go home and wait until next time she is told that her daughter wants to call her.

It is not a very reliable mode of communication.

Access to the phone depends on family relations or friendships. Family members from Polanco or another *barangay* may come to receive phone calls instead of using a phone closer to their home, whereas a number of people in the *barangay* will not have access to receive calls. If they are not on good terms with the *barangay* captain, and in particular with his wife, the message may not be passed on.

In addition, it is almost impossible to keep the contents of a phone call secret. When leaving a message it is difficult not to say what the call is about, and in a Filipino household you are unlikely to be alone while receiving the call. In fact, asking to be left alone may be considered a little odd, like insisting on cleaning your fingers after shaking hands with someone.

The *barangay* captain is hesitant to lend out his cellular phone for outgoing national or international calls. Such calls are expensive and he cannot record the price of each call or make collect calls from the cellular phone. Except for calls by his own closest family, outgoing national and international calls are normally made from the PT&T office in Dipolog. It takes a minimum of two hours to make such a call, if one includes the trip to and from Dipolog and waiting time before a phone is available.

---

[10] The term "sales lady" is commonly used in the Philippines. It is gender specific, as are the persons designated by it.

Moreover, even though the PT&T shop is open until 9 or 10 pm,[11] there is almost no public transport in the evening, so people from the *barangay* must either make their calls during the day or stay the night with family in Dipolog after making the call.

Finally, calling a family member who works in an office and asking him or her to pass on a message is not an ideal immediate mode of communication for several reasons: it is considered impolite to refuse a request, so the family member working in an office may out of politeness agree to pass on the message, even if unable or unwilling to do so; even if the family member working in an office wants to pass on the message, it may be impossible to get the message to the receiver in time; it is only possible to call within office hours.

In one instance we wanted to invite a family member to come and visit us. He lived about a 5-hour bus journey away. We called on the Monday and reached his daughter, who worked in an office. She said that her father would like to visit us the next Friday. However, he did not turn up on the Friday, and we spent about two hours going round to the houses of different members of the family and asking if they had seen him. The office was closed over the weekend, and the daughter had the Monday off. She was out of the office when we managed to call on Tuesday, so we were unable to reach her.

We thought about what had happened, and if we might have misunderstood the message. However, our visitor turned up on the following Wednesday. One of his neighbors had died on the Friday; he had to attend the burial and had no way of getting a message to us.

In general, phone calls are made only when there is no alternative. This is in contrast to normal use in the USA and Europe, where one tends to call when possible and go personally only when one has to.

Part of that is because access to a phone is difficult, and it is often just as easy to go in person. When visiting members of the extended family, one does not call in advance. You assume their house is always open. It is considered more than a bit peculiar that people in Europe tend to call before making a visit, even though it saves them from going when the people they want to visit are not at home.

If a child for some reason cannot go to school, you will give a letter to another child in the neighborhood, who can take it to the teacher. You do not try to phone the school. In a similar manner, you often send a child with a message, when in Europe or the USA one would make a phone call. The child will normally get a small snack after having delivered the message.

---

[11] It is open from 8 am to 9 pm on Saturday and Sunday, and from 7 am to 10 pm, Monday to Friday.

If someone is ill, the family or neighbors will load him or her into the back of a truck or jeepney (a converted jeep used as bus) and drive him or her to a doctor or to the hospital. They will not call and expect a doctor or an ambulance to come.

Nor do you call the police. It is unlikely that the police could arrive in time, so if you are in trouble you grab a machete and prepare to defend yourself and your home. If you want to file a complaint, you go to the police station.

In general, unless you want to contact a member of your family, you do not call an office, but go in person. One reason is that Philippine public offices are paper and not computer based. Even if you can get assistance immediately, it is necessary to wait for the relevant papers to be found. It is therefore normally not possible to get a case resolved within an acceptable length of a phone call. In addition, some offices have far more requests than they can handle. If such an office offered assistance by phone, their phone system might break down.[12]

Even persons applying for a job in another city go there personally. If a sailor from the *barangay* wants to find a job in Manila, he spends 1,600 pesos on a return ticket[13] and travels for three days by boat to get there and go round the employment offices. He cannot call in advance and inquire if there are any jobs available. This may be a matter of supply and demand. When there is a surplus of qualified persons willing to go to the employment agencies, there is little incentive to handle requests by phone.

The most important use of the phone is for resolving practical matters with or offering emotional support to family members who live in other regions or outside the Philippines. Filipinos have strong family ties in both the close and the extended family, and compared with Europe or the USA they rely more on the extended family for help and emotional support (Andres and Ilada-Andres, 1987).

Approximately 10% of the population of the Philippines are employed outside the Philippines as overseas contract workers or undocumented or illegal workers (Gonzalez, 1998). A comparable number from small cities and rural areas work in the larger cities, such as Manila.[14]

---

[12] *Philippine Daily Inquirer*, August 10, 1999 (www.inquirer.net).

[13] William Gothong and Aboitiz, a shipping company.

[14] In addition to the overseas workers, there are Filipino women married to Australian, American or European husbands. However, a report for the United States Immigration and Naturalization Service by Robert J. Scholes (1999) indicates that their number is much smaller than the number of Filipinos in temporary employment outside the Philippines. It reports 19,000 marriages between Filipinos and foreigners a year (both men and women), indicating a total of fewer than 300,000 married Filipino women outside the Philippines. That figure should be compared with the 7 million Filipinos, of whom about two-thirds are women, in positions of temporary employment outside the Philippines.

The majority employed outside the Philippines are younger women, and a substantial proportion of them are mothers who have left their husband and children behind, normally with an aunt or another member of the extended family helping with the children (Gonzalez, 1998). Phone access is then crucial for keeping the family together – for decisions and emotional support or for discussing practical and monetary matters.

The cheapest national postage is only 5 pesos, and the cheapest international postage is 15 pesos. However, it typically takes eight days between a letter being sent in the Philippines and a reply arriving, and it takes at least fourteen days for an international letter. That is too slow in times of crisis.

The family at home is often dependent on the income from the person working in a larger city or outside the country. If a member of the family gets ill, or if the tuition fee is raised in the younger sister's school, a phone call is the only means of discussing the problem and asking for money with a minimum of delay.

In a similar manner, the person working in a larger city or outside the country is dependent on emotional support from the family. Substantial psycho-social stress is caused by being separated from the family and possibly alone in a different culture (Gonzalez, 1998). These problems are aggravated if the person working away experiences a deterioration in the relationship to children left behind, a breakdown of marriage, abuse or another crisis (Gonzalez, 1998). In such situations, the person needs contact to the family for support and advice on whether to stay and save money or to go home.

As a result there is a substantial number of national and international calls in comparison with local calls. These calls are necessary, even though the family often has to make a difficult choice between emotional needs and the cost of phone calls. For example, a sales lady in Manila has to work for 70 minutes to pay for a 3-minute call home.[15] A similar call from Hong Kong costs US$0.96,[16] and a woman working as maid in Hong Kong has to work for at least 90 minutes to pay for the call.[17] The costs and salaries are similar for someone working in Singapore, but salaries often are lower and the cost of calls about three times higher for someone working in the Middle East.[18] In addition, many calls cannot be completed in 3 minutes. In times of crisis it may take 10 or more minutes to sort things out by phone.

[15] Salaries for sales ladies are higher in Manila than in Dipolog. The calculation is based on a monthly salary of 4,000 pesos and a seven-day week of 10-hour days.
[16] Call price from Cheapcalls2 (www.cheapcalls2.com), November 1999.
[17] The term "maid" is gender specific. The figures are based on a monthly salary of HK$3,800 for a seven-day week of 11-hour days (at most she has half a day off every week).
[18] Prices from Cheapcalls2 (www.cheapcalls2.com), November 1999.

A further problem is that the different times of phone access do not coincide. Someone working in Manila or abroad can receive or make phone calls only at specific times of the day, and these times may not be the same as the times when the family can make a call from the phone in the *barangay*, an office or Dipolog.

The lack of phones often leads to waste of time. As an example, we went to visit a family in Dipolog, but when we arrived only their youngest child of about seven years was home. He said that his parents would be back later in the afternoon. We talked about what to do, and told the boy to tell his parents that we would return in about two hours. However, we got delayed, and it took about four hours before we were back. The family had then been waiting two hours for us.

This situation is similar for most meetings in Philippines, whether in educational institutions or businesses. The expression "Filipino time" describes how most people are either waiting or late, or a combination of the two. However, that is probably not caused by some strange genetic twist in Filipinos, but rather is a consequence of the lack of phones. People in Western Europe or the USA may not be much more punctual, but they can call and say they are late or ask for the meeting to be postponed.

### Comparison with expectations

It is interesting to compare the actual use of phones in the *barangay* with what might have been expected if no empirical observations had been made.

Anecdotes suggest that the quality of phone services is much lower in the Philippines than in Europe or the USA, whereas in fact it is difficult to perceive any difference in the normal service level. That is a consequence of the multi-tier economy. Most people who can afford a phone have comparable relative incomes and standards of living to the middle class in Europe or the USA, and they want and can pay for a similar level of service. The problem for the majority is not a low service level, but a lack of affordable access to phones.

Discussion of phone access in Europe and the USA often focuses on safety aspects: you need a phone to call for help in an emergency. That aspect is hardly mentioned at all in the *barangay*, where people are forced to accept much greater risks in their daily lives than people in Western Europe or the USA. The combination of heavy traffic and unsafe vehicles, in particular tricycles, leads to a high rate of traffic casualties. Medical assistance, clean water and adequate protection against mosquitoes are difficult to get or prohibitively expensive for the majority. In comparison with such problems, phone access in emergencies is not important.

Another feature of Western Europe and the USA is the high proportion of local calls. In the *barangay*, because calls are expensive and difficult to make, you go in person instead of making a local call, whereas it is necessary to make national and international calls to family members in larger cities or abroad.

Finally, you might expect more payphones. However, when people in the area adapt their demand to the supply of phones, the supply of phones tends to adapt to the demand.

## Conclusion

Access to telephones and their use to make calls are shaped by the economy. The people in the *barangay* waste a lot of time going in person instead of making phone calls but, given the actual situation, their choices are completely rational. They are adapted to limited access to electronic communication. Because it is used so little, the benefits of using it become even smaller.

As regards access to communication, the people in the *barangay* are not much better off than a hundred years ago. Although they do have some access to electronic communication, significant numbers of family members today live and work 700 or 7,000 km away, whereas a hundred years ago the family lived within a day's travel.

## References

Andres, Tomas B., and Ilada-Andres, Pilar B. (1987). *Understanding the Filipino*. The Philippines: New Day Publishers.

Gonzalez III, Joaquin L. (1998). *Philippine Labour Migration*. Singapore: De La Salle University Press.

Scholes, Robert J. (1999). "The 'Mail-order Bride' Industry and Its Impact on U.S. Immigration." Appendix A of *International Match-making Services: A Report to Congress*. United States Immigration and Naturalization Service, 4 March. Available on http://www.clas.ufl.edu/users/rscholes/writeup.htm, accessed July 10, 2001.

# 18    Beginnings in the telephone

*Emanuel A. Schegloff*

I come to the theme of this volume – "Mobile communication, private talk, public performance" – as a student of conversation and other forms of talk-in-interaction. The sort of work my colleagues and I do is focused on the "stuff" of quotidian interaction, as encountered in naturally oc-curring settings, as captured by modern recording devices which allow repeated examination of particular specimens, and thereby facilitate our overcoming the relentless blinders of familiarity which can keep us from seeing what is really going on, and how it gets to be that way. That is how I came some years ago to take as an analytic target talk on the telephone – the ordinary, fixed, wired telephone; it is that analytic experience which is my credential for this volume, and is the basis for what is offered in what follows.

The title of this volume – "Perpetual Contact" – reminds me of a similar-sounding phrase introduced some years ago – "a continuing state of incipient talk" (Schegloff and Sacks, 1973). The phrase referred to certain interactional circumstances (and a form of overall structural or-ganization of conversation) in which the parties' co-presence is shaped by contingencies independent of the character of their talk. Familiar venues in which one finds continuing states of incipient talk are members of a family or other living arrangement sitting together in a common room; members of a car pool en route to or from their destination; seatmates on an airplane or train; and the like. Unlike many other conversational circumstances, gaps of silence at topic or sequence boundaries are *not* taken to occasion the launching of the closing of the conversation. The parties are taken to be together for the duration, a duration set by con-tingencies and constraints other than those of the talk – such as arrival at a destination, or the setting being their "home base."

In a continuing state of incipient talk, a stretch of talk structured by topic or by some course of action can come to a close and have silence set in, silence that can be allowed to grow into a lapse – one that can

This chapter is a revised version of the keynote address to the "Perpetual Contact" workshop at Rutgers University, December 9, 1999.

last a very long time, conversationally speaking. The lapse is one in which talk can break out again at any moment (hence "*continuing* state of *incipient* talk") with no "hello"s to start it, just as there are no "bye bye"s to end the talk before the lapse.

It may serve as a kind of reality check on the novelty of the topic of the volume to recall that continuing states of incipient talk have been with us humans for a very long time. They have *not* been limited to interaction with kinfolk or intimate acquaints either, although those have probably predominated. But the seatmates on an airplane, the co-riders on the airport shuttle, etc., surely give evidence that this is not criterial.

Clearly, the "perpetual contact" of this volume's *raison d'être* is quite different from a continuing state of incipient talk, not least of all in that each spate of talk requires the launching of a new conversation, a *new making* of contact. In fact, I mean to spend some time on just that *differentia specifica*. What is perpetual here is not contact itself but the possibility of *making it*, through the variety of devices that occupy the spotlight – pagers, car phones, mobile phones, cell phones, and who knows what else.

The air is full of anecdotes about the impact of these devices on our social life – some of a public health character (like the effect on traffic safety of talking on cell phones while driving), some concerning their effect on interaction. These anecdotes can merit serious attention – some for the access they may give to the symbolic value they have for the networks in which they circulate, others for the ways in which they epitomize their protagonists' understanding of the social worlds they inhabit. Let me mention only one.

In a paper several years ago about a famous confrontation between then Vice President Bush and news correspondent Dan Rather (Schegloff, 1988/89, 1992), I made the point that the "interview" from which this confrontation emerged was not only a matter of the contextual definition of the genre supplied by the network studio, the camera and the professional personas of the participants; it was at bottom a matter of the parties' orientation to the talk and the practices they employed to co-construct the talk.[1] And some of the anecdotes we hear about mobile communication devices may be understood to document the same point, only not for institutional contexts but for so-called "private" ones.

Consider, for example, the following anecdote, reported to me by an old friend from graduate school days, among the smartest people I have known, now an attorney in New York. She is on the train home to Long Island from Manhattan. A young woman is talking on the cell phone, apparently to her boyfriend, with whom she is in something of a crisis.

---

[1] When those practices changed, the occasion stopped being an "interview," though the context remained unchanged.

Her voice projects in far-from-dulcet tones. Most of the passengers take up a physical and postural stance of busying themselves with other foci of attention (their reading matter, the scene passing by the train's windows, etc.), busy doing "not overhearing this conversation" (as students or other visitors to one's office may do if the phone rings while they are there, carefully examining your bookcase from a distance, or their fingernails). Except for one passenger. And when the protagonist of this tale has her eyes intersect this fellow-passenger's gaze, she calls out in outraged protest, "Do you mind?! This is a private conversation!"

Now nothing in the setting would support the conventional understanding of this assertion. There are many people around in this public space in a railroad passenger car. She is talking quite loudly. None of the contextual features we associate with privacy are present. And yet it is not that she is just being shameless. She is almost literally in two places at the same time – and the railroad car is only one of them. The other place that she is is "on the telephone." And she may well understand that to be a private place; after all, commercial and governmental agencies explicitly alert one to the possibility that, for quality control purposes, someone other than the caller and the service representative may listen in on the conversation that has been placed to the agency. That is taken to be an intrusion on privacy that callers may legitimately assume is theirs. And *this* young woman is talking to her *boyfriend*, about intimate matters, in the usual conversational manner – except for the argumentative mode, and this also, perhaps *especially*, makes it a private conversation. What is different here is that the portability of the phone has transported all of this into a full railroad car in New York, a place full of overhearers pretending not to hear, a pretense with which she collaborates in a *folie à deux* multiplied by a very large factor indeed.

But this intersection of worlds, this transportation of one social setting into the middle of another from which it remains disengaged, did not start with cell phones. I recall, for example, years earlier, being startled by the increasing numbers of people in public places – on campus, in buses or at the airport, on sidewalks – who appeared to be marching almost literally to a different drummer; whose body tonus and body idiom, as Erving Goffman used to call them (1963), stood in sharp contrast to those of others in the setting. The pace and shape of their movements, the character of their demeanor, was calibrated not to the environment which we shared, but to one to which I had no access. They were, in an important sense, not there at all.

At first I thought these folks were drunk or stoned or in a schizophrenic break with local reality. Only gradually did I learn to look for the telltale wire leading from belt to head, to look through the longish hair to spot the round black circles covering their ears. They were some place else than I was – in an auditory environment pulsating with sounds I could not hear but which dominated their consciousness and seemed to have taken command of their muscle control. In recent years, the effect has lessened, in large measure, I think, because people listening to their Walkman or portable CD player are more resistant to yielding up their bodies to the discipline of the music.

But in substantial ways those talking on a cell phone are quite like these marchers to a different drummer. To paraphrase Gertrude Stein, they are not in the same "there" as the rest of us are; there are two "theres" there. In the occurrences I will be concerned with, both "theres" are occasions of talk-in-interaction, which is what I know something about.

First of all, how do I come to be represented here, in this volume? I must confess at the outset that I do not now, nor have I ever, owned a mobile phone, a cell phone, a pager or any other mobile or perpetual accessibility device. Nor have I had the opportunity to examine data on the use of such devices. So it is not by virtue of any expertise on the new wave of communication devices that I am represented here. I suspect that my involvement has to do with my having wandered by accident into an engagement with an *ancestor* of these devices, the telephone – an earlier way of persons being made accessible to one another directly in real time without being "co-present" in the sense of being within earshot or voice-reach (depending on whether you take the speaker's or the hearer's point of view). And I do mean "wandered by accident"; it had never entered my mind to study the telephone as an object of inquiry. Let me fill you in on how came to do so, for it has a bearing on other of the themes that I will be touching on.

In the mid-1960s, building on an exposure to the work of Erving Goffman on interaction (1963 and 1967 *inter alia*) and that of Harold Garfinkel on ethnomethodology (1967), my friend and colleague Harvey Sacks and I were exploring ways of working at the confluence of those sets of interests, although we were not explicitly thinking about it in those terms. Sacks came upon a set of tape recordings of telephone calls to a suicide prevention center, where he was a scholar in residence. I came upon a body of telephone calls to the police in the aftermath of a major disaster and a comparable body of calls on "normal watches." Several features of these materials quickly became apparent and extremely attractive.

First, they were naturalistic data of an extraordinary kind. They embodied a record of what had transpired in the natural course of events in an ordinary setting of the society. By "natural" and "ordinary," here,

I mean only that the events on the tape were not the product of scholarly or scientific intervention in the world to engender the occurrence of the events; and that they were the sorts of events for which the setting was the proper home. And the form in which the events had been captured and made available for repeatable inspection was free of the sorts of scholarly and scientific intervention that involve memory and recollection to create field notes, paraphrase, description, analysis, coding, reporting by lay observers in what we call "interviews," and the like. Indeed, even the processes of tape recording, which attenuate the sound signal being preserved, were of comparatively little moment given the signal attenuation already introduced by the technology of telephony. It seemed that this was as good as naturalistic data on live interaction among humans were going to get.

Second, and even better, in those days when there were substantial limitations of technology and cost on gathering the visually accessible data of interaction – limitations barely imaginable in today's world – these telephone materials appealed on other grounds as well. For studying co-present interaction with sound recording alone risked missing embodied resources for interaction (gesture, posture, facial expression, physically implemented ongoing activities, and the like), which we knew the interactants wove into both the production and the interpretation of conduct, but which we as analysts would have no access to. With the telephone data, the participants did not have access to one another's bodies *either*, and this disparity was no longer an issue.

So we did not ignore the telephonic nature of the data; we appreciated it and embraced it. But, having harvested these benefits, we got on with it, and went to work on the interaction being prosecuted through these materials, not the telephonic medium in which they were being conducted. Until there was reason to do otherwise.

The work I had undertaken to pursue – an ethnomethodological theme appropriate to that time – concerned the relationship between vernacular and technical discourse, between lay input and professional organizational response. Specifically, I was interested in how the police transformed or reconciled the common-sense terms in which citizen callers report their troubles and request police intervention, on the one hand, with the legal and organizational terms – that is, the technical terms – by reference to which decisions to "send a car" had to be made, on the other. Accordingly, I began by looking at, and listening to, the citizen callers' utterances in which they start to do their business, that is, in which they either report their circumstances, or articulate their requests, or both. It was not long, however, before I found that those utterances appeared to be sensitive in various ways to the talk that had immediately preceded them; and that *that* talk in turn was contingently related to the talk that preceded *it*, and so on, in the familiar process that close students of interaction may be tempted to call "a barely finite regress."[2] Each utterance bore the marks of orientation to its prior, and each prior utterance posed the task of providing some analytic characterization of *it*, so as to have some sense of how it constrained the talk that had followed it.

And so I came to what appeared to be the limit of this regress – the first bit of talk in these telephone calls, which generally took the form, "Police Desk," or "Police Desk, can I help you?" But as I tried to register some basic observations about this highly recurrent first utterance in these exchanges – who said them, what they were doing, how did that person come to be saying them and to be doing the action or actions they were implementing – it became obvious that, although these were the first utterances, they were not the first *contributions* to these conversations. These utterances were themselves *responses*. Responses to what? Well, to some signal that had served to secure their speakers' attention.

And so I found myself dealing with little sequences, I called them "summons/answer sequences," one of whose recurrent deployments served to mobilize the attention and the aligned recipiency (Goodwin, 1979, 1980, 1981) of their target as a way of launching an episode of interaction. Like calling out, "Hey Jim?" and having Jim redirect his gaze at me or say "What?" Or like knocking on the door and having someone say "Come in." Or like tapping someone on the shoulder and having them turn around or look up. In other words, these sequences – or, rather, this sequence *type* – were hardly specific to calls to the police, nor were they specific to the telephone. The sequence type was endemic to interaction, for deployment under certain contingencies, to do actions associated with those contingencies.

But in my data the first part of this little sequence took the form of the ringing of the telephone, a ringing that had been made to happen by someone at a considerable distance, doing various things mechanical and electrical that made just this phone start ringing. And, with that, I found myself having to think what else might be special about this particular class of interactional contexts, in which the parties were not directly accessible to one another. I found myself studying the telephone – or rather studying interaction in ways that accepted the relevance to the conduct of the interaction of the fact that it was being conducted over

---

[2] For work that addresses the actual work done between police and citizen callers, see Whalen and Zimmerman (1987, 1990, 1992); Zimmerman (1984, 1992).

the telephone, because the participants' conduct was oriented to this being a conversation on the telephone. They were doing "talking on the telephone." It was an aspect of these specimens of conversation.

I must say that that is where my interest in the telephone has always remained. And one central theme of this chapter comes to the fore here. It is that studies of new technological developments will frequently be best pursued not for the technology as itself the interest of the first order, but rather for the technology as a device through which are refracted other phenomena, a proxy for interests that are more analytical in character. Such an orientation will require of investigators that they have a clear notion of the more general processes or domains of phenomena they study, and what analytic status the new technology or its products has within that universe. The technology, of course, changes – often before the publication comes out. To avoid premature antiquarianism, one needs to have captured the way in which that technology embodied the value of some variable with greater staying power, however transiently; and the consequence of that value of the variable is the payoff for understanding that analytic domain. My analytic domain was interaction, and talk-in-interaction in particular. The telephone affected talk prosecuted through it and gave me a special kind of access to the organization of talk thereby. The domains of interest to other students of the telephone – and now the cell phone – are surely different; but I believe it may be worthwhile to think about the form my point here takes for any investigator's work.

So what was the relevance to the conduct of the interaction of the fact that it was being done over the telephone? Let me take up just a few things about summons/answer sequences and about interactional openings, which turned out at the time to be affected by certain features of the telephonic medium of interaction.

One of the first things I noticed was the contrast between the ways in which summonses were issued in co-present and telephonic interaction respectively, and the ways in which they were answered in co-present interaction and on the phone. Noticing this was facilitated by the difference in the way they are answered on the phone in domestic contexts and in institutional or work ones (Schegloff, 1970b). The initial simple observation about "Police Desk" is that it is a kind of self-identification, whereas "Hello" is not. (Of course, in some other cultural contexts, domestic phones are also answered with a form of self-identification – Houtkoop-Steenstra, 1991; Lindström, 1994 – but for now let us stick with the American practice.)

And that prompted a next observation: that there is an asymmetry of information between the caller and answerer about who the other is, or is likely to be. A caller knows at least who the target of the calling was *meant* to be – what number was intendedly dialed and whose number, as we conventionally say, it is; which is to say, who are the possible or likely answerers of it. The person reaching out to a ringing phone, on the other hand, did not ordinarily have such information – except for special circumstances, like the one in which my wife's Aunt Ida could know that the phone ringing in her kitchen on Tuesday evening at 7:00 pm was her dutiful daughter, checking in.[3] And this is in large measure because the summons has taken the form of a standardized mechanical ring; there is no summoner's voice to be detected and recognized as familiar or not, as male or female, etc., and no format to the summons that might indicate the relationship the summoner claimed – as stranger or intimate, for example, by virtue of an "excuse me" or a calling out of a first name.

But the structure of summons/answer sequences entailed an interactional consequence ironically at odds with this distribution of interactional knowledge: the answerer – the *less* informed party – was in the position of talking *first*. And the alternative forms of answering differed precisely with respect to this feature. In the work or institutional context, answerers addressed themselves to this identity issue and confirmed what the caller ought already to have supposed. Often enough the caller's identity was of little concern, and did not involve the caller being recognized. In the domestic context, on the other hand, the answerer did *not* speak to this issue in responding to the ring, except insofar as the "hello" they said provided a voice sample that the knowing caller could recognize or not. Indeed, in such so-called "personal" or "private" or "domestic" calls, who the parties were, and who they were to each other, was the very next order of business after establishing contact – one dense with interactional issues, with jockeying for position, with claims on one another's recognition to underwrite ratification or revision of the terms of the relationship, and so on. I cannot here take up these themes in any detail, except to recall

---

[3] Or, to cite an actually recorded exchange of this sort, one in which the connection between anticipation of who the caller is and the choice of response term is made explicit:

```
Marsha and Gina:    Cooking Dinner
        Marsha:     Hello
          Gina:     Hi
                    (0.2)
        Marsha:-->  I almost said hi
                    (0.4)
          Gina:     hi?
        Marsha:-->  yeah I felt I figured it was you [ yeah        ]
          Gina:                                      [oh it is me: ]
        Marsha:     'sept I'm in da middle of coo:ken dinner
          Gina:     oh I was just about to start < I just called to
                    tellya that I wasn't going be able to ta:lk to you
        Marsha:     OH=
```

that there appeared to be a preference to be recognized – whether caller or answerer – over having to identify oneself, a preference that could lead not only to elaborate, nuanced exchanges to allow such recognition to occur, but to cheating as well, that is, claiming recognition when none had in fact occurred, as in the following opening (taken from Schegloff, 1979; p. 43):

```
1 Alice:  Hello
2 Robin:  Hi:
3 Alice:  Hi:
4         (0.3)
5 Alice:  Oh Hi Robin
```

Alice's re-greeting at line 5 – marked with the "change-of-state" token "Oh" (Heritage, 1984) – betrays the pretense of her previous claimed recognition at line 3.

The detailing of these phenomena came, of course, not from studying the telephone but from studying the talk – how it was organized, what actions the parties were accomplishing, and by what practices they were implemented, following the data wherever they led in an unmotivated way – all the while keeping in the back of one's mind that this was on the telephone, because that would have been, and demonstrably *was*, a matter of continuing orientation for the participants, and therefore shaped and constrained what the participants did, how they did it, and what needed specially to be managed differently by virtue of its being on the telephone. Of course this *did* render a view of the telephone – the telephone as practice-d object – a view embodied and reflected in the interactional practices of talk fashioned to be implemented on it.

Eventually this work issued in an account of a more or less canonical form to which conversational openings on the telephone seemed to be oriented (Schegloff, 1968, 1979, 1986). This account has prompted a small cascade of further work comparing American telephone conversation openings with those elsewhere: for example, France (Godard, 1977), the Netherlands (Houtkoop-Steenstra, 1991), Lebanon (Hopper and Koleilat-Doany, 1989), Sweden (Lindström, 1994), Taiwan (Hopper and Chen, 1996), Germany (Berens, 1980), Greece (Sifianou, 1989), Japan (Park, forthcoming), Korea (Park, forthcoming).

This body of work does take on the appearance of a kind of comparative study of telephony and its impact on interaction, as well as the more commonly emphasized theme – the telephone conversation opening as a kind of Rorschach test for national culture. But, as I have recently argued elsewhere (Schegloff, forthcoming), this seems to me to miss the point. What should most matter about these studies of telephone conversation openings is their providing an analytic resource for understanding what happens *subsequently* in these conversations. For things of moment can and do occur in openings, sometimes by their omission, and these affect what happens later in the interaction. In order to understand that later trajectory, one needs tools for the analysis of the openings, including what may have failed to occur there, and that requires empirically grounded accounts of what canonically *does* occur there. The point, then, of having accounts of telephone openings in France or Japan is not in the first instance to juxtapose them to telephone openings in America, but to empower the analysis of the subsequent trajectory of telephone conversations in those cultural contexts. Again the point of these studies is not conversation on the telephone per se, and not the telephone as a comparative diagnostic tool for culture, but the telephone as another tool for the analysis of talk-in-interaction, as especially constituted in this technologically shaped context.

It is striking to see how the technological developments of recent years have borne out the interactional analyses of *those* years. The development in recent years of such new wrinkles as "Caller ID" reflects directly the commercial exploitation of aspects of conversational openings revealed in those early analyses. The development of "Caller ID blocking" allows us to see that *callers* have exploited the asymmetries of knowledge and wish to preserve them, as *answerers* have suffered them and welcome the possibility of neutralizing them. We conversation analysts like to ground our claims by reference to the orientations of the parties, but never has such grounding been carried through in this commercial arena and on this scale! That the technologists set out to make this feasible, and that they – and we – were right that it would matter to the users, is a different kind of encouragement than we have had before. The importance people attach to Caller ID and its neutralization reflects not only the structure of conversational openings and the special form it takes on the telephone, but the whole rest of the organizational practices that make talk-in-interaction the activity it is – most notably that, once someone has gotten you into a conversation, you may find it problematic to get out, and so wish to regulate the getting in before it goes too far.

I should add, however, that we have no studies that I am aware of that tell us what the consequences of Caller ID have been for the actual conduct of talk on the telephone, and their openings in particular. In principle, Caller ID could change the asymmetries of information noted about past telephone interaction by making it possible for the recipient to know something before lifting the receiver. But exactly *what* the answerer knows may be unclear, not only to researchers but to the parties themselves. The answerer may know whose phone is calling, but not who is using it at the moment; and the caller may not know what the answerer knows. So what do these openings sound like? Is there a caller recognition sequence? Are these openings made to sound the same as in the past so as to mask that Caller ID is in use? Do they succeed? And are there consequences for the trajectory of the talk that go beyond the squaring away in the opening?

One upshot of the preceding discussion is that setting conversation in the context of the telephone intersects various of its practices and organizations of practice in ways that are not wholly anticipatable. Perhaps it might have been anticipated that removing visual access from participants otherwise accustomed to it would have an impact on the use of demonstratives such as "this" and "that," but not that it would engender a wrinkle in how getting-to-know-who-the-other-is gets accomplished. Here is *another* wrinkle, drawing on features of early work of mine that are rather less well known (Schegloff, 1970a, published for the first time in Appendix B in this volume). The target of these observations remains the summons/answer sequence, but another facet of its operation.

In ordinary, visually accessible, co-present interaction, the circumstances for doing a summons and responding to it appear to include a set of assessments that underwrite its relevance and its appropriateness. Ordinarily a summons is done only "for cause," and ordinarily it is understood to have been done "for cause." Because it is understood to serve to mobilize its addressee's attention and provide for the addressee's alignment as a recipient, its use is warranted only when the attention and aligned recipiency of the target are in question, or appear to be impaired or attenuated – typically by involvement in some competing activity or activities. As the summons serves to make relevant for its addressee a reallocation of attention and involvement, the respective claims of the currently ongoing activity or activities, on the one hand, and the ones heralded and projected by the summons, on the other hand, can be an issue.

It is in this light that we can appreciate that a summons not only launches a course of action, but is the *culmination* of one. That is, a prospective summoner can be understood to have assessed the relative claims of the current activities of the prospective target of a summons and the activity on whose behalf the summons is being done. The assessment can go to the issue of relative priority or gravity, of relative temporal duration (a "quick question" being so formulated for the rights thereby accrued for doing it interruptively), and of the waxing and waning and boundary placement of the current activity (as in waiting until some segment of it appears to be over before undertaking to intervene with the summons). One who issues a summons thereby claims that the incipient activity for which the summons serves as a wedge has passed a test that somehow combines these aspects, and that the timing has been carefully assessed and designed as well (interrupting in the middle vs. having visibly held off until a sub-boundary or temporary hiatus).

And the summoned party regularly takes the issuance of the summons to testify to the *outcome* of such assessments on the summoner's part. This is critical because of the power of the summons; ordinarily it makes answering the summons the priority next thing for the addressee to do, and that means – if the summons has been done for cause – the at least temporary interruption or abandonment of whatever addressee involvement was in progress that prompted the summons. Addressees of summonses can tolerate letting their ongoing activities be subject to this kind of interruption as long as they can rely on its being initiated only under constraints, only after passing some sort of priority assessment. And so they do. If they judge the assessments to be error prone, for example because an onlooker could not know how serious the current matter is, or how delicate the moment at which it has arrived, they can hold up their hand and hold the summoner off or wave them off. Otherwise, assured that the summons has been done after judicious balancing of priorities, temporal demands, etc., they respond to it promptly. The most familiar resistance to doing so comes when the summoner can *not* be trusted to have done the priority assessment, or to have the savvy to have done it right – most notably the care-giver's unresponsiveness to the summonses of children, in the form of "Mommy, mommy, mommy, etc." These observations pertain to co-present interaction. With the introduction of the telephone, problems – or *other* problems – surface.

Anyone whose sensitive conversation has been interrupted by the phone's ring, who has waited patiently in a service line only to find themselves displaced by the phone's ring when their turn for service has finally arrived, will have experienced the problem of the absence of the priority analysis. For the demand of the summons for response "next" is insistent, and most phone "owners" respond to it. A variety of solutions have been developed or adapted to dealing with it.

The constraints on summoning that I have referred to by the terms "for cause" and "priority and temporal analysis" are, of course, like much of the infrastructure of talk-in-interaction, largely tacit and not ordinarily accessible to what Giddens (1984) has called "discursive consciousness." They become accessible mostly in the breach, whether the breach is artificially induced, as in *Candid Camera* or Garfinkel's (1967) classic demonstrations, or naturally, as in the case of not-yet-competent children. But another way they surface is when technology provides for transforming the capacity for interaction and, with it, its settings and their fit to interaction's infrastructure.

With the introduction of the telephone, the capacity to summon another to interaction was disengaged from spatial proximity and was relocated to the spatial proximity of a legitimately usable telephone instrument. But, although the telephone instrument made the voices accessible, it did not permit the visual access to the other in *advance* of initiating interaction that allowed a potential caller to assess the appropriateness of undertaking to initiate a conversation *then*. Persons in interaction thereby became vulnerable to promiscuous intervention in their activities, including their co-present interactions, where by "promiscuous" I mean only intervention not subject to – or subjected to – otherwise appropriate constraints, and not hearable as having met those constraints.

There were various solutions to the consequent problems, some of them adaptations of other resources, designed for other problems. Secretaries were one such adaptation in institutional settings; the boss could be freed from such promiscuous intervention in his (and I use the pronoun advisedly) activities by interposing a secretary to answer his phone and assume that vulnerability herself. Then screening calls via the answering machine became another serendipitous resource for this problem in domestic environments. Neither resource, to be sure, had this as its primary job. In any case, the devices we are concerned with have bypassed these solutions.

It may be worthwhile to discriminate briefly among different mobile communication devices and to explore the different ways in which they affect conversation. If I understand how they work correctly, pagers make known the presence of someone's interest in initiating conversation, but do not themselves initiate the contact. Their intervention in the interaction that they intersect may be only momentary, involving the signal that announces their activation, a signal that may be accessible to all parties to the co-present interaction, who may then defer to it and its owner's need to check the source of the signal, or may *not* do so. Even this interruption may be avoided by making the signal take the form of a silent vibration – clearly an effort to minimize disruption of ongoing local activities and interaction. Most important, the recipient of the signal can in some instances then carry through a version of the priority and duration analysis that summoners otherwise do before doing a summons, and can then decide whether or not to intervene in the co-present interaction in order to respond to the pager, and how to time that intervention relative to the trajectory of the co-present interaction. So the pager poses several issues for its owner: to look to see the source or not (and this may be different if it is registered by sound hearable to others or by vibration, not accessible to others); to move to respond or not, and if so, when? At the next "break" in the talk? Interruptively of what's going on at that moment? Interruptively of the topic? Of the sequence? Of the turn at talk?

Mobile phones and cell phones intersect an ongoing interaction differently. Their owners can either turn them off, or tolerate the insistent ringing of an unanswered phone, or respond and find themselves immediately in a conversation, rather than with a decision as to whether to get into one, and therefore in principle answerable to two sets of interactional others at the same time.

Can we not therefore anticipate at least the following two sorts of issues for pursuit in both inquiry and policy? First, how should we understand cell phone use: is it like any other phone use, or do the new technological affordances modify the terms under which such conversations are initiated and conducted? And, second, how should we understand the effects, if any, on co-present interaction and its settings of their vulnerability to unmeasured intrusion by cell-phone-initiated conversation – if that is indeed what develops.

Anecdotal evidence suggests that there are issues to be pursued under both headings. For example, with respect to the former, it is readily observable that callers to cell phones ask answerers – often just after contact is established – "Where are you?" This is a question that has in the past not been unusual when asked "the other way around" by call recipients to callers. On some occasions, the query reflected on ongoing orientation to an activity-in-progress; for example, the caller might have been on the way to the answerer's place, from a greater or lesser distance, and the question sought to track the caller's progress or ascertain the cause of a delay in arrival. On other occasions, the question was occasioned by some aspect of the conversation. For example, in a telephone conversation between two young women recorded by one of them in the late 1960s, the recipient inquired at one point, "You home?"

```
 1 Ava:  YOU HO:ME?
 2                  (0.4)
 3 Bee:  No,
 4 Ava:  Oh I didn't think so.
 5 Bee:  nNo,
 6                  (0.9)
 7 Bee:  You are, hhnhh [hnhh! ·hhh
 8 Ava:                 [Y'sounded too fa[r a- ]
 9 Bee:                                  [Ri:gh]t? hh =
10 Ava:  = Yeh. =
11 Bee:  = See? hI-I'm doin'something right t'ay finally, [·hh
12 Ava:                                                   [Mm
13 Bee:  I finally said something right. (0.2)You are home.
14       hmfff
15 Ava:  Yeh- I believe so. [Physically anyway.
16 Bee:                     [°°hhm hhh
17 Bee:  Yea-a-h.°Not mentall (h)y (h) though (hh)
18 Ava:  °No, khhhh!
```

Here, almost certainly, the inquiry was prompted by the attenuated acoustic signal caused by the recording process at Bee's end of the connection, which in those days caused a marked weakening of the signal. Ava, whose home was apparently not far from Bee's, would have registered a volume which sounded "far away," and this could prompt a query such as "You home?" What is even more striking, however, is the exchange at lines 7–18. Throughout this conversation, these two young women – apparently friends since childhood – have been continuously not meshing. When Bee says (at line 7) "You are [at home]," this is virtually guaranteed to be correct, for Bee has called Ava at home and reached her. For this interaction, what is so striking is that Ava finds a way to call even this "given" into doubt (at line 15); for our topic, what is so striking is that the issue of a call recipient's location is now routinely open to serious question by the caller – and this is the "Where are you?" question so often anecdotally reported about cell phone contacts.

But anecdotes are not enough. In coming to terms with these preoccupations for inquiry and policy, it will be critical that work be grounded in real data. Although this chapter was not based on cell phone data, it *was* based on what we have learned from real data on the telephone and co-present interaction. And the study of such data – recorded data drawn from media and settings with which we were already acquainted from practical experience – has regularly yielded observations and findings contrary to what might have been plausibly supposed from ordinary common-sense experience, and, more important, observations and findings that made salient matters we did not even know enough to have suppositions about. It remains to be seen what is to be learned from comparable recorded data on the use of the new media of perpetual contact.

For the many who appeal to other sorts of data to ground their inquiries, let me just suggest again the long-term payoffs of setting new technological inventions in the proper context, an analytically conceived context. For they are like naturalistic versions of experimental stimuli: given precise analytic characterizations of the field into which they are introduced, their effect can be revelatory. Examined as objects in their own right, they may yield only noise.

### References

Berens, F.J. (1980). "Dialogeröffnung in Telephongeschprächen: Handlungen und Handlungschemata der Herstellung sozialer und kommunikativer Beziehungen" [Dialog Openings in Telephone Conversations: Actions and Action Schemata of the Construction of Social and Communicative Relationships]. In P. Schröder and H. Steger (eds.), *Dialogforschung:*

*Jahrbuch 1980 des Instituts für Deutsche Sprache.* Düsseldorf: Schwann, 402–417.

Garfinkel, H. (1967). *Studies in Ethnomethodology.* Englewood Cliffs, NJ: Prentice-Hall.

Giddens, A. (1984). *The Constitution of Society: Outline of the Theory of Structuration.* Berkeley: University of California Press.

Godard, D. (1977). "Same Setting, Different Norms: Phone Call Beginnings in France and the United States." *Language in Society* 6: 209–219.

Goffman, E. (1963). *Behavior in Public Places: Notes on the Social Organization of Gathering.* New York: Free Press.

(1967). *Interaction Ritual: Essays in Face to Face Behavior.* Garden City, NY: Doubleday.

Goodwin, C. (1979). "The Interactive Construction of a Sentence in Natural Conversation." In G. Psathas (ed.), *Everyday Language: Studies in Ethnomethodology.* New York: Irvington Publishers, 97–121.

(1980). "Restarts, Pauses, and the Achievement of Mutual Gaze at Turn-Beginning." *Sociological Inquiry* 50: 272–302.

(1981). *Conversational Organization: Interaction between Speakers and Hearers.* New York: Academic Press.

Heritage, J. (1984). "A Change-of-State Token and Aspects of Its Sequential Placement." In J.M. Atkinson and J. Heritage (eds.), *Structures of Social Action.* Cambridge: Cambridge University Press, 299–345.

Hopper, R., and Chen, C. (1996). "Languages, Cultures, Relationships: Telephone Openings in Taiwan." *Research on Language and Social Interaction* 29: 291–313.

Hopper, R., and Koleilat-Doany, N. (1989). "Telephone Openings and Conversational Universals: A Study in Three Languages." In S. Ting-Toomey and F. Kevizing (eds.), *Language, Communication and Culture.* Newbury Park, CA: Sage, 157–179.

Houtkoop-Steenstra, H. (1991). "Opening Sequences in Dutch Telephone Conversations." In D. Boden and D.H. Zimmerman (eds.), *Talk and Social Structure: Studies in Ethnomethodology and Conversation Analysis.* Cambridge: Polity Press, 232–250.

Lindström, A.B. (1994). "Identification and Recognition in Swedish Telephone Conversation Openings." *Language in Society* 23(2): 231–252.

Park, Y.-Y. (forthcoming). "Recognition and Identification in Japanese and Korean Telephone Conversation Openings." In K.K. Luke and T.-S. Pavlidou (eds.), *Telephone Calls: Unity and Diversity in Conversational Structure across Languages and Cultures.* Amsterdam: John Benjamins.

Schegloff, E.A. (1968). "Sequencing in Conversational Openings." *American Anthropologist* 70: 1075–1095.

(1970a). "Opening Sequencing." Unpublished Ms.; published in this volume (Appendix B).

(1970b). "Answering the Phone." Unpublished Ms. To appear in G.H. Lerner (ed.), *Conversation Analysis: Studies from the First Generation*, in preparation.

(1979). "Identification and Recognition in Telephone Openings." In G. Psathas (ed.), *Everyday Language: Studies in Ethnomethodology.* New York: Irvington Publishers, 23–78.

(1986). "The Routine as Achievement." *Human Studies* 9: 111–151.

(1988/89). "From Interview to Confrontation: Observations on the Bush/ Rather Encounter." *Research on Language and Social Interaction* 22: 215–240.

(1992). "On Talk and Its Institutional Occasions." In P. Drew and J. Heritage (eds.), *Talk at Work*. Cambridge: Cambridge University Press, 101–34.

(forthcoming). "Reflections on Research on Telephone Conversation Openings: Issues of Cross-cultural Scope and Scholarly Exchange, Interactional Import and Consequences." In K.K. Luke and T.S. Pavlidou (eds.), *Telephone Calls: Unity and Diversity in Conversational Structure across Languages and Cultures*. Amsterdam: John Benjamins.

Schegloff, E.A., and Sacks, H. (1973). "Opening up Closings." *Semiotica* 8: 289–327.

Sifianou, M. (1989). "On the Telephone Again! Differences in Telephone Behavior: England versus Greece." *Language in Society* 18: 527–544.

Whalen, M., and Zimmerman, D.H. (1987). "Sequential and Institutional Contexts in Calls for Help." *Social Psychology Quarterly* 50: 172–185.

(1990). "Describing Trouble: Practical Epistemology in Citizen Calls to the Police." *Language in Society* 19: 465–492.

(1992). "Telling Trouble: Citizen Calls to the Police." In R. Frankel (ed.), *Language in Institutional Settings*. Norwood, NJ: Ablex.

Zimmerman, D.H. (1984). "Talk and Its Occasion: The Case of Calling the Police." In D. Schiffrin (ed.), *Meaning, Form, and Use in Context: Linguistic Applications*. Washington, DC: Georgetown University Press, 210–228.

(1992). "The Interactional Organization of Calls for Emergency Assistance." In J. Heritage and P. Drew (eds.), *Talk at Work*. Cambridge: Cambridge University Press, 418–469.

# 19    Conclusion: making meaning of
# mobiles – a theory of *Apparatgeist*

*James E. Katz and Mark A. Aakhus*

## Span of consequences

The preceding chapters analyze how mobile communication changes the nature and quality of social behavior and organization. These changes are not restricted to the industrialized countries, but are pandemic. Whenever the mobile phone chirps, it alters the traditional nature of public space and the traditional dynamics of private relationships. The technology itself offers people an opportunity to modify preconceived uses, and, consequently, the way in which its design and vector develop relies on these modifications. This chapter spotlights selected changes and their significance. Our purpose is not only to make sense of the myriad social and thematic issues raised but also to suggest a novel theoretical orientation.

The contributors to this volume demonstrate the *prima facie* evidence that times are changing owing to the mobile phone. Communication among teenagers is more intense, and novel forms of intimacy and distancing emerge. Relationships between teens and parents are altered by the existence of the mobile phone. In social relationships among adults, mobile communication leads to different forms of coordination, cooperation and conflict. The organizational structure of businesses is changing as well. In the physically mobile, but socially "in touch" workforce, corporate managers must deal with new forms of supervision, while employees must deal with new forms of monitoring. Questions of folkways, norms and cultures of adoption and opposition also arise. New forms of marketing and advertising emerge that prey on the human consciousness. Potentially gross abuses exist too; these include mobile phone spam messages that would fill up and deny voice mailbox use, or, worse, attacks similar to e-mail worms that have led computer networks to falter. Even the struggle for hierarchy and status is shifted to a new ground: people compete now based on who has the smallest and classiest-looking mobile device.

The contributors also make clear that, although the mobile phone can mend and enhance social relationships, it can also severely erode privacy at both the individual and societal levels. Robbins and Turner (chapter 6 in this volume) are appropriately sensitive to the kinds of locational monitoring of users that can occur in the USA. Another source of privacy invasion can be the companies themselves. Mobile phone giant Vodaphone has a system that "segments and profiles each and every one of its customers quickly and simply" based on the calling patterns of each network user (Quadstone, 2000). This capability is available to any mobile phone service provider. Despite the fact that mobile phone use can allow detailed monitoring of users, there appears to be almost no public reaction against the technology on this ground. Public interest advocates who specialize in civil rights, such as the Electronic Privacy Information Center, have effectively registered their concern, however. Although quiescent now, the privacy/monitoring issue could become of paramount importance to the future quality of human rights (Katz, 1999, ch. 11).

In many countries, the social landscape is changing as a result of people working out the routines and rituals that incorporate mobile communication and the mobile telephone into everyday life. How people socialize and behave in public spaces, including cafés and train stations, is modified and shaped by the presence of and response to the mobile. The physical landscape is also changing. Billboards abound encouraging people to subscribe to a mobile phone service. Ungainly signal transmission towers are prominent features of one's view of the panoramic landscape. Public space and public buildings are becoming modified to accommodate (or in some cases impede) the use of mobile devices. It is also noteworthy that these changes are surprisingly universal with respect to levels of economic development and social hierarchical structures, despite the fact that the cultural traditions from which the behavior must spring varies widely.

The chapters in this book have also emphasized the psychological changes precipitated by the mobile telephone, substantiating what we might call the feel or texture of life. The predicate of one's interpersonal relationships has been altered. New points of orientation in conversations – for instance, "Where are you?" – have been added to the features of social navigation. The impact on social control, and especially on intimacy, has been discussed in depth in the chapters. Some chapters have also pointed out the way that mobile communication unsettles further the "at home within oneself" nature of the lived experience (Wynn and Katz, 1997).

Yet we do not wish to become fixated on a given technology. Rather, our interests are social processes and how mobile communication helps us understand them, as well as how the mobile character and richness of the technology change and initiate new social processes. Although our case derives from the mobile telephone, it does not rely on it exclusively. Support comes from an examination of the effects of other communication technologies (for instance, the portable CD player and transistor radio, citizen band radio, pagers, personal digital assistants and computer notebooks). Moreover, as Gergen (chapter 14) points out, the mobile phone is unique in the capacity it gives people to communicate. As the Internet and mobile phone continue to converge, the impact of mobiles can only grow. Indeed, it is reasonable to expect that more people will soon be accessing the Internet via mobile phones than more conventionally through personal computers.

As noted earlier in the volume, the ordinary communication capabilities of today's mobiles are beyond what had been historically attributed to divine beings. Our technology is pushing still further. The ambitious dream of a generation of telecommunication engineers is becoming realized: we will be able to have at least potential contact with most anyone at any time or place. Ordinary people, with a modicum of resources (money, for instance), will be able to access the world's information trove from most points of the populated landmasses. For those who are interested, the entire history and documentation of their own lives will be available for recording and rifling. We will be able to monitor or even interact with satellites exploring the solar system or astronauts operating a space station. Perhaps, from small screens on our bodies, we will be able to watch archival video of our own birth or replay our youthful lover's departing message breaking off our relationship. We can have perpetual contact, enjoying instant or asynchronous communications from around the world or the heavens above.

These are not future dreams but achievable today. In this context, we seek to identify consistencies and novelties in what people do with these technologies, and what patterns are repeated and embroidered. This impression shifts our thinking from the material plane of the physical capabilities of the technology to the plane of ideas: how these technologies are recreated in the interests of the users, and with what intended and unintended consequences.

## Tackling theoretical issues

To formulate an adequate answer to this question, the way people use, modify and relate to personal communication technologies (PCTs) requires careful scrutiny. Hence, we broaden our focus from mobile phones to this larger category, which includes video-cassette recorders, TVs, interactive voice response units (VRUs), beepers and e-mail. We perceive consistencies in what we might call the strain of the direction of change. There seems to be movement toward certain inherently consistent patterns in the way people use PCTs. This occurs even when such consistency is not predicated by the design aims of the creators or marketers of the technology in question.

For their part, our contributors have captured the manner in which people redeploy communication devices in their environments to serve their interests, and how those technologies in turn modify the communication environment. They have also shown the interaction between social actors who use the resulting folk theories and observations to reconfigure their behavioral repertoires. The result is that they are modifying their rationalizations of PCTs and constantly reinventing their use of technology. This means that the use of communication tools themselves will be dynamically adjusted to maximize the needs and comforts of their users and even to explore and invent new needs and interests.

Theorists have sought to generate a framework for understanding behavior in a socio-technological environment. They often highlight agency, structure, interaction and change as essential concepts. Much of use can be gained by using these frameworks. At the same time, we note, as have others, the problematical aspects of this endeavor. Popular social theorists such as Allan Mazur, as well as many others, note that social science is generally interested in developing "context-free knowledge," whereas the "stocks of knowledge employed by social actors in social life" require them to have "practical mastery of the demands of everyday activities" (Giddens, 1978, p. 246). Like Giddens and others such as Goffman (1968), we argue that social actors are self-aware of at least the lower levels of the operational principles of their immediate locales, and that numerous "classic" theorists have not given sufficient consideration to this in their models. Like Innis (1950), and later Giddens (1978), we see space–time as a pivotal but too often neglected dimension in understanding human behavior. Extended critiques have been offered that suggest the importance of considering the value of network externalities and critical masses (Sitkin, Sutcliffe, and Barrios-Choplin, 1992) or the discrepant value of later adopters (Shapiro and Varian, 1999). Finally, like Giddens, who coined the term "structuration," we see the need for a new term to describe social change and its interaction with social institutions within the technological communication context.

In terms of structuration theory itself, many schools of thought have sought to grapple with the role of information and communication technology. Orlikowski (1992) argues that that there is a "duality of technology." She echoes Giddens' argument about the duality of structure, saying that technology both shapes and is shaped by human action. Poole and DeSanctis (1990, 1992) propose the "adaptive structuration theory" to explain how people appropriate advanced information systems into their work. They say that the spirit of the technology, which is the normative intent of the technology design, is realized (or disturbed) by human action. The two approaches are concerned with the manner in which technology is adopted into organizations. Another variation on structuration is the "domestication" theory proposed by Silverstone and Haddon (1996). Their theory applies to the integration of personal technology into everyday domestic life and in particular puts forward a description of the stages involved in this process. They also underscore a moral economy perspective on choices concerning technology usage. Common to all these approaches are assumptions that the social world is complex, and that individuals exhibit limited rationality subject to particular configurations of heuristic learned rules of reasoning, conditioned by social and cultural circumstances. Indeed, technology is the result of chains of cooperative human activity and is socially constructed in people's actions.

The family of structurational theories is a reaction to strong technological determinist accounts of technology. The structurational approaches have brought people back into the picture, but in so doing become preoccupied with technology's effects in particular domains. However, critics say that adherents to this approach have not been successful in producing predictive statements (Cummings and Kraut, forthcoming). To us it is clear that both sides of the equation need to be considered. Yet we wish to draw attention back to the technology without ignoring human will. We suggest that there is logic associated with communication technology. Indeed, this logic antedates the particular technologies we are currently with, but was unable to be expressed without the medium. This logic is grounded in broader ideologies that are rooted in historical, materialistic, religious and ideational ontologies, and that have dominated human attempts to contextualize and make meaningful their life experiences.

### Articulating the neologism *Apparatgeist*

To convey the logic associated with our concept of communication technology more effectively, we coin the neologism *Apparatgeist* to suggest the spirit of the machine that influences both the designs of the technology as well as the initial and subsequent significance accorded them by users, non-users and anti-users. The neologism has its origins in Latin and is derived currently in the Germanic and Slavic word *apparat*, meaning machine, which includes both the technical and sociological aspects. English speakers are familiar with the term and concept, embodied in the word "apparatus." For instance, the American Heritage Dictionary (third edition) defines the primary meaning of the term as "the materials needed for a purpose such as a task." Another one of the meanings is "the totality of means by which a designated function is performed or a specific task is executed." "Equipment" is emphasized throughout the definitions of "apparatus."

Also, we often associate the term "apparatus" with gadgetry. In addition, it clearly means being able to accomplish a task, often an important or complicated one. The term also encompasses a social operation, an organized group that can achieve some end, often in an efficient way, and usually with a political objective.

We draw too upon the German word *Geist*, which denotes spirit or mind. We adopt Hegel's sense (Hegel, 1977) and use it to denote a directive principle within historical entities, and guiding their existence, that unfolds in historical time and expresses itself in the creations of the denizens of the society so animated (Rostenstreich, 1973, p. 491). Although the term has contested meanings, and is frequently misused, we find that Hegel's interpretation of terminology as stemming from the intellectual or rational, which defies empirical analysis, instead signifies a fundamental theme that animates the lives of human cultures. The term *Geist* is popularly associated with another Germanic philosophical thesis, namely the *Zeitgeist*. The *Zeitgeist* can be only indirectly observed. Although this spirit is actually directing human activities, in a broad sense, it can be only indirectly observed throughout the intellectual, moral and cultural climate of an era. Hence, folklore, poetry, popular myths and folk theories are all indicative of the more profound unified thesis of an era. The *Zeitgeist* transcends popular culture and other areas of a society, including religious beliefs, intellectual endeavors, social policy and political structures. Hegel himself asserted that the *Zeitgeist* was a spiritual and intellectual force that truly existed. With respect to our term *Apparatgeist*, we cannot embrace such an intangible concept.

The term *Geist* implies a sense of movement, a direction and a motive. This sense we encompass in our framework as well. The notion of goals connected to movement, though, is not included in our meaning. It does not have a sense of rational pursuit of ends, or *Zwecksrationalität*. Rather, it has only the rationality of means, the algorithms or rules that guide decisions on a moment-to-moment basis. It has then a sense of becoming rather than a sense of being, if we invoke the terms of the fascist philosopher Martin Heidegger (1996).

We also intend to link the word to the Hegelian notion of historical movement. Hegel (1977) argued that there were certain latent urges of each historical period that culminated in its idealized expression and manifestation; metaphorically speaking, much like a tree in autumn that sheds its leaves and revitalizes in the spring, the historical momentum decays, rebuilds and manifests itself in another time. He also argued that there was an underlying *Geist* to history, which he likened to the expansion of freedom. For our part, we use the term to imply spirit in the way of incremental change followed by occasional, unpredictable bursts of drastic change in history.

The term *Apparatgeist* ties together both the individual and the collective aspects of societal behavior. That is, the cultural situation and the limitations of extant technology determine individual behavior, which also takes place within a group or collective. Yet, it is not a term that requires technological determinism. In fact, we argue that technology does not determine what an individual can do; rather, it serves as a constraint upon possibilities. Much as a cafeteria menu will not offer infinite meal choices, but rather presents a finite selection of meal courses, so too historically bound technology offers us a flexible menu of extensive, but not infinite, choices. The *Apparatgeist* refers to the common set of strategies or principles of reasoning about technology evident in the identifiable, consistent and generalized patterns of technological advancement throughout history. It is through these common strategies and principles of reasoning that individual and collective behavior are drawn together.

### The logic of perpetual contact

We see that there is a logic, or nascent philosophy, about personal communication technology. It is both a logic that informs the judgments people make about the utility or value of the technologies in their environment, and a logic that informs the predictions scientists and technology producers might make about personal technologies. Our goal is to articulate this logic and to demonstrate the content of this spirit. The logic that informs the *Apparatgeist* is perpetual contact, at least in potential terms, or, as Emanuel Schegloff says in chapter 18, incipiency.

Perpetual contact is a socio-logic (Goodwin and Wenzel, 1979) of communication technology. A socio-logic is neither a formal logic nor the natural cognitive processes of an individual, but is located in the "socially developed sense of practical reasoning" that results from communities of people "thinking and acting together over time" (Goodwin and Wenzel, 1979, p. 289). The compelling image of perpetual contact is the image of pure communication, which, as Peters (1999) argues, is an idealization of communication committed to the prospect of sharing one's mind with another, like the talk of angels that occurs without the constraints of the body. Pure communication is the image deeply embedded in the logic of perpetual contact that underwrites how we judge, invent and use communication technology. Like the image of perpetual motion that has driven the technological development of machinery over the past two millennia (Whyte, 1962), the development of personal communication technology presupposes perpetual contact. Whereas the idea of perpetual motion concerns the means of production, perpetual contact concerns the means to communicate and interact socially, which is fundamental to humans.

Although there is clearly a logic and pattern to people's reasoning, individually as well as collectively, about the adoption and use of PCTs, it is not always available for direct inspection. The chapters in this volume help solve this problem through empirical findings and illuminating analysis. Moreover, these contributions provide multiple convergent vantage points from which to understand perpetual contact as the logic of *Apparatgeist*. We see in the emergence of mobile communication, in a wide variety of nations, how the mobile phone initiates new questions about appropriate contact and renews contests over communication competence when new means for communicating require a new practical mastery of everyday activity. In the chapters on mobile communication in Finland, Israel, Italy, Korea, the United States, France, the Netherlands, and Bulgaria we see shifts in communicative habits to accommodate mobile communication that undermine long-standing routines and rituals in making contact with others. It is not that what went before stood in opposition to perpetual contact but that those rituals and routines were geared toward different capacities for achieving the ideal of perpetual contact. Indeed, the coming of the telephone to a Filipino village (Strøm, chapter 17) dramatizes the gap that can exist between extant communication rituals and routines and the needs and demands that stem from an ideal of perpetual contact.

The chapters on private talk and public performance go further in explicating the content of *Apparatgeist* as it is realized in the socio-logic of perpetual contact. Ling and Yttri (chapter 10) and Kasesniemi and Rautiainen (chapter 11) offer detailed analyses of how teens integrate the mobile phone into their lives. These reflect a common, though likely implicit, orientation among teenage user groups about communication competence now that mobile communication is a real part of their lives. This common orientation is given expression in the results of Skog's survey of Norwegian youth (chapter 16). The differences between gender in regard to mobile phones is built on an extraordinary similarity in orientation to both the technology design and the purpose of the technology as a means of communication and perpetual contact. Gergen's analysis (chapter 14) that the mobile phone presents a radically different solution to the phenomenon of absent presence than traditional mass media and the Internet (as an information retrieval tool) articulates aspects of the rationale implicit in the orientation identified in the empirical research on teens. The mobile telephone is a means to regulate one's social environment through integration of social contact rather than simply inviting socially dispersing media into one's life. The logic of perpetual contact makes it possible to take sensible action in the conditions of the contemporary societies.

Yet the logic of perpetual contact has other sides. As personal technology successively approximates the ideal of pure communication, it gives way to new behavior that is unanticipated, often objectionable, and open to redress. Rule, de Gournay, and Nafus and Tracey articulate the contests over the ideological and material conditions of communication precipitated by the media of perpetual contact, and highlighted by the national comparison chapters. In each case, extension of the logic of perpetual contact has an unanticipated consequence. Rule (chapter 15) outlines a paradoxical loss and gain for individual control over communicative environments afforded by the particularizing tendencies of the media of perpetual contact. The result is more personalized relations with entities such as firms and agencies. De Gournay (chapter 12) identifies how mobile telephones foster informal conversation at the expense of formal conversation and the etiquette necessary for generating a public sphere. Nafus and Tracey (chapter 13) show how perpetual contact helps people realize the traditional value of individuality while undermining social boundaries, such as the household, that in the past made individuality possible. These chapters put into perspective the frustration people experience with personal technologies. These authors may have also identified the by-products of a perspective that lead to its evolution. Thus, the cunning of the *Apparatgeist* may lie less in the current class of solutions it presents than in the class of frustrations it presents.

The contributions to this volume point in a direction that we choose to call *Apparatgeist*. However, we would like to go further in articulating and formalizing *Apparatgeist*. One reason this is important is that, although the family of structurational theories has brought people back into the picture of social and technological change, these theories emphasize the process of socio-technical environments and change at the expense of the content that animates socio-technical environments and change. We redress this balance here by focusing on the individual, with a full sensitivity that individuals and their relationship to their media are embedded in a social context and history.

The investigations of perpetual contact bolster our position that there is a socio-logic of perpetual contact. Katz (1999), for instance, has shown that people regard telecom technologies in a coherent conceptual way. Moreover, in our own unpublished research with student focus groups, we find that, in describing their decision-making processes, subjects oscillate between explicit reasons (form, function, price) and implicit ones (how others perceive them, beliefs about the usefulness, appropriateness to one's concept of "self"). Both these levels, which Merton tagged as manifest and latent functions, are required for a full understanding of PCT's role in people's lives, or what we call *Apparatgeist*.

In table 19.1, we present both the manifest and latent salient points in people's reasoning, further breaking them down into technological and social aspects of PCTs. These reasonings or functions move along an upward vector of, say, 45 degrees, representing the increased capabilities of PCTs. Imagine, if you will, the vector encased in a spiral spring, representing the movement of people's thinking and needs listed in each cell in table 19.1.

The premises in each cell in table 19.1 (identified in italics) have a dual quality. On the one hand, these premises can be used to generate empirical predictions about communication technology. They enable the individual, and, in turn, collective entities, to make predictions about the performance of and uses for a technology. On the other hand, these premises are used to formulate normative judgments about communication technology, its uses and its users. The premises refer to presuppositions about preferences for the social and communicative arrangements technology makes possible. The fact that these premises are both empirical and normative justifies the creation and utilization of the perhaps inherently paradoxical term *Apparatgeist*.

The direction of the *Apparatgeist* is evident in the premises of perpetual contact. *Apparatgeist* can be broadly vocalized because universal features exist among all cultures regarding PCT; technology itself tends to assume certain standard features independent of place or time. Regardless of culture, when people interact with their PCTs they tend to standardize infrastructure and gravitate towards consistent tastes and universal features. Throughout the history of technological advancement, the tendency is for people to operate by identifiable, consistent and generalized patterns, and to rely on a common set of strategies or principles of reasoning despite individual creativity and worldwide cultural diversity. For instance, people and corporations worldwide create and gravitate toward common designs for airports, cars, bicycles and computers, regardless of cultural diversity. Another vital point is that users operate within a networked environment. That is, behavior relative to the system is affected by who else is available, currently and potentially. Though this can be seen most clearly with the telephone, it is useless when there is only one person with a telephone. Its value increases as does the number of potential users. Decisions about adoption and use are carried out with at least latent recognition of this quality.

Having addressed *Apparatgeist* content from the perspective of the individual, we look now at how *Apparatgeist* moves forward through

Table 19.1 *Premises supporting the drive toward perpetual contact*

| | Technology | Social relationships |
|---|---|---|
| **MANIFEST REASONING** | Qualities of attractive technology (design)<br>*These are specific and manifest attributes that are sought after in the design process, and what potential users might want*<br>Smaller<br>Faster<br>More places<br>More functions if cheap and easy to operate<br>Lower cost<br>Higher status or luxury marker<br>Easier to use<br>Better control of information<br>Better filtering of outsiders<br>Control over others<br>Escape control of others<br>Efficiency in personal life<br>Automate routine and repetitive tasks | Qualities of technology's potential social role (social context)<br>*These are the manifest qualities and processes of the local social context of the potential user, hence, to the extent the technologies can "fit," they will be of interest*<br>Efficient information seeking<br>Social roles<br>Personal needs<br>Local interests<br>Norms (patterns of behavior)<br>Values (principles of what is desirable and worth pursuit)<br>Social system's action – reward/punishment matrix<br>Network externalities (changing character as more users and activities added to system) |
| **LATENT REASONING** | Qualities of attractive uses of technology (performance and personal applications)<br>*These are the latent issues concerning the technology that potential users weigh in their adoption and use of technology*<br>Symbolic affirmation of values<br>Socially appropriate behavior of relevant technology<br>Exploit to loosen monitoring over self<br>Exploit to increase monitoring over others<br>Reproduction of moral regime<br>Selective access<br>Media exposure<br>Social learning | Social setting in which technology will be used (social applications)<br>*These are latent social dimensions that factor into decisions about adoption and usage*<br>Reference group (attraction/avoidance)<br>Perspectives (*Weltanschauung*)<br>Network of social ties based on:<br>Sentiment<br>Interest<br>Obligation<br>Predicates of action folk theories<br>Advancement of self within group, but retention of affiliation and integration<br>Advancement of group within society, but avoidance of conflict<br>Advancement of values within culture, diminution of values of others<br>Synergies of additional participants in network |

history. Systematic reinforcements (and dissuasions) affect the directions of technological development as well as the filters through which people see these technologies. Table 19.2 illustrates how *Apparatgeist* evolves through several domains of incentives and disincentives by an individual's assessment of PCT. Some of the reinforcements that give life to *Apparatgeist* include folkways and folk theories, social learning and the mass media's tendencies to advertise technology in terms of the new, the dramatically changing, the threatening and, most of all, the entertaining. It is important to note that the individual in this model is firmly rooted in a social context.

## The pertinence of the *Apparatgeist* theory

Through our theory of *Apparatgeist* we intend to advance the state of communication theory concerning personal technologies. Understandably, much of communication theory draws from face-to-face interpersonal communication and mass media modes. Beginning in the 1970s, a third and increasingly visible branch of theory was evolving, centered on understanding human–computer interaction. Although these lines of inquiry have been fruitful, we see that it is now appropriate to speak of a fourth form of communication mediated through personal technologies. Although it is an intangible concept in terms of the horizon of the communication discipline, we anticipate it represents the shape of things to come.

There have been several laudable attempts to develop perspectives on this topic, the most prominent and widely embraced of which is the domestication theory, pioneered by Roger Silverstone and Leslie Haddon (1996). Among the valuable insights offered is a moral economy of these technologies, which directs our attention to the importance of the emotional and symbolic dimensions of PCTs. However, the development of a "theory" is probably too ambitious. Rather than a formal theory per se, they aspire to offer a perspective or a viewpoint, by which the use of technology is embraced and assimilated in the household (Haddon, 2000).

For our part, we seek to introduce the rudiments to establish a formal theory. However, these are only modest first steps in a long and complex journey. The task we set for ourselves is to create statements that enable us to investigate the nature of social reality and change as adequately as possible. We see that mobile phones are used in many facets of life. Yet despite the great variation in cultures – from teen dating to family arrangements and from economic bases to social hierarchies – the use and folk understanding of the mobile phone seem to be pressing toward

Table 19.2 *Evolution of Apparatgeist through domains of individual decision-making*

| | Individual's assessment of personal communication technology | | | |
|---|---|---|---|---|
| | Disincentives | | Incentives | |
| Level of analysis | Avoidance motives | Individual psychological domain | Material contingencies | Social symbolic/affiliative aspects |
| Symbolic | Anti-symbolic | Cultural/social location of individual | Technology possibilities | Pro-symbolic |
| Usability | Perceived difficulty using | Self-image/competence | Ease of use | Mastery in social settings |
| Affirms group affiliation | Anti-reference groups | Relational | Family and friends ties/co-workers | Reference groups and social class |
| Economics | Cost | Reallocation of disposable income | Promotions and ads, social learning, media exposure | Relationship to body and self |
| Operational environment | Desire not to complicate environment | Immediate control of environment | Demands on individual; network size and externalities | Perceived social role |
| Folklore | Negative folk theories | Personal values | Positive folk theories | Cultural ideals |
| Body orientation | Physical discomfort | Physical needs | Personal and economic resources | Physical pleasure |

conformity and uniformity. Because PCT affects so many facets of life, we cannot avoid calling it something, and we find *Apparatgeist* a viable term.

People seldom pursue one prevailing interest; instead, they seek to work several avenues of interest at one time. They apply a variety of perspectives to any given issue. In our research on folk theories and attitudes toward the mobile phone, we note that people's multiple perspectives are often simultaneously logically incompatible. There is no reason to think that the mobile phone is unique in this regard. These perspectives constrain and guide people's behavior; however, we also realize that many of these perspectives are constructed retrospectively to justify behavior in which the actor was engaged.

Social actors must constantly perform a series of ever-changing and highly complex social roles. They must also deal with other actors who themselves are performing a series of ever-changing and highly complex social roles. This in itself represents an uncertain and complex scenario in which communication takes place. Indeed, PCT is powerful enough to affect national leadership. Take for instance, the drama that occurred during the US election of 2000 when heavily utilized mobile phones and pager devices delivered timely information and strongly affected serious decisions. Vice President Albert Gore had been en route in a motorcade with the intention of delivering a concession speech, when an aide in another vehicle in the motorcade received the breaking news via a pager system. The aide used his mobile phone to contact the staffer, who in turn revealed that the margin between the presidential candidates was becoming slimmer. Based on a rash of mobile phone calls, the Vice President decided not to deliver his concession speech on November 8, 2000. Thus, the sequence of communication via PCT served as a critical intervention tool in light of the fact that massive public confusion would have prevailed if Gore had given his concession speech. According to an Associate Press wire story, Gore policy adviser Greg Simon said, "We had no TVs. Everyone was on their cell phones. People were calling us from everywhere, telling us, "Don't concede" " (Sobieraj, 2000). Because of PCT, intervention was possible and helped to avoid embarrassment and confusion. The anecdote illustrates how these technologies can alter the course of American and, indeed, world history.

## Conclusion

The chapters in this book seek to make sense of the phenomenon of mobile communication by analyzing its many manifestations and meanings. By assembling these insights, we wish to lay a foundation that could serve many different theoretical perspectives. Yet we also see them in service of a specific perspective, which we call *Apparatgeist*. We see emerging from it the rudiments of a theory that explains, and that makes testable predictions about, the phenomenon of personal communication technology. Thus, in Popper's (1963) sense, we seek to migrate the insights captured in this book from a context of discovery to one of justification where ideas must stand the test of theoretical and empirical refutation.

To summarize, we have suggested how the functionalist and structuration theories, though they deal with important issues and provide valuable insight, fail to deal with or account for what we see as some core aspects of the way people use mobile and other personal communication technologies and the way they make meaning from them and their use. Functionalist theories emphasize instrumental, goal-oriented rationality at the expense of the symbolic. Structuration theories emphasize process at the expense of the values that animate processes. With our approach, *Apparatgeist*, we wish to draw attention to several issues that we feel are insufficiently dealt with by these approaches. These issues include the way that people use mobile technologies as tools in their daily life in terms of tools-using behavior and the relationship among technology, body and social role. They also include the rhetoric and meaning-making that occur via social interaction among users (and non-users). That is, unlike the functionalist approach, we do not just see mobile phones as a narrow way to achieve a specific purpose. Rather, they are both utilitarian and symbolic. Indeed, the symbolic importance is often paramount. And, unlike the structuration approach, we do not see that, as technologies become institutionalized, they are rendered invisible. Instead, a technology's being taken for granted is the result of a large amount of prior evaluation and resolved choices of people concerning technology. Their evaluations and choices are based not only on the function of the technology but on their own social roles, status and values. An important aspect of this process is the competition for status and prestige as well as public perceptions of competence and the management of social roles and commitments. Moreover, we do not take for granted the axiom that the habituation and institutionalization of personal technologies flow from exploitation or conspiracy. Rather we regard these as matters for investigation and demonstration, which indeed may very well show that the exploitation can flow in the opposite direction than would have been predicted by these models, and that conspiracies can take place on many levels, for many ends. In this regard, *Apparatgeist* also spotlights how personal technology can be used creatively to empower some individuals, often at the expense of others.

We see a consistent interaction between the functional and social needs of potential users, their perceived values and status concerns, and their choice of which technologies to use and where to use them. This interaction has directionality in the sense that there is a consistent strain to manage competing needs for connection and autonomy and the various boundaries people construct to manage the social world. These competing demands and the struggle to define appropriate boundaries between public and private are evident in the design and use of personal technology and the folk discourse praising and blaming personal technology. As a result, we see that a certain degree of predictability can be attained in terms of who uses which types of new technologies. Because these tools have a life of their own, people must deal with the tools in their social environments even if they do not adopt the tools themselves. This extends not only to new users, but to those who will be "drop-outs" or active rejecters, or who will simply ignore technology. These stances toward technology are grounded in deeper communicative principles outlined in *Apparatgeist* theory and should be reflected in the personal theories of technology that people develop and their routine and ritual behaviors relevant to the technology.

Given the extraordinary impact of communications technology on virtually all cultures, there is a need to understand still better how people fit these new devices into their lives and to what effect. Certainly these issues have been explored with insightful results using perspectives drawn from, among others, world systems, post-modern, developmental, feminist and ethnomethodological perspectives. However, although these perspectives can be used to create post hoc explanations of how people's technology use changes over time, they have had only limited success in predicting future states (Cummings and Kraut, forthcoming). For instance, the above theories, to the extent they offer predictions at all, suggested that work uses would expand at the cost of social uses. After their initial inception, this certainly does not appear to have been the case with mobile phones. Hence it seems we could benefit from a theory that would predict uses and meanings within a social setting and in light of potential connectivity.

We believe our proposed perspective, *Apparatgeist*, is helpful in this regard. Our theory sets parameters that may aid in explaining and understanding the role of the machines we choose as "intimate partners" in our daily lives. The perspective should facilitate understanding the role of communication devices such as the mobile within the complex realm of social interaction as well as from the multifaceted perspectives of users. This is especially true as new forms and uses of PCTs inevitably arise.

In conclusion, it seems that certain conceptual perspectives arise in people's minds as a result of their interaction with technologies, and these are remarkably consistent across cultures. If this is indeed the case, future research should continue to detect this phenomenon. It then becomes the job of theorists to provide a conceptual justification. We have offered our own theory that might account for this process and result. Further investigation may be merited on the heuristic value of this theoretical perspective in terms of understanding the social dimensions and reciprocal path dependencies of these new personal communications technologies. The empirical findings of this volume doubtless are valuable since they add to the extraordinarily slender literature on the human uses and meanings of mobile communication technology.

## References

Cummings, Jonathon N., and Kraut, Robert E. (forthcoming). "Domesticating Computers and the Internet." *The Information Society*.

Giddens, Anthony (1978). *Central Problem in Social Theory*. Berkeley: University of California Press.

Goffman, Erving (1959). *The Presentation of Self in Everyday Life*. Garden City, NY: Doubleday.

Goodwin, M., and Wenzel, J. (1979). "Proverbs and Practical Reasoning: A Study in Socio-logic." *Quarterly Journal of Speech* 65: 289–302.

Haddon, Leslie (2000). Personal communication, June 3.

Hegel, G.W.F. (1977). *Hegel's Phenomenology of Spirit*. Trans. A.V. Miller. New York and London: Oxford University Press.

Heidegger, Martin (1996). *Being and Time: A Translation of Sein und Zeit*. Trans. Joan Stambaugh. New York: State University of New York Press.

Innis, Harold A. (1950). *Empire and Communications*. Oxford: Clarendon Press.

Katz, James (1999). *Connections: Social and Cultural Studies of the Telephone in American Life*. New Brunswick, NJ: Transaction.

Orlikowski, W. (1992). "The Duality of Technology: Rethinking the Concept of Technology in Organizations." *Organizations* 3(3): 398–427.

Peters, J. (1999). *Speaking into the Air: A History of the Idea of Communication*. Chicago: University of Chicago Press.

Poole, M. S., and DeSanctis, G. (1990). "Understanding the Use of Group Decision Support Systems: The Theory of Adaptive Structuration." In J. Fulk and C. Steinfeld (eds.), *Organizations and Communication Technology*. Newbury Park, CA: Sage.

(1992). "Microlevel Structuration in Computer-supported Group Decision-making." *Human Communication Research* 19: 5–49.

Popper, K. (1963) *Conjectures and Refutations: The Growth of Scientific Knowledge*. London: Routledge.

Quadstone (2000). "Quadstone Solution Helps Vodafone Gain Customer Insight." Media Release, November 13, Boston, MA. Located at: http://www. quadstone.com/info/press/2000/11_13.html. Accessed on December 1, 2000.

Rostenstreich, Nathan (1973). "Volksgeist." *Dictionary of the History of Ideas*, vol. 4. New York: Scribner's, 490–496.

Shapiro, C., and Varian, Hal (1999). *Information Rules*. Cambridge, MA: Harvard University Press.

Silverstone, Roger, and Haddon, L. (1996). "Design and the Domestication of Information and Communication Technologies: Technical Change and Everyday Life." In R. Mansell and R. Silverstone (eds.), *Communication by Design: The Politics of Information and Communication Technologies*. Oxford: Oxford University Press, 44–74.

Sitkin, S., Sutcliffe, K., and Barrios-Choplin, J. (1992). "A Dual-capacity Model of Communication Media Choice in Organizations." *Human Communication Research* 18(4): 563–598.

Sobieraj, Sandra (2000). "The Story behind the Near-Concession." Associated Press Wire story, November 8, 16:33 EDT.

White, Lynn, Jr. (1962). *Medieval Technology and Social Change*. Oxford: Clarendon Press.

Wynn, Eleanor, and Katz, James (1997). "Hyperbole over Cyberspace: Self-Presentation in Internet Home Pages and Discourse." *The Information Society* 13(4): 297–329.

# Appendixes

Whereas the exploration of perpetual contact and mobile communication in the previous chapters has been contingent primarily on comparison across cultures and nations, across the micro–macro divide, and across time, these appendixes provide a different vantage point from which to understand mobile communication. In a rigorous, searching examination, *Emanuel Schegloff* discusses the interplay between technology and social science with particular reference to the way the telephone set in motion a substantial interest in what today has become known as conversation analysis. The field arose out of a need to analyze the fossil residues of human communication – namely, naturally occurring telephone conversations – and this has led to insight into both human behavior and the way people use technology in their everyday life. As part of his analysis, a heretofore unpublished essay written more than a quarter-century ago is presented, along with an intertextual interpretation. This analysis illumines what is a constant in human intention despite the proliferation of electronic forms of those contacts through cellular phone and other mobile and increasingly semi-automatic communication technologies.

# A    On "Opening Sequencing": a framing statement

*Emanuel A. Schegloff*

One central theme of my contribution to this volume (chapter 18) is that inquiry into new technology – like the several technologies of "perpetual contact" – is most likely to be productive of new ideas and knowledge if the technology is examined not (or not only) as an object in its own right, but by reference to its intersection with things toward which we already have a cogent analytic stance. In the case of my own work and experience, the technology of the telephone – the old-fashioned, wired, fixed telephone – served as a prism through which were refracted the practices of ordinary talk-in-interaction. The result not only pinpointed some interactional issues that were brought to the fore on the telephone (as noted in chapter 18), but provided the impetus for noticing, registering and describing practices of ordinary talk-in-interaction that pervade conversation when persons are co-present. Seeing the ways in which these practices of talking were modified on the telephone brought their very existence into sharper focus and required an account of them in non-technologically mediated contexts to allow a specification of their transformation when implemented through a new technological medium.

The document published in Appendix B presents an example of this intersection, and one that played a role in the development of Conversation Analysis. Studying the openings of telephone calls to the police in the aftermath of a disaster provided the occasion for isolating for careful description common practices for initiating conversation in a delicate, yet "routinized," aspect of interpersonal interaction, and, more generally still, for explicating how a great variety of practices of talking in interaction, and efforts to carry through a variety of courses of action, get organized and packaged in well-structured sequences of turns at talk.

A bit of background about this text is in order. An earlier version constituted the second chapter of my dissertation (Schegloff, 1967), a revision of which was published in the *American Anthropologist* (Schegloff, 1968). Around the same time as this publication, Erving Goffman, who had recently relocated from the University of California, Berkeley (where he had chaired my dissertation committee), to the University of Pennsylvania, contacted me regarding a series that he and Dell Hymes were to co-edit for the University of Pennsylvania Press under the title "Conduct and Communication." It was to include as its inaugural volumes his own *Strategic Interaction* (1969) and a collection of Ray Birdwhistell's work under the title *Kinesics and Context* (1970); could they include a revised version of my dissertation as another of the inaugural titles? I spent the summer of 1970 working on the revision of the dissertation manuscript (and of the paper published from it) to see if I could fashion a book I would be content to publish. I completed the revision of two of its chapters – the second and fourth – before deciding that I no longer felt that the sort of work being developed under the rubric "conversation analysis" could be defensibly done that way, and I declined the invitation.[1]

To this day I am not sure whether this was the right decision, either for me or for Conversation Analysis as a mode of inquiry. It surely affected my life in major ways. But publishing a piece of work is in effect an endorsement of a way of working, and, at the time, I felt that there was too much in even the revised version that I could neither endorse as a way of working and presenting results nor remove without undermining the viability of the work as a book.

Most problematic was the recourse to "plausibly recalled" data, so-called "field notes" of scenes observed once in real time, clippings from newspapers, and the like – much of it familiar from ethnographically based research and especially from the body of Goffman's work, but hardly defensible in view of the growing evidence of the decisive and "surprising" relevance of "detail" discoverable from recorded data but inaccessible to once-in-real-time observation or occasioned and "interested" recollection. In participating in the development of a distinctive mode of research, it seemed ill advised to publish a piece of work that took the adequacy of such data apparently for granted and used it to support the sorts of analytic claims we were finding could be made compellingly. An observation key to the whole work of the dissertation was, after all, my noticing of a single second of silence from the answerer after the phone had been picked up. Although we did not yet have much well-transcribed recorded data (hence the recourse to other types of material), it no longer seemed defensible to ground claims on data that were out of keeping with what we were trying to do, whatever their role in previous inquiry.

That said, I do think there is much that was – and is – correct in these revised chapters, some that is important and has since been further developed, and some that is potentially important but is not yet developed. I publish it here under the auspices of historical documentation; conversation-analytic work has developed to the point that there is no risk (I hope) of anyone thinking that I am endorsing the ways of working I found problematic thirty years ago. And perhaps some of its substantive findings can be of use. As noted at the outset, in the context of this volume it may serve to illustrate how the technological features of an interaction medium can lead investigators who are pursuing an analytic goal to advance our understanding of features of interaction that are by no means technology specific.

For the development of conversation analysis, this chapter offered a variety of themes and analytic tacks, such as the positioning of objects within a turn and the organization of a turn, an orientation to sequences of sequences, and the ways in which interactional practices and constraints set the context and limitations on unilateral determination of interactional outcomes – here with respect to the very availability of persons to interact. If particular advances in the larger enterprise were to be singled out, developed largely in my interaction with Sacks, they might include:

- A systematic account of a sequence type. This included (a) the identification of a particular sequence type used to do a particular activity – the summons/answer sequence; (b) the specification of an account of the notion or unit "a sequence"; (c) an important step in the development of the notion of preferred and dispreferred responses in sequences, previously introduced in the notion of asymmetric alternatives (Schegloff and Sacks, 1973, but first developed for the conference presentation of that paper in 1969), further specified here (at pp. 358–368) and later further developed by Sacks in his 1971 lectures (1992, II, pp. 414–415) and subsequently 1987 [1973]), by Pomerantz (1984), and in Schegloff (1988).
- One piece of the early study of what we term "the overall structural organization of the unit 'a single conversation'." Aside from Sacks' inquiries discussed in the *Lectures* (and some papers taken from them, such as Sacks, 1975), the work on openings taken up in this chapter is further pursued in Schegloff (1970, 1979, 1986, and forthcoming), and the work on closings was pursued in Schegloff and Sacks (1973) and Jefferson (1973).
- The notion of practices and actions done "for cause," and the linkage of that to the priority claims such actions make on their recipients.
- An exploration of what might be involved in an exhaustive exploration of a single turn or turn type, and a very brief and formulaic one at that, and doing it in a fashion compatible with what was known about other targets of inquiry.
- The first piece of work to take on an aggregate of data. The single turn or turn type was explored through a collection of 500 instances of that

turn type, and this at a time when inquiry had been limited to intensive examination of single occurrences.

- Through working with collections of instances, the introduction to this domain of inquiry of the notion of a deviant case, apparently at odds with an analytic claim, "testing" the claimed finding, allowing reformulation of the finding, finding indirect support in the apparently incompatible instance(s), and allowing further specification of the finding.
- The first efforts to deal with what I have come to call "granularity" (Schegloff, 2000).

This work, then, did spawn a line of research for which the technology involved was central – a whole genre preoccupied with telephone conversation. At the same time, the technology served to spur the development of a whole modality of research to which it was fundamentally peripheral, but to which it provided a contextually varied glimpse of its basic data. Who knows what the view in retrospect thirty years from now will reveal to have been the major payoffs of research set in motion by the devices that have engendered "perpetual contact"?

## Note

1 The two chapters I revised were for a long time known only to my friend and colleague Harvey Sacks, with whom I discussed them at the end of the summer in 1970; they have since been read by a few people to whose work they seemed relevant. The document published here is the 1970 version of chapter 2 (modified only to accommodate publishing conventions adhered to by Cambridge University Press); Chapter 4 is to appear elsewhere (Schegloff, 1970). Chapter 1 was introductory and literature-review-ish, in the genre style of dissertations at that time. Chapter 3 had concerned something I had termed "the method of the call" in developing the dissertation work, a line of analysis that Sacks had pursued in his 1968 lectures (1992, I: 773–783 passim) under the rubric "the reason for the call." The central topic of chapter 5 – transformations of the identities or "capacities" in which the participants are to be talking – turned out to require prior work (at the time still undone) about mutual identification and recognition in so-called "personal" conversations, that is, ones not in institutional contexts or with a "business" character. That work was subsequently undertaken (Schegloff, 1979), and the dissertation material on the matter in an institutional context is treated thematically in Schegloff (forthcoming).

## References

Birdwhistell, R.L. (1970). *Kinesics and Context: Essays on Body Motion Communication.* Philadelphia: University of Pennsylvania Press.

Goffman, E. (1969). *Strategic Interaction*. Philadelphia: University of Pennsylvania Press.

Jefferson, G. (1973). "A Case of Precision Timing in Ordinary Conversation: Overlapped Tag-Positioned Address Terms in Closing Sequences." *Semiotica* 9: 47–96.

Pomerantz, A. (1984). "Agreeing and Disagreeing with Assessments: Some Features of Preferred/Dispreferred Turn Shapes." In J.M. Atkinson and J. Heritage (eds.), *Structures of Social Action: Studies in Conversation Analysis*. Cambridge: Cambridge University Press, 57–101.

Sacks, H. (1975). "Everyone Has to Lie." In M. Sanches and B.G. Blount (eds.), *Sociocultural Dimensions of Language Use*. New York: Academic Press, 57–80.

(1987 [1973]). "On the Preferences for Agreement and Contiguity in Sequences in Conversation." In G. Button and J.R.E. Lee (eds.), *Talk and Social Organisation*. Clevedon, England: Multilingual Matters, 54–69.

(1992). *Lectures on Conversation*, 2 vols. Ed. by G. Jefferson, with Introductions by E.A. Schegloff. Oxford: Blackwell.

Schegloff, E.A. (1967). "The First Five Seconds: The Order of Conversational Openings." Unpublished Ph.D. dissertation, University of California, Berkeley.

(1968). "Sequencing in Conversational Openings." *American Anthropologist* 70: 1075–1095.

(1970). "Answering the Phone." Unpublished Ms. To appear in G.H. Lerner (ed.), *Conversation Analysis: Studies from the First Generation* (in preparation).

(1979). "Identification and Recognition in Telephone Openings." In G. Psathas (ed.), *Everyday Language: Studies in Ethnomethodology*. New York: Irvington Publishers, 23–78.

(1986). "The Routine as Achievement." *Human Studies* 9: 111–151.

(1988). "On an Actual Virtual Servo-Mechanism for Guessing Bad News: A Single Case Conjecture." *Social Problems* 35(4): 442–457.

(2000). "On Granularity." *Annual Review of Sociology* 26: 715–720.

(forthcoming). "Reflections on Research on Telephone Conversation Openings: Issues of Cross-cultural Scope and Scholarly Exchange, Interactional Import and Consequences." In K.K. Luke and T.S. Pavlidou (eds.), *Telephone Calls: Unity and Diversity in Conversational Structure across Languages and Cultures*. Amsterdam: John Benjamins.

Schegloff, E.A., and Sacks, H. (1973). "Opening up Closings." *Semiotica* 8: 289–327.

# B    Opening sequencing

*Emanuel A. Schegloff*

It is an easily noticeable fact about two-party conversations[1] that their speaker sequencing is alternating. That is to say, the sequencing of speakers in two-party conversation can be described by the formula "ababab," where "a" and "b" are the parties to the conversation.[2]

The "abab" formula is a specification, for two-party conversation, of a basic rule for conversation: *one party at a time*.[3] The strength of this rule can be seen in the members' practice that, in a multi-party setting (more precisely, where there are four or more participants), if more than one person is talking, it can be claimed not that the rule has been violated, but that more than one conversation is going on. Thus, Bales can write (1950, p. 461; emphasis added):

> The conversation generally proceeded so that *one person talked at time*, and all members in the particular group were attending the *same conversation*. In this sense, these groups might be said to have a "single focus," that is, *they did not involve a number of conversations proceeding at the same time.*

When combined with an analytic conception of an utterance, the "abab" specification has a variety of other interesting consequences, such as allowing us to see how persons can come to say "X is silent," when no person in the setting is talking – as in Bergler's (1938) title, "On the Resistance Situation: The Patient Is Silent."

The "abab" formula, in common with techniques for speaker sequencing in multi-party conversation (see Sacks, 1992), operates on an utterance-to-utterance basis. It relates each speaker's turn sequentially to the previous one, the completion of one speaker's turn serving to occasion a transition to a next speaker's turn. This mode of operation may be seen to generate two associated problems: a termination problem, i.e. how to deprive some turn's completion of its relevance for a transition to another speaker (for a preliminary report see Schegloff and Sacks, 1973); and an initiation problem, i.e. how coordinated entry by two parties into an orderly sequence of conversational turns[4] is managed. It is the latter problem that is to be addressed below.

One way of specifying the initiation problem might be to ask: "Who talks first?" The problem would thus be seen as an allocation problem, concerned with the assignment of the term "a" in the "abab" formula to one or another party. A completely general solution would be one that, for any two possible co-conversationalists (or for any $n$ co-conversationalists), would give a determinate finding on "who goes first." No such general solution seems operative. One reason for this might be that such a solution would seem to require some identification or categorization of the prospective participants, in terms of which an allocation might be decided. However, first, it does not appear that any collection of identification terms for members is uniformly a locus for rights of first-speakership (for example, the collection "Protestant, Catholic . . . " is not, nor are most such collections). Secondly, Sacks (1972a) has shown that, as between alternative identifications or categorization terms and as between alternative collections of them, there is a selection problem which is general, and consequently a problem of convergence in the selection of identification terms. The consequence of this is that, even if all identification terms were the locus of first-speakership rules, convergence on some set of terms would be required for an unambiguous determination of first speaker to be arrived at. Thirdly, it is not the case that the identifications that may make it relevant for the parties to talk in the first place yield a determination of who should talk first. Were that the case, a solution as general as was needed would be available, any determination of the relevance of talk being simultaneously a determination of who should begin it.

More to the point, however, is that the initiation problem formulated as an allocation problem is not general. Rather, the problem in that form arises only in a restricted class of cases. In many of the cases in which the allocation problem is seen as relevant, it is by virtue of some already selected identification of the parties. That is, "who goes first" is a problem only given some already relevant identification of the alternatives. For example, when participants are already relevantly formulated as "officer–private" or "adult–child," a rule such as "don't speak until spoken to," addressed in part to the allocation problem, is in point. Similarly, given the relevance of formulations of the parties such as "master, servant," or "clerk, customer" (and some formulation of the "setting" – for example, in the latter case, being in a business establishment the clerk serves and the customer is then patronizing), the allocation problem may be found to be relevant.[5] In view of the fact that the relevance of the allocation problem in many cases presumes some formulation of members and setting (from a restricted set of such formulations), it is hardly surprising that available discussions of it typically offer in their findings solutions couched in terms of those formulations (typically involving some hierarchicalized set of identifications, for example age-grade, social status, organizational rank, etc.; see Albert, 1964, and Goffman, 1963, p. 91, for examples).[6] There are other than categorical ways in which the "who first" problem may be found relevant, for example in terms of interpersonal histories, when there is an issue about who will "break the ice" after some breach in a relationship, but those are clearly not general.

One domain in which the problem seems relevant, and within which there seems to be a generally used solution, is that of telephone conversations. There, a "distribution rule for first utterances" is: the *answerer speaks first.*[7] The distribution rule can hold generally in its domain because it formulates the parties in terms of identification categories which are "this-conversation-specific" for any conversation in the domain, rather than in terms of categories "external" to the conversation (on "external" identifications and attributes, see Goffman, 1961, pp. 19–34). The categories "caller, called," or "caller, answerer" are relevant to participants for other parts of the conversation as well, for example in closings (Schegloff and Sacks, 1973; for another description of the relevance of "caller, called" to conversational openings, see Lewis, 1969).[8]

I shall not elaborate here on the details of the distribution rule as a solution to the allocation version of the initiation problem for telephone conversation (see Schegloff, 1968, pp. 1076–1080). In the corpus of data with which we start, it holds for all but one of the roughly 500 conversations. In the vast majority of these, the dispatcher (when calls were made to the police) or others (when calls were made by the police) spoke first. In several cases of simultaneous talk at the beginning of the conversation (occurring because the caller was still talking to the switchboard operator when the dispatcher "came on the line"), a resolution occurred by the caller withdrawing in favor of the called. That is, either the caller stopped and the dispatcher continued, or both stopped and the dispatcher went on.

```
#364
D: [ Police Desk.
C: [ First aiders with me.
D: Police Desk.
C: Hello?
D: Yes.
C: Uh, this is...(etc.)

#66
D: Police Desk.
C: ((simultaneously giving phone number 54377
   in background to operator))
```

```
D:  Hello
C:  I am a pharmacist. I own...(etc.)
```

#43
```
D:  [ Police Desk.
C:  [ Say, what's all the excitement...
D:  Police Desk?
C:  Police Headquarters?
D:  Yes.
C:  What's all the excitement,...(etc.)
```

Simultaneous talk is of special interest because it is the converse of "abab," which requires that only one party talk at a time. The resolution of simultaneous talk at the beginning of telephone conversation by reference to the distribution rule would support a claim for its status as a general solution to an "allocation" problem in that domain. A fully adequate demonstration might involve giving a precise explication of the notion of one party's "withdrawal," perhaps by reference to some utterance unit, for example a sentence, begun but not finished. The available data do not allow such a demonstration here.

One case clearly does not fit the distribution rule:

```
#9      Police make call; receiver is lifted,
        and there is a one second pause:
        (1.0)
Police: Hello
 Other: American Red Cross
Police: Hello, this is Police Headquarters...er,
        Officer Stratton,...(etc.)
```

In this case the caller talks first, whereas the distribution rule would require that the first line be "American Red Cross," the utterance of the called party.

In dealing with this datum, we come to find that the distribution rule, although it holds in most cases, is best understood as a derivative of more general rules. The more general formulation is relevant to unmediated interaction as well as to telephone conversation. By reformulating the initiation problem, we are enabled to deal with aspects of the opening structure on which the distribution rule is mute. A shift in focus from "who talks first" to how the initiation of conversation is done leads to a description of a solution for *that* problem, a solution that in turn provides for alternative "first speaker" outcomes. The distribution rule can then be understood as one specification of the more general formulation, and data such as #9 above as another, both in that sense being special cases subsumed under it.

## The problem of availability

Many activities seem to require some minimum number of participants to do them. For thinking or playing solitaire, only one is required; for dialogue, at least two; and, for "eristic dialogue," at least three.[9] When an activity has as one of its properties a requirement of a minimal number of parties, then the same behaviors done without that "quota" being met are subject to being seen as instances of some other activity (with a different minimum requirement, perhaps), or as "random" behavior casting doubt on the competence or normalcy of their performer. Thus, one person playing the piano while another is present may be seen to be performing, whereas in the absence of another he may be seen to be practicing. Persons finding themselves waving to no one in particular by mistake may have to provide for the sense of their hand movement as having been only the first part of a convoluted attempt to scratch their head.

Conversation, at least for adults in this society, seems to be an activity with a minimal requirement of two participants. Reference to such a feature seems required for the analysis of observations such as the following.

Buses in Manhattan have as their last tier of seats one long bench. Two persons were observed sitting on this last bench next to one another but in no way indicating that they were "with each other" (Goffman, 1963, pp. 102–103). Neither turned his head in the direction of the other and, for a long period of time, neither spoke. At one point, one of them began speaking without, however, turning his head in the direction of the other. It was immediately observed that other passengers, within whose visual range this "couple" was located, scanned the back area of the bus to find to whom that talk was addressed. It turned out, of course, that the talk was addressed to the one the speaker was "with." What is of interest to us, however, is that the others present in the scene immediately undertook a search for a conversational other. On other occasions, however, similar in all respects but one to the preceding, a different sequel occurred. The dissimilarity was that the talker was not "with" anyone and, when each observer scanned the environment for the conversational other, no candidate for that position, including each scanner himself, could be located. The observers then took it that the talker was "talking to himself" and the passengers exchanged "knowing glances."[10] The issue here could be seen to involve what Bales (1950, pp. 87–90) has called "targeting," and to be sure that is what the persons in the scene appear to have been attending to. It is to be noted, however, that it is by reference to the character of conversation as a minimally two-party activity that the relevance of seeking a target is established in the first place. In this connection, it may be remarked that such phenomena as "talking to the air" (Goffman,

1953, p. 159) or glossing one's behavior by "talking to oneself" are best understood not as exceptions to the minimal two-party character of conversation, but as especially noticeable by virtue of it, and frequently ways of talking to others while not addressing them (of which other examples are given in Bales, 1950, pp. 89–90).

For activities that require at least two parties, an initial problem of coordination is the problem of availability; that is, a person who seeks to engage in an activity that requires the collaboration of two parties must first establish that another party is available to collaborate. For conversation, that problem may be specified as follows.

I noted earlier that one basic feature of conversation, its speaker sequencing organization, operates on an utterance-to-utterance basis, the completion of one speaker's turn occasioning a transition to a next speaker's turn. If recognizable conversation requires the effective operation of the rules that are relevant to achieving this completion–transition, then one seeking to launch a conversational course of action must attend to the likelihood that at the first relevant point the rules will operate. That point might at first appear to be the completion of his first utterance. What is required is that that point be recognized by a co-conversationalist; that is, that the first speaker's completion be recognized and be made the occasion for a transition to the next speaker, that the co-conversationalist then talk.

However, more is required. For something would be amiss if a next speaker, having "recognized" the first speaker's completion, and having effected a "transition" by speaking "next," produced talk that was not analyzably related to the first speaker's talk. Should that occur, then what might be seen is that the fact that the second speaker did not talk until the first had completed was "accidental," i.e., was not the product of the second speaker's analysis of the first speaker's utterance to find that, and when, it had been (possibly) completed, that serving as the occasion to start talking. Such a finding of non-listening when an utterance is not analyzably related to a prior one can be made not only at the initial exchange of a conversation. An illustration of this point occurring well into an ongoing conversation is the following, drawn from another body of data (BC – a corpus of calls to a radio talk show):

```
A: You know it's a funny thing, any man who hires
   anybody, has a choice between relatives and strangers.
B: Yeh.
A: When a man hires relatives,
B: Yeh
A: in a private business,
```

```
B:  Yeh
A:  Nobody gets excited.
B:  Yeah.
A:  Why?
B:  Yeh. I unnastan dat // (    )
A:  Butchu didn' hear a word I said.
```

In addition, then, to simply being a "next speaker," the second speaker's utterance should exhibit attention to, and analysis of, the one it follows. The requirement that utterances be "fitted" to one another independently of managing the transition of one speaker to another adequately (without interruption or pause) is further suggested by the following. When conversations are started with initial "substantive" utterances (for example with a question), next speakers will frequently, in their first turn, ask for a repetition, for example "What?", "Huh?". For instance,

```
Standing near a bulletin board:
A:  What's Koto?
B:  Pardon me?
A:  It says here, ''Koto lessons.'' What's Koto?
B:  Oh. It's a Japanese musical instrument.
```

From their production of such utterances as "pardon me" as non-interruptions, it is clear that members can have found that completion had occurred and transition was relevant. But when an utterance fitted to the prior utterance and the activity it was doing is not done, the alternative is not any talk at all that would accomplish the transition to a next speaker, but rather a repetition request. A repetition would allow that analysis which is necessary to producing an utterance fitted to the prior utterance.

Given the relevance of "utterance fitting," we can see that the problem of providing that the sequencing rules will operate, and thus that a course of conversational action is being initiated, may have its locus earlier than the first completion–transition point, though it is at that point that the fruits of the collaboration may first be exhibited. Insofar as the second speaker's utterance after the first completion–transition point should exhibit an analysis of the first speaker's utterance, then "possible second speaker's" attention may be required from the *beginning* of the first speaker's utterance, thus allowing him to analyze that utterance as it is produced, find its possible completion, and be prepared in closely paced order to produce an utterance at the transition point that will exhibit his analysis of the first utterance.

The availability of another, a prospective co-conversationalist, for participation can thus be seen to involve the possibility of his analyzing a first utterance as it is produced. That availability can be open to inspection. That is, an analysis by a prospective first speaker of the appearances of a setting may yield as its product the availability of another (or some specific other). What such an analysis consists of I cannot describe here, though some categorization of others, their involvement in activities not combinable with conversation,[11] distance, noise, etc., would seem to be involved. When such an inspection and analysis do not show a prospective co-conversationalist to be available, when there is reason to expect non-hearing or non-analysis of a prospective first utterance, then interactional procedures may be employed to address the problem of availability. The use of such procedures is, thus, "for cause." A description of such procedures, which can constitute solutions to the problem of availability, will serve at the same time as descriptions of the accomplishment of coordinated entry into a conversation.

I turn, then, to a description of one such procedure – summons–answer sequences – and seek to describe its components, organization and properties, and show how it serves as a solution to the problem of availability and thus as a mechanism for coordinated entry into the "abab" formula.

## Summons–answer sequences

What the "answerer" referred to in the distribution rule is answering is a summons, for that is the class to which telephone rings are assimilated when analyzed by members (unless explicitly agreed upon on an ad hoc basis otherwise, for example as signals of leaving, requests for return call). Summonses are not restricted in their occurrence to telephone conversation or to conversational openings. They may be used whenever members attend availability as relevantly problematic, including, for example, in the course of an already ongoing conversation (as in data excerpt #398 cited below). And mechanical devices (such as telephone rings or office buzzers) are only one sub-class of summonses, others being terms of address ("John?", "Doctor?", "Mr. Jones," "waiter," "Mister"), courtesy phrases ("Excuse me," "Pardon me"), and a variety of non-verbal actions and paralinguistic productions (a tap on the shoulder, a wave of the hand, a cough, throat-clearing).

The various items that can be used as summonses may be used to accomplish other activities as well; the finding that summoning is being done is, therefore, the product of (members') analysis. Consider, for example, terms of address. An item is a term of address if on some occasion of address it is usable. (Although that it is usable on some occasion of address will not guarantee that it is usable on all occasions of address, or on any next occasion of address; for example, "Hello, stranger," may be usable only once at the beginning, and not thereafter in the same interaction. In particular, there may be a distribution of rights to use some particular term of address, some being entitled and others not, and some terms of address may vary in appropriateness with some formulation of the setting, for example endearment terms and obscene nicknames being inappropriate in a mixed public setting). This test may generate such sub-classes of address terms as first name, last name, title plus last name, nickname, some occupational titles (but not others – "Doctor," "Nurse," "Rabbi," "Officer," for example, but not "Secretary" or "Plumber"), kinship terms, and others.[12] The use of a member of any of these sub-classes of the class "terms of address" as a whole, can be seen as doing the action "addressing." But doing the action "addressing" in this sense is regularly (perhaps invariably) seen as accomplishing some other action as well when the term of address is produced as a complete utterance. For example, a term of address may be used to accomplish greeting, sanctioning, warning, pleading, invoking an action (as in the surgeon's "Nurse" at the operating table), or summoning. Just as not every term of address is appropriately usable on every occasion of address, so not every term of address is usable to accomplish any of these actions. But on any occasion of use, it is a matter for analysis what action is being done. And although the prior examples have concerned instances in which a term of address is produced as a complete utterance, similar analyses may be relevant in other contexts. For example, a hearer may have to distinguish between a term used as a simple addressing and a use as summons. The following considerations may be relevant to such an analysis.

First, when addressing, the positioning of a term of address is restricted. It may occur at the beginning of an utterance ("Jim, where do you want to go?"), at the end of an utterance ("What do you think, Mary?") or between clauses or phrases in an utterance ("Tell me, John, how's Bill?"). As summons items, however, terms of address are positionally free within an utterance. (This way of differentiating the usages has a "one-way" character; that is, it differentiates only when an item occurs where terms of address, as non-summons items, cannot. When it occurs within the restrictions on placement of terms of address, it clearly is non-differentiating.) As a mere address term, an item cannot occur between a preposition and its object, but as a summons it may, as in the following excerpt from the data:

```
#398
C:  Try to get out t' -- Joe?
D:  Yeah?
C:  Try to get ahold of...(etc.)
```

Secondly, summons items may have a distinctive rising terminal juncture, a raising of the voice pitch in a "quasi-interrogative" fashion.[13] This seems to be especially the case when a summons occurs after a sentence has already begun, as in the above datum. It need not be the case when the summons stands alone, as in "Jim," when trying to attract Jim's attention.

Thirdly, a term of address is "inserted" in an utterance. By that I mean that, after the term of address is introduced, the utterance continues with no break in its grammatical continuity; for example, "Tell me, Jim, what did you think of..." When a summons occurs in the course of an utterance, it is followed by a "re-cycling" to the beginning of the utterance. The utterance is begun again, as in datum #398 cited above. Although in that datum the original utterance is altered when started again, alteration is not intrinsic to what is intended by the term "re-cycling." Thus,

```
A:  If you think -- Gary, if you think -- Gary?
B:  (Looks at A)
A:  If you think that's bad...(etc.)
```

Similarly, as the names I have used to refer to them may suggest, the other classes of items that are used to do summoning – "courtesy terms," paralinguistic productions such as coughs, and so on – are not intrinsically summons terms; they are used to do other actions as well. That they are on some occasion of use doing summoning is the outcome of an analysis by co-participants, an analysis to which the production of the utterance may be oriented to ensure its proper outcome.[14] That availability is possibly problematic is one consideration relevant to such an analysis.

The analysis of some utterance as a summons may involve at the same time an analysis of the kind of summons it is. In this respect it is relevant not only that the terms that can be doing summoning can be doing other actions as alternatives, but that utterances used as summonses may be selected for consistency with other features of the setting, or may be vehicles for the accomplishment of other aspects of the interaction. For example, "Excuse me" may, as alternatives to summoning, be used as an apology or as part of a micro-ecological maneuver, as when getting past someone in a crowded setting. In analyzing which of these actions is being done on some occasion of use, however, it is relevant that, as a summons term, "Excuse me" is typically selected when summoning "strangers" and is not used when summoning "acquaintances" (if so used it may be immediately corrected, as in "Excuse me," other turns around, "Oh, Jim, I didn't know you were here"). "Excuse me" can then be seen to display some analysis by a possible summoner of the prospective interactants as "non-acquaintances," serving as a vehicle for a proposed typing of the upcoming conversation as between "strangers" and being selected as consistent with such an identification of the parties. When the parties both know, and know each other to know, that such an identification (as "strangers") is incorrect, then the analysis of the utterance "Excuse me" as a summons may be rejected; for as a summons it is mis-selected, while as an apology or as part of a micro-ecological maneuver it is correctly produced.[15] Where the term selected is consistent with alternative analyses, errors may in fact be made, as in the following observation.

Two policemen are conversing in front of the rear door of a bus. A lady carrying a young child approaches and says, "Excuse me." One of the policemen looks at her and says, "Yes, ma'am." The lady says, "Excuse me." The policemen step away from the door, and the lady moves toward it.

One resource, then, in deciding between alternative analyses of an utterance that can be used for both summoning and other actions is the organization of possible summonses into classes, selection of which is intendedly consistent with, serves as vehicle for, or accomplishes other features of the setting and interaction (such as a proffered characterization of the co-participants).

As summonses can be done by any of a range of terms, some of which are relevantly seen as organized into standard classes, so answers may be accomplished through a range of terms, whose class membership is also relevant to what they can be analyzed as doing. One class, what Goffman (1963) calls "clearance cues," includes such answers as "Yeah," "What," "Uh huh," as well as such non-verbal availability displays as directing the eyes on, or repositioning the head or body towards, the summoner. The other class is heterogeneous, including a variety of utterances and non-verbal actions, not necessarily precluding availability but making it, and possible conversational sequelae, problematic. Because the class is heterogeneous, each of its members as an answer to a summons requiring particularized, situated analysis by the co-participants to determine its consequences, there is relatively little that can be said about the class per se. I shall return to a discussion of this class of "problematic answers" to summonses and their consequences below, after a discussion of some features of sequences made up of summonses and "clearance cue" answers.[16]

## Non-terminality of summons–answer (SA) sequences

The sequence[17] that a summons initiates is intendedly preliminary or prefatory to some further conversational or non-verbal activity. Whether at the beginning of a conversation or in its course, to produce or hear an utterance as a summons is to produce or hear it as initiating a sequence (a pair) intendedly introductory to something that will follow it. When followed by a "clearance cue," a summons–answer sequence cannot properly stand as the final exchange of a conversation. Such sequences have "non-terminality" as a specifically relevant feature.[18] They are, then, members of a class Sacks (1992, I, pp. 685–692) has called "pre-sequences," a term collecting such specific forms as "pre-invitations," "pre-offers," "pre-warnings." SA sequences might, accordingly, be called (especially when occurring other than in the course of an already ongoing conversation) "pre-conversationals."

Given the relevance of some continuation upon the completion of an SA sequence with a clearance cue, two constraints may be noted here (another will be discussed below, p. 342) that are relevant to the continuation.

One constraint concerns the party whose "responsibility" it is felt to be. The non-terminality property is produced by the obligation of the *summoner* to talk again upon completion (by the summoned) of the SA sequence. This might seem to be tautological, since the completion of the answer occasions a next speaker's turn, and, in a two-party conversation, the next speaker is necessarily the summoner. The seeming tautology arises in part from the difficulty in two-party conversation of distinguishing between what a party does as formulaically generated next speaker and what he does by virtue of having in his last turn produced a summons. In multi-party conversation, however, there are other possible next speakers (other than the summoner) after the answerer; and the obligation of the summoner to talk again may be seen to select him from among the others, if a clearance cue answer is produced.[19] This point should not be taken as indicating that the summoner's obligation to talk again operates in multi-party, but not in two-party, conversation; only that it may be more clearly analyzable in the former. Sequencing rules seem to operate as general rules, that is for $n$-party conversation. That two-party conversation seems to have a sequencing formula "abab," whereas multi-party conversation does not, is not a product of special sequencing rules, but is a derivative specification for two-party conversation of mechanisms generally operative. Even within two-party conversation, the non-redundant character of the summoner's obligation to talk again after a clearance cue answer may be appreciated, if we note that, although the answer to a summons (for example "Yeah" or "What") can be a complete utterance, it need not be. The sequel could be produced by an obligation for the answerer to continue, as is the case, for example, when a chairman calls on a next speaker in a pre-set order of speakers:

```
Chair: Mr. Smith
Smith: Yes. I'd like to suggest...(etc.)
```

or when the initiator of a broken-off interaction is re-contacted by his erstwhile co-participant. These sorts of occurrences are to be distinguished, and are distinguished by members, from SA sequences. Even within two-party conversation then, the summoner's obligation to talk again is an independent sequencing mechanism. With rare exceptions (themselves having orderly consequences), the summoner fulfills this obligation and talks again. It is the routine fulfillment of this obligation that produces data in which conversations beginning with SA sequences do not terminate there.

The force of the non-terminality feature, specified in the obligation of the summoner to talk again, may be appreciated by observing what regularly occurs when the summoner, for whatever reason, does not wish to engage in the activity to which the SA sequence he originated may have been preliminary. Here we characteristically find some variant of the sequence: "Sam?", "Yeah?", "Oh, never mind." Note that in the very attempt to withdraw appropriately from the obligation to continue after a completed SA sequence, the summoner in fact conforms to it, and is not simply silent. (Note also that hearers, and the reader, "naturally" hear that he is withdrawing, or canceling, what he was otherwise about to initiate; they do not hear that he summoned the other in order to say "never mind.")[20] Even in telephone contacts between mutually anonymous strangers, where maintaining the intactness of a relationship or a reputation would not seem to be at issue, the obligation to continue talk upon completion of SA is regularly fulfilled. For example, in calling an establishment to learn if it is open, that fact may sometimes be established when the ringing phone (summons) is lifted and "Hello" or the establishment's name is heard. Rather than hang up, callers will often continue with the already answered question "Are you still open?" (although there is a common tendency to append to it some seemingly less superfluous inquiry). Similarly, even when a caller can detect from the answerer's first utterance that he has reached a wrong number, he may fulfill the obligation to talk again (CF corpus):

```
A:  Hello.
B:  Uh, I called the wrong number, 451 instead of 251.
    I am getting absent-minded. Excuse me.
A:  Alright.
```

Another constraint on the sequel to SA sequences is imposed by another feature – their non-repeatability. Once a sequence has been completed, the summoner may not fulfill his obligation to continue with another summons to the same party. A contrast may be helpful here with
question–answer sequences (QA). QA is a sequential unit like SA (see
next section), and may also be used in conversation as a pre-sequence.
For example, A: "Remember Mary Jones from high school?" B: "Yeah."
Further talk from A would seem to have been made relevant, the question
having been specifically preliminary to it. The obligation to talk again can
be satisfied by another question (for example, A: "And remember the guy
she used to go around with?"). Although a questioner may be (except for
special classes of question and appropriate context) constrained not to
ask the same question again, he may choose some question to fill the
next slot. A summoner is barred not only from using the same summons
again, but from doing any more summoning (of the same "other").

The effectiveness of this restriction depends upon the clear recognition
that an answer has been returned. This recognition normally is untrou-
bled. However, trouble sometimes occurs by virtue of the fact that some
lexical items may, in some circumstances, be used both as summonses
and as answers. That "Hello" may be so used in telephone conversations
can be seen at D5/S5 of the following datum:

```
#IPD 237
D1:  Yeah.
S1:  Listen uh is this the dispatcher?
D2:  Mm hmm.
S2:  Listen, how's the ambulance situation?
     Have you got enough of 'em?
D3:  Well, hold on, let me check for you.
S3:  Well (now) listen, we can jury rig uh
     some uh ambulances out of our motor tenders
     if necessary.
D4:  Uh huh, hold on, let me check.
S4:  Alright
     (pause)
D5:  Hello.
S5:  Hello.
D6:  No, they've got... (etc.)
```

In some circumstances it may be impossible to tell whether such a term has been used as summons or as answer. Thus, for example, when acoustic difficulties arise in a telephone connection, both parties may attempt to confirm their continued mutual availability. Each may then employ a "hello" as a summons to the other. For each of them, however, it may be unclear whether what he hears in the earpiece is an answer to his check, or the other's summons for him to answer. One may, in such circumstances, hear a conversation in which a sequence of some length is constituted by nothing but alternately and simultaneously offered "hellos." Such "verbal dodging" may be resolved by one party's use of an item on which a second is conditionally relevant (see next section) where the second is unambiguously a second part of a pair (such as a QA sequence, "Can you hear me?"). In unmediated interaction, the difficulty can arise in situations where physical barriers make it difficult for the summoned person to indicate his having heard the summons and having initiated a course of answering. If the summoner does not hear the answer of the other and repeats the summons, the answerer may treat the second summons as over-insistent.[21] Continued knocking on the door or ringing of the phone may be met with the complaint, "I'm coming, I'm coming."

To sum up, the summoner's obligation to talk again cannot be satisfied by initiating another SA sequence to the same other. This does not mean, however, that one might not find two SA sequences in tandem in the opening of a conversation. If the non-terminality property is not met – that is, should the summoner not fulfill his obligation to talk again – the answerer of the first SA sequence may start another with a summons of his own, as in lines 1–3 below:

```
E has called M.  S
1  M:  McNamara    A
2      (pause)     Ø
3  M:  Hello?      S
4  E:  Yeah.       A
5  E:  John?
6  M:  Yeah
7  E:  I uh just trying to do some uh intercom here
8      in my own set up and then get a hold of you
       at the same time.
```

One further observation on the operation of the non-terminality property, concerning a possible misunderstanding of the use of a name, can allow us to note how the orderliness of "mistakes" in interaction is based on such formal properties. Names as address terms may be used, as suggested earlier, as both greetings and summonses (to cite but two of their uses). Should a name intendedly uttered as a greeting be heard as a summons, the hearer will expect a continuation whereas the speaker may not be prepared to give one. This may occur if A calls B's name and waves. A greeting will have been intended, verbally and gesturally accomplished. The lexical item perceived alone, for example if the gesture is not seen, may be heard as a summons, and one who hears it as a summons may then answer and await the activity to which it was expectably preliminary. The misinterpreted initiator may then feel required to say, "I was just saying hello," thereby honoring an obligation he was mistakenly seen to have assumed.

It is worth noting about such occurrences that misinterpreted persons can see how they were misinterpreted. Such availability of the nature of an error may have important consequences, such as the following.

First, it is not only "correct" or "sequentially appropriate" utterances that can be analyzed as methodically produced, but errors can be seen as methodically produced as well (by participants and therefore by analysts). Here the error turns on the ambiguity of an address term, its usability to do alternative activities, in this case "summoning" and "greeting," where there is a differentiating feature of two otherwise closely related sequences. The non-terminality of SA sequences stands in contrast to the possible terminality of greeting exchanges; whereas an SA sequence is properly followed by further talk, an exchange of greetings can be (but need not be) all of a conversation (A: "Hi," B: "Hi"). The comparison of SA sequences and greeting exchanges is in point, for analysts and for participants, because of the special status both have as openings. Greeting exchanges properly occur as openings, that is, as the initial exchange.[22] Although SA sequences may occur throughout a conversation "for cause" (that is, when the other's availability may be problematic), one place they regularly may be in point is as an initial exchange. Both greetings and SA sequences, as compared with other utterances, are then especially relevant to the opening slots of a conversation: that is, the opening slots are one place one can look for them on the one hand, and on the other hand they are preferred solutions to an analysis (by members) of utterances occurring in those slots.[23] The usability of some utterance (for example a first name) both for a summons and as (a component of) a greeting can lead to an error of analysis because either is a preferred analysis for such an item in a first slot; it can lead to a *consequential* error, since each calls for a different response, and the possible terminality of the exchange differs between them. But the error can be seen to be methodically produced via the sequential similarities of the exchanges, and the relevant differentiating feature of terminality. When one mistakes a greeting for something else, it is not anything else it may be mistaken for;

the mistake stands in an orderly relationship to a correct analysis of the utterance.

Secondly, given that there was an error, a misinterpreted person can see how it was produced. It is in point to note further that a misinterpreted person can see that there was an error. Although I cannot undertake a full explication here, I can note that detecting that an error was made in the analysis of the first utterance turns on the relevance of different sequelae to different interpretations of the first utterance. If a first utterance was a greeting, then another greeting, a greeting return or a greeting answer are relevant (respectively, "Hi," "Hi"; "How are you?", "And *you*"; "How are you?", "Fine"). If a first utterance was a summons, then an answer is relevant.[24] Although some utterances may be possible second parts of either sequence (for example, "Hello"), for the most part the class of utterances that can be second parts of greeting exchanges, and the class of utterances that can be answers to summonses, are not overlapping. It is via the occurrence of a member of a class that is "incorrect" as a second item that the occurrence of an error of analysis can be detected by a first speaker.

Thirdly, being able to see that an error has been made, and being able to see the methodical basis of the error upon its occurrence without extended investigation, allows immediate correction and choice of relevant correction, correction being relevant because of the difference between the sequences with respect to possible terminality.

Fourthly, that members can detect and find the basis for mistakes in differentiating greeting usages from "summons" usages, and do so methodically, gives some basis for hope that analysts will be able to do so.

Non-terminality is an outcome of the summoner's observation of his obligation to talk again. Corollary to that obligation is the obligation of the answerer, having answered the summons with a clearance cue, to listen further. Just as the summoner, by virtue of his summons, obligates himself for further interaction, so the answerer, by virtue of his answer, may commit himself to staying with the encounter. An orientation to these respective obligations may enter into the selection of an answer to the summons. Should an answerer not be in a position, or not be willing, to attend the otherwise obligated next utterance of the summoner, he may select other than a clearance cue as his answer. For example, "sometimes the reply may contain an explicit request to hold off for a moment" (Goffman, 1953, p. 197). But why should one who has been summoned reply immediately with a request to hold off for a moment, rather than hold off for a moment and then reply with a clearance cue? Several issues are involved here. First, an explication of the internal structure of summons–answer sequences and their temporal organization will

allow me to examine the timing considerations just raised. Second, I shall
have to give some attention to non-clearance cue answers to summonses,
though they do not appear in my data.

## Conditional relevance in SA sequences

Throughout the preceding discussion, there has been repeated reference
to summons–answer "sequences." In employing the term "sequences,"
more is intended than to refer to the feature, always present where consecutive rather than simultaneous organization holds, that one event follows
another; more is intended than subsequence. Although the relationship of
subsequence, and especially adjacent subsequence, is pervasively relevant
to conversation (the placement of utterances, and especially what they are
placed after, being central to the analysis of their use), the present use of
the term "sequence" is intended to take note of a specific organization of
utterances employed by members, which makes of the sequence a unit
in its own right. Such "sequences in the strong sense" have determinate
numbers of parts; frequently they are two-part sequences (pairs), but
they may have more parts (as in "rounds"). And they have determinate
components; given the first part of the sequence, some member of a restricted class of utterances will be relevant, will be a component required
to complete the sequence. Thus question–answer sequences, or greeting
exchanges or story rounds require contributions from a restricted class
of components. The term "conditional relevance" (which, together with
several of the ensuing observations related to it, is borrowed from Sacks,
1972a) is used to refer to that property. When one utterance (or member
of a class of utterances) is conditionally relevant on another, or when
one action is conditionally relevant on another, attention is called to their
treatment by members as a "sequence in the strong sense." Given the
occurrence of the first, the second is expectable; upon its occurrence it is
seen (analyzed) by members as second to the first, as the second part of
a pair, as produced "responsively."

The formulation of the property "conditional relevance," and the sequencing unit it serves to constitute, allow us a way of dealing in an analytic way with "absences." Members (professional analysts among them)
make reference to things that did not occur, things that were not said,
actions that were not taken, and so on. In principle, an indefinitely expandable list might be assembled of utterances, actions, etc. that did
not occur at some point in a conversation. By reference to such a list,
observed absences might be trivializable; a remarked upon or noticed
absence might not be discriminable from any other on such a list. Of
the indefinitely expandable list of non-occurrences however, only some

have such a relevance that allows them to be seen as absent. Some are, so to speak, "officially absent," and it is in point to search for the bases of "official absence" – that is, the orderly procedures whereby some items, actions, utterances or classes of them are discriminable from others such that their non-occurrence is relevant, is "absence." Conditional relevance is one basis for such official absence. Just as the occurrence of an utterance or action that is conditionally relevant on some other (as "answer" is on "question") is seen as paired in strong sequence with it, so its non-occurrence is its notable, official, relevant absence. Such an "absence" is an event in its own right, constituting adequate grounds for explicit conversational comment (in the ongoing or some subsequent conversation), for further action or modification of action, and/or for appropriate inference, as I shall have occasion to note below in the case here under discussion, summons–answer sequences, in which an *answer is conditionally relevant on the occurrence of a summons.*

Before focusing on conditional relevance as a property organizing the utterances making up a summons–answer sequence, however, we can note that the non-terminality of SA sequences can be seen as the outcome of the conditional relevance property operating at a different level of organization. If the utterances that accomplish the activities of summoning and answering together constitute an organizational unit – the summons–answer sequence – then that unit can itself be subject to organization, not to utterance-to-utterance organization, but to the organization of sequences of utterances. Non-terminality can then be seen to be the consequence of the conditional relevance of further talk on the completion of an SA sequence (in which the answer is drawn from the sub-class of clearance cues). It is the completion of the sequence that makes further talk (or further activity that can be analyzed as the "reason" for the summons) relevant. Should it not be forthcoming, it will be seen as officially absent; and should the answer be not a clearance cue, but one that seeks to block further talk (for a discussion of this class of answers to summonses, see below), the summoned can later ask the summoner what "he wanted" earlier, treating that as something that had been specifically absent (though on good grounds).

The consequences of absences similarly provide a convenient way of noting the operation of conditional relevance in constituting a summons–answer sequence. If one party produces a summons and no answer (of any class, not just no clearance cue) occurs, that may provide the occasion for repetition of the summons. The non-occurrence of the answer is treated by the summoner as its official absence, and its official absence provides adequate grounds for repetition of the summons. "Adequate grounds" are in point in view of the rule, previously formulated, that the summoner

may *not* properly repeat a summons if the sequence has been completed.[25]
A similar rule seems to hold for greetings: one per co-participant per occasion, if answered. The absence of an answer is thus treated as an event
in its own right, being usable to warrant modification of the rule on non-
repeatability, and as the occasion for consequent courses of action. The
conditional relevance of an answer on a summons and the unit that it
constitutes – the summons–answer sequence – should, therefore, be seen
to operate prospectively. The summons–answer sequence is not a higher-
order sequencing unit built up out of the separate component utterances
once they have occurred, aggregating two utterances and constituting
them an emergent unit. When the summons has been produced, an answer will be "relevant," whether or not it occurs. The answer "slot" has
been provided for; it may be found to be filled or empty. The summons–
answer sequence is thus an autonomous unit; it may be operative even in
the absence of the occurrence of one of its components. That the SA sequence operates retroactively as well can be seen when, after a lapse in the
conversation, and particularly when the other(s) are not physically present
but are within recallable range, one party produces an item that may function as an A to S, such as "Yeah" or "What." Then, another in the scene
may hear that an unspoken summons had been heard, and may "reply,"
"I didn't call you." To cite a specific observation (EAS, Field Notes):

```
Boy playing in sandbox:  What mommy...what mommy...
                              (starts climbing out of sandbox)
                         what mommy...
                              (running towards mother)
                         what mommy,
Mother:                  I didn't call.
```

We have here another case of immediately graspable error, such as was
remarked on earlier. The conditional relevance property may then be an
operative feature, and a conversational resource, even when one or the
other of the parts it relates is absent.

Two qualifications must be introduced at this point, one dealing with
the extendability of repetitions of S, the other with the temporal organization of those repetitions in relation to the initial S. To take the second
point first: in order to find that an A is absent (thus warranting repetitions
of S), the summoner need not wait for posterity. In principle, unless some
restriction is introduced, the occurrence of an S might be the occasion
for an indefinite waiting period, at some point in which an A might occur.
This is not the case. In noting this point, a modifying property related to
the issue of "pacing" may be added to the conditional relevance of A on
S – the property of immediate juxtaposition.

In question–answer (QA) sequences, a considerable silence may follow the question before an answer is given. Although the "pause" may be grounds for inferences such as "he's thinking," "stumped," etc., an answer may remain "awaited." If certain constraints are met by the ensuing utterance (in some cases having to do with their relation to the "substance" of the question; for one proposed set of constraints, see Harrah, 1963), it may be heard as an answer to the earlier question. Even if the utterances following the question are not analyzable as an answer to it, if that talk meets certain constraints it can be heard not as displacing an answer (thus as, for example, "evasive") but as prefiguring it, and some later utterance can be awaited, and then analyzed, as "the answer." (For example, X1: "Have you seen Jim?" Y1: "Oh, is he in town?" X2: "Yeah, he got in yesterday." Y2: "No, I haven't." YI–X2 may be called an "insertion sequence," being inserted between the components of a question–answer pair. For a more extended discussion of insertion sequences, see Schegloff, 1972).

In SA sequences, however, the conditional relevance of an A on an S must be satisfied within a constraint of immediate juxtaposition. That is to say, if an item that may be used as an answer to a summons is not produced by the summoned in close order, it will not be awaited but found absent. (It should be pointed out, however, that SA sequences do seem to allow a limited class of insertion sequences; for example, X1: "Jim." Y1: "Did you call me?" X2: "Yeah." Y2: "Just a minute.")

Although this point introduces a temporal constraint on the SA sequence, it is far from clear that "elapsed time" is the relevant consideration. Rather than clock time, a more relevant temporal ordering turns on a notion of "nextness" or priority with respect to other, ongoing action sequences. Upon the occurrence of a summons, an answer should be the "next" action of the summoned. This can be seen especially when the summoned is engaged in some action sequence or course of action that is treated as non-combinable with conversation.[26] Then, he may be often found to place his answer to the summons before some next action in the course of action he had been engaged in when summoned. A clear case can be found when a telephone rings during an ongoing face-to-face conversation. Then, answering the summons may have priority over continuing the conversation until it is brought to a close, although the co-conversationalists may use the occasion to bring the ongoing conversation to a close, possibly using an analysis of where they are in the structure of the conversation to find that as a possibility, and closing the conversation before the phone is answered.[27]

This last qualification suggests the double relevance of doing an answer to a summons "next." For to place an utterance "next" requires a conception of "units" out of which the ongoing course of action is assembled, and in terms of which there will be some unit that may be "interrupted" and/or some unit whose completion can serve as the occasion for answering the summons as a "next" action; that is, a notion of a unit with respect to which nextness will operate ("next after what").[28] If the ongoing activity is conversation, such units as an extended utterance (story, argument), action, utterance, sentence, phrase, word, or syllable may be treated as units for this purpose, the end of the unit being the occasion for invoking the priority of answering a summons. There is no one fixed order of unit that is invariably the relevant one in terms of which nextness is made operative. Rather, a summoned party can select an order of unit that he will employ on a given occasion. The selection he makes – choosing to complete an extended utterance before answering, breaking off a sentence, or word, or syllable to answer – can be treated by co-participants as indicative of the relative importance or priority accorded the ongoing activity as compared with the expectable activity the summons is initiating (expectable by virtue of the status of the summons as a pre-sequence).[29]

Although no fixed order of unit is invariably the relevant one, speakers may demonstrate that an utterance-in-its-course is being interrupted to answer the summons. One way of showing that an utterance has not been completed relies on the use of the sentence as a "constituting unit" for utterances (see Sacks, 1992, I, pp. 647–655 passim); since utterances are regularly produced in integral numbers of sentences, one way of displaying that an utterance has been interrupted, has been left incomplete, is by leaving a sentence incomplete.

It should be noted that the priority of an answer to a summons is attended to not only by the summoned party, but by others with whom he may be engaged in a course of action as well. If one party to an ongoing conversation is summoned, for example, it is not only he who has responsibilities in dealing with it. If someone other than the summoned is speaking when the telephone rings, the speaker may leave some unit incomplete to allow the summoned to attend to the priority answer (the non-combinability of one conversation with another otherwise forcing the summoned to choose between listening to the speaker in the conversation he has been in or answering the summons). If the summoned party is the speaker at the time the summons is done, and he leaves some unit, for example a sentence, incomplete to answer the summons, then other parties will not complete it (as they might in other circumstances where a speaker leaves a sentence incomplete). If the summoned completes his utterance, or if, without completing it, the action it was doing is nonetheless analyzable, others will not direct a response to him, or with normal pacing produce a next action in that course of action.

```
Kit:  Well, I'm sure the cover charge isn't very much.
Bob:  It's probably about two-fifty.
Kit:  Oh Hell!
Bob:  What'd'ya mean, ''Oh, Hell!''
Kit:  O.K. Let's call up that place.
Bob:  Shit. Well, look (telephone rings) most places
      charge, uh (answers telephone). Hello. Uh, this
      is her husband, uh could, uh, I uh, if it's an
      emergency, I'll take it. Could you inquire if it's
      an emergency? Sure, she'll be home in another, about
      fifteen or twenty minutes. Okay, Okay, thank you,
      good-bye. She sounded like she had a charge on.

      (Throughout the telephone conversation, the two
      girls present talked, but their talk was
      untranscribable.)
```

When a party to an ongoing conversation is summoned, the summons has consequences for all the parties to the conversation, regardless of who the speaker is at the moment the summons is produced. Answering the summons, and the course of action the summons is a pre-sequence to, can take priority over the ongoing conversation, and an integrated set of actions by the parties is produced to manage this. Not only do the parties to the ongoing conversation no longer direct utterances to the summoned party, but they may undertake to be visibly dis-attending the conversation he has been called to. If the prior conversation was two-party, then the single party left after the summoned has turned to the interrupting course of action regularly averts his eyes, inspects the surroundings, engages in various "auto-involvements" (see Goffman, 1963, pp. 64–69), begins reading. He will, if possible, appear to engage in some action that is treated as non-combinable with listening to conversation. If the prior conversation was multi-party, then the remaining non-summoned parties may adopt, as a way of showing they are not listening, a conversation among themselves (a way of showing non-listening by virtue of the non-combinability of one conversation with another). Given that there are tasks for everybody when one party to a conversation is summoned from outside it (clearly the consequences are different when he is summoned by another party to the conversation; others in the conversation then properly listen instead of properly "not listening"; should others start to talk, it would be a violation of the one-party-at-a-time feature, although it is not a violation if they talk when the summoned has turned to the second conversation, etc.), though the summons may be directed at a particular party, the interruption is done to the course-of-action or the occasion.

The priority or "nextness" constraint on answers to summonses, combined with the pre-sequence character of SA sequences and the relevance of the sequence to all pre-present parties, allows us to see the basis for the treatment a summons may get as an "interruption," even when it is placed by a summoner so as not to coincide or be simultaneous with another's talk, and not to break a larger sequencing unit (such as QA). Since it makes an answer to the summons a priority next action for the summoned, since it makes relevant a correlative set of tasks for other parties to an ongoing conversation, and since the SA sequence is properly a pre-sequence to further talk, then, though no utterance or strong sequence is interrupted by the summons, an action sequence is interrupted, and extendedly so (potentially; that is, the summoned may not answer with a clearance cue). Although a greeting addressed to someone engaged in a conversation may have a response inserted into that ongoing action sequence, the ongoing sequence can continue because an exchange of greetings can be terminal. That is not the case with an SA sequence, which projectedly interrupts the ongoing action sequence. One can, then, exchange greetings with another otherwise engaged and leave him otherwise engaged; one cannot so summon him, though similar lexical items, similarly placed, may be employed.

Correlatively, whereas SA sequences share the conditional relevance property with greeting exchanges and QA sequences, SA sequences appear to be more constraining, and more effective therefore, as interruptions. Thus, when QA sequences are employed with someone engaged in another course of action (for example a conversation) they may fail; the question may fail to get an answer. Upon that failure, a summons may be used, and may succeed. Thus:

```
A:  Can I have a glass of water please?
      (pause)
A:  Miss.
B:  Yes.
A:  Can I have a glass of water?
B:  Yes sir.
```

Or:

A dog ran by.

Margaret said, "Doggie," in a quick, mandatory tone.

She called out loudly, "Do you know who he is?" and looked expectantly toward the two women.

The women were chatting and ignored her question.

Even more loudly and insistently, she repeated, "Do you know who he is?" and a slight scowl appeared on her face.

Still no response from the two women on the porch. Then she said impatiently and in an irritated way, "Grandma!"

The grandmother finally looked up and asked calmly, "What?"

Margaret said, "Do you know who he belongs to?" in a teasing, playful fashion. The grandmother said, matter-of-factly, "No."

Margaret said proudly, "Ellen."[30]

To summarize: the operation of temporal constraints on the occurrence of an answer when a summons has been produced provides the basis for finding an answer "absent," rather than having "not yet" occurred, and thereby the occasion for repetition of the summons. (It is these constraints that preclude the possibility of substituting for a "Just a minute" with a subsequent "Yeah," a pause until the summoned is available.) The empirical outcome has the form: S – short pause – S – short pause – S – short pause . . . It is curious to note that when the actual performance of the summons is turned over to machines, the machines are built to follow this form. If each ring of the telephone be considered a summons, then it is built to summon, wait for an answer, ring, wait for an answer, and so on (Clearly, it could have been built to produce one sustained ring.) And some persons, with apparent regard to the status of a ring as a summons and thus an utterance of sorts, decline to interrupt, and wait, hand on receiver, for the completion of a ring before answering.

To this qualification concerning the temporal organization of SA sequences that affects the initiation of repetitions[31] of S must be added another concerning the extensiveness of repetition of S upon the official absence of A. It is empirically observable that S is not repeated without limitation until an A is returned. Although it seems that repetitions of S do not exceed three to five, it does not appear that "counting" or "numbers" are the central consideration, just as clock time is not at the heart of temporal organization (but see note 32). There would appear to be some orderly basis for ending repetitions of S, although there does not seem to be anything like a "restriction" or "terminating rule" involved. Indeed, it is not quite accurate to speak of a basis for "ending repetitions," for what is ended is not "repetitions" but "summoning," not successive use of summons items, but continuing attempts to start a conversation by establishing availability. The needed qualification concerning the "extensiveness" of repetitions of S involves the summoner's finding not only that availability has not been established but that it cannot or ought not be. One element relevant to such a finding appears to be an orientation to the summoned party's expectable respect for the property of immediate juxtaposition; by reference to that it may be found that, if several repetitions of S fail to elicit an A, further repetitions will do no better. Some inferences based on the absence of an A that may support such a

finding will be discussed shortly (for example, the inference "no answer –
no person"). It is perhaps the recognition that summoners employ such
considerations that leads the telephone company to advise callers to allow
at least ten rings to permit prospective answerers time to maneuver their
way to the phone.[32]

It was remarked earlier that the official absence of an item conditionally relevant on another was an event in its own right, remarkable upon,
constituting good grounds for consequent action and modification of
otherwise relevant rules, and warranting a variety of inferences. In turning now to the last of these features, we can note that the conditional
relevance of an item (utterance, action) removes it from the domain of
"naive option." It is not that answering a summons is "obligatory," or
that it can be "enforced," but that the absence of an answer supports a
variety of strong inferences, and a member who does not answer does so
"at the peril" of one or another of those inferences being made. Indeed,
an explication of the notion "no naive option" involves that the legitimacy
of *some* inference cannot be denied. If some particular inference is proposed, then, in denying it, a summoned party who did not answer offers
a substitute, thereby conceding the legitimacy of *an* inference, though
not perhaps of a *particular one*. If questioned as to the warrant for his
inference, a summoner may refer to the absence of an answer, and this
stands as adequate warrant. A sequence constructed to exemplify these
remarks might be:

```
Summoner:  Are you mad at me?
Summoned:  Why?
Summoner:  You didn't answer when I called you.
Summoned:  No, I didn't hear you.
```

Conversely, the following observed exchange suggests what is intended
by "naive option" in the character claimed for "hair playing":

```
A:  What are you thinking about?
B:  Who says I'm thinking?
A:  You're playing with your hair.
B:  That doesn't mean anything.
```

The inferences for which the absence of an answer can be good grounds
are "fitted" to the circumstances in which the summons was done. Without pretending to exhaustiveness, or to adequate attention to detail, it
may nonetheless be useful to point to some classes of circumstance and
relevant possible inferences.

It was proposed early in the present discussion that SA sequences
are employed when availability is analyzably problematic. One kind of

problematicalness is whether there is another, potential co-participant, present and interactionally "in play" (for example, not asleep; the term is from Goffman, 1963). (I use the "kind of problematicalness" without being able to describe how a scene is analyzed to find its relevance.) One inference based on the absence of an answer to a summons, seemingly related to this circumstance, is "no answer – no person (co-participant)." Someone who dials another on the telephone and hears no receiver picked up may announce, as a matter of course, "Nobody's home" or "No one there." A man returning home, seeking to find out if anyone else is already there, may call out the name of his wife, for example, and upon not receiving an answer may take it she is not home or not "in play." (Indeed, he may take it that no one is home; others may hear in his summons that he is seeing if *anyone* is home and, if they are, they should answer; it may be no excuse to say, "But you didn't call *me*." Accordingly, attending to the way others will analyze his summons, he may find "no answer" supporting the inference not only that the one summoned is not there, but that nobody is there.)[33] It is not a primary inference that, although present and in play, they chose not to answer.

In unmediated (that is, non-telephone) interaction, the occurrence of an answer (whether clearance cue or not) may serve to establish presence (though the absence of an answer does not *require* the inference "no person"), but it does not establish availability; for that, the selection of the answer (that is, a clearance cue) is relevant. Similarly, in telephone interaction, a distinction must be drawn between presence and availability. The lifting of the receiver serves to establish the presence of a person at the number called. It does not, however, establish the availability of that person for further conversation. That person can sometimes be heard to be continuing a conversation they were engaged in while answering the phone. And the "deviant case" introduced earlier was one in which, though the phone was picked up, the summons was not answered to indicate availability, and accordingly elicited a repeat of the summons by the caller. Indeed, this can be a matter of explicit comment and joking for members:[34]

```
Operator: Hello, Mister Lehroff?
Lehroff:  Mm hmm,
Operator: [Mister Savage is gon' pick up an' talk to ya.
Lehroff:  [Alright.
          (52 seconds intervening)
Operator: Hello.
Lehroff:  Yes.
Operator: Did Mistuh Savage ever pick up?
```

```
Lehroff:   If he did, he didn't say 'hello
Operator:  Oh, o alright, smarty, just hold on.)
Lehroff:   [heh! heh heh heh heh heh heh
Operator:  [hhh.
```

Where presence is not problematic (for the co-participants),[35] the absence of an answer may be taken as warranting the inference "didn't hear." Although I can again not describe those features of a scene that permit members this analysis, it can be noted that this is one inference some scenes can support. It is, in a way, an inference especially suited to the circumstances; for the very conditions of "problematic availability" – that is, uncertainty that a hearer will be available for an utterance – that may warrant the use of an SA sequence in the first place may be invoked in seeing what is involved in the absence of an answer to the summons, namely that there was no hearer for the summons.

The inference "didn't hear" has the following importance: as long as it is made, although the absence of an answer may be an event, and thereby warrant repetition of the summons etc., it is not seen as an action of the summoned; it is not an event the summoned produced. As in other conversational circumstances, however, establishing hearing or, more precisely, establishing "having heard" gives the ensuing occurrences the status of actions. So, for example, parents may follow up an unheeded request or command to children with the question, "Did you hear me?" or "Did you hear what I said?", potentially converting the inaction to defiance. And a prospective passenger running after a bus leaving the bus-stop yelling, "Hold it," can be told the character of the event he has just lived through by the remark of a passerby, "He heard ya!" (Field Notes.)

Similarly, the absence of an answer in a setting that for members will not support the inference either "no person" or "didn't hear" may be transformed into a "refusal to answer." It is thereby a resource for members who wish to "ignore," "show pique," "sulk," "insult," "act superior," "give the cold shoulder." It is also for them a limitation; for, to accomplish those activities by withholding an answer, they must be able to be seen to "be withholding" rather than "not hearing." And the summoner may then have fine discriminations to make in deciding whether some bodily behavior (for example turning away) that a summoned party produces after a summons in a setting that could possibly support the inference "didn't hear" is to be seen as an extrapolation of behavior he was otherwise engaged in (or perhaps as "auto-involvement"; see Goffman, 1963), or as intendedly responsive. If the latter, then such inferences as "mad," "arrogant" or "piqued" may be supported. In settings that will not support the inference "didn't hear," then, members can "choose" to not answer a summons but they cannot do so "naively"; in the absence of inferences about their hearing, other inferences as to their character or mood will be made. But at this point we are talking no longer about the "absence of an answer" but about answers of a particular sort, ones that are not clearance cues but make the continuation of the interaction problematic. In seeing them produced responsively, a summoner can see that he has had a hearer for his utterance; and although the hearer may have indicated a preference for hearing no more, that is a preference a summoner may not feel himself required to respect. He may then go on to talk further, a sequel summoners do not regularly produce (except in repeating summonses) if they find "no answer" after their summons. I shall return to non-clearance cue answers below.

This discussion of hearership suggests a more general point: hearership should be displayed or acknowledged. After any first utterance, if some other (or targeted intended other, if that is analyzable in the scene) does not display or acknowledge in some way "having heard" and the setting will sustain the inference "didn't hear," one may then get from the first speaker the initiation of an SA sequence. If there is no acknowledgment of having heard and the scene does not sustain the inference "didn't hear," then "ignoring," "arrogance," etc. may be found. In scenes that will not sustain the inference "didn't hear," then, such inferences may be made in the absence of acknowledgment following any initial utterance. A variety of tokens of acknowledgment are used – smiles, nods, "uh huh" – as well as extended utterances. Some of these (for example nods and "uh huh," and its variants) have continuing use in conversation as claims of hearership,[36] although they may have other uses as well, such as showing (when constituting the whole of a speaker's utterance) an appreciation that the other speaker has not yet completed an utterance or activity he is doing (serving then as "continuers"). Speakers building extended utterances or activities may, accordingly, allow places for the display of claims of continued hearership, as in slight pauses at clause or sentence boundaries; and they may treat the absence of such displays (typically when several consecutive slots for them are not filled) as grounds for suspecting the continued availability of the interlocutor, and thus as occasion for the use of SA to (re-)establish it. At the beginning of a conversation, the absence of hearership acknowledgment after the first utterance may have the same consequence, as was noted above.[37]

A consequence of this "relevance of acknowledgment after first utterances" is that the initial two slots of a conversation regularly resemble a pair in structure and "feel"; for the non-occurrence of the acknowledgment is treated as its official absence,[38] with all the possible consequences suggested earlier. It is not, however, that all conversations begin with utterance pairs,[39] that is, units that have the pair construction wherever they occur in conversation (such as QA and SA). It is not by reference to the pair as a unit that this phenomenon is to be understood. It is rather by reference to the overall structure organization of the unit "a single conversation," whose first two slots are regularly organized by the conditional relevance property, that these effects are to be appreciated. And that is why it is useful to keep distinct the notion of an "utterance pair" and the property of "conditional relevance," for, though the former is in large measure constituted by the latter, the property organizes utterances or slots that are not properly called an utterance pair, operating as they do at a different level of organization.

While the conditional relevance property may then relate the initial slots in a conversation whether it is an SA sequence that is being accomplished there or not, SA sequences are also a pair (that is, they constitute a unit in its own right) and they are pre-sequences. It was noted earlier that this pre-sequence, or non-terminality, property could be reformulated as the conditional relevance of further talk (or non-verbal interaction) on the SA sequence (when the A is a clearance cue). Thus, in telephone conversation, if a called person's first utterance is treated as an answer to the phone ring's summons, it completes the SA sequence (regularly with a clearance cue, although sometimes a "just a moment please" is appended) and provides proper occasion for a next utterance by the caller. If the conditional relevance of further talk on a completed SA sequence is not satisfied, we may find the same sequel as is found when an A is not returned to an S – repetition.[40] For example:

```
#86
D:  Police Desk                A
    (pause)                     Ø
D:  Police Desk                A
    (pause)                     Ø
D:  Hello, Police Desk.        A
    (long pause)                Ø
D:  Hello                      A or S
C:  Hello                      A or S
D:  Hello                      A or S
    (pause)                     Ø
D:  Police Desk?              A
C:  Pardon?
D:  Do you want the Police Desk?
```

This discussion of the problem of availability and SA sequences was undertaken because it did not seem that the initiation of conversations could be formulated as a general problem in terms of the allocation of first turns. It is therefore in order to see if the preceding discussion is responsive to the concerns that motivated it. It will be recalled that the datum inconsistent with the distribution rule began as follows:

```
#9 Police make call; receiver is lifted, and there
     is one second of silence.
Police:  Hello
Other:   American Red Cross
Police:  Hello, this is Police Headquarters...
```

In this datum, the caller produces the first utterance, whereas the distribution rule required that the called party make the first utterance. The distribution rule provides no resources for dealing with this case, other than simply to call it a violation or use it as grounds for rejecting the distribution rule. Examining the datum in terms of the "analytic machinery" for the initiation of conversation allows us to see it as equally a rule-governed phenomenon as other opening interchanges are. The ring of the phone being treated as a summons, an answer is conditionally relevant on its occurrence, and is relevant in immediate juxtaposition, as a next action. The non-occurrence of an answer is its official absence, and such an absence warrants a repetition of the summons (that is, a repetition of summoning; a different summons item may be used for the repetition). For telephone conversation, lifting the receiver establishes the presence of another but not his availability for interaction, the feature to which SA sequences are addressed. In #9 we have the occurrence of a summons (in the ring of the telephone), the establishing of presence (in the lifting of the receiver) and the absence of an answer in immediate juxtaposition (in the second of silence). A repetition of the summons is thus claimably warranted, and it is a claimably warranted action for the initial summoner (the caller), who thus produces the first utterance. Although an initial "Hello" in a telephone conversation is thus most frequently an *answer* to a summons, and therefore is produced by the summoned or the called, here it is *a repetition of the summons* in accord with a mechanism that provides for the repetition of summonses, and is produced by the summoner or the caller. The datum that was deviant with respect to the distribution rule is thereby assimilated as a methodically produced outcome; and the typically occurring sequence formulated by the rule "the called talks first" is similarly generated by the conditional relevance of an answer on a summons. As was suggested earlier (p. 329), the description of the methods for the initiation of conversation generates alternative possible "first-speaker" outcomes.

Attention to the initiation of conversation was focused on a problem generally relevant there (in contrast to the allocation problem, which did not appear to be generally relevant), the problem of availability. The problem of availability is relevant to any activity that requires at least two participants; it is relevant to conversation because conversation has such a requirement. That requirement is not satisfied by the mere co-presence of two persons, one of whom is talking. It requires that there be both a "speaker" and a "hearer." To behave as a "speaker" or as a "hearer" when the other is not observably available is to subject oneself to a review of one's competence and "normalcy." Speakers without hearers can be seen to be "talking to themselves." Hearers without speakers "hear voices" (but see Hymes, 1964b, on cultural variations in the definition of participants in speech events). Inferences about those who try to engage in an activity whose *n*-party requirements are not met aside, availability of co-participants is an operational problem for a person seeking to initiate such an activity. For conversation, that problem was specified earlier in terms of its constitutive sequencing structure (the issue of a next speaker talking upon completion of the first speaker's utterance) and the required fitting of utterances (the issue of a next speaker's utterance displaying attention to, and analysis of, its sequential placement after some last utterance or sequence of utterances). What is required is a co-participant's attention from the beginning of the first utterance, allowing its analysis as it is produced. Where inspection does not allow the finding of availability in this sense, procedures may be available for establishing it.

SA sequences are such a procedure. Their features are fitted to the work they are asked to do. The production of an item that can be an answer to a summons (in contrast to other answer terms) displays that a summoned party has heard (and was thus available to hear) the initial (summons) utterance, and analyzed it to be doing summoning. To have so analyzed it is to have analyzed it as a pre-sequence, as an activity specifically prefatory to another to follow; to have answered with a clearance cue answer is to have committed oneself to be available to the activity the pre-sequence was preliminary to. In the absence of an answer, repetitions of the summons may be warranted, any one of which may have these consequences. Alternatively, in the absence of an answer, a variety of inferences may be warranted, each of which is directly relevant to the problem of availability. "No answer–no person" settles the availability problem negatively; the activity to which S is a pre-sequence is normally estopped. "Didn't hear" may serve to verify that there is an availability problem; that is, the SA sequence having been used "for cause," it shows there was indeed cause. Again, though possibly more temporarily, the finding is "no availability," and the pre-figured activity is estopped until the SA sequence can be completed. When completed, it will have shown "hearing" and availability for the analysis of a next utterance. The SA sequence, then, can establish availability if it can be established, and can show its absence if it cannot. There is, however, an intermediate possibility, suggested earlier in another sort of inference that can be warranted by the absence of an answer, when the "no person" and "didn't hear" inferences are not supportable, namely "unwillingness" of various sorts (pique, condescension, sulking). It was suggested that here we were dealing not so much with the absence of an answer as with an answer of a special kind; not clearance cue answers, but problematic answers. We shall turn to them shortly.

Before doing so, it may be in point to remark on telephone conversation in particular, since that is the character of the corpus of data with which we started. It might be claimed that, certainly for telephone conversation, the issue is much simpler, and more technically physical, than this discussion would suggest. It is simply the issue of opening some acoustical channel to serve as the medium for conversation. That is certainly a problem. But it should be noted that that problem could be solved technically in a variety of ways. For example, dialing a number could in itself open a channel to the telephone dialed, no action on the receiver's part being necessary (just as visually no complicity is required of an object seen). In fact, however, the technical problem's solution has been assimilated to the SA format, a format that involves some element of "listener's choice." Although that "choice" or "control" is circumscribed, as was suggested above, by an inferential structure, it is operative. One central resource for hearers (that is, summoned persons) is the selection of answer terms, and that selection includes a set of possible answers to which repeated allusion has been made. This chapter will conclude with some discussion of "problematic answers" to summonses, a discussion that is necessary for completeness but that is necessarily speculative in the absence of relevant data.

### Problematic answers to summonses

By "problematic answers" I intend to refer to the class of utterances after summonses, including utterances such as "Just a minute," "What now?" "I'm busy," "I'm in the shower," "I'm doing X," "Z is talking," "Go away," "Leave me alone," "Don't bother me," as well as eye aversion, body realignment away from the summoner, and so on. These are possible answers, because when placed after a summons they can be analyzed by members as produced in sequence to the summons, as responsive to it; they satisfy the conditional relevance property; on their occurrence, repetition of the summons may not be warranted. They are problematic because they make proceeding with the interaction to which the summons was a pre-sequence problematic, and this finds expression in the SA sequence itself. Some of the features claimed for SA sequences when the A is a clearance cue do not hold, or hold problematically, when the answer is a member of this class. For example, the non-terminality property holds only problematically when a summons is answered with "Don't bother me" (the sense of "problematically" used here is to be explicated below). As another example, the immediate juxtaposition feature of the conditional relevance of further talk (or non-verbal interaction) on a completed SA sequence is modified if the A is "Just a minute"; as was suggested earlier, such an answer may be selected specifically with an orientation to the nextness constraint on further talk (and the corollary obligation to listen assumed by the answerer), and serves to suspend that feature while some other course of action is continued, to be reinvoked when a clearance cue answer is later produced. In suspending the nextness constraint on the relationship between the SA sequence and further interaction, that constraint operating on the relationship between an A and an S is respected. That is one reason for giving a "Just a minute" answer immediately, and a clearance cue later, rather than simply waiting until later to give a clearance cue. If the latter were done, it might warrant the finding "didn't hear" and repetition of S.

In suggesting that problematic answers may modify the features of SA sequences as they have previously been described, the adequacy of that description may be called into question. Should we not reformulate the account of the opening sequence so that the features of SA sequences with problematic As are naturally assimilated, rather than being treated as modifications? Or, if the basic description of SA sequences is to be formulated for one class of answers and not both, why not formulate the basic description on sequences that include problematic As and then consider clearance cues in terms of that description? Neither of these procedures is preferable.

First, the classes "clearance cues" and "problematic answers" are not symmetrical alternatives. Although the occurrence of a summons makes relevant the occurrence of an answer, without specification of the class of answer it is not a matter of indifference which class is drawn on – not a matter of indifference to the summoner. If the summons is produced as a pre-sequence utterance, then it is produced in search of a clearance cue answer. One feature of pre-sequences as a class is that whether or not the base sequence (that to which the pre-sequence is "pre") is produced may turn on the outcome of the pre-sequence. Thus certain answers to "pre-invitations" (for example, "Are you doing anything?") can have the consequence that no invitation is offered. Given the occurrence of a pre-sequence item, parties can see that some returns to it are produced to allow the occurrence of the base activity (perhaps with intended guaranteed results; for example, the invitation will be accepted),[41] whereas others are produced to block the occurrence of the base activity or to make it problematic. In either case they are responses to the presequence utterance, and attend it as a pre-sequence to some base activity. But they are not, on that account, symmetrical alternatives. (We can note without elaboration here, for example, that problematic responses are regularly accompanied by, and sometimes constituted by, accounts, excuses, apologies, etc., whereas clearance cues are not.) In the case of SA sequences, clearance cues are the centrally relevant answers, problematic answers being marked and specific alternatives. Problematic answers are alternatives to clearance cues; the reverse is not the case. For the basic formulation of SA sequences, therefore, it is non-arbitrary to work with the assumption of a clearance cue answer. As was suggested earlier, some problematic answers may be designed precisely to deal with some feature of basic SA sequence structure as formulated on that assumption.

A second feature, related to the asymmetry of the classes "problematic answers" and "clearance cues" as answers to summonses, is the "complexity" of the former class and the "simplicity" of the latter. (I use the terms "complex" and "simple" in a manner similar to that of Sacks, 1972a, in his discussion of the contrast set "joke–serious" in the analysis of utterances.) Whereas the utterances which may be used as clearance cues may serve as the vehicles for other interactional accomplishments (as was suggested earlier re personal style, and will be elaborated below), and are in that sense not "simply" answers, with respect to the first-order business of SA sequences the class "clearance cues" is simple; any of its members, whatever else it accomplishes, in whatever setting, for whatever parties, with whatever anticipations concerning what will be done in the ensuing conversation, is produced and heard to be produced to allow the occurrence of the base activity, further interaction. And what properly follows is some interactional activity for which the SA can be seen to have been a pre-sequence. The class "problematic answers" is not "simple" in this sense. In referring to the class as "problematic," attention is drawn to the feature that occurrence of members of this class does not per se preclude proceeding to the interaction that was pre-sequenced. It makes proceeding a problematic matter (in a sense to be discussed below); and attention to this problem – deciding whether to go on or not, and, if to go on, whether to go on with what was otherwise being pre-sequenced[42] – requires particularized attention to the problematic answer employed, the setting, the parties, and so on. It is in this sense that the class "problematic answers" is complex, and does not have a single homogeneous analysis and consequences over members of the class.

A fully adequate discussion of the "problematicalness" of problematic answers to summonses would require detailed analysis of a range of actual occurrences. Such data are lacking, but it may be useful nonetheless to suggest some aspects of that issue, for this may add to our understanding of SA sequences with clearance cue answers as well.

In referring to such things as "problematic answers," let us consider for what and how they are problematic. In terms of the problem to which we originally proposed that SA sequences are a solution – that is, the availability of a second party as a hearer for the first utterance and prospective producer of a second fitted utterance – the production of an answer to a summons, or the analysis by the summoner that a response has been produced, establishes availability in the sense employed, *whatever the character of the answer*. To have analyzed some behavior as an answer is to have seen that the other heard the initial utterance, analyzed it as a summons and behaved responsively to it. Whatever the answer, a completed SA sequence establishes availability, as that was earlier formulated. The consequence is that the option of proceeding is available to the summoner; in other words, to continue the interaction will not subject him to reviews of competence such as "talking to himself."

What is problematic, then, is not whether he *can* continue, but whether he should. However, that issue involves doing not the activity "conversation" or "interaction," but whatever activity might have been undertaken through conversation. (Or it may involve doing conversation per se, if that was the pre-sequenced activity, i.e. "just to talk"; also some problematic answers, whose business is to suggest the impaired character of the relationship, an impairment extending to "not talking," may make the task or problem "talking" as a way of repairing the relationship.) So problematic answers can go to three issues: "not talking," "not talking now," "not doing through talk what it might be figured was to be done through talk (now)." The particular problematic A selected poses for the summoner the issue of finding which of these is being done, with consequences for his further continuation, given that continuation is possible, availability in the technical sense having been established. For example, a finding that what is being made problematic is a range of actions doable in conversation that require consequent actions from the summoned (which an answer of the form "I'm Xing" is designed to show may not be forthcoming) may be consistent with proceeding with the conversation if what is to be done is an action that does not require a consequent action (other than, for example, acknowledgment) from the summoned, for example an announcement ("I'm leaving"). Or it may be consistent with not proceeding with the conversation for the duration of the activity in which the summoned announces himself to be engaged (if it and the pre-sequenced one are non-combinable; if they are combinable then the conversation may proceed). Or it may be consistent with proceeding with the conversation, given a claimed assessment of the relative priorities of the ongoing activity and the pre-sequenced one ("Jim." "I'm working." "The house is on fire"), or their relative prospective duration (as for example when a single request for information is to be done).

To elaborate a bit on the preceding, consider the different sorts of work accomplished by, or analyzable out of, "Just a minute" on the one hand, and such forms of problematic answer as "I'm Xing," "I'm busy," "I'm in the middle of X," on the other. (I omit here utterances such as "X is talking," which is used mainly with children, and typically when what is thereby announced is in any case available to inspection. In that case, such an utterance is used for socialization and/or sanctioning, re interrupting. When the form is used with adults, announcing what is otherwise available to inspection, "I'm Xing," it is heard as testy and insulting, perhaps because its base use is with children as a sanction.) First, announcements of the latter sort offer an account for the absence of a clearance cue. Second, they appear to be used when summoned by one not in visual range, or when what the summoned is doing is not available to inspection ("thinking," "listening to the music"). In those circumstances, it may be seen that the summoner has not fitted his summons (and, in such cases, his interruption) to some assessment of the ongoing activity. The selected formulation by the summoned of what he "is doing" can then be seen to select an order of priority for the ongoing activity, in terms of which the summoner should assess the proposed prospective activity to decide whether to proceed or not, in terms of dimensions such as were suggested earlier. "Just a moment" does not lay that burden of comparative assessment on the summoner, but leaves the control of the timing with the summoned. It seems to be based on some assessment by the summoned of where he is in the ongoing course of action in which he is engaged, being used when the completion of that course of action, or some sub-unit of it, and consequent readiness to attend to the summoner, fall within some relevant temporal constraints. But here, it should again be noted, we are dealing not with availability but with readiness to engage in the interaction.

It should be clear that the "problematic" character of the answer is non-definitive; it does not preclude a continuation, but requires a particularized, situated analysis. The consequence is variability in the terminality/non-terminality feature, although in many cases the outcome is similar to that noted earlier, in which, after a clearance cue, the summoner seeks to withdraw, and does so not by silence but by some utterance that thereby respects the non-terminality feature. So, with problematic answers, the summoner may withdraw with "Sorry," "Never mind," "O.K.", "It's not important," thereby achieving non-terminality, and perhaps also showing that the incident has not been taken amiss and has not been seen as suggesting the impairment of the relationship. Should the summoner not talk again, the non-observance of the non-terminality feature may be warranted by the problematic answer. (We may note in passing that in SA pre-sequences we find a sequel also found in other sorts of pre-sequences; when the outcome of the pre-sequence is to block the base sequence, the initiator of the action may announce what he would have done had he had the opportunity to proceed. In pre-invitations, this takes the form, "I was gonna say, let's go to a movie"; in pre-conversationals, one may find such sequences as "Alice?" "Go away," "I was just gonna say I'm sorry.")

In noting that answers of the form "I'm doing X" may be used when the summoned's ongoing activity is outside the summoner's visual range or is not subject to inspection and has thus not been available for comparative assessments of priority with respect to the pre-sequenced activity, it is further suggested that, when a summons is done under conditions of visual access, the summoned may take it that the comparative assessment has been made, and the outcome was the production of the summons. That may be one reason for not using the form "I am Xing" where that is open to inspection and for hearing it as "testy" when it is used. It further suggests that summons are heard to introduce interaction that has passed some priority test, and therefore that SA sequences will not often be found as pre-sequences to, for example, "Gesundheit" (and, if they are, then it may be heard that it was not merely acknowledging the occurrence of a sneeze, but sharing some common private joke or allusion, and thus the SA was preliminary not to the ritual but to the intimacy). If it is the case that potential summoners of those otherwise engaged (that is, potential interrupters) engage in some assessment of the comparative priority of the ongoing versus the prospective activity, and that those summoned treat the summons as having been produced as the outcome of such a comparative assessment, then we should expect that only infrequently will we find (under conditions of visual access) problematic answers; for, on the one hand, potential summoners will forbear when priority cannot be claimed for the prospective activity, and, on the other hand, summoned parties will hear the claimed priority finding in the fact of the production of the summons. Here, in the assessment of the comparative priorities of activities, is one place "status" may enter as an important feature in conversation, the lesser activities of higher-status persons taking priority over the activities of lower-status persons; that may therefore become a procedure for claiming status, or "pulling rank."

It may be noted in passing that the once frequently discussed complaint about the telephone's capacity for the "invasion of privacy" is related to the inability of a summoner to analyze ongoing activities to assess comparative priorities, and the summoned's inability to do so before answering. No alignment is therefore possible. When, in addition, status differentials are introduced, an "important man" finding his activities interrupted for activities of little comparative weight, the import of interposing a secretary to make such assessments, and provide problematic answers ("He's not in," "He's in conference") is clear,[43] as is the competition that is rumored to go on between executives and executive secretaries as to who should get on the line first.

It has several times been suggested in passing in the preceding discussion that temporal assessments may be relevant to the selection of an answer to a summons when the summons has been produced as an interruption to some ongoing course of action. The simple use of the term "interruption," however, glosses two distinct types of occurrence. One sort of interruption occurs when some ongoing unit of action is stopped (or is subject to an attempt to stop it) before completion, and is seen as not, as a matter of natural course, to be resumed after the interruption. Interruptions of utterances are regularly of this sort (see, on "interruptions," Sacks, 1992, I, pp. 624–646). Utterances, or component sentences, are not regularly resumed at the point of interruption once the interrupting utterance has been completed. The interrupting utterance may become the one to which subsequent utterances are fitted. When resumed, interrupted utterances are typically pointedly accomplished as "resumptions"; that is, they are not simply re-begun from the point of interruption, or from their initial beginning, but are marked with an "As I was saying . . ." or "Anyhow . . ." "Resuming" in this fashion may then be heard as a way of taking notice of the interruption, and perhaps of "complaining" about it, and may draw an apology from the interrupter (an apology rather than a counter-complaint, which is another possible return, because the first-order activity is not "complaining" but "resuming"). Interruptions of which the above is descriptive are regularly interruptions by other co-participants in the ongoing conversation.

Different from these are "interruptions" that are "insertions," that is, where it is taken that the interrupted course of action is held in abeyance while some other course of action is inserted. Upon completion of the inserted course of action, the abeyance is lifted and the interrupted activity is resumed as a matter of course. Such interruptions may be seen as intended when the interrupter is not a participant in the ongoing conversation; what is then seen as interrupted is not an utterance (though the interruption may have been initiated so as to intervene in the course of an utterance) but the conversation, and the conversation may be held ready for resumption upon completion of the interruption.

For "insertion interruptions" a temporal assessment seems relevant within which there is attention to a proper "ratio" of the extensiveness of the interruption (the "insertion") to the interrupted course of action (a ratio that may itself be shifting, depending on assessments of comparative seriousness, importance, priority, and so on). When the interruption begins to exceed certain boundaries, the party common to both interactions (the interrupting and interrupted) may feel he should cut short (or in any case bring to an end) the interrupting activity to return to the interrupted ("Can I call you back?"), an obligation to which the interrupter may also be sensitive ("I don't want to keep you any longer"). The parties to the interrupted course of action who are not parties to the interruption may feel restive, and may use the event to terminate the interaction (or occasion) in which the other course of action was being pursued (an action they may also take upon the occurrence of the interruption to relieve the party involved in both courses of action of the obligation to cut the one short to return to the other; hence the observation earlier, p. 346, that persons in a conversation when the phone rings may use the occurrence of that event to bring the conversation to a close). What started as an interruption, subject to constraints on its proper extensiveness when inserted into an ongoing course of action, may thus have its status changed in its course and be relieved of those constraints. And "Just a moment" as an answer to a summons may be selected to allow completion of some ongoing course of action and the undertaking of the pre-sequenced conversation as a course of action in its own right, subject to its own temporal development, rather than as an insertion interruption.

An orientation to this "relative extensiveness" propriety concerning interruptions and interrupteds may require of a prospective interrupter some pre-assessment of the possible temporal requirements of his interruption, adding this temporal assessment to the assessment of comparative priorities discussed earlier. Similarly, it may warrant a reliance by those interrupted that the interruption will stay within appropriate temporal boundaries, since it would not have been proposed if it could not be expectably accommodated temporally into the ongoing activity. Those who have a priority matter that may not fit to the temporal requirements of an insertion interruption may as alternatives ask the relevant engaged party to leave the ongoing conversation or may request the termination of the ongoing course of action in favor of the priority one.

As with assessments of comparative priority, the circumstances in which telephone conversations are initiated may partially preclude such temporal assessments (partially only, because callers may time their contacts so as not to coincide with what they know to be busy times of the day for others). Not knowing whether any courses of action were in progress at the time of the initiation of the call, callers may not know whether or not they are engaged in an insertion interruption, and whether, therefore, the temporal boundaries appropriate to such interruptions are relevant (this circumstance is not limited only to telephone conversations; it holds as well for un-prearranged dropping in on someone's home or office). In such cases, the initiator of the possibly interrupting contact may, as an utterance early in the conversation or prior to some expectably extensive part of it, inquire about the matter. One may then find what have elsewhere (Schegloff and Sacks, 1973) been referred to as "pre-topic closing invitations," such as "Are you busy?" "Are you in the middle of something?" "Are you preparing dinner?" It is the inability to monitor for those possibilities before doing the interruption, for example before summoning, that contributes the telephone's capacity for "invasion of privacy."

I have suggested that some problematic answers may force a reconsideration by the summoner of the grounds for starting up a conversation, especially if starting up a conversation involves interrupting some ongoing course of action in which summoned is engaged. The issue of "adequate grounds for starting up a conversation" or "adequate grounds for interrupting an ongoing course of action" is distinct from the issue of the availability of a hearer and of the utterance-to-utterance organization of summons–answer pairs that is addressed to it. Although these are separate issues, operating at different levels of organization of conversation, the opening pair is a site for the working out of both. Although the opening slots have a "local" utterance-to-utterance organization (one instance of which is the summons–answer sequence organization), that "local" structure may be seen to be in the service of, or under the jurisdiction of, higher-order levels of organization.

One higher-order level of organization relevant to conversational openings (and also to conversational closings; see Schegloff and Sacks, 1973) is the articulation of the conversational course of action with the occasion or setting in which it occurs. For a prospective conversation, one feature of the setting includes courses of action relevantly already in progress (where "relevantly" intends that the ongoingness of those courses of action has consequences for whether, and how, the prospective conversation is to be accomplished). The articulation of a prospective conversation with its occasion or setting can first of all affect the selection of conversational opening; thus, problematic availability can make relevant the use of a summons–answer sequence as the opening structure. Further, however, the articulation of the prospective conversation with the setting is effectuated through the properties of the structure that accomplishes the opening. There is a fit between the assessment of the comparative priority of the ongoing and prospective courses of action and the priority occurrence of an answer upon the occurrence of a summons. If a summons is used, and heard to be used, properly only upon a finding of priority for the activity that its use pre-sequences, then upon its occurrence that priority is given effect by the priority occurrence of an answer, a clearance cue for that priority activity. Conversely, were the priority that is accorded an answer within the local organization of the pair not fitted to the restraints on the use of the first part of the pair by the relevance of a priority analysis of what it pre-sequences, then perhaps some other way of ordering competing courses of action within a setting would be needed. It is perhaps because children early acquire the local structure of the SA sequence, and its power, while not yet (in adult eyes) making acceptable assessments of comparative priorities, that children's interrupting summonses so frequently go unheeded (with the understanding that "he just wants attention").

It is a pervasively relevant issue for parties to a conversation concerning any utterance in it, "Why that now?" The import of the above discussion is that, for the occurrence of a summons, the answer to that question may be found on different levels of organization. The pre-sequence use of SA sequences entails one answer: more to come. Its relationship to the availability problem entails a search for the scenic features that have made availability seemingly problematic. And where those include some ongoing course of action, the use of the summons entails, as an answer to "Why that now?" the claimed priority of the "more to come" over ongoing courses of action. The use of the summons initiates one articulation of a prospective course of action with ongoing ones, and lays an immediate constraint on the summoned. Alteration in the initiated course of action must be done within the local structure already under way.

This discussion has focused almost exclusively on one regular occasion for the use of problematic answers, that is, when the summons has been used as one way of accomplishing an interruption, or when it is interrupting "by the way." The involvement of a summoned party in some ongoing activity, not combinable with a prospective conversation, is one basis for possibly problematic availability, and thus is one place where SA sequences are regularly used (as is the absence of the prospective co-participant from visual monitoring range), and where there is a settled basis for the selection of a problematic answer as one component. Another circumstance in which problematic answers may be employed, another analysis a summoner may make of the use of a problematic answer, is severe impairment of the relationship or the summoned's declining to initiate one (as in looking away from a beggar on the street). Such circumstances cannot be described here.

Several points suggested by the preceding discussion may serve to close, for now, the consideration of the sequencing of openings. The relevance of assessments of relative priority and temporal fit that the possible use of problematic answers reflects has the consequence that, when a prospective initiator of conversation finds that such an answer might be employed, and might warrantedly be employed, he may not produce the summons, and the talk the summons was to pre-sequence may not be initiated. When, further, such assessments yield a clear analysis that problematic answers would not be warranted, then no summons may be produced, the talk being initiated without need for a special opening sequence. When there is no clear outcome of such assessments, an SA sequence may be initiated; but the option of forgoing the sequence and the talk it might initiate if the prospective answer to a summons is possibly a problematic answer makes the centrally relevant sequel to a summons a clearance cue answer. For the summoned, the summons can be seen to have been produced as the outcome of an assessment by the summoner of the prospects of a warranted problematic answer, and can be seen to have "survived" such an analysis of relative priority and temporal fit. Responding with a problematic answer may then be seen not merely as making availability problematic, but as reflecting on the adequacy of the summoner's assessment, for example as having insufficient respect for one or for one's activities. (Persons, categories of persons or relationships may develop histories in this regard, in which the values in terms of which assessments of relative priority and temporal fit are made are found inappropriate, or are contested. Thus, the regular inattention to the summonses of children, mentioned earlier, may be an instance where this applies to categories of persons.)

These considerations lead to a modified understanding of the notion of "availability" with which this discussion began. "Availability" is better thought of not as a "state of the other" with respect to possible prospective conversation (a state that it is the initiator's business to figure out and be controlled by), but rather as a matter of "relative states" of the prospective initiator and his intended co-participant, each assessing the prospects of initiating a conversation, and each oriented to the other's assessments in doing his own. For each, then, an analysis is required that is oriented to the particularities of the instant case, the present possible co-participant, the currently ongoing and possibly prospective activities, the relevantly formulated setting (i.e. the local situation), and the relative states and circumstances of the parties in it, not some absolute characterization of some candidate co-participant. Availability is, therefore, thoroughly interactional, not only in being a prerequisite to interaction but in being interactionally assessed.

Once availability is seen to be, for members, a matter of relative states of the co-participants, then it can be seen as well that availability is a matter of continuing interest throughout the course of a conversation, once initiated, and not only as a condition for its initiation. The suspension of conversation by co-participants when one of their number may be responsible for a ringing phone as a priority matter (on persons' responsibility for answering, see Schegloff, 1967, ch. 4, and forthcoming) reflects this attention to the relative states and competing priorities of co-participants. And members may be attentive to others' so-called "wandering attention," that is, their continuing availability throughout the course of an initiated conversation. Because availability is a matter of continuing concern, the conversational sequence that supplies one resource for dealing with it, SA sequences, may be found to be used not only at conversational beginnings but throughout their course. In this respect, SA sequences are one of a range of resources that may be addressed to fluctuations in availability, another being, for example, "voice raising." An exploration of the range of devices addressed to problems of continuing availability and the basis for selection among them is yet to be undertaken.

The structure of SA sequences described in this discussion is in many respects applicable to their use across variations in setting or context. In some respects, however, there are important modifications in their use in telephone conversation.[44] In discussing the utterance forms that are the components of SA sequences in telephone conversations (which supply the corpus of data with which we started), some attention will have to be given to the ways in which SA sequences are treated differently when the conversations being initiated are telephonic.

### Acknowledgments

This text is a revision, completed in 1970, of chapter 2 of my PhD dissertation (Schegloff, 1967), modified only to accommodate publishing conventions adhered to by Cambridge University Press. Parts of that dissertation chapter, in revised form, appeared in the *American Anthropologist* (Schegloff, 1968). The text presented here does not, however, include all the text of Schegloff (1968), and it incorporates extensive revision and expansion of what did appear both there and in the dissertation. Chapter 1 of the dissertation had included a description of its data, to which reference is made in the text that follows. Briefly, the data consisted of a corpus of some 500 telephone calls to the police of a mid-western city in the immediate aftermath of a disaster. Calls were routed from a central switchboard to a so-called "complaint desk," at which point the recording of them by the Police Department began. The material was made available to me by the Disaster Research Center, then at The Ohio State University, which had collected it for its own studies of community response to disaster. Work on these materials was supported by the Advanced Research Projects Agency, Department of Defense, through the Air Force Office of Scientific Research under Contract number AF 49 (638)-1761, administered through the Bureau of Applied Social Research, Columbia University.

## Notes

1 I use "conversation" in an inclusive way. I do not intend to restrict its reference to the "civilized art of talk" or to "cultured interchange" as in the usages of Oakeshott (1959) or Priestly (1926), to insist on its casual character, thereby excluding service contacts (as in Landis and Burtt, 1924), or to require that it be sociable, joint action, identity related, etc. (as in Watson and Potter, 1962). "Dialogue," while being a kind of conversation, has special implications derived from its use in Plato, psychiatric theorizing, Buber, and others, which limits its usefulness as a general term. I mean to include chats as well as service contacts, therapy sessions as well as asking for and getting the time of day, press conferences as well as exchanged whispers of "sweet nothings."

2 I am indebted to Sacks (1992, I, pp. 95–103) for suggesting the significance of this observation, and some of its implications.

3 For an extensive development of the consequences of this and other fundamental features of conversation, see Sacks (1992, I, pp. 523–524, 633–684; Sacks, Schegloff and Jefferson, 1974).

4 Notice that I do not mean to identify a "turn" necessarily with any syntactic unit or combination of units, or with any activity. In the former case, it should be clear that a turn may contain anything from a single "mm" (or less) to a string of complex sentences. In the latter, it is crucial to distinguish a single turn in which two activities are accomplished from two turns by the same party without an intervening turn by the other. An example of the latter occurs when a question must be repeated before it is heard or answered; an example of the former is the line, following the inquiry "How are you?" "Oh, I'm fine. How are you?" A "turn," as I am using the term, is thus not the same as what Goffman (1953, p. 165) refers to as a "natural message," which he describes as "the sign behavior of a sender during the whole period of time through which a focus of attention is continuously directed at him." There are, of course, other views of the matter, such as using a period of silence or "appreciable pause" to mark a boundary (as in Stephen and Mishler, 1952, p. 600, or Steinzor, 1949, p. 109). But unanalyzed pauses and silences are ambiguous (theoretically) as to whether they mark the boundary of a unit or are included in it (as the very term "pause" suggests).

5 A less usual case may be found in a story in the *New York Times* of January 12, 1968, reporting on an interview with the official executioner of Canada on the occasion of the abolition of capital punishment. Among other things, the *Times* reports: " 'Those condemned died quickly and painlessly,' he said, adding that before he got down to business he sometimes talked 'with them about whatever they want to talk about.' However, he added that the condemned man had to start the conversation."

6 "Who starts" is treated as related to, and indicative of, stratified status even when such matters are far from the topic under investigation. For example, in Berelson, Lazarsfeld and McPhee's (1954) study of *Voting*: "The people who talked with equal or higher occupations were more likely to have *started* the discussion themselves than those who talked with lower occupations" (p. 104, emphasis in original), although it is unclear whether it is the initiation of the conversation or of the topic that is involved.

7 The term "answerer" is used in preference to "called" to avoid the implications of intentionality in the latter, the rule holding even if a wrong number is reached.

8 The orientation of members to "caller–called" as a relevant formulation of the parties, its status as a preservable and reportable feature of a conversation, and the sort of conversational features it may be used by members to account for are suggested by the following:

```
A:  Hello.
B:  Hi.
A:  Oh!! i!! 'ow are you Agnes?
B:  Fine. Yer line's been busy.
A:  Yeah, my fu(hh)! hh my father's wife called me.
    hh So when she calls me!! hh I always talk fer a
    long time. Cuz she c'n afford it 'n I can't.
    hhh//heh ehhh.
    (NB, 4 calls, call.2)
```

9 I touch here only tangentially on a larger area – what might be termed "*n*-party properties and problems." What is suggested by that term is that, for activities that have a common value for *n* (two-party activities, three-party activities, etc.), there may be, by virtue of that common feature, some common problems or properties. For example, two-party activities may share some problems of coordination, or some properties as compared with three-party activities. Alternatively, activities that have a minimum-number-of-parties requirement may have common properties as compared with those whose relevant parameter is a maximum number of participants. It is the latter possibility that is being touched on here.

On "cristics," see Perelman and Olbrechts-Tyceta (1969, p. 166): "Were there any need for a clear sign enabling one to contrast the criterion of eristic dialogue with that of the other kinds, it would be found in the existence of a judge or arbiter charged with giving the casting vote between the antagonists, rather than in the intentions and procedures of the adversaries themselves.

Because the purpose of the debate is to convince not the adversary but the judge; because the adversary does not need to be won over to be beaten; for this very reason the eristic dispute is of no great interest to the philosopher."
10  Similar observations are reported from elsewhere. For example, on Thailand:

While sitting in a small sidewalk coffee shop in Bangkok, I noticed that a Thai man sitting alone at a table across the aisle was talking. Beside the proprietor and myself, there were only two other people in the shop, neither of which were seated at the same table as this man. As the man spoke, all of us looked at each other in an unsuccessful attempt to see who was the object of his conversation. No one spoke back to him, and a few moments later he said something else, again not appearing to address his remark to anyone in particular. (The second remark, as I recall, was a mildly profane comment about some unspecified male; I did not understand the first remark.) At this second remark, the proprietor said something in a low voice to each of the other two customers, which elicited the identical replies of 'mai lu' (don't know). The proprietor then asked me in English if I knew the man, to which I replied no. A third remark by the man was then spoken, and it was again disparaging some unknown male. At this point, the proprietor asked the man, in a rather impolite manner, to whom he was speaking, and indicated that only crazy people talked to themselves. When the man didn't reply, the proprietor told him to leave. After some hesitation, the man did (without paying, I might add). For the next several minutes, his behavior was the subject of an animated conversation between the proprietor and the two remaining Thai customers. (I was left out, presumably because I was a foreigner.) The conversation was interspersed with many comments of 'ba' (crazy).

I am indebted here to an unpublished paper by Francis K. Lengel.
11  Which activities are combinably doable by an actor and which are not combinable seems to be part of the corpus of common-sense knowledge defining competent membership. In much of Western culture, for example, conversing and reading are not combinable, whereas conversing and knitting are. The consequences of such treatments are various, including, for example, whether one is "interrupting" another or not; to begin talking to one who is reading is to interrupt him; to do so to a knitter is not. The availability of a single member physically "just sitting" may thus turn not only on whether he is "doing nothing" or doing a one-party activity such as "thinking," but also, in the latter case, whether that activity is combinable or not with another; in the case of "thinking," it is in this society not seen to be combinable with conversing; whether or not it is combinable with "listening to music" is sometimes a matter of dispute.

Concerning the presumed non-combinability of reading and conversing (that is, speaking and/or hearing), I take it that it is by invoking that common-sense "assumption" as a resource that the "point" can be made in the following report (*New York Times*, February 14, 1970):

The Premier denied that there had ever been a difference of opinion among Cabinet members about Israel's position, although by now it is fairly generally conceded privately by Government officials that Foreign Minister Abba Eban and a small group in the Cabinet were outnumbered when they tried Sunday to raise an old proposal that a conciliatory approach to the Arabs be tried...Defense Minister Moshe Dayan is said to have read a newspaper while Mr. Eban was speaking.

12 For an extensive bibliography on terms of address, see Hymes (1964a); for a recent discussion, see Ervin-Tripp (1969).

13 Bolinger (1958); "quasi-interrogative" because American English seems not to have an intonation pattern that is necessarily and invariably interrogative.

14 Such analysis is subject to error, as will be suggested below. That the utterance of a name could be analyzed as a summons can lead to various circumlocutions to avoid that possibility. For example, Westermarck (1926, I, p. 263) accounts for the elaboration of circumlocutions to refer to evil spirits (the "jnun" or "jinns") by noting that, for the Moroccans, "[t]o pronounce their name would be to summon them."

15 Another possibility is that it will be heard as an ironic summons, using a form intentionally mis-selected, the irony being done, perhaps, as comment on a "distance" between intimates that hints of being "strangers." For another case of mistake and irony as alternative analyses, see the comments in note 33 below on answers to summonses and answers to roll-calls.

16 At that point, a rationale will be offered for treating sequences completed with "clearance cue" answers, instead of ones including "problematic" answers, as the point of departure. See the first three paragraphs (pp. 358–360) of the section below, "Problematic answers to summonses."

17 The sense in which "sequence" is used here will be explicated below in the section on "Conditional relevance in SA sequences."

18 It is this feature that especially fits "summonses" for the work of reopening otherwise completed conversations. Conversations that have been properly closed – a properly initiated closing section having been completed with a terminal exchange (see Schegloff and Sacks, 1973) – can be reopened even after the completion of the terminal exchange; one regularly employed method for doing so involves the use of a summons. For example, after interaction is brought to a close, two parties walk in opposite directions. About 25 yards apart, "A" turns and yells:

```
A: Jerry...Jerry...Jerry
B: Yeah
A: I forgot to ask how are things with you.
```

Or, in a case of telephone conversation (NB: 9/10/68, 1:1),

```
A: Hello
B: Is Jessie there/
A: (No) Jessie's over et 'er Gramma's fer a
   couple days.
B: Alright Thank you.
A: Yer welcome/
B: Bye
A: Dianne/
```

19 It is crucial that the obligation is contingent on the answer. Otherwise, it might appear that, in relying on this sequencing structure, a member could, by starting an SA sequence, self-select as second-next speaker, and this would undermine, or be an exception to, the utterance-to-utterance organization of speaker sequencing. Determination of next speaker may be seen, by contrast, to be in large measure under the control of the one to whom a summons is directed; clearance cue (and some problematic) answers do select the summoner as next speaker, but other utterances may select others. Summoners cannot, therefore, unilaterally select themselves as second-next speaker.

20 Sequences of the latter sort do seem to occur, as when A has asked B to do something, and, before B has done it, one gets the sequence: A: "Sam?," B: "Yeah," A: "Never mind." The sequence cited in the text differs from this in the "Oh" attached to the last utterance; this suggests the use of "oh" as a marker of unplanned utterances, and may be used here to allow a hearer to distinguish which course of action the "never mind" is being placed in, the "local" utterance sequence or the course of action in which the request was an action.

21 Sacks (personal communication, 1966) has pointed out that "repetitions," as contrasted with second occurrences, are distinctively done as "repeats." Even if the first was not heard, the second can be heard as a "repeat." It is this that allows us to see how someone can respond, "I didn't hear you," without either lying or raising the puzzle how he could know there was something he didn't hear if he didn't hear it.

22 See Sacks (1992, I, pp. 96–99 passim); Schegloff (1967, ch. 4); Schegloff (forthcoming).

23 By "preferred solution" I intend to notice the following. Some persons improvise in answering the phone; their initial utterance is a grunt, or some unorthodox sound. That does not appear to make problematic for callers "what he said" or "whether he answered" (though it may make it problematic whether the caller reached the one he was trying to reach, especially if it is the first time he has encountered such an "answer"). Rather than making it problematic whether that sound was "an answer," it may be heard as "the way he answers the phone," as his "style" (alternatively it may be treated as displaying "mood," to non-natives it may display "regional practice," etc.). While, in a literal sense, one who answers his phone "hello" has that as "*his* way" of answering the phone, it is not so heard; though he answers that way, it is not his way of answering. This treatment seems to involve seeing that it is a standardized way. The recognition of style, of someone's "way of doing things," therefore, seems to imply a recognition that it is not a standardized way, and therefore an orientation to the availability of standardized ways.

One consequence of this point is that, when reference is made to classes of terms usable as summonses or as answers, and to those classes as bounded (i.e. there are utterances that are not members of them), it does not follow that a summons or answer can be done only by selecting some member of those classes. The consequence may be that a "standardized" summons or answer is done by selecting from those classes. Where sequential placement is critical, as in second slots of utterance pairs, a much wider range of terms inserted there will be analyzed as proper (for example as answers) if they can be; "answer" is a "preferred analysis" of utterances placed in the second slot of an utterance pair whose first slot had a summons. The non-use of a standard class member is then one way of displaying personal style (or mood, etc.).

This discussion has the following outcomes: class membership (in classes such as summons, answer, term of address) may define not possible use but possible standardized (or unmarked) use. This is quite aside from the point that selection from among members of the standardized class can serve as a vehicle for marking features of the conversation or setting, as "Excuse me" displays an analysis of prospective co-participant as "stranger." And one strategic place for accomplishing "personal style" is where sequential placement is especially relevant, where a wider range of terms will accomplish the relevant first-order action because of a preferred analysis of utterances placed there. Although in the first place doing the work of establishing availability, SA sequences, through the selection of their components, can be used as vehicles for other accomplishments as well, a theme to be elaborated below.

24 For the sense in which "relevant" is used here, see the next section below.

25 See above, p. 339.

26 See note 11 on combinable activities; for example, reading and conversation may be treated as non-combinable, as may a second conversation with a first.

27 For further discussion, see below, pp. 347–348, 365.

28 As is suggested by the unexplicated use of terms such as "action sequence" or "course of action," the notion of "nextness" (a property not specific to the organization of conversational events, but possibly relevant to all kinds of activities) involves us in a series of very knotty problems. Most centrally, how are courses of action organized within streams of simultaneously ongoing events that are not part of them? Or, observationally, how are some events selected out of a large set and isolated as an organized course of action? For example, when one asks an "expert" (for example a car mechanic) what he "is doing" and he says "X," one may not know (if one lacks any of the relevant expertise) whether only the thing he is doing at the moment is X, or whether what he started ten minutes ago and will finish in five minutes is X but what intervenes is not. Nor, perhaps, does one know what is X about it, not being able to distinguish which parts or aspects are his personal style, which are idiosyncratic contingencies of this case and treatment of it, or which are paradigmatically, and definitionally, X; that is, what is the "course of action, X." Or consider the directions A may give B for getting somewhere or instructions for making something. Such directions, instructions, recipes may have explicit, but at least implicit, "nexts" between the steps ("Do A; next do B; ..." or "do A; then do B ..."). Now we observe B "following the instructions." We may find him to have followed them correctly, although many nameable actions or activities may have occurred between any two steps of the instructions, steps that were to stand in the relationship "next." Nonetheless, the "nextness" property is not found to have been violated on that account. For "next" may be used not only, perhaps not even primarily, to intend "immediately following" but also "in the proper sequence" or "immediately following in *that course of action*," the course of action being foregrounded from other events in which it is embedded. "Nextness" and "correct sequence" are respected when the events named in the instructions are produced in the order in which they are named in the instructions, all other events not being counted; when

the instructions, transformed in tense from the imperative or future to the past, stand as a description of what was done. Accordingly there seem to be "orders" of events that can enter into some course of action, and others that are of a different "order of event." (Some such issue seems to be involved in the strangeness of children's telling and retelling of stories; for example, "First he ran away from home, then he took a horse, then he went to the city, then he picked his nose . . . ," where an item from a different order of events seems to adults to have been misplaced into a course of action. When the storyteller is adult, and is telling a mystery story for example, it may be seen that this otherwise misplaced item, drawn from a different "order of event," will turn out to be crucial.) And from events of a same order, some will be parceled into different courses of action, as when someone instructed to go to X street and then turn left goes to X street and turns right, "into a café for coffee," before continuing on his way, where "into a café for coffee" serves to indicate that a separate course of action is inserted into the one he is otherwise pursuing.

The problems of organizing a stream of events into different orders, or layers, and those into courses of action seem to be fundamental problems of cognitive order underlying normative order. They are relevant to all action, not only conversation; they involve relations not only of nextness but also of intermittence (or, rather, may involve as a discovery for both analysts and members that what might otherwise be seen as discrete is organized by intermittence, or what might be seen as discrete or intermittent is to be seen as organized via nextness, thereby providing for the "discovery" of a "covert" course of action where accident might have been supposed). Since an explication of "immediate juxtaposition" in SA sequences seems to require at least some reference to these considerations, it is worthwhile to consider superficially for a moment the iceberg whose tip is making an appearance.

29 As evidence that attention may be paid to the order of unit completed or interrupted in an ongoing course of action in the face of the claims of a competing course of action that intervenes (of which the occurrence of a summons in an ongoing conversation is one instance), and that the relative priorities thereby displayed may be treated as evidence of characterological features, consider the following account of an attack on the American embassy in Saigon:

With no warning, the wooshing sounds of a projectile, then a bang, flooded into the room from the open veranda along one side. The other explosions followed at once, the whole series lasting perhaps five or ten seconds.

Most people flinched. Some women ducked behind their husbands. General Westmoreland, resplendent in black tie, gold braid, a short white jacket and medals, did not so much as blink. He *finished a sentence in conversation with friends without interrupting himself*, and then commented evenly: "It sounded like recoilless-rifle fire to me, and incoming." (*New York Times*, November 1, 1967; emphasis added)

30 From unpublished data of Roger Barker's group at the University of Kansas. I am indebted to Harvey Sacks for bringing it to my attention, and for suggesting that I try to elaborate the notion of "immediate juxtaposition" in terms of "nextness."

31 Reference to "repetition" of S does not intend that the same lexical item need be repeated. Rather, successive utterances are each drawn from the class of items which may be summonses, though the particular items may change over the series of repetitions. There may be shifts from one term of address to another (from "Jim" to "Jim Smith," as, for example, when trying to attract someone's attention from the rear in a crowded setting), from a ring of a door bell to a knock on the door, from a mechanical ring of the phone to a lexical item (for example, "Hello" when the receiver is lifted and nothing is said, as in the deviant case introduced earlier and to be reconsidered below), or from one car to another, both stopped for the same traffic light (A: "Excuse me." [pause] A: "Hello." [other turns to summoner] A: "Is Route 25A ahead?"). In addition, as was noted earlier, repetitions may be given distinctive intonation that allows them to be heard as repetitions without hearing earlier occurrences; and some summons terms, in some settings, may be specially used as "summons repeats" (as I think may be the case for "hello" in face-to-face interaction, for example, in the data just cited).

32 In telephone contacts, "number of rings" supplies a temporal measurement system for the relation of answer to summons. Thus, the "ten rings" referred to in the text; and the following report in the *New York Times* (March 18, 1969, p. A12) about the Prime Minister of Israel:

When Mrs. Meir, who is 70 years old, knew Israeli soldiers were going out on a military operation, she would say, "Phone me when the boys come home," Mr. Dinitz said, adding: "I'd be called by the army and then I'd phone Golda – at 2, 3 or 4 in the morning. She always answered at the first ring."

And the following incident in an interview with an actress:

The phone rang, and the 5-foot-5-inch, 110 pound actress reacted like a child who has just heard the Good Humor Man's bell on an August day. She grinned mischievously, jumped to her feet, and ran so fast she caught it on the second ring. It was her husband in Toronto, just wondering how she was, and she talked to him – in animated French – for about 10 minutes. "We are really still newlyweds," she explained, blushing, as she hung up. ("Who's Playing Saint Joan? Genevieve Bujold?" *New York Times*, October 22, 1967, Section 2)

Just as, if some number of rings pass without an answer, that may be treated as evidence that no one is home (see below), so one who answers at the first or second ring may be seen (for example by the caller) as "waiting for the (a) call," "being eager," etc. And prospective answerers may give attention to what a caller may make of the number of rings, rushing to answer if many have passed and pausing so as to avoid answering "too quickly." Recognition that it is the rings and not the silences between them that are counted, that the caller counts them as well and that answering after one or two may display eagerness or uninvolvement in other activities, thus prompting a waiting before answering, leads to an alternative account (suggested by Harvey Sacks) of the earlier observation about persons who wait, hand on phone, before answering; namely, that in waiting to answer after a reasonable number of rings they thereby wait to answer after some particular ring, it being the number of rings, and not the completion of *a* ring, they are waiting for.

33  Where SA sequences are initiated to address this sort of availability problem, a clearance cue answer will entail subsequent talk, even if only greeting exchanges. I note this point to suggest that, although this usage may seem to be a kind of "roll-call," it bears all the features of SA sequences, whereas roll-calls do not. That roll-calls are different can be seen from the following:

(1)  Roll-call exchanges may be terminal for the two parties in a single exchange (A: "Jones." B: "Here").

(2)  The class of answer terms is different from the class of answer terms for summonses, terms such as "here" and "present" being members of one, but not the other, class. There are terms that are members of both classes, for example "Yes" or "Yeah." The class of answers to roll-calls is a class especially open to innovation; where standards of formality have been relaxed, persons (especially persons well into the roll) may employ a wide range of terms and sounds to indicate presence. The partial overlap of the classes of answers to summonses and roll-calls is treated as providing a resource for levity and playfulness, by using roll-call answers in responding to summonses (for example, A: "Jim." B: "Present." A: etc.) or answers to summonses to respond to a roll-call. In this connection, it is interesting to note that the levities are not combinable; those who play by using a roll-call answer to respond to a summons use a "standard" roll-call term ("Here," "Present") and not an innovation, though innovations may be used to respond to roll-calls. It is also interesting that using an answer to a summons as a response to a roll-call can often be immediately seen as ironic, and not as an error; that is, the caller of the roll can see that the roll was being correctly answered with an incorrect term, rather than that his activity was incorrectly analyzed as a summons, and thus corrective action need not be taken. This may be a fruitful site for the investigation of irony, but this is not the place to undertake it.

(3)  They occur only at beginnings (or re-beginnings, for example after intermission) of occasions or meetings (whereas SA can be used throughout a conversation).

(4)  They are used only in multi-person settings.

(5)  They typically involve the use of a list, so that attention to the prospective calling of one's name is focused by an attention not to availability problems but to how lists are ordered (alphabetically, ecologically, etc.). Consequently, only the first person called is likely to have to analyze whether a roll-call or an availability summons has been done, although persons can display their non-attention to the "official goings-on" if they respond to a calling of their name well down the list in a roll-call with an item that shows they are answering a summons (this being an analysis alternative to irony). For another case where persons are expected to have been analyzing the proceedings so as to see that a calling of their name is not a summons, see Sacks' 1967 and 1968 lectures (e.g. 1992, II: 65), and the following item from the *New York Times* (cited by Sacks in a lecture from the Spring 1967 set not included in the published version):

As the President spoke, he looked across from his armchair to a sofa on which Secretary of Defense Robert S. McNamara sat with General Earle G. Wheeler, chairman of the Joint Chiefs of Staff, and General William C. Westmoreland, commander of American forces in Vietnam. "The troops that General Westmoreland needs and requests, as we feel it necessary, will be supplied," Mr. Johnson said. "Is that not true, General Westmoreland?"

"Yes, sir."

"General Wheeler?"

"Yes, sir."

"Secretary McNamara?"

"Yes, sir."

34 I am indebted to Gail Ziferstein (now Jefferson) for calling the datum to my attention.

35 How, for members, the "presence" of another is established is not entirely clear. "Seeing" the other is not definitive; one may see him at a great distance and not count him as present, or not see him because he is in another room, yet take his presence for granted. The latter point suggests that, at the least, "not seeing" is not definitive. With respect to the former point, it may be that "exchanged seeing" – seeing the other, the other seeing one, and each seeing that the other saw and saw one see – may be definitive.

That finding another's presence is a member's achievement, the methods for whose accomplishment remain to be described, suggests that the analyst's term "co-presence," which has been taken as referring to an unambiguous, transparent and entirely non-problematic property not only in sociology but in disciplines such as animal ethology, should be seen as problematic indeed. For whether two persons (or objects) are "co-present" or not may depend on the order of place formulation in terms of which the matter is considered. Two persons not "co-present" in a room may be in an apartment. This exercise can be extended for the range of place formulations at will. Since the selection of relevant place formulation can be considered problematic, and solutions to it orderly (Schegloff, 1972), features such as "co-presence" that are dependent on the formulation are equally problematic. For analysts, this entails not using "co-presence" as an intrinsic or transparent feature with direct consequences for actors' behavior, but attending to members' findings of "presence" and "co-presence" as achievements. In writing in the text "where presence is not problematic," I intend that, for the summoner, some place formulation is established as relevant and techniques employed by reference to which he and the summoned are co-present, and which he takes it would be the same for the summoned.

Another sense of "presence not problematic," and of subsequent usages in the text such as "will not support the inference 'no person,'" is relevant in the case of some items of common-sense knowledge concerning places that are always "staffed" (for example hospitals, operators' switchboards). Persons calling "operator" may not use the fact of "no answer" after "many rings" as evidence for "no person"; presence not being treated as problematic (and the "didn't hear" inference also not being supportable), inferences regarding "being busy" or "inefficiency" may be treated as warranted.

36 It is important to see that these are *claims* of hearership, claims that may be discreditable or discredited. Thus, the following remark by a disabled girl concerning her attempts on the phone to get officials to keep a service for the disabled operating:

... and I'd be giving my all and I could hear him say, "Yes, yes ... I understand," and I know he wasn't listening and wanted me to hang up. (*New York Times*, August 18, 1968, p. 92)

To notice that such hearership claims are discreditable is not to say that they are regularly so treated by interlocutors; that is, to say "claim" is to not be heard as intending "false claim." It is only to contrast it implicitly with hearership displays that *show* hearership, by, for example, completing an utterance in a syntactically and semantically coherent way, thereby demonstrating that the completer had been hearing and analyzing the utterance to that point. Harvey Sacks has developed the consequences of this last point extensively in his unpublished lectures (now Sacks, 1992). The possibly subversive use of hearership claims are recognized in a standard joke, in which a husband, returned from work, is absorbed in the newspaper, while his wife recounts the day's troubles, regularly leaving a slot of silence into which the husband inserts a "Yes, dear." Aware that all is not as it is claimed to be, she says, "Dear, you're ignoring me," to which he replies, "Yes, dear."

That "hearership" be seen as a locus of rules, and a status whose incumbency is subject to demonstration, is suggested by some of Sacks' work (1972b; 1992, I, pp. 236–266).

37 The not infrequent occurrence of "Pardon me?" (or variants) as the second utterance in a conversation may be related to this phenomenon. Acknowledging hearership requires some utterance or substitute, and not all acknowledgment tokens may appropriately follow any initial utterance; thus, in some circumstances, it may be required to in fact hear in order to acknowledge hearing appropriately. This may be especially in point if the first utterance was at least heard to be a question, or was not heard not to be a question; for many of the acknowledgment tokens are answer terms if used after a question (nods, "uh uh," "yes," etc.), and what is produced as an acknowledgment of hearership may in effect become a positive answer if the question was a "yes–no answerable" one, and self-evident disproof of hearership if it was not. On the other hand, acknowledgments may be made of utterances that were "not heard," as in the following, in which A makes a remark while passing B and C who are seated together:

```
A:  (                        )
B:  Mm hmm.
C:  What'd she say?
B:  I dunno.
```

38 For example, it is noticeable and reportable, as is shown several times in the following report on a visit by Vice President Agnew to Singapore; the report is used to characterize his trip as "not illustrious":

Mr. Agnew spent a total of five minutes in the Fung apartment. His visit went like this: He shook hands with Mrs. Fung, with her sister, Rosey Tan, and with her mother, Chionh Kim Lien. He looked at the Fung's son, Daniel, $3\frac{1}{2}$ years old, standing shyly behind his mother and said, "Hi, young man, how are you?" None of them responded.

The Vice President then said: "Certainly is nice of you to let us see your house. We appreciate it." He looked through the kitchen door at the bright sunlight and said: "It's nice and cool up here, isn't it? Breezy."

Again no one responded. Mr. Agnew's hosts merely smiled and watched him as he went past a door on which a bumper sticker proclaimed "Zoom with the Supershell Girl."

He looked into Daniel's sparsely furnished bedroom and exclaimed, "There are a few toys in there."

Then the Vice President peered into the parents' bedroom, turned quickly and walked into the kitchen. He dallied there as American photographers were ushered out and Singapore photographers were escorted in, and left within minutes. (*New York Times*, January 11, 1970)

Smiles may, of course, sometimes be recognized as acknowledgments.

39  For example: A and B at a bus stop; A tamps down some snow with his boot.

```
B:  They really should clean that away.
A:  Pardon me?
B:  They really should clean that away so people can
    get on the bus.
A:  Mm hmm.
```

It does not appear that either BA sequence is properly considered an utterance pair, though the AB sequence may be a QA pair.

40  And there are association inferences should no further talk be forthcoming; for example, "wrong number," "crank call," "prankster," "crossed wires."

41  Here, as throughout the discussion of pre-sequences, I am indebted to Harvey Sacks.

42  The notion "what was otherwise being pre-sequenced" suggests a set agenda. That such a notion is used by members where SA is involved can be seen, as was suggested earlier, in the practice of later asking one who has unsuccessfully summoned earlier "what he wanted."

43  That the selection among problematic answers can be a delicate matter, and its sequential placement in the conversation analyzed to find how it was selected, is suggested in the following advice to doctors:

*Is your aide careful not to be too abrupt in asking who's calling and why?* Getting even such basic facts as these requires the tactful wording of questions. Suppose, for example, your aide asks who's calling and *then* says that for some reason you can't take the call. That's enough to make the caller suspect you'd have talked to him if he'd been somebody more important... if you prefer to have all calls screened, your aide will get the best results if she says something like this: "Yes, Dr. Williamson is here, but I'm not sure he's free to talk. May I tell him who's calling, please?" That way, she has an out if you decide not to take the call. But it's not a transparent out and thus doesn't irritate the caller. (Morgan, 1967; emphasis in original)

44 There are other sorts of occurrences than face-to-face conversational exchanges that seem to be produced and recognized in terms of the SA structures, as described above or with modifications. For example, the act of "entering a commercial establishment" seems to be treated as embodying an SA sequence structure. The action "entering" for such places seems to serve as a virtual summons to some service person there. The developing features of interactions in such settings appear to be produced by reference to such a model. For example, after a person enters an eating establishment and seats himself at a table or counter (if there is no host(ess); if there is, the sequence will be played out by arrival and the host(ess)), a service person may approach without any further communication or signal, and upon arrival produce as the initial utterance, "Yes sir."

Though in such a circumstance the service person talks first, what he produces is not a "first utterance." That utterance, and others that may be produced in that slot (for example, "Can I help you?"), are occasioned utterances, some basis for their production having to be available to warrant their occurrence. The warrant seems to be that the act of entering is treated as initiating a course of action related to the formulation by which the establishment presents itself (see Schegloff, 1967, ch. 4, and forthcoming, for discussion of self-identification forms of answering the telephone). The structure of that initiation is an SA structure: it is seen as intendedly pre-sequential, an answer (of some form) is seen as conditionally relevant, further interaction is conditionally relevant on the completion of the sequence, etc. When that structure does not supply the form of the initiation of interaction, violations may be found by the participants and/or observers to occur, as in the following observation:

```
Customer:  You look like you're waiting for something.
Waitress:  You look like you want something.
Customer:  Well, we don't, so go away and just leave
           us alone.
```

Observers of this scene in an eating and drinking establishment may comment that the waitress was warranted in standing by the table and waiting for an "order" that was expectably forthcoming. The "waiting" is conditionally relevant on the virtual summons the customers accomplished in entering and seating themselves. It is warranted. The customer's first utterance, in seeming to treat its warrant as unclear or unestablished, might be treated as intendedly nonserious, as "Kidding around with the waitress," and not as questioning the warrant that his own action had provided. His seeming insistence in his second utterance on the seriousness in questioning the warrant is then analyzable as converting the whole sequence into a violation, making the act of entering and seating into a "naive option," one with no interactional consequences, which is not an enforceable version of such an action unless that is in some way announced. The self-service format is one way of providing that one's entrance will not be treated by service personnel as a summons directed at one of them.

Several other points may be mentioned to relate "entering establishments" to SA sequencing structures, and to suggest some modifications in that structure adapted to this use of them. In the settings under discussion, a greater lag between summons and answer may be "tolerated" by summoners than was suggested in the prior discussion. Still, the relationship of nextness is relevant in the relation of summons and answer, the answer being expectably "next" after some unit of ongoing activity. In the present context, the intervening activity after which an answer to any particular customer's summons should come "next" is expanded to accommodate other summoners whose summonses are seen to have temporal priority – the phenomenon of the queue. One does not, therefore, get repetitions of S if an answer is not "immediately forthcoming"; one does get them when the "nextness" of one's own "next" is violated; it is then that customers may wave, call "Waiter" or "Miss," or seek eye engagement with service personnel, though the latter may also be sought to establish one's place in the queue.

Similarly, the conditional relevance of further interaction on completion of the sequence is treated as relevant. Customer–service person talk may be treated as having priority once the virtual SA sequence is completed (as it may be when someone has entered and been seated and a service person "comes up to them," and faces them, though no utterance has yet been produced). A couple sitting at a table may, for example, "suspend" their conversation (leaving an utterance in its course incomplete) when the service person arrives. Here, then, there may be a period of asymmetric availability, the customer being committed to availability by his entrance, it being the servicer's availability that he awaits. When the latter is established, the summoner's further talk is conditionally relevant "next," it has priority.

It is by reference to the status for some places of "entering" as a virtual summons that we may, in part, understand utterances such as "I'm just browsing" after a salesman's, "Can I help you?" Such utterances seem to be structurally equivalent to the "Never mind" after conversational SA sequences such as were discussed in the body of this chapter.

What has been done here is to start with some conversational occurrence; describe some of its properties; and then locate other occurrences that do not have or may not have the conversational parts, but that have the same properties and thus appear to be members of the same class of events. A way may thereby be furnished for seeing the interactional texture of otherwise seemingly uninteresting non-verbal events, indeed for seeing them *as* events, and for warranting some formulation of the actions they accomplish.

## References

Albert, E. (1964)." 'Rhetoric', 'Logic', and 'Poetics' in Burundi: Cultural Patterning of Speech Behavior." In J.J. Gumperz and D. Hymes (eds.), *The Ethnography of Communication*. Washington, DC: *American Anthropologist* (Special Issue), 66(6), part 2, pp. 35–54.

Bales, R.F. (1950). *Interaction Process Analysis: A Method for the Study of Small Groups*. Reading, MA: Addison-Wesley.

Berelson, B.R., Lazarsfeld, P.F., and McPhee, W.N. (1954). *Voting: A Study of Opinion Formation in a Presidential Campaign*. Chicago: University of Chicago Press.

Bergler, E. (1938). "On the Resistance Situation: The Patient Is Silent." *Psychoanalytic Review* 25: 170–186.

Bolinger, D. (1958). *Interrogative Structures of American English*. University of Alabama Press.

Ervin-Tripp, S. (1969). "Sociolinguistic Rules of Address." In L. Berkowitz (ed.), *Advances in Experimental Social Psychology*. New York and London: Academic Press, 93–107.

Goffman, E. (1953). *"Communication Conduct in an Island Community."* Unpublished Ph.D. dissertation, Department of Sociology, University of Chicago.

(1961). *Encounters: Two Studies in the Sociology of Interaction*. Indianapolis: Bobbs-Merrill.

(1963). *Behavior in Public Places: Notes on the Social Organization of Gathering*. New York: Free Press.

Harrah, D. (1963). *Communication: A Logical Model*. Cambridge, MA: MIT Press.

Hymes, D. (1964a). *Language in Culture and Society*. New York: Harper & Row.

(1964b). "Introduction: Toward Ethnographies of Communication." In J.J. Gumperz and D. Hymes (eds.), *The Ethnography of Communication*. Washington, DC: *American Anthropologist* (Special Issue), 66(6), part 2, pp. 1–34.

Landis, M.H., and Burtt, H.E. (1924). "A Study of Conversations." *Journal of Comparative Psychology* 4: 81–89.

Lewis, D.K. (1969). *Convention: A Philosophical Study*. Cambridge, MA: Harvard University Press.

Morgan, B. (1967). "How's Your Aide's Telephone Technique?" *Medical Economics*, April 3: 219–223.

Oakeshott, M.J. (1959). *The Voice of Poetry in the Conversation of Mankind. An Essay*. London: Bowes & Bowes.

Perelman, C., and Olbrechts-Tyteca, L. (1969). *The New Rhetoric: A Treatise on Argumentation*. Notre Dame, IN: University of Notre Dame Press.

Priestly, J.B. (1926). *Talking*. New York and London: Harper.

Sacks, H. (1972a). "An Initial Investigation of the Usability of Conversational Materials for Doing Sociology." In D.N. Sudnow (ed.), *Studies in Social Interaction*. New York: Free Press, 31–74.

(1972b). "On the Analyzability of Stories by Children." In J.J. Gumperz and D. Hymes (eds.), *Directions in Sociolinguistics: The Ethnography of Communication*. New York: Holt, Rinehart & Winston, 325–345.

(1992). *Lectures on Conversation*, 2 vols. Ed. by G. Jefferson, with Introductions by E.A. Schegloff. Oxford: Blackwell.

Sacks, H., Schegloff, E.A., and Jefferson, G. (1974). "A Simplest Systematics for the Organization of Turn-Taking for Conversation." *Language* 50: 696–735.

Schegloff, E.A. (1967). "The First Five Seconds: The Order of Conversational Openings." Unpublished Ph.D. dissertation, University of California, Berkeley.

(1968). "Sequencing in Conversational Openings." *American Anthropologist* 70: 1075–1095.

(1972). "Notes on a Conversational Practice: Formulating Place." In D.N. Sudnow (ed.), *Studies in Social Interaction*. New York: Free Press, 75–119.

(forthcoming) "Answering the Phone." In G.H. Lerner (ed.), *Conversation Analysis: Studies from the First Generation*.

Schegloff, E.A., and Sacks, H. (1973). "Opening up Closings." *Semiotica* 8: 289–327; reprinted in John Baugh and Joel Sherzer (eds.), *Language in Use: Readings in Sociolinguistics*. Englewood Cliffs, NJ: Prentice-Hall, 1984.

Steinzor, B. (1949). "The Development and Evaluation of a Measure of Social Interaction." *Human Relations* 2: 319–347.

Stephen, F.F., and Mishler, E.Y. (1952). "The Distribution of Participation in Small Groups: An Exponential Approximation." *American Sociological Review* 17: 598–608.

Watson, J., and Potter, R. (1962). "An Analytical Unit for the Study of Interaction." *Human Relations* 15: 245–263.

Westermarck, E. (1926). *Ritual and Belief in Morocco*. London: Macmillan.

# Index

absence of answers, 343–344, 345, 350, 351, 352–353, 356
absent presence, 227–231
  cultural reverberations of, 231–236
  mobile phones and, 236–239
access to phones, in Philippines, 276, 278–279, 282, 283
accessibility, 9, 23, 115–116, 118, 119, 140, 152, 194–197
  management of, 8, 24, 54, 115, 154–155
  teenagers and, 149–150, 262
acknowledgment calls, 186
address, terms of, 333–335
adolescence
  role of, in contemporary society, 147–149
  role of mobile phones for, 149–151
  *see also* teenagers; young people
aesthetics, 54, 59–60, 61
age, and use of mobile phones, 51, 63, 84, 104, 124
  in Finland, 20–21, 28
  *see also* teenagers
allocation problem, 327–328
answering machines, 123, 186, 237
*Apparatgeist*, 11, 305–312
  theory of, 312–314, 316
appointment-making, 70–71, 143–144, 198
artificiality, 58
Aspden, P., 83, 84
asymmetry of information, 196–197, 290–291, 293
asynchronous discourse, 159–161
attitudes to mobile phones, 52, 53, 208–209
  non-users, 116, 117, 119
  users, 88, 116, 117
audacity (*chutzpah*), 39–40
availability, 22, 108
  of another party, for conversations, 331, 333, 353, 357–358, 361, 368–369

control of, 9, 102–104, 203
gender and, 23
for teenagers, 149–155

Bezeq (Israel), 31, 40
bonds, maintaining, 105, 106, 108
Bourdieu, P., 256
boys, 256, 261, 271–272
  and functional qualities of mobile phones, 262–263, 268
  use of language in text messages, 184, 185
Brown, M.E., 230
Bulgaria, 18, 126–128
  mobile phone use, 130–133
  in emergencies, 134
  mobile phones in popular culture, 135–136
  promotion of mobile phones, 128–130
business use, 21, 68, 118, 301
  *see also* work, and leisure

Calhoun, C., 141
call waiting, 120, 122
Caller ID, 120, 122, 293
Calling Party Pays (CPP), 82
care-giving, remote, 145–146
CDMA (Code Division Multiple Access), 81
Cellcom, 32–33, 37
chain messaging, 158, 179–180
chatting, 116, 124
children
  mobile phone use, 28, 213
  telephone lines for, 120
  text message users, 172
class, 215
  and mobile phone use, 208, 256, 259–261, 267–268
clearance cues, 336, 337, 359, 360
collective orientation, 71–72
collective text messaging, 181–182